This is a book that was written twenty-five years ago. Louis Bromfield was a pioneer then, in the truest sense of the word: for he had decided to return to the land, to feed and nurture it, recognizing that living off the land was a process of give-and-take, that the earth itself is a living organism which will die if it is endlessly depleted.

Malabar Farm was a triumph—a way of living, a philosophy that brought an arid tract ruined by exploitation back into the cycle of life. This is how it was done, this is the tale of the joys and satisfactions, the work, the fun. This is the message that carries a promise for all of us.

## More Ballantine Books
## You Will Enjoy

ISLAND IN THE SOUND, Hazel Heckman          $1.25
Anderson Island in Puget Sound—The distinctions
of this island and its people, its lore and its history,
are what this beautiful book is all about.

THE POPULATION BOMB, Dr. Paul R. Ehrlich     $.95
*The national bestseller!*
Overpopulation is now the dominant problem in all
our personal, national, and international planning.
Dr. Ehrlich clearly describes the dimensions of the
crisis in all its aspects, and provides a realistic eval-
uation of the remaining options.

THE ALIEN ANIMALS: The Story of Imported Wild-
life, George Laycock                        $.95
Case histories which reveal the tragic results of
transplanting an animal from one environment to
another because insufficient consideration was given
to overall ecology. *An Audubon/Ballantine Book*

A SAND COUNTY ALMANAC, Aldo Leopold         $.95
First published in 1949, Aldo Leopold's A SAND
COUNTY ALMANAC is now an established en-
vironmental classic. Beginning with a beautifully
written description of the seasonal changes in nature
and their effect on the delicate ecological balance,
the book proceeds to examples of man's destructive
interference and concludes with a plea for a Wilderness esthetic which is even more urgent and timely
today.

*For a complete list or to order by mail, write to:
Dept. CS, Ballantine Books, 36 West 20th Street,
New York, N.Y. 10003*

# MALABAR
# FARM

## Louis Bromfield

*with Drawings by*
### KATE LORD

BALLANTINE BOOKS • NEW YORK
An Intext Publisher

Grateful acknowledgment is made to *The Atlantic Monthly*, *Liberty Hyde Bailey* and *The Land* for permission to reprint material in this book. Also to Oxford University Press for four selections from *The Georgics of Virgil*, translated by C. Day Lewis; copyright 1940, 1947 by Oxford University Press, Inc., New York.

BALLANTINE BOOKS, INC.
101 Fifth Avenue, New York, N.Y. 10003

## DEDICATION

Again for all those at Malabar who have
found in the Valley the delights and
satisfactions of the life and the
accomplishments in which all of us have
participated.

For right and wrong are confused here, there's so much
      war in the world
Evil has so many faces, the plough so little
Honor, the laborers are taken, the fields untended
And the curving sickle is beaten into the sword that
      yields not
There the East is in arms, here Germany marches;
Neighbor cities, breaking their treaties, attack each other;
The wicked War-god runs amok through all the world.
      —*The Georgics of Virgil*

# CONTENTS

# AUTHOR'S NOTE

For the sake of those interested in the identity of the various persons mentioned in the Malabar Journal—Mary is the author's wife and Anne, Hope and Ellen his daughters. George is his business manager. Nanny is the Englishwoman who has been nurse, great friend and housekeeper at the Big House and in Europe for twenty-one years. Reba is the cook at the Big House and Tom the indispensable man of all work. Charlie is in charge of the communal gardens which feed the families at Malabar. Bob is the farm manager and Virginia his wife. Kenneth is the farmer-mechanic who both farms and runs the machine shop. Martha is his wife and Bob and Jim Cook are his sons. Jim recently out of Ohio State Agricultural College now shares responsibility with Al for the big dairy herd and the hundred and fifty head of dairy heifers and baby-beef steers. Max is the first manager of the farm who set up the organization and later left to head the Northern Ohio Breeders Cooperative, one of the biggest organizations of its kind in the country where he has made an outstanding success. Jenny, a neighbor, is the expert buttermaker Jesse is the general man of all work, an experienced character who knows how to do everything from run a buzz saw to setting posts and feeding hogs.

L. B.

# PREFACE

## *A Letter to a Sergeant in Okinawa*

MY DEAR SERGEANT:

Thank you for your interesting letter. Okinawa is indeed a long way from Ohio.

I wish I could answer your letter as I would like to do but your questions are so varied and so provocative that it would require a whole book to answer them even with a modest adequacy. I'm glad you liked *Pleasant Valley*. In that book I tried to answer some of the questions you ask, not dogmatically but out of my own experience, speculatively, because although the world has made great progress during the past generation along the lines of a better agriculture and the understanding of natural and universal laws regarding soil, production, nutrition, and many other phases, there are still many things, remaining in the realm of the unknown, which we do not understand. As we discover new laws and facts and gradually dissipate the fog of mystery, we make strides toward improving the conditions of the human race, its health, its happiness, its living standards, its whole future and, not the least, the possible realization of its hopes for peace; because in this shrunken, complex, modern world peace and war are largely determined by the world supply and distribution of food, of raw materials and of markets. As the population of the world increases at the rate of twenty-five a minute while food sources appear to diminish, food becomes the primitive and dominant factor.

Agriculture is the oldest of professions. Yes, it is older even than the one you are thinking of, for it began when Adam and Eve were expelled from the Garden and prostitution did not begin until at least one more woman entered the world. It should be remembered that both professions spring from fundamental urges in man: (1) The necessity to eat; (2) The urge to propagate, legitimately, indiscriminately, or otherwise. They exist in the above order, since to exist at all man must eat and to insure his continuation on this earth he must propagate. Both urges have been since the beginning of time subject to debasement and greed and ignorance. There is as much original sin in poor agriculture as there is in prostitution, and a good deal of the agriculture practiced in this country is in itself no more than prostitution. The speculating wheat farmer, the farmer who "wore out three farms and was still young enough to wear out a fourth," the miserable one-crop cotton farmer are all cases in point. All three represent a whorish agriculture and certainly such an agriculture has been until recently as prevalent in this country as prostitution itself. It is difficult to say which is the more devastating to the welfare, morality, health, and security of the individual or the nation.

It is a whorish, greedy, ignorant agriculture which fastened the label "hick" to the farmer of the last two generations. It made him the butt of vaudeville jokes before cheap, city-bred audiences. It very largely produced the "hill-billies," the "white trash," the army of unemployed migrant workers which, during the Great Depression, afflicted parts of the nation like locusts. Indeed, the social and economic diseases spread by a poor agriculture have been and still are as bad as or worse than the diseases spread by the prostitute.

Oh, I am aware that many factors have contributed to the waste and dissipation of our abundance—the absentee landlord, tenant-sharecropper systems in which the evils of a parasitic agriculture are doubled, subsidies by government which tend only to preserve and maintain such systems, and with them in the Deep South one of the worst agricultures practiced anywhere in the world. Poor and indifferent means of distribution, exploitation of the farmer by fertilizer and feed merchants, commission merchants, meat packers and livestock yards have contributed their share to the debasement of the farmer in the bad period between the frontier and the New Agriculture. All of these things must be considered but they were superficial in relation to the fundamental fact that all real solidity, security, and prosperity are

4

dependent upon the fertility and production per acre of the farmer's soil and the efficiency with which he cherishes and manages it.

And do not be misled by cries of "surpluses" and "What shall we do with surpluses?" For a thousand years there have been no real surpluses of food produced on the farms of the world or of this country. There has been only poor and inefficient distribution, exploitation of the buyer, and high prices for which this distribution is partly responsible. These things—poor distribution and high prices—create artificial surpluses which have no reality in a world where half the people suffer all their lives from malnutrition and the diseases arising from it, and where at least 500 million people are born and die without ever having had enough to eat one day of their lives.

Government might well have helped the American farmer and the national economy by spending the billions it has spent not upon bribes, parity, guarantees, subsidies, ever-normal granaries and other artificial methods of propping up an imperilled economy, but in finding the proper, efficient and economical means of getting American-raised food to other nations and peoples or even to the Americans themselves who need it but are prevented from buying it by high prices which they cannot afford. Who, knowing anything about economics, can doubt that the market for beefsteak at thirty-five cents a pound would not be at least twenty-five times greater than the market for beefsteak at ninety cents a pound? My point is merely this—that the farmer *could* produce profitably beefsteak at thirty-five cents a pound (with all other agricultural food products in similarly priced relationship) if we had a really good and productive agriculture.

As a nation we produced record amounts of food during the war but never has any nation at any time produced such expensive food. Indeed it was produced so expensively that many kinds of high-protein foods, important to the health of the nation, had to be subsidized with taxpayer's money to induce production anywhere approaching the demand and the need. This was so because our agriculture was and is, largely, unproductive and inefficient. In simple words we farmed much too much land in order to produce the record of food production we attained. To put it even more simply, when we farm five acres to produce a hundred bushels of corn, it costs us five times as much in terms of taxes, interest, investment, labor, seed, and general wear and tear than when we farm one acre to produce the same amount. It is probable that, if we had an agriculture as good as that of France, Holland, Denmark, or Belgium, or as good as that practiced by 10 per cent of our own farmers, the price of food could come down at least a third from the levels of 1939 and our farmers would be making 20 per cent more than they are making today. Among the nations mentioned above, there is no such thing as a poor farmer either in the economic or the agricultural sense. In those countries the word "farmer" is synonymous with the words "rich man." And what makes a rich farmer? Production and efficiency, or exactly the same methods which make rich industrialists and make the wages of our industrial workers higher by from 40 per cent to 90 per cent than that of the industrial workers anywhere else in the world.

That great authority on practical agriculture, E. R. Babcock of Cornell University, has declared and proved clearly enough that if every American lived upon a proper diet, we could not, at our present agricultural production levels, produce enough food. Dr. Lowdermilk, the great soil authority of the U.S. Department of Agriculture, estimates that we could produce on a fourth less land than is now under cultivation enough food to feed 250 million people at our present dietary levels whereas we are actually afflicted with too-high prices and at times actual shortages in our effort to feed 140 million. And we are managing barely to hold that level with all the vast aid of mechanization, hybrid corn, new seeds, weed-killers, subsidies, parity guarantees, bribes, and all the rest of what might be called technological or money aids.

One truth, of course, is that in our agriculture we have neglected largely the fundamentals—the soil, its preservation, its maintenance and restoration, and with these things we have overlooked the natural and universal laws for which there is no short cut even through Socialism, Communism or Nazi dictatorship. Nature is still unconquered by man and when he attempts to upset or circumvent her laws, he merely

6

courts disaster, misery, low living standards, and eventual destruction.

The truth is, of course, that for the last century, while industry has been moving toward the assembly lines, massproduction, and efficiency which give our citizens more telephones, automobiles, plumbing, and radios than all the rest of the world put together and her industrial workers the highest living standards in the world, agriculture has been moving in the opposite direction toward a lower and lower production per acre, per man hour, and per dollar invested. For if one writes off the immense technological and money aids listed above, the small increases in yield per acre reported in recent years by government satisticians are quickly nullified and indeed annihilated and it becomes evident that we are still going down hill.

And bear in mind, Sergeant, that these technological and money aids are tricky and might be called both superficial and artificial. Mechanization can be destructive as well as constructive. These things can serve the good farmer as a means by which he can increase his income and lower his prices to the consumer. They can also help the poor farmer to destroy his land many times more rapidly than he has destroyed it in the past. And I repeat that a subsidized agriculture must always be a burden to the average citizen in terms both of taxes and high prices. He is forced to pay the high prices either directly across the counter or in terms of taxes for subsidies out of his other pocket. Actually in these times, under present conditions, he is paying both ways. A subsidized agriculture is necessarily a static agriculture in which progress toward production, efficiency, low prices, and many other desirable ends is averted. Subsidies serve merely to protect and maintain the poor and inefficient farmer or absentee landlord who is always looking toward high prices rather than production per acre to give him economic solidity and prosperity. They serve also to maintain the socially and economically destructive absentee landlord, tenant-sharecropper system in its worst exploiting form.

And it would be well to remember that at least 60 per cent of our American farmers practice in one form or another a whorish, greedy agriculture. Thirty per cent are moderately

7

good farmers and ten per cent bear the burden, out of all proportion to their numbers, of feeding the nation. Food, according to labor organizations, is the principal item in the living cost budget of city dwelling industrial and white-collar workers. It is the cost of food, increasing steadily since the Civil War, which sets off (according to labor economists) the demands for constantly increasing wages among industrial workers, white-collar workers and city dwellers generally, raises which are passed on in the prices of everything all of us buy including *both* industrial and agricultural commodities. What all of us need is not *more* dollars but dollars which buy *more*. That is the only way in which any of us ever gets a real raise in pay whether we are keeping books or making automobiles or producing hogs.

How better can a start be made toward stabilizing our economy on a productive, not a speculative, basis than by achieving a really productive, efficient agriculture with lower costs to consumer and higher profits to the producer? As with all else in our modern, highly integrated world, high production per man hour, per dollar invested, is the answer and never scarcity and high prices.

In all of this we are driven to fall back upon the great fundamentals—the soil and its productivity and maintenance. Under a whorish agriculture we have wasted our soil by erosion, by bad and greedy land use. We are still wasting it at a frightening rate, so rapid and so frightening that as population increases and yields per acre remain static or decreasing, there appears on the horizon a cloud "no bigger than the hand of man" which may turn into a disaster such as that of India or China where crude grain is so precious that it cannot be used as feed to produce eggs or butter or milk or meat, and where prices are so high and wages so low that 90 per cent of the population rarely tastes what we call high-protein foods. There comes at last the ultimate misery of populations where millions live and die without ever having had enough to eat one day of their lives.

At present, high protein foods are available in sufficient quantities to only about 60 per cent of our population because the prices are too high. Raising industrial and white-collar wages serves only to increase in turn the cost of food. The answer lies with a better and more productive agricul-

8

ture which lowers the price of food and increases the value of every man's dollar.

What I am trying to say is that the farmer, the good farmer, has in a starving world become an increasingly important and vital citizen. No young man with any aptitude for agriculture could undertake a more fascinating and, probably in these times and for years to come, a more profitable career than agriculture or one in which he could do more for the welfare of mankind. The *good* farmer or livestock man is no longer a "hick," as indeed he never was. He must always be an intelligent man of parts, knowing perhaps more about more things than any other citizen. He must know and understand something of markets, the weather, distribution, machinery, economics, history, ecology, disease, bacteriology, and many other things, but most of all he must understand the earth and the laws of God and nature which govern its maintenance and productivity. This last is a vast field and it is a startling fact that, although agriculture is the oldest calling worthy of the name of "profession," it is only recently that we have begun to understand beyond the realms of superstition, the laws which govern its relationship to our economy, our health, and indeed our survival as decent, comfortable, happy citizens. There is much that we still have not discovered or understood. In the field of experiment and research alone there exists a whole unexplored world of great fascination, for in a cubic foot of good productive soil one can find the pattern of the laws which govern the universe—laws before which political ideologies, manipulations of currency, short cuts, and all manner of man-made dodges become singularly silly and puerile.

I haven't answered a tenth of your questions. You are indeed a smart fellow with a mind that works. Of that fact, you should be proud in a world which needs desperately that kind of mind and in which all the expensive machinery for education appears to produce more and more citizens who seem merely able to read and write and do not especially distinguish themselves even in these primary steps toward civilization.

Since the publication of *Pleasant Valley* I have received thousands of letters, half of them from GI's like yourself stationed in what to many an American boy seemed out-

9

landish places like Okinawa, the Solomons, India, North Africa and from little towns in Germany and France and Austria. Some of them were "thank you" notes because *Pleasant Valley* had somehow assuaged a deep homesickness for the home landscapes and living of New England, of Texas, of the Middle West, of the South or of that great empire, the Northwest. Most of them, together with all the correspondence from civilians, asked questions, endless and important and fundamental, about how we were getting along at Malabar or questions regarding soil and livestock or health or economy.

The sum total of letters and questions represented a mass of correspondence which, if answered or merely discussed intelligently and conscientiously, would have occupied all my time for a period of years. Since I have to make a living both by farming and writing, it was impossible to answer adequately and beyond mere acknowledgment more than a very few, so I am writing *Malabar Farm*, which is no more than a second volume of *Pleasant Valley* recounting largely what we have accomplished in achievement, observation, and experiment during the period of nearly five years since *Pleasant Valley* was written. For all of us at Malabar the whole experience has been exciting and as satisfactory, I think, as any human experience can be. In the following pages you will find a lot of the things about which you asked in your letter. I hope you'll get as much enjoyment out of *Malabar Farm* as you did out of *Pleasant Valley*.

Anyway, when you come back, come and see us here. I'd like to show you some remarkable things. In any case there is a great job to be done in the field of agriculture from one end of the world to the other. Never forget that agriculture is the oldest of the honorable professions and that always the good farmer is the *fundamental* citizen of any community, state, or nation. Never in the history of the world has this fact been more evident than in the disordered times in which we live. It is likely to remain equally evident for the rest of man's existence upon this earth.

Good luck. Let us hear from you how things are going and pay us a visit.

Yours faithfully,
LOUIS BROMFIELD

# I: MALABAR JOURNAL

## Autumn 1944

We are but farmers of ourselves; yet may
If we can stock ourselves and thrive, uplay
Much, much good treasure for the great rent day.
—John Donne

AUGUST 31: The drought broke today with a heavy, slow, soaking rain which began during the night and continued all through the day. Forty-six days without rain, save one or two thunderstorms, has left the corn that was planted early in the season parched and dry with only undeveloped nubbins as ears. Without water the chemical fertilizer has not been available to the plants. We have just finished filling the four silos with the corn that was planted to provide feeding corn during the winter, leaving the corn planted later for silage to

---

NOTE: The Journal—which makes up five of the eighteen chapters of this book—is merely a record of the life at Malabar Farm during a period roughly of one year. It was not kept as a daily record but was written when the weather was bad and the work light—in short, when there was time to set down the record. On a modern, well-managed farm there are no slack periods. Modern farming has become a business like any other, save that outdoor life, sport, nature and independence all play larger roles than in the lives of the banker, lawyer, businessman, and industrial and white-collar worker. There are no killing peaks of labor in spring, summer, and autumn and no sitting around the village store spitting into the stove during the winter months. And everybody has a vacation. During the disturbed year recorded, Malabar Farm like all America, felt at times the impact of the events taking place in the world outside. This is reflected in the Journal itself.

develop into feeding corn. That is one of the tactics weather sometimes forces upon the farmer. If the frost holds off we shall have a good crop despite the drought, now that rain has come at last.

Drought in our green Ohio country where it is seldom expected is a shocking experience. It raises in good Ohioans a sense of indignation and outrage. Each day under the hot sun the fields and bluegrass pastures grew a little drier and

browner, the cattle a little more nervous. Day after day clouds came up on the horizon only to move on to some more fortunate region, very possibly the middle of the Atlantic since this year the late drought has extended eastward through Pennsylvania and the seaboard states.

Here at Malabar we are proud of the fact that not one of our fifteen or more springs, big or little, showed any signs of drying up. All through the heat and drought there was good cold spring water for the livestock in every pasture on the farm. Switzer's Creek got as low as I have ever seen it but there was always plenty of water and the big swimming hole in the Jungle was always clear and cool all through the dry hot weather. It is a natural pond made by the water pouring over a big fallen Sycamore which made a dam. It is deep, with a spring in the bottom, and across it leans a huge and ancient willow the branches of which provide diving platforms at varying heights. During the hot weather the boys on the farm lay off work a couple of times each day to go there for a swim. Almost all day long it was full of children and dogs.

All our contour plowing, cover crops, and strip cropping have paid us great dividends. Throughout the drought when farms all over Ohio were hauling water, our springs kept up their flow, because the methods we took to stop erosion and the run-off of surface water had stored up great quantities of water underground. When we came here about 80 per cent of the water in a heavy rainstorm ran off the place; today we keep on the place 80 to 90 per cent of the rain that falls, trapped by sod, contours, and strips. It sinks deep into the earth to replenish the reservoirs in the great crevasses in the underlying sandstone rock.

In the middle of the night I awakened from a deep sleep to hear the sound of rain. It was a soft, pleasant sound, scarcely loud enough to disturb a cricket, but after long weeks of waiting my subconscious mind was alert, impatient to hear that wonderful sound. I lay awake for a long time listening to it, afraid to go to sleep again lest the soft patter would stop, and presently I rose and walked out of my room, which is on the ground floor, onto the terrace to *feel* the rain. Two of the dogs, Prince and Baby, went with me and stood there enjoying it as much as myself. Baby, the big Boxer, who is a natural clown, lifted his head, opened his mouth and let the water, dripping from the eaves, fall into it.

When I returned to my bed I slept better than I had slept for weeks. It was almost as if I could feel the earth, the pastures, the fields of corn and soybeans drinking up the falling rain.

It continued all morning and after lunch I went for a long walk in the rain over a large part of the farm. It was warm, slow, heavy rain and you could feel the thirsty earth drinking it up as you walked.

A week before the rain came, we turned all the livestock, sheep, beef cattle, and hogs into one 50-acre field in which there were ten acres of corn and about ten of soybeans. The rest was knee-deep in second growth alfalfa. After the sparse bluegrass the animals were in paradise and could not make up their minds whether they preferred the corn, the lush soybeans, or the deep green alfalfa. They went from one to the other eating for a few minutes in each strip, the giddy heifers running and kicking with pleasure. We turned them in on the crops because the permanent pastures had grown short in the drought. Turning livestock into good soybeans and corn very nearly broke manager Bob's heart, but it gave me pleasure to see beasts enjoying themselves. Surprisingly none of the cattle showed any signs of bloating, perhaps because the diet was so varied.

There is some curious factor controlling bloat in cattle which we have not yet discovered. I suspect that bloating is related less to the gorging of lush new grasses than to the presence or the absence of some element in the soil. In the region around Lexington, Kentucky, where hundreds of steers are run among the horses on the same kind of bluegrass and white-clover pasture which we have at Malabar, bloating is a very serious problem each spring. On our glaciated Ohio soil we have never had a case of bloat on bluegrass—white-clover pastures, or even upon rich ladino and alfalfa. To be sure we never turn *hungry* cattle suddenly into a rich field, but neither do the cattlemen at Lexington. In that region cases of "spring bloat" occur even after the steers have been on pasture for weeks. Our theory is only a theory born of observation but it might well be explored by research men.

We have also observed that where cattle are turned into fresh, heavy legume pasture they will instinctively take care of themselves provided there is some form of dry roughage or even coarse weeds available. They will "balance" their own forage by mixing large quantities of dry stuff or weeds with the lush green forage. For this reason many wise farmers provide dried hay placed in an accessible spot. Cattle on new heavy pasture will consume large quantities whereas later in the season when the pasture is less rich and its mineral content much higher, they will merely pick at it or not touch it at all. We have also observed that during the rich months of early spring they will consume quantities of mint, dock, nettles and other weeds which later in the season go entirely untouched.

For the first four or five days neighbor after neighbor stopped in to tell us the livestock were in the corn. To some of them the turning of cattle into a field of unharvested crops seemed a violation and a sacrilege.

I know of nothing more comical than a hog making a hog of himself. The hogs were, as usual, both comical and intelligent. They would stand chewing great mouthfuls of alfalfa for a few minutes and then dash with grunts and pig excitement into the corn to snatch up the ears knocked off by the beef cattle. Then back again with excited noises to chew alfalfa. They didn't get to the soybeans until the second day. Once they discovered them, they lived on a three-course diet. The cattle followed out the same menu, but more calmly. The sheep as usual behaved with stupidity. They huddled together for two days in the alfalfa before they discovered either corn or beans. On the third day I drove them through the gate into the bluegrass pasture where the water was. Eventually they would have found it but they lacked either the cleverness of the hogs or the sound instincts of the beef cattle which always leads them to water. The hogs and cattle will keep going down hill until they find it. Now with the rain, they will all have the best diet livestock can have— corn, soybeans, alfalfa, bluegrass and wild white clover with the finest and cleanest of spring water.

When I think of our lush Ohio pastures and the burnt-up sage brush of the western prairies I wonder how western cattle survive.

For the agronomist or the livestock breeder nothing can be of greater interest than a study of the eating habits of animals. I have spent many hours watching them as they grazed across permanent bluegrass pasture and the record is almost always the same. They do not, as supposed, *prefer* the bluegrass and white clover to *all* other vegetations. On the contrary they show a great liking for all kinds of weeds and even the leaves of many trees. The pattern seems a fairly uniform one. The cattle will graze for a few minutes on the lush bluegrass and then turn aside to eat common dock, mint, and other coarse weeds, even young nettles and thistles. It is clear, I think, that they are seeking something, probably minerals or even flavors, which the shallow-rooted bluegrass and white clover do not contain. The deep-rooted dock and thistles undoubtedly

15

bring up minerals, particularly trace elements,[1] from the deep layers of minerally rich glacial, gravel loam and the nettle, as has long been accepted in superstition and witchcraft, possesses special properties and curative qualities. In France young nettle shoots are fed, chopped finely, to young turkeys as a specific against virtually all young turkey ills. In some regions the young shoots are sometimes eaten like asparagus or made into soup for human consumption. The shoots are used much as the American pioneer used sassafras tea—"to clear the blood in the spring."

Basing my deductions upon the belief that any animal knows better how to balance its diet than any professor or feed merchant, I have come to the conclusion that pasture or hay all of one kind or one or two kinds, however lush and beautiful, is not necessarily the *best* pasture or forage for top nutrition and health of livestock. With this in mind, most of the farm meadow pastures of pure brome grass, alfalfa and ladino (the most rich, high-protein food) connect with permanent bluegrass pastures where, despite constant clipping, dock, thistles, mint, nettles, and many other "weeds" are available to the animals along ditches and creek beds, in fence corners and on patches of wet unclipped ground. We have noted many times in the feeding barns that cattle being fed the finest quality pure alfalfa hay will, after a week or two, turn away from it to eat their oat straw bedding, either from boredom or in a search of something which is lacking in the pure alfalfa. It need not be simply minerals, for our farm-grown alfalfa is, of course, not only a deep-rooted plant but its mineral content runs about o6.5 which is considerably above the average mineral content of alfalfa. The more subtle facts of animal nutrition, beyond the primary protein, carbohydrates, principal mineral needs and balances, are still largely unexplored.

It is probable that the most nutritious pasture and forage

[1] The expression "trace elements" means the rarer mineral elements which appear only in such small quantities that their percentage cannot be measured, hence only a "trace." They are generally boron, cobalt, manganese, copper, magnesium, iodine, fluorine. zinc and sulphur, and some others, as compared to the major elements such as nitrogen, phosphorus, potassium and calcium.

in the world is the high mountain pastures grown on a rocky soil and composed of a great variety of mixed grasses, wild flowers and weeds with a high proportion of legumes. There are areas in the Rockies and in Switzerland where cattle, fed on such pastures, actually grow fat as if they had been fed grain. A similar pasture once grew on the calcium-impregnated Great Plains region but it has been largely destroyed by overgrazing and burning over. The health and vigor of the cattle on the Southwestern Plains covered by sparse vegetation probably arises from two factors—the considerable variety of vegetation plus the high mineral content in the unleached soils of areas of low rainfall formed from an agglomeration of broken-down rock.

Although Bob's heart was broken and some of the neighbors were outraged by the rape of the corn and soybeans, we shall in the end benefit by it. It will send all the livestock into the barns for the winter sleek and fat and healthy. We shall have been saved the labor of harvesting the corn and beans and alfalfa and all will be turned into beef, mutton, and pork before we plough the land for wheat. It will take less corn to carry the breeding stock through the winter and to fatten out the steers. Once animals have been permitted to go backward it takes twice as much feed to put them back on their feet.

As I walked through the rain, it was obvious to me that the livestock were enjoying the warm downpour as much as myself. The cattle were standing knee-deep in the alfalfa with the rain running off their backs. The sheep were huddled under the trees near the old graveyard and the hogs were industriously making wallows for themselves where any water collected in the field.

The rain will make the wheat plowing easier. One field—the poorest on the Fleming Place—we are plowing for the first time in four years. It has been limed and has had a crop of coarse sweet clover pastured off in the second year by the cattle. The poor spots have had a coating of manure and following that it was seeded to a mixture of ladino and alsike. The native wild white clover seeded itself, and some bluegrass has come in. For two years it has been pastured, thus receiving directly the manure of sheep and cattle and, most valuable of all, the urine. It should grow an excellent crop of wheat. After that it will be seeded to a mixture of alfalfa, red clover,

17

brome grass, and ladino to serve the triple purpose of grass silage, hay, and emergency pasture. After two years of trampling in all weather by the cattle it has been hard to plow. It is a rough steep field pitching in all directions with streaks of glacial gravel. All of us have taken turns wrestling with the plowing of it. The rain will help soften it.

The longer we farm this hill country the longer it becomes clear that grass farming is the way to do it. It is surprising how beef cattle will grow and wax fat on bluegrass, white clover, or alfalfa when there is plenty of lime and phosphate in the soil.

Crossing this pasture, I found the first mushroom of the season. And then another near it and another. The warm rain had brought them out. The spawn had been there all along in the hard, baked earth and with the night's rain they pushed their way through the bluegrass. They were fresh, young and damp, some of them no more than buttons, others opened up with the gills showing tender and flesh-pink. The sight of them sent me through the dripping woods up the long steep hill to the Ferguson Place where the big fields are ancient pastures more than one hundred thirty years old. They have been pastures since the forest was first cleared away.

There, "up Ferguson way" as everyone in our valley calls it, one is high up against the sky. For a long time I stood on the highest part of the pasture where there is an unobstructed view over the fields and valleys and forests of three counties, watching the rain falling over the parched woods and fields.

In the old orchard near the empty hole which marks the spot where the burned farmhouse once stood, I found two very old peach trees with the fruit ripe and dropping to the ground. One tree bore white peaches and the other yellow ones. They were small but of a delicious, concentrated flavor, partly because they were "old-fashioned" and partly because the dry weather had concentrated their flavor and sweetness. The possums and raccoons and perhaps the foxes had been sampling the ones that lay on the ground. There were tiny sharp teeth marks in nearly all of them.

There was a quality and flavor in the peaches which city people rarely know. They get only "improved" varieties of fruits and vegetables which are bred not so much for flavor as to ship and keep well, or for convenience in canning or quick freezing. They rarely receive the old-fashioned varieties of strawberries, peaches, cantaloupe and lima beans which are often far superior to the new sorts developed not for flavor or excellence but for utilitarian purposes. We have inherited many old varieties of fruit which are now virtually unobtainable off the farm—rambo and russet apples, tender, juicy, white clingstone peaches, the old small variety of Jonathan apples that are of an intense, tangy flavor. And in the vegetable garden we have each year planted some of the old-fashioned vegetables and small fruits which are no longer obtainable in the markets.

On the way home I passed one of the wild apple trees descended from the ones planted by Johnny Appleseed which are scattered over our hills and pastures. The apples are small and sour and with a tangy flavor of their own. Some of them are excellent and they are much favored by possum, raccoon, and rabbit.

I returned home through the dripping woods with a hatful of young, fresh mushrooms. I was soaked to the skin but that was a small matter considering that the drought was broken. In the woods there was a warm, steamy mist coming up from the decaying leaves. It smelled of decay and fungus and the promise of new life.

SEPTEMBER 1: Slept late after having made a talk last night in Mansfield. Unfortunately when I went to pick up my wife, Mary, at the Prestons on the way home, I had a drink or two and fell into conversation. It was three-thirty in the morning when we set out on the fifteen-mile drive down the Pleasant Valley road. There was a full moon setting but very brilliant and the valley never looked more beautiful. All five Boxers and Dusky, the Cocker, were still up waiting for us, most of all, I think, to have their "snacks" which they are accustomed to every night at midnight. Prince and Baby had had a fight and apparently Baby had gotten a good hold on Prince's ear and chewed it for some time.

Worked all morning on articles and propaganda in behalf of the plan to reorganize all agencies having to do with the natural resources of Ohio—soil, water, forests, parks, mines, highways, fish, game, and so forth. All of these agencies are interlocked but in the past each has operated separately

19

without much co-ordination and with a great deal of confusion and red tape. A sensible plan is in the course of development under the Post War Planning Commission, headed by Paul Herbert, the Lieutenant Governor, who is doing a good job. Murray Lincoln, head of the Farm Bureau, is chairman of the Natural Resources Committee and I serve on the Soil Conservation subcommittee.

After lunch although work was piled up on my desk I couldn't resist going out on the farm. The rain had stopped and the air was cool and clear. Picked a half bushel of mushrooms. Would have plowed but all the tractors were busy, two disking the ground on the high hill above the old Bailey Place where we are sowing rye for late fall and early spring pasture. Fifty acres of rye will permit us to keep the cattle out of the barns three or four weeks later in the autumn and get them out that much earlier in the spring. With one hundred head of cattle and a couple of hundred sheep that means a great saving of labor, and of hay and silage and grain which are generally put up during the summer. By disking the ground the rye can be seeded in only two or three days and serves as an excellent cover crop. In the spring after the cattle go on the bluegrass, the fifty acres will be disked and sowed to alfalfa, brome grass, and ladino in the way Dr. Borst developed it at the Zanesville Soil Conservation Station—using alfalfa as a poor-land crop, seeded directly into a trash mulch,[2] without all the old coddling nonsense. With us it has been strikingly successful. It produces one of the most valuable crops and builds up the soil at the same time.

The third tractor was mowing the third cutting of alfalfa and the fourth was out with the pick-up baler. Bob went to help out Herb Briarly, whose main barn burned during a recent thunderstorm. He has one barn left but it is too small to take all his soybean hay and straw put in loose. If it is baled he can store it. Although it comes at a busy time and, like everybody else, we are terribly short of help, we felt we had to help him out.

---

[2] The expression "trash mulch" means disking or "working" into the soil the residue of grass, straw or weeds left in the fields after harvesting.

Doc Wadsworth came to patch up the red Guernsey who jumped a barbed-wire fence and cut her udder. Always enjoy seeing him as do the dogs who know him well. I like this because it makes me know that when the dogs are with him, they are happy. His favorite is Gina, the grandmother of them all. What a dog she is! She leads an independent life and takes no nonsense from her children or grandchildren. She really "brings them up," teaching them good manners and disciplining their natural Boxer boisterousness. She can make them quail simply by making a ferocious face at them and she can certainly make ugly faces.

When Doc left, I took Susie, the Angus heifer, down to the Fleming farm to turn her in with the beef herd. She is more or less a pet having been brought up in the big barn with the dairy calves. She has a determined and comic character and twice has jumped the fence to return to the girl-friends she has been brought up with. But she is old enough to breed now and must find out the facts of life and go to work producing. To my surprise she went with perfect docility the half mile down the road to the Fleming Place. But I don't trust her. I expect to wake in the morning and find her back with her friends the Guernsey heifers.

Susie's father Blondy, the big Angus bull, simply knocked out the side of the barn this morning in order to rejoin his harem half an hour after he was shut in a box stall. He runs with the shorthorn cows the year round and resents being separated. To return to them, he jumped two fences and smashed a floodgate. I can't blame him. What real bull would like to leave the corn, alfalfa, and soybeans, not to mention the harem? We shall have to start all over again to-morrow trying to keep him shut up as we want to avoid his breeding with his own daughters, the crossbred blue-roans.

Went up this evening with Bob and Harry, and Ma to look at the forty-acre alfalfa seeding on the Ferguson Place. Despite the drought it looks pretty well. If it gets through the winter we shall have a fine field for hay and emergency pasture.

Ma, my mother, is extraordinary. At eighty-three she takes the liveliest and most intelligent interest in everything that goes on at Malabar—fertilizer, seedings, livestock, pasture treatment, orchards. She insists on going everywhere with me in the old Ford, across streams, ditches, rough ground, always with six dogs in the back of the car. And she is very smart about it all and passionately interested in new farming developments. She loves livestock and if she can pay a daily visit to the beef cattle, she is happy. She is a farmer's daughter, my grandfather having been one of the best farmers in the state and one of the founders of the Ohio Grange.

The Ferguson Place was as always very beautiful, with its enormous view of farms, forest, streams and lakes. The sun was setting as the full moon rose over Pleasant Hill lake and the white houses and barns in the Darling settlement far below in the valley.

When at last, our venerable Ford, like "the one hoss shay" fell apart, we replaced it with a jeep which has proved invaluable in the operation of a big farm in hilly country. It serves as conveyance and emergency repair wagon, and can do all kinds of farm work. In bad weather nothing but a Ford or a jeep can cope with some of the lanes and the rough ground. Mr. Ritter, President of the State Golfers' Association, is also an official of the Willys-Overland and was telling me at dinner last night the great virtues of the jeep and its possibilities. I have made an engagement to visit the Sorensen farm on the sixteenth to see jeeps in operation.

To bed early to read Aldous Huxley's new novel which begins well. Many ordinary readers say they don't believe his characters exist in real life, but they do. I think you would have to know Europe during the past twenty-five years to understand that their counterparts do exist and have had an appalling amount to do with the tragic-foolish history of our times.

SEPTEMBER 3: Yesterday and today had better be entered as one day since they are hopelessly mixed up in a procession of people and work. In the morning Mr. Harrison of the Redpath Bureau appeared with the joint purpose of seeing the farm and inducing me to sign up for lectures with his bureau. He was a very sympathetic and agreeable salesman and an intelligent and good companion. We didn't talk lectures until the last minute and then it did no good because I despise lecture tours. By the time we got round to business after three hours on the farm, we had become old friends and it was not difficult to make him understand how I felt.

I don't dislike people or talking or even making speeches but I can't make lectures to audiences who have paid $1.50 to come and see a show. I like political speeches and talking to farmers and businessmen and to people who share common interests. I tried to explain this, saying that I make a hundred or more speeches a year for conservation, for political reasons, on soil, on gardening, even at times on Europe and India. I get paid little or nothing for all this and turn over the proceeds to the Friends of the Land or to charities. Usually I pay my own expenses. Happily I can afford to talk when and where I please and about what I please. I explained that I could make more money by staying at home minding my farming and writing than I could ever make on a lecture tour, even at the high fees suggested, and I keep my independence and freedom and am not bored by repeating over and over night after night the same speeches.

The interesting part of Mr. Harrison's visit was entirely devoted to horticulture and agriculture. I think his real interests were his fruit farm in northern Michigan and his wheat ranch in Texas. The valley looked beautiful after the big rains and several shades greener than a week ago. I was proud of how well our crops looked and how well our springs flowed after nearly fifty days without rain. Mr. Harrison promised to send us a crate of his best cherries next July.

The car that took Mr. Harrison to Mansfield brought back Dalpeggeto and Herbert Spencer, two young ensigns and friends of Hope's, who have been at the University in a special Navy course. They have been spending week ends here during the summer. Nice and very smart kids they are. If the whole of the younger generation is as good, the future of the country is safe.

A Mrs. Johnson called from Antioch College saying she was from Connecticut and was interested in the soil program we had here in relation to human nutrition and in the cooperative side of the farm. I told her to come and reserved a room at the hotel in Mansfield. I have learned a certain caution about strange visitors. Some times they turn out to be charming and intelligent and stimulating people and sometimes they turn out to be bores and cranks. If they turn out all right they're moved from the hotel to Malabar.

We have had strangers come to pay an hour's visit, remain

for lunch, then the night and finally stay for a week or ten days. That is what happened with the Robertsons from South Africa. He is the editor of *Libertas*, a South African publication resembling our own *Life Magazine* and a great advocate of American soil conservation methods. South Africa has suffered devastation by erosion, both wind and water, even greater than our own, if this were possible. Dr. Bennett of the U.S. Soil Conservation Service is making a trip there this winter at the urgent request of the South African government. I made several talks on the subject by short wave radio for the OWI during the war at the request of South African government officials, *Libertas* and the Johannesburg newspapers. I hope to follow Dr. Bennett's route during 1948. Countries all over the world are turning to our Department of Agriculture and principally the Soil Conservation Service for aid and instruction in the New Agriculture developed here. This is a little-known fact in which Americans should take pride—that out of the widespread ruin of our originally rich virgin land we have built the principles of a New Agriculture of great value to every nation in the world.

Before supper the boys and I gathered two bushels of yellow and white tomatoes, carrots, onions, and celery from the garden. After supper Nanny and Tom made it up into a drink which we worked out for ourselves and found much more interesting and stimulating than ordinary tomato juice. There is no water involved, only the juice of the tomatoes for a base with half a peck of onions, two dozen carrots and eight big bunches of celery, tops and all, the greener the better. Sometimes spinach is added, and always three or four cloves of garlic, parsley, bay leaves, celery and mustard seed, salt, pepper and a dash of Cayenne. When boiled and strained it looks and tastes like the finest consommé; jellied it is wonderful in hot weather; served hot, it is a delicious, clear soup. You can also drink it as you drink orange or tomato juice. We whipped it up as an experiment two years ago and have put up several dozen bottles of it each year since then. Nanny calls it "Doctor Bromfield's Special Vegetable Compound and Celery Tonic." The chief difficulty is to stop drinking it.

After supper the two ensigns, Dal and Herb, and I went plowing while there was still light. We used the Ford-Fergusons—which make plowing a pleasure. In fact I know

24

nothing that gives me more pleasure or satisfaction than turning over rich soil, mixing sod, manure, rubbish of all sorts into the earth to raise big crops. The field was on the Fleming Place—the same field I described the day of the walk in the rain—and presented a tough job. It was a steep field which before we got the farm had been used to grow row crops in the old-fashioned up-and-down-hill method, which had allowed the top soil to be washed off the slopes by the time we arrived on the scene. The rain had softened up the ground and the plowing was easier. The boys were fascinated by the power and maneuverability of the neat little Ferguson tractor.

We had hardly gotten started when George came down to say that Frank and Jane Lausche were at the Big House and I left the plowing to the boys to go and see them. Two nicer or finer people do not exist. Frank is the Democratic candidate for Governor and had been campaigning in the southern part of the state. He wanted to talk about his campaign. He was a little discouraged by what he felt was the "isolationist" feeling he had encountered. I tried to persuade him that he had not gotten a fair picture of Ohio during his trip since he had visited only five or six counties, strongly German in ancestry and in open rebellion against the New Deal, where Gerald Smith, Father Coughlin and their friends had taken advantage of the discontent to muscle their way in. In one of the counties a faction of the farmers, in open rebellion, smashed up the OPA and the AAA offices and burned the records after seizing a cornpicker without a WPB priority.

Frank and Jane stayed late but would not spend the night. They had to return to Cleveland as the Graphite Bronze Company, one of the most important war production plants, is in the throes of one of the most irresponsible and shameful strikes, and Frank wanted to return and do what he could as Mayor of Cleveland to end the situation.

After they left everybody went to the kitchen and finished bottling the "Vegetable Compound" and as usual the evening finished with us—everybody from Patti Aldrich and Ellen and Sigrid Meisse who are twelve to Ma who is eighty-three—sitting around eating cantaloupe from the garden and drinking milk and talking about the war and India and international politics. Dal and Herb, displayed remarkably sound

25

grounding in all subjects and offered some good contributions concerning the past, present, and future of this wretched world.

Finally to bed after hearing the midnight news that American troops were in Belgium and near the German border. In bed, read an excellent article in *Fortune* on the political monkey-business that went on at both party conventions in Chicago. I saw them both from the inside and certainly neither one was an especially elevating spectacle.

SUNDAY MORNING: Rose late after a night interrupted a couple of times by the exit, entrance, and barking of the dogs going courting with Bob's bitch Kitchee. Yesterday Bob was boasting how he had fixed them by keeping Kitchee locked in the garage but this morning he admitted that the dogs (and nature) had won out by making sleep impossible and by Kitchee's rescue and escape from the garage, aided by Prince, Baby, and Smoky, who simply chewed and tore a big hole in the garage door. This morning Kitchee was all smiles and wriggles. At times the fertility of this place, like that of India, becomes terrifying.

Herb Spencer drove to Mansfield to fetch the mysterious Mrs. Johnson, and Dal and I and the dogs drove to the Bailey farm where Kenneth Cook and his boys, Bob and Jim, and Bob Huge and his brother-in-law were busy with the tractors, fitting[8] the ground and drilling rye in the sixty-acre field above the house. It will be good to see those hills green once more. The worn-out soil has been bare for too long.

The longer I watched the operations and co-operation involved the more it seems to me that co-operation in one form or another is the solution to many problems afflicting agriculture today. Nobody asked the boys to work on Sunday; they did so on their own because it was to everybody's interest and they did it as a kind of lark. Kenneth's boys, Jim and Bob, work in a factory during the week and on the farm evenings and Sundays, laying aside money for their education. No one would have worked on Sunday save that we are, like all farmers, desperately short of help. We need four farmers and two hired men and actually we have only

---

[8] "Fitting" means preparing the earth for seeding.

three farmers—Bob, who manages things and works like a dog in the fields, Harry who has thirty head of Guernseys and 1200 chickens to care for, and Kenneth who has all the machinery to keep in order, in addition to the bulk of the actual farming. This year we haven't even been able to find a man or boy to cut weeds. The three high-school boys from Cleveland—Johnny Rudhuyzen, Dave Stamper and Jimmy Caddick were whirlwind workers during the hay part of the year but they had to go back to school. This, their second year, they did the work of full-time hired men and were a lot more intelligent than the average hired man.

On the Bailey hill we again picked a shirtful of mushrooms, many of them growing out of the bare clay on poor ground which seemed to indicate that fundamentally the apparently worn-out soil was better than it seemed.

Went through the corn originally planted for silage, and if we have any luck with the frost holding off, we shall have a good crop of corn despite the drought. Luckily we had the sense to put the half-ruined corn crop into the silo and let the silage corn benefit by the rain that came at last. The drought was very nearly a disaster but out of it we have learned many valuable things about soil and crops, most of all about the priceless value of humus and organic material as a means of soaking up and preserving moisture.

Mrs. Johnson appeared and turned out to be very intelligent, having had many years of experience working along dietary and nutrition lines. She was very interesting about her experiences with the dreary Okie camps in California during the bad years. She agreed that after the post-war boom dies down, we shall have the armies of migratory workers, dispossessed from poor, worn-out land, back on our hands, a liability, not only in relief and taxes but a moral, physical, and spiritual liability to the nation. The economic-human problem of the "poor whites" and "Okies" is an extremely complex one which in the end can be solved only by dealing with fundamentals—soil, diet, and education in that order. Poor, worn-out soil produces specimens handicapped physically, mentally, and morally from the very beginning. Food grown on such soil from which calcium, phosphorus, and other vital minerals and elements are exhausted can only produce sickly specimens, both humans and livestock. Wretched

27

diet aggravates sickliness, and poor, undernourished, stupid people make bad farmers who only destroy the soil still further. Education comes third because it is useless to attempt education with people sick physically and mentally from deficiencies of vital minerals. It is no good trying to solve the problem by taxes, WPA, charity and relief, although these may be necessary in time of acute crisis.

Reba is off for the week end in Mt. Vernon so Tom and Nanny cooked lunch aided by bits of advice, some corn-husking and potato-paring by the rest of the family. And a good lunch it was—young White Rock broilers, mashed potatoes, gravy, cauliflower and sweetcorn fresh from the garden, quantities of fresh butter churned Thursday, tomatoes like beefsteak and the first limestone lettuce, newly made peach butter and freshly made pickles put up by Nanny and Jenny Oaks, ice-cold cantaloupe watermelon, big bunches of Niagara and Concord grapes and fresh peaches, ice-cold glasses of Guernsey milk or fresh buttermilk with little globules of butter still floating in it. Everything on the table was produced on the place.

We were fourteen in all in the big house—from Butch who is seven to Ma who is eighty-three. It reminded me of the meals at my grandfather's farm long ago when farmers somehow lived better than most of them do today. I believed it could be done and it has been done, but best of all every other family on the place was having the same kind of meal. Today the acres at Malabar support *more* people than ever before in their history. And the families live better, having more comforts and a higher standard of living than any living on the same land in the past. We have dispossessed nobody. On the contrary we have been able to make much of the land, poor and run down when we took it over, do a better job than when it was virgin soil, freshly cleared of forest.

As we left the Sunday dinner table three cars of people—men, women and children—arrived from Wooster to go over the place to see what we had accomplished. Two of the men and one of the women were doctors. I had met them all when I went to Wooster last spring to speak under the auspices of the Izaak Walton League and the State Agricultural Experiment Station.

The farm was in an interesting condition, its springs flowing despite the drought, its corn and beans and pastures greener than those on most farms, part of it plowed for wheat, part of it "trash-farmed" without a plow in order to conserve moisture. The cattle, despite the drought, were looking sleek and well from a summer on bluegrass and white clover, supplemented by corn, soybeans and alfalfa, and the calves fat and happy. The story was all there—the results spread before the eyes of any who wanted to see. The "new fangled" ideas were paying big dividends.

In our old Ford station wagon there were six dogs, Mrs. Johnson, Ma, the two ensigns and Ellen and her two friends. We finished up in the big spring house at the Bailey Place where a whole brook of ice-cold water flows out of a crevasse in the sandstone. It was a hot day and never did that clear, cold water taste so good.

When the Wooster party departed, Charley Schrack and his son Hilbert arrived. Hilbert has been nearly four years in the Army—four of his best years as he is now twenty-eight—for the idiotic reason of war. This time Hilbert brought back a wife and year-old son his parents had not seen before. He is bringing them over tomorrow.

Managed to get a half hour off and went to the swimming hole in the Jungle. No ladies this time so we went in the good old-fashioned way—George, Butch, the two ensigns and myself. The day was hot but the spring in the bottom of the pool made the water very cold. On arriving back at the Big House found Todd and Sadie Chesrown. I know of nobody I love more than Todd and Sadie. Todd went to school with me and last year won the award of the Cleveland City Farmers Club for having done the best job in restoring a run-down farm to productivity. They have built up their farm and raised eight children and are giving them all college educations, without asking help of anybody. It's a damned shame there are fewer and fewer Americans with that spirit and more and more who want the government to take care of them. I don't know any happier couple. They gave us the guinea fowl which insist on roosting in the big catalpa tree just outside the bedrooms and make the most god-awful noises when any intruder comes within five hundred yards of the place. But they are wonderful eating in the winter—all breast and white meat with a delicious wild flavor because they live wild, like pheasants, roaming over the farm all the year round. Roasted and basted with butter in which celery, parsley, and dill have been chopped, and served with bread sauce they are better than any pheasant. Todd and Sadie have one of our Boxer pups which they love with the same passion which afflicts all owners of Boxers. Mr. Hunter, superintendent of the Ashland schools, his wife and grandson, came with Todd and Sadie.

The supper bell rang and Todd left saying the American Legion Band wanted to come over some Sunday evening before the end of September for a picnic and serenade. We decided on the twenty-sixth as I have to be in New York next week end.

Usual Sunday night supper is by co-operative effort in the kitchen and pantry. After supper Mrs. Johnson and the ensigns left, one for California and the others for Columbus, and my cousins Catherine, Roy, and Johnny McGinty arrived. Catherine brought a lot of old photographs and daguerreotypes of our common ancestors on my father's side of the house. It gave one an extraordinary feeling, going back and back into the past to great-great-grandfathers and grandmothers sitting primly before the camera. Some of them whom I remembered only as very old people were remarkably handsome and beautiful as young people. It gave one an intense feeling/of the continuity of life and of immortality. All of them are Ohioans. We came here in the very beginning and are still going strong.

Catherine brought a big watermelon, and, in return, we gave her a bushel of tomatoes for canning and a half bushel of the little yellow and orange tomatoes for making tomato butter. Roy is having fireblight in his one Bartlett pear tree.

The dogs all got in their chairs and went to bed early. They had had a hard day, covering miles of hunting while we made the farm tour. Prince got a groundhog, his second this week and tried proudly to bring it into the crowded station wagon and had to be restrained by force.

Marshall Bullitt wired and asked me to stay at Oxmoor while in Louisville. It is one of the oldest and most beautiful houses in Kentucky. He has a famous herd of Jerseys and is immensely proud of the thick yellow cream.

SEPTEMBER 4—LABOR DAY: One of the pleasant things about living in the country is that there aren't any holidays. One day is like the next and if you want a day off you can take it when you like. It doesn't have to be on the same day ninety million other people are having a holiday.

Worked all morning with George getting caught up with letters. They pile up at such a rate that if you let them go for two or three days you are swamped and it takes a day or two to dig out. I try to be conscientious about answering the letters of people who take the trouble to write, but it sometimes becomes physically impossible. The letters of every Service man and every farmer get answered and the letters of people who want information. The cranks, whose number is legion, the abusive letters, and naturally the anonymous ones go unanswered. There are advantages and disadvantages to a large correspondence. It brings in friends from all over the world but it takes an enormous amount of time. As someone said, most letters if left unanswered long enough, answer themselves.

In the middle of the morning Eula Stander came in with two women friends. All the husbands were over at Maxwalton Farm looking at Ernie Hartman's and Wallace Campbell's Shorthorns. The purebred Shorthorn and Angus people look on me as if I had married a Hottentot because we cross Angus and Shorthorn. The final indignity is that we are gradually eliminating purebred beef cows altogether and are building up a herd of blue-roan (crossed Angus and Shorthorn) cows and breeding them to a Shorthorn bull. We're not interested in pedigrees or show cattle but in producing quality, top-market beef with a minimum of sickness and feeding and I think we've made some progress. The calves of the blue-roan heifers bred to a Shorthorn bull look like miniature fat steers from the day they're born. Some of the crossbred blue-roan heifers give more milk with their first calves than some of our registered Guernsey heifers. Why, I do not pretend to know.

All the beef cows—that is, the blue-roans of the Angus-Shorthorn cross—are actually black and polled, and the bull, a Shorthorn, is pure white. Their offspring, the calves, come in all mixtures of blue and strawberry roan and calico. There are two which like their father—two-thirds Shorthorn, one-third Angus—are pure white, a dazzling white, with black noses and black eyes. Prettier animals I have never seen. On the rich pastures the coats of the black cows actually shine in the evening sunlight.

The day was hot and muggy and at noon big black clouds piled up behind the hill above the house. For three hours we had another good heavy soaking rain. Kenneth had just finished drilling twenty acres of rye on the Bailey hill. It will be sprouted by day after tomorrow. It is the first time we have worked that ground and I discovered that the earth there is filled with chipped and broken rocks, stratified like limestone but unlike the clean pink and red sandstone that crops out all along the valley. It must have come from the bottom of a pre-glacial lake and ought to enrich the soil as it disintegrates. It is great soil for alfalfa.

Watching the rain from the top of the hill was a magnificent sight. Butch Aldrich and George Cook, aged seven and eight, were there and told me that Bob was giving them cheques for their summer work. They both helped with loading baled straw. Bob let them take turns steering the big truck in low gear, but after a couple of hours they learned all about shifting gears and began to drive. It almost makes one believe that their generation is proof of inherited instincts.

Went with Mary, Ma, Bob and Virginia to the ice-cream supper at the valley church. The money is to be put into "the electric." The romantic side of me can't help being a little sorry over the prospect of "the electric." I liked the natural gas that comes right out of our earth here, but electricity will be more convenient.

The little church is built of red brick and sits by the roadside on the edge of the Douglass woods which still has a lot of virgin oak in it and in spring is filled with the white clouds of dogwood. Below the church lies the little valley and Charley Schrack's rich fields, and beside it an old churchyard where sooner or later all the valley people are buried. Tonight after the big rain the earth is steaming and a white cottony mist lay over the valley. During the evening a big, red harvest moon came up behind Charley's woods silhouetting the branches of the big trees. For a moment when old

32

Miss Andrews saw it and said, "Look," and the word spread, a silence came over the crowd in the churchyard. Most of the people stood watching as the moon, which seemed no further away than the Andrews farm, rose above the trees. I had never stood still before watching for a time the rising of the moon and had no idea how rapidly it comes up out of the horizon. Said old Miss Andrews watching it, "It's a wonder we don't all just fly right off the earth."

While the women washed dishes and served sandwiches, the men stood about in groups talking. Some of the talk was of crops and the beneficent rains, but most of it was of politics and how soon the war would be over and the bad effect of the industrial boom and the high war wages on juvenile delinquency and adult morals, on citizenship generally. Here in rich agricultural Ohio, studded with big industrial cities like Cleveland, Akron, Youngstown, Toledo, Canton, Cincinnati, Dayton and many others, the gap between the farmer and war labor is very great indeed, and sometimes the animosity runs high. All efforts by organized labor to unionize farmers have been dismal failures and will continue to be so, since nearly all farmers, even tenants, are individual proprietors and not employed labor. There are, however, great possibilities for better understanding between farmers and organized labor in the establishment of co-operatives, with the farmer on one side as the producer and union labor on the other as consumer. Some of the farm people were bitter about the administration's coddling of labor. Most of the men present were middle-aged or elderly men who had been carrying on somehow, working with their wives and young children twelve and fourteen hours a day. Nearly all the farm boys have been taken in the draft and the few who remained were ill or handicaped. Short of machinery, of spare parts, harassed by questionnaires and all sorts of regimentation, their profits checked during the first prosperous period they have had for a long time, they have done one of the heroic jobs of history. Old man Tucker, eighty-six years old, was there. Living alone he has farmed his 120 acres single-handed for two years because there was *no* help to be had. He did not quit and go on relief. Nobody in that community had gone on strike because a toilet floor wasn't swept, or because the A.F. of L. was trying to horn in on the C.I.O. or vice versa or because some labor leader had to produce results or lose the next union election.

I went home feeling both elated and depressed—proud because there were still in America people like those at the valley church festival and depressed because there were too few of them and too many of the other kind, looking to Government to support them. The big industrial cities are the curse of the nation, perhaps of the whole world. What they have brought us in bad health and morals and insecurity and misery are not worth the gains in comfort and convenience that come from the machinery they turn out.

Charley Schrack's boy Hilbert came over with Charley to introduce his new wife and baby. Hilbert met and married his wife in Wyoming where he is stationed. They were married there and the baby was born there in a couple of inadequate and inexpensive rooms which was all they could find to live in. The wife is a handsome, strong girl, raised on a Nebraska farm, with plenty of strength and courage. She said, "We're so tired of living like cattle. We'd like to have a decent home of our own." There are so many like them—young people trying to get along, dislocated, living from day to day as best they can, all because of this damned war. Four years out of your life between the ages of twenty-four and twenty-eight is a pretty terrible price for young people to pay. The baby is eight months old, very pretty and bright. Hilbert and his wife have one day more before they go back to the dreariness of that Wyoming camp. Hilbert has lost twenty pounds in the last year and is becoming discouraged about his future. He'll have to begin all over again as if he were a boy of eighteen instead of a man of thirty which he may well be before he is demobilized.

After the festival Bob and his wife Virginia came up to the house and we sat talking until one in the morning, mostly about the handicaps which great inherited wealth placed on young people and the need to find the right groove early in life. We also talked about cattle-breeding and the value to us of crossbred cattle rather than purebred beef stock.

At one o'clock we went to the kitchen and had sandwiches, milk and cantaloupe before going to bed.

SEPTEMBER 5: Joe Connolly of International News Service called up to try to straighten out the difficulties over whether I am to write a series of special political articles for International News or for Scripps-Howard. The whole business had become tangled, through no fault of my own. The mix-up involves the Bell Syndicate which publishes my column, Scripps-Howard and the Hearst papers. Sometimes I should like to take to the woods and live the rest of my life in a cabin.

The radio brought the good news that the British and Canadians are on the outskirts of Rotterdam and the first rumors (denied) of German capitulation. Lindsay of the Mansfield *News Journal* telephoned two days ago to say that Senlis, the town where we lived for sixteen years in France, had been liberated. It was good of him. Soon we shall be receiving a lot of letters from friends who have been shut off from us for four years or more. They are as good and close friends as any we have here in our own country. From time to time we have had messages from them through the Underground or through Mademoiselle Vuillemin, the translator of my books, who is French-Swiss and was allowed by the Nazis for a time to go back and forth between Geneva and Paris as a newspaper correspondent. She would see our friends and when she returned to Geneva write us the news.

Antwerp has been liberated and I shall be hearing shortly from my friend Willy Van Hove who is a master pilot on the Scheldt. I heard from him every week until Germany declared war on us. The letters came by airmail from Antwerp to Lisbon to Richland County. The Germans permitted it, I think, in the hope of getting information from the letters written in return. They didn't get much save the kind of news they didn't want to hear.

SEPTEMBER 16–17: The usual busy week end. Herbie Spencer and Dal, the two ensign friends of Hope, came up as usual from Columbus for Saturday and Sunday. I find the younger generation remarkable, both in information and intelligence, superior to my own generation and far superior to the generation before mine. Most of that generation has never grown up at all. The record of my own generation isn't too good but these kids seemed intelligent, balanced, and mature. This

35

is their last week end. Dal goes to the Pacific and Herbie to the Atlantic, both in command of destroyer escorts.

Herbie and I spent most of Sunday on the Ford-Ferguson tearing up a soybean field to plant rye. Dal ran the big John Deere, disking the cornfield into which we turned the cattle. Between the cattle, hogs, and sheep they have eaten it bare. Both the kids get a kick out of the farm.

Most of the talk while I was in New York among old friends was of France, of Senlis, of all the French friends and acquaintances out of the past—the Polignacs, René de Chambrun and José Laval, the Rochefoucaulds, the Archbishop of Senlis, the mayor, the neighbors, the Swiss who rented our house—and the rumors and gossip concerning some of them. Bernard Fay is sharing a cell at Drancey with Sacha Guitry. Also speculated regarding Camilla Acheson who married a boy called Von Schaffenburg, cousin of the man who tried to kill Hitler. Mary and I went to their wedding in London and have known Camilla since she was a little girl. Her family have heard virtually nothing from her for four years.

SEPTEMBER 19: Home from Columbus at noon. Barbara Wood, Ben's wife, drove over from Lima with her aunt for lunch. She and her husband are stationed in Texas where Ben is a flying instructor. She was most interested in beef cattle and we went to the bottom pasture to see the blue-roans and the calves of the blue-roan heifers by the Shorthorn bull —as fine beef calves as I've ever seen.

Went to see Vane Close who was spreading lime with a manure-spreader and a Ford-Ferguson manure-loader equipped with a homemade scoop. The combination solves our lime-spreading problem and does away altogether with the slow, tiring process of *shoveling* lime. With this set-up one man can do much more quickly and efficiently the work that would take two or three men to do in the past. It solves one aspect of our problem of labor shortage and the big acreage we have to cover.

We talked of the hard-shell conservatism of many of the farmers in our neighborhood who will go down into bankruptcy rather than try new ideas. Their fields wash out under their feet, their crop yields go down year after year and still they go on criticizing the more progressive farmers who are aware that the old ways of farming in America are no longer good enough. Some of them have come round and have been imitating Vane and Roy Mengert and ourselves and are getting results but if you should remark on the methods or results they would probably abandon the new methods and go back to the disastrous old ones just "to show you" and vindicate their sense of independence. It is a curious psychology, as old as agriculture itself and has some aspects which are both grim and humorous.

Finished the fitting of the wheat ground on the strips near the big house, using spring tooth and spike tooth, the one behind the other. It is almost unbelievable—the increase in the humus content, the moisture and the workability of the soil over what it was when we came here.

Grass farming and livestock are gradually becoming the established program with us. It has come about through experience and day by day experiment. It is ideal country for such a program—well-drained glacial hills that raise wonderful bluegrass and wonderful ladino and alfalfa with the low ground given over to row crops. The cattle grow fat on such pasture and the calves grow like weeds and the soil gets better and more productive all the time. There is no satisfaction like watching the earth grow richer because of what you do with it.

SEPTEMBER 20–21–22: Three busy days. Another heavy rain which has brought on the rye pasture and filled the ground with moisture for the wheat planting. Unfortunately it caught us with some soybean hay still down, but the wind and sun dried it out quickly and today we are baling it. Yesterday I drove the big John Deere all day fitting wheat ground for planting after the twenty-sixth when it should be safe from Hessian Fly. While working the ground, I was struck again by the miracles that can be done with poor soil. The change in mineral as well as humus content, even in a few years, is extraordinary. One would believe that it was not the same soil we found when we came here. And production has jumped as much as 300 per cent to 400 per cent. Wherever alfalfa or sweet clover has been plowed under the change is phenomenal.

Worked at night on a chapter on "Decentralization of

37

Cities" to be included in a book edited by Elmer Peterson and published by the University of Oklahoma Press. Elmer, Paul Sears and other writers on agriculture and economics are contributing.

Thursday's mail brought a letter from Sandro D'Ostiani, an old friend, still a prisoner in North Africa where he was captured. Nothing makes war seem more futile and tragic than the way in which it destroys people's lives. Sandro, a painter and philosopher, an anti-Fascist, a hater of war, has lost the best five or six years of his life and now sits in a prison camp in North Africa, guarded by American soldiers.

Also had a letter from an American officer named Taylor, saying that he had seen and talked with Louise Pesch who for years was our friend and cook in Senlis. He could not, owing to censorship, give me her address and no civilian mail is yet going to or from France. She is a remarkable woman with a tragic life. She began with the little band— César and Marie Ritz, Escoffier et al.—and rose with them through the Ritz in Paris, the Savoy and Carlton in London and then went to America where she had a table d'hôte restaurant in New York in the Twenties and later a *charcuterie* in New Jersey. After that she returned to France to retire and live on her savings. These were wiped out by the inflation and she came to work again with us when she was well over sixty. She stayed with us until the work grew too heavy for her. Like all French people she was politically minded and well informed. No one understood better than she did the weakness of the Popular Front and the meaning of the British political maneuvers, Munich, sanctions, the Spanish Civil War, Russia. We used to talk European politics by the hour in the red-tiled kitchen. If Daladier, Reynaud, Chamberlain, Léon Blum, Halifax or Sir John Simon had been as wise and able and honest as Louise, the history of the world might have been different and there might have been no war. She told Taylor that her one hope was to revisit America and that she hoped to visit us.

Blondy, the big Angus bull, has escaped again and crossed five fences with no difficulty, to rejoin his harem which, unfortunately, contains some of his own daughters. No box stall or pen would hold him and so we set up an electric fence about him, inside the barn. He wouldn't go near it and from time to time we shut off the current. When that happened the ticking of the transformer would stop. After a while he apparently discovered the connection between the ticking and the current and waited for the ticking to stop before breaking out. Anyone who lives closely with animals can't help respecting their intelligence and be led almost into a belief in reincarnation. He is a gentle, amiable bull, very beautiful, and will come up to you in the field to have his ears scratched. He gets on very well with the young white Shorthorn bull save in the case of rivalry. The Shorthorn bull has the advantage of horns but Blondy manages to keep him under domination. I can't help preferring the beef cattle to the dairy herd—more personality, I guess. The dairy herd just eats and gets milked, but the beef cattle are always raising hell of some kind.

SEPTEMBER 24: A man named Darnell called early asking if he could come out and go over the farm and talk of his plans for setting up a farm of his own. He came down from Mansfield at nine-thirty and it turned out that he was a New York businessman of about forty who had had enough of city and business life and wanted to invest his savings in a farm where he could live the rest of his life. He had been doing a lot of reading and investigating and was very well informed, with few illusions concerning the business of farming. Very intelligent about it all. One of the finest things about the Malabar adventure is the contacts it brings with intelligent and well-informed people of broad interests.

Charles Kimmel, the County Game Warden, came to get a contribution for the new Boy Scout's camp and to talk over the soil and game conservation film which he and Floyd Dent are making here in the county on colored film. They have been at it for eighteen months and have some beautiful material. We expect to get it pieced together soon and titled. I'm doing the titles and paying expenses which is the smallest part of the job. When finished it will be available for showing throughout the state and elsewhere. Charley and Floyd have done wonders by organizing the scouts and high-school boys from towns and villages in the county to continue the planting of seedling trees in Mohican State Forest after war shortages of labor very nearly killed the forestry project.

At noon went up to Mansfield to talk to the State Convention of the Credit Managers Association on the decentralization of cities and the value to the national economy of small landholdings by industrial workers and white-collar people.

Came home about two-thirty and finished fitting the field by the old graveyard for wheat. Our working on Sundays scandalizes some of the more conservative and cantankerous of our neighbors, but it seems to me that real faith and religion begins in people with love and respect for the earth and for animals. I have to work on the farm when I get a chance and I am sure the Lord understands. Some of those who are horrified would do better to make less of a public display of piety and take better care of their soil and livestock.

Blondy, the bull, wasn't content with breaking out of the barn and rejoining his harem. This afternoon he broke down a fence and led them all off on an excursion through the woods and up to the Ferguson Place. He is just too damned smart.

Bob and Virginia came up tonight and we talked farm and financing. Things go better and better each year with really good prospects ahead. We are finding out a lot of answers, the hard way, but that makes it interesting and when you learn the hard way, you learn for good and are on a sound basis and anything is better than standing still. The conservatism of the farmer is sometimes his worst handicap.

SEPTEMBER 25–26: Worked on the baler with the last of the soybean hay. It was too dry and the dust was thick, with the result that I had chills and fever in the evening from it. Protein poisoning!

Had the first real letter out of France today from Jean de Sourian. The last we had heard from him was a letter actually written on the beach at Dunkirque calling despairingly for us to send help. He wrote that all the country around Senlis was a shambles and that the De Montfort and Harcourt boys were both killed. His mother, English by birth, was in a concentration camp for a while. Jean, who is twenty-two, joined the American army on the day after it arrived in Paris. Half-English, half-French he is extraordinarily American in his outlook and likely, I think, to end up here.

Finished tilling the upper field on the Anson Place (Faulkner method).[4] It has been treated that way for two years and the increase of humus is striking, especially in contrast with the soybean field on the Fleming Place which was like cement in spots. The record of better moisture content in the Anson field as compared with the Fleming field is striking. I begin to suspect that the real system is trash farming (Faulkner method) for two or three years and then a really deep plowing to bring up the glacial subsoil every third or fourth year. On our soil man can create in five or six years what it takes nature thousands of years to do, but it can only be done by using nature's own method, speeding it up enormously.

Went with Ma up to the Ferguson Place where, as we guessed, Blondy had taken most of his harem. The others are in the bottom bluegrass pasture with the white Shorthorn bull. Blondy, apparently, still has more sex appeal as most of the cows had followed him. The calves from the crossbred blue-roan heifers are big and fat and vigorous. They are only a little over four months old and as big as the ordinary beef calf six or seven months old. There was a tree of late peaches ripe near the ruins of the burned down Ferguson house. They were touched by the frost and delicious. We gorged ourselves.

[4] Edward Faulkner is the author of a remarkable and controversial book on agriculture called *Plowman's Folly* published in 1943. It outsold most novels and nonfiction books of the year and has attained a sale of near to one million copies. He advocated the abandonment of the conventional moldboard or "turning" plow and the universal employment of "trash farming" which mixes all surface residues *into* the soil rather than turning them under. His book did much to promote the farming methods since largely adopted over the wheat-growing areas of the Great Plains which are very largely responsible for checking dust storms, conserving moisture and achieving record production. He is a neighbor of Malabar Farm and a constant visitor and observer. He recently published a second valuable book called *A Second Look* in which he modified some of his earlier contentions and set forth new controversial material. His greatest contribution to American agriculture has probably been his capacity for stirring up controversy and injecting life and interest into the whole of the vast field.

The first frost came Sunday night (September 24). The average date is supposed to be October 4 in this area. We have drilled to date something over ninety acres of wheat and about sixty of rye and are not behind schedule. This is remarkable considering we are 50 per cent undermanned. The answer to our problem is, I believe, first-rate machinery, good management and grass farming. Bob who has been here for about eighteen months had done one of the most remarkable jobs I've ever seen or heard of being done. With Max's illness and absorption in other things and my own absence, the place was in a mess when Bob came, plus the awful burden of the run-down Bailey Place which we bought in March. We did not want another worn-out farm at that time but it fell into our laps and we had to seize the opportunity.

This afternoon Kenneth drilled more wheat in the cemetery field while Bob and I got in all the soybean hay. I helped with two loads until we discovered two of the registered Guernsey calves were missing from the old orchard paddock. I went to find them in the top Anson field. Blossom, one of the Holsteins, had a heifer calf during the morning.

I know few satisfactions greater than getting in a field of good hay green and in prime condition. The barns are bursting with hundreds of tons of alfalfa and soybean hay that looks good enough to eat. The silos are filled and the grain bins. Only the corn crop will be short but under OPA ceilings no farmer can afford to fatten out cattle with corn save for his own use. It's getting so that the only good steaks are to be found at home. And there is butter and buttermilk and cream and a quick freeze filled with strawberries, sweetcorn, lima and string beans, cauliflower, broccoli, and red raspberries. Soon the root cellar will be filled with apples, potatoes, squash, carrots and celery. The cellar shelves are groaning under jars of homemade tomato juice, jams, jellies, pickles, canned peaches, blackberries, elderberries and "Dr. Bromfield's tonic." A farm life is a good life. Nanny and Jennie Oaks have done nobly this year with the canning and freezing.

Some of the corn is shocked in the valley and the evenings are growing frosty with mist lying white in the moonlight over the lower pastures and over the ponds. The rye on the distant Bailey farm hill turns a more brilliant emerald green

42

every day. In the bottom fields at Bailey's, the new contours are showing up in strips of different shades of green. Ladino clover is wonderful stuff: seeded in a mixture over the poorer bottom fields without lime or fertilizer it has spread in a mat over the whole field.

Charley started preparing ground for the new peony collection given me by the Chamber of Commerce of Van Wert, Ohio. It is the center of the peony growing industry in America and they are giving me a collection of 75 of the world's finest peonies in return for making a speech there on "soil." I can't think of any better payment. We are planting them in a semicircle in front of a row of climbing hybrid perpetual and rugosa roses which begin to bloom at about the same time as the peonies.

The County Commissioners are widening the bridge just outside the garden and are making a tiny new pond by excavating soil from the runway where the cattle come down from the orchard paddock to drink. Bob says I will end up by having the whole farm under water. Well, there's never too much water on a farm with livestock.

Four farmers from Palestine turned up this week to spend the day and to investigate our soil conservation and soil building program. Unfortunately I was not at home but Bob turned over the day to them. They were tough and horny-handed specimens (as they need well be for the job they have undertaken in rehabilitating ruined, half-barren Palestine). Three were from Poland and one from Roumania. They had escaped somehow out of the shambles of Central Europe three or four years ago. They spoke very little English but Bob knows German and by "wrassling" with Yiddish and German they managed to communicate with each other and both sides had a profitable day. Bob said their knowledge of modern agriculture was remarkably varied and sound. I was sorry to have missed them. Scarcely a week passes, even in wartime, without visitors from some remote part of the world as well as from all parts of the United States.

OCTOBER 21: This morning when I went down to the big bottom pasture to have a look at the new carload of Holstein heifers which arrived during the night from Wisconsin, I started up all kinds of game birds in the marshy land along the creek and ponds. I started up snipe, four woodcock and

43

a whole flock of that rare and beautiful bird, the golden plover. Apparently, like the common killdeer plover, they were gathering to migrate southward. The golden plover, still very rare, became at one time almost extinct and are now protected from all shooting. Apparently their numbers are increasing for I have seen a few each season. This flock behaved in the regular plover fashion. After I started them, they circled around and settled in a wheat field where the freshly seeded wheat is only a few inches high. When I went nearer to investigate them, I could not at first discover them at all. It was not until I nearly stepped on one that I discovered they were all hiding there in the newly grown wheat, pressed tightly against the bare earth. The coloring was so exactly the same as our brown glacial soil that they were practically indistinguishable. The bird that took to wing made a short circle of flight and settled back among its immovable companions. Only when I walked into their very midst did they again take to the air as a flock.

The flight of the woodcock is one of the swiftest and most erratic of all birds. They start up from under foot in a flight which can best be described as the zigzag course of a streak of lightning. I am certain that no sportsman has ever brought down a woodcock except by accident—Annie Oakley included.

The red-winged blackbirds have all gone. I miss their beauty and their song. They live in our low lands in summer in great numbers.

The first hell-divers have appeared in pairs on the ponds where they have made themselves completely at home and refuse to be disturbed. They will be followed shortly by wild ducks of every sort, and with luck, by a few geese.

The proper use of the land plus a simple program of game food and cover has certainly paid big dividends in fish, birds, and game. Everywhere at Malabar, since we established the farm as a game propagation area, the population of wild life has doubled and redoubled, again and again. Once the area becomes saturated, the excess population moves off into the neighboring territory where it provides sport for hunters. We do not shoot on the farm and allow no shooting but the sportsmen benefit enormously by the closed season on this large area. Big fox-squirrel, fox, raccoon and rabbits are especially abundant. Of course there is always plenty of quail (on which in Ohio there is no season) and some grouse and pheasant although the foxes kill off the latter pretty rapidly.

It is easy to see why the quail escape the foxes. Almost from the day they are hatched, they leave the nest and are able to fly. Again and again in midsummer I have started up a covey of newly hatched quail so small that but for the presence of the mother among them I would have taken them for a flight of good-sized grasshoppers.

The delight of the sudden flight of a bird or the sight of the secretive muskrat migrating with his undulating, ripple-like motion down a rapidly flowing stream or the glimpse of a herd of deer among the dogwood and wild grapes has an extraordinary power to dissipate all feelings of worry and depression and restore a sensation of confidence and even delight on the most trying of days.

The new heifers, on the whole, look pretty good. They seem very quiet but their coats are rough and shaggy compared to the coats of our own heifers brought up on our pasture. Ours are sleek and they shine as if they had been groomed for a stock show.

August has begun to slip toward winter but the barns and silos are full, the cattle are looking sleek and bright-eyed, and the wheat and rye spread vigorous and emerald-green across the fields.

# II: THE PASSING OF A PATTERN

> For horticulture and good husbandry are eternally liv-
> ing professions, constantly growing and changing their
> methods and manners, and subject to all manner of
> pressures from economy and science and philosophy.
> —Voltaire

IN PLEASANT VALLEY much space was given to "The Plan"
under which Malabar Farm was set up. It was a cooperative
plan with a good many goals which appeared Utopian. The
important point is that these goals were recognized in the
very beginning as Utopian and most of them as perhaps
unattainable. The Plan was something to aim at and after eight
years it is remarkable how many of those goals have been
attained. War intervened and took away Pete and Wayne,
which was a great loss, and Max, after organizing the farms
and setting them in operation, stepped out, to head the
Northern Ohio Cooperative Breeders Association, one of the
most important American centers of artificial insemination
with all its vast implications of better economic conditions for
the farmer-cattle breeder throughout the nation. Max, I
think, regretted leaving and I know we all regretted seeing
him go. But it was a job and an opportunity for which he has
been specially trained and for which he had a great enthusiasm,
and then Bob Huge stepped in to take his place. And finally
the pattern became set to include four families and ourselves
and it appears likely that it will change little for years to come
save for the addition of another family or two from time to
time as our acres continue to increase their yields.

Of these original goals certainly one—a good life with
mutual enthusiasm and cooperation in an undertaking—has

been attained. And certainly the checking of all soil and water loss and the restoration of eroded or depleted land has been realized and far more quickly and to a degree far beyond anything even the most optimistic of us had hoped. The change in the very landscape from one of abandoned fields, of gullied desolation of hills brown and red with sorrel and broom sedge to greenness has been as remarkable as the steadily darkening color of the soil as the fertility rose with gains in production ranging from 50 to 1500 per cent per acre. Where once the same acreage could scarcely feed thirty head of cattle, winter and summer, ten times that number could flourish today with abundant forage, grain and pasture always in reserve. Abundance, not only in crops and livestock but in living as well, has been brought into being and the actual value of the land on the Federal Land Bank basis of appraisal has increased three or four times.

And there have been many less tangible satisfactions— such things as mutual enthusiasm and interest and the deep pleasure of having succeeded at a tough job. An enthusiasm and a pleasure shared not only by all those living permanently at Malabar but as well by the boys who come each summer to bale the hay and the straw and clip the pastures and fill the silos. They must all have been happy for each year they return during the school months to spend a great part of their Christmas and Easter holidays working with us in the big dairy and feeding barns. We have seen them grow from boys into men and go off to war as new and younger teams came in. They return to visit us and bring back their girls to meet us and all during the war we had letters from the older ones at least once a month from Okinawa or Calcutta or Stuttgart or other remote and unlikely places. The oldest ones are getting married and before long will make a grandparent of Malabar Farm. The contact with these boys and the character and the sense of responsibility they have shown has certainly been one of the richest of our experiences and has served to raise a great confidence in the future of the nation which produces such specimens.

And of course there has been the satisfaction and the pleasure of friendship and cooperation with the neighbors and the people of the surrounding villages in a life far removed from the neurotic, snarling life of the city subway.

And there have been scores and hundreds of new friends coming from all parts of this country and from all over the world whom we should never have met save for Malabar Farm and a mutual interest in agriculture and scores and hundreds of letters from all parts of the world.

Not the least of the satisfactions has come from the visitors, the thousands of people, mostly dirt or city farmers or scientists who come on Sundays from late April to well into November. They come in shiny cars, in jalopies, in motor buses—from two hundred to a thousand each Sunday throughout the summer, in such numbers that mere curiosity-seekers have long ago been eliminated and sent on their way and the boys have had to set themselves up on Sunday afternoons as traffic cops with a log chain and tractor always ready to pull stray cars out of a ditch or mud hole. There have been Farm Bureau groups, Granges, 4-H Clubs, Future Farmers of America, Soil Conservation District Association, G. I. Vocational classes, City Farmers Clubs, many of them coming by bus from as far as Flint and Saginaw in Michigan and Buffalo in New York State.

Most of them are good and serious and successful men —the City Farmers as well as the dirt farmers—most of whom, like ourselves, are making contributions to cattle, swine and poultry breeding and to the New Agriculture. More than half of them are young men and many of them are boys—the group which will have to cherish our soils and feed not only ourselves but a large part of the world from now on until Doom's Day. They are of all stations of life and all degrees of affluence, from the symbolism of the big shiny Cadillac to that of the jalopy containing a young tenant getting a start with a wife beside him and four or five children in the back seat. But they all have one thing in common—an eye which shines at sight of a beautiful heifer or a shiny fat steer or a thick, heavy stand of lush pasture and a willingness to sit on the fence and talk farming and cattle breeding until darkness falls. At Malabar we have learned much from the new friends who come on Sundays.

In long processions on foot or in cars they follow the long winding lane to the top of the Bailey hill which Phillippe, one of the boys, long ago named "Mount Jeez." The name might be indelicate or even blasphemous but for the fact that it came about spontaneously and reverently. From the top of the hill there is certainly one of the most beautiful views in the world, across wild woodland and both rich and desolated fields, of all Pleasant Hill lake, Pleasant Valley and the valley of the Clear Fork. On a clear day you can see into four counties. From the top of Mount Jeez the whole landscape tells its own story both of weedy, abandoned fields, ruined worn-out land, pastured sickly woodlots and of farms which are green, where the soil is dark and rich and the crops stand strong and opulent in the fields. The green farms—our own and those of some of our neighbors stand out like jewels. They make you feel good, and they make you see what all our valley and all our state and nation could be under a good agriculture. Up there on the hilltop with the whole of Malabar laid out like a map below, the talk goes on for an hour, two hours, sometimes three, and afterward, those who haven't already left to go home to do the chores, move down to the ancient spring house on the Bailey Place and drink their fill of the icy water which gushes directly out of the sandstone cliff behind the house to rush through the watercress beds on its way to the big fish pond across the road.

One by one, family by family, the crowd slips away, until at last there remains as the sun begins to go down only a handful of farmers gathered, usually in the milk parlor where Al and Jim are doing the evening milking. Sometimes Sunday is a long, hard day but always it is a rewarding and satisfactory one. By ten o'clock bed feels pretty good and there isn't any trouble about sleeping.

In the original Plan for Malabar set forth in *Pleasant Valley* great emphasis was placed on diversified farming and self-sufficiency. These two goals have not been reached, not because we failed in the attempt but because under the changing pattern of modern economic life both goals have become, in so far as such a unit as Malabar is concerned, uneconomic and even expensive. Although Max had always had doubts concerning the soundness of both goals in modern agriculture, I had held out strongly for both of them. Looking back now, I think there were two reasons for my insistence: (1) The fact that I had recently come from Europe where war appeared inevitable, and because of having lived for years outside the United States, I knew the hardships and deprivation brought about by wars, rationing, inflation and the consequent disruption of human society. (2) A nostalgia born of memories of my grandfather's farm where virtually everything but salt, pepper, coffee, tea, and spices was supplied from the farm and where the cellar, the attic and the fruit house were always groaning with food.

During the war years the self-sufficiency goal was a satisfactory and sound policy. In the years when butter, bacon, beef, lamb, poultry, honey, maple syrup, and many other things were either available only at fantastic black-market prices or not available at all, the four families at Malabar and all the countless visitors lived well and richly. In the case of another war or the disruption which might arise from political disorders, the self-sufficiency program would again be useful and economic and could be quickly re-established. But for periods of fairly normal peacetime existence we found that we could *not* at Malabar *afford* a program of 100 per cent self-sufficiency nor could we afford a program of highly diversified farming on the plan of my grandfather's "General Farm."

My own miscalculations regarding the goal arose from the fact that in the beginning I was not thinking of the intricate, co-related world in which we live today, but of the world as it existed in my grandfather's time and even into my early youth. It was a world in which there were few fast trains, no automobiles, no telephones and no radio and little means of communication, a world in which neither time nor labor were expensive, where there was no electricity and the principal use of gasoline was for the patent lamp in the parlor. It was a world born of the frontier or prairie and forest, a pattern of life which grew up of necessity in America as it grew up in South America and Australia and South Africa and wherever families had to lead the lonely life of the frontier. It was a pattern of farm life which, save in remote areas, has not existed in Europe for generations and even centuries. The pattern became known as the "general farm," and throughout the horse-and-buggy days on comparatively new, still fertile soil, it prospered. It built many fine barns and farm houses and piled up small fortunes upon which farmers could retire and "live in town."

The pattern of the general farm has, I think, outlived its usefulness and its economic justification and to a certain extent so has the pattern of self-sufficiency. The successful farmer of the future in the United States will be, as he has long been in Europe, not a frontier farmer living in a little world of his own with a few cows, a few hogs, a few chickens, ten acres of corn, ten acres of oats, ten of hay and ten of wheat with a little primitive, untended pasture land on the side, but a businessman, a specialist and something of a scientist. I suspect that the old-fashioned, frontier-pattern general farm has already become obsolete and that in the future save for a few farmers who stubbornly prefer that pattern and are willing to sacrifice profits to hard work and low income, the general farm will cease to exist within a generation or two. It is not a prospect which I, personally, regard with any pleasure but my own preferences or those of anyone else are of small importance where the pressures of economic law in the industrial era are concerned.

I hasten at this point to add that by the passing of the general farm I do not mean the passing of the family-sized farm. Size has nothing to do with it. It is a question of program and of land use. I know some families who on fifty acres or less make far more money every year than other families who operate ten to twenty times the acreage. *Reviewers please note* and do not accuse me of predicting the passing of the family-sized farm or of speaking of it with derogation. The family-sized farm is still, and I hope will remain, a bulwark to our agriculture, and our economy, and our democratic ideals. I mean simply that it cannot survive on the old overdiversified pattern of the frontier general farm.

The obsolescence of the pattern is one part of the enormous revolution in agriculture which has taken place almost unnoticed and which is still taking place. Many things have contributed to it—mechanization, better and quicker distribution, specialization (within reason), efficiency, health regulations, increasing markets and populations, rapid means of communication, rural electrification and the immense advances in agricultural discoveries and knowledge made during the past generation. All these things and many more have,

I think, made the old-fashioned, overdiversified farm as obsolete as the wooden plow. And it has, generally speaking, reduced the general farmer not only to a standard of living far below the level of that of his more advanced, specialized, mechanized brothers but has made him a burden to the taxpayers of the nation. It is my guess that if an analysis could be made of those farmers who need subsidies, parity supports, bribes, etc., 80 per cent (excluding the blighted cotton areas) would fall in the category of general farmers who work upon a plan so overdiversified that they can afford little mechanization and all of whose efforts and energies become in turn so diversified and so splintered that they can at best achieve only a maximum of hard work and a minimum of profit.

If I had not observed these things at Malabar and among neighboring farmers they would have been forced upon my attention during agricultural trips which I make each year into some forty states. To be sure, Malabar is not in the pattern of the general farm or even the family-sized farm. It is a farm of about 1,000 acres, including 140 acres of woodlot, cooperatively run and making a much better than average living under modern conditions for five families. It is made up of five farms, four owned and one rented, which had been originally operated on the old general farm plan. Despite the differences many of the things which we discovered through our own operations nevertheless apply to all farms and nearly all of them apply to all big farms.

In our own case we have moved gradually but surely away from the original pattern of the general farm on an expanded scale toward a program of specialization. We set out on the original 640 acres with a pattern which included dairy and beef cattle, sheep, hogs and chickens and a field program which included corn, wheat, oats, hay, soybeans, pasture and an orchard of some 200 trees. Bit by bit we discovered that if we stuck to such a program and were efficiently and self-sufficiently mechanized, we should have too big investment in machinery and that we did not have enough acreage or production in hay to support a baler, enough acreage in corn to support a corn-picker or enough acreage in small grain to support a combine. To justify this mechanization as well as the investment in other incidental mechanization one of three courses was necessary: (1) to acquire more land; (2) to raise production per acre to such a point that the yields justified the investment in machinery; or (3) to do custom work in order to augment the cash income to a point where it justified the mechanical equipment.

We could not raise production per acre over night and if one or two of us went out on the machines doing custom work it meant that we were taking time away from the urgent needs of a farm where not only were the normal operations in progress but also an intensive program of rehabilitation. The first choice was taken and we acquired by purchase and lease 350 more acres. Even with the additional acreage, however, the high degree of mechanization was still not justified in the economic sense because the production per acre on the eroded, depleted farms was so low—not higher in total production possibly than the production of an average, well-managed 200-acre farm. In other words, such a 200-acre farm on a highly diversified program could no more really afford such a degree of mechanization than we could on our 1,000 acres. (Eventually the rapid gains in production per acre did justify the purchase and maintenance of some of our machinery.)

Then gradually we began to discover that we could not afford to operate the 200-tree apple orchard. If we operated it with any degree of efficiency, the investment meant mulching and mowing, five or six sprays, picking, sorting, and packing the apples. Two hundred trees did not justify the investment in spraying apparatus and if we hired the spraying done the cost had to be added to the cost of other operations and even a bumper crop could be produced and marketed only at a loss. Added to this we should have had to take time off away from the other important and profitable operations. The point was that we could not afford to operate the orchard. If we had had 5,000 apple trees we could have made money, but with only 200 trees we were neither in nor out of the apple business so the orchard was abandoned or leased out to neighbors who quickly found themselves in the same situation and quit their leases after one year.

One story concerning potatoes parallels that of the orchard. For three or four years under our self-sufficiency program we grew a supply of potatoes sufficient for all of us with a little over. "All of us" means about an average of forty people the year round. The small acreage involved did not merit elaborate planting, spraying, digging machinery, so beyond the plowing and fitting much of this work was done by hand and therefore, together with plowing, fitting and cultivating, consumed considerable valuable man-hours which might profitably have been employed elsewhere. Because we always had to steal time from other more important tasks to take care of the potatoes, they were neglected and both the yield and the quality were poor.

It was only after three or four years that the light struck us. We could go down the road to a neighbor whose business is potato growing on a scale of thousands of bushels and buy all the potatoes we wanted far more cheaply than we were raising them in terms of seed, labor, and fertilizer, and they were much better potatoes. He in turn came to us for meat and dairy products because that was our business and we produced them much more cheaply and efficiently than he could on his own place.

In a tiny way, the potato story illustrates one economic phase of a changed world. It has been true also that at times we could buy peas or string beans cheaper than we could raise them. We have not done so because we prefer the freshness and better flavor of the vegetables grown in our own communal garden. We have also used that garden as an experimental plot and we find pleasure in raising good vegetables, but all of these elements are outside the realm of pure economics and of course a world controlled by pure economics, devoid of luxuries and pleasures of the spirit, would be a poor and dreary world indeed.

Next we found that save for a couple of years with occasional high prices we could not afford to operate the laying houses with only 1400 pullets, no matter what records they made. Each year the hen house showed a profit, but if we charged up labor and the time taken away from the operations more vital, the profits largely vanished. Again it was the same story. We were neither *in* nor *out* of the egg business. If we had had 5 thousand or 25 thousand pullets we could have operated efficiently and even made large profits but none of us liked chickens well enough to sacrifice all other operations to them. The same story held true of heavy chickens, especially when OPA ceilings made it impossible to produce them at 28 cents a pound even when fed cafeteria system on our own grain. So the flock was reduced to enough merely to supply eggs and poultry for the farm with an occasional small surplus for sale purposes. The expense in labor and feed and time were all slight and justified, especially during the war years when eggs and poultry prices not only were high but when both were for a large part of the time either in the black market or altogether unavailable.

And so, once the usefulness of the sheep as consumers of poor pasture came to an end, the sheep went the way of the orchards and the poultry. We were neither in nor out of the sheep business and could not afford them. (They were fine-wool Dorset crossbreeds.) Registered sheep of high individual value might have been a different story but ordinary sheep are a low profit per head and it requires a great many to show any substantial profit.

Hog-raising soon went the way of the sheep, the poultry and the orchard, for we quickly found it much cheaper to buy weanling pigs to run after the cattle in the feeding barns, than to keep an array of sows the year round with all the labor, housing and feeding costs involved. In any case, our hill country is naturally grass country and not hog and corn country.

Gradually as the fertility of the fields mounted, we found ourselves moving deeper and deeper under the pressure of common sense and economics into streamlined, efficient, specialty farming and a program based upon small grains and grasses. We moved toward a pattern which today is firmly and permanently established. We have become a factory for grass in all its forms—hay, grass silage, and pasture. Our livestock has become incidental to the main specialty. They are merely the factory which processes the raw material we produce in the form of grass. The factory in the livestock barns processes it into milk, cheese, veal, baby beef and dairy heifers which we ship to the eastern markets. Within another year or two we shall probably grow no corn at all, put the remaining corn land into grass, buy what corn we need, and make money by doing so. We still raise oats and wheat because both give us at present a high-priced cash crop while we are reseeding meadows and because we consume a considerable amount of oats in our program. We are going up hill all the time, concentrating all our efforts upon a definite, streamlined program of grass and cattle, building our fertility instead of tearing it down and making more money per acre than any general farmer can make and more than most corn and hog farmers are making. (The reasons are set forth in the chapters "Grass, The Great Healer.")

We know where we are going, what we are doing and what to expect in returns from year to year. Bad weather, not even drought (in our country), nor rains, nor frosts, affect seriously our grasslands production. The books are simple and easy to keep and the turnover is constant and stable. Not only is our income much higher than we should have off a general farm with a little of this and a little of that but we have done away with headaches which go with over-diversified farming. We can operate with our hay baler (for hay, straw, and making silage) one combine, two mowers, two side delivery rakes, four tractors and the usual fitting tools on something over a thousand acres. Four men do the work with the aid of the boys who bale and fill silos in summer. Working upon our original general-farm plan we should need at least two or three more men. We also have the satisfaction of doing one or two jobs well instead of doing a dozen indifferently.

The truth is, of course, that the general farm cannot afford a high degree of mechanization because its gross income is not so high as that of the specialized farm doing one or two or three things expertly, efficiently, and well. The higher income of the specialist provides an economic base for still greater mechanized efficiency per acre and per man-hour, reduces drudgery to nil and permits still higher gross production and profits. Without mechanization it is difficult for the general farm to compete on even terms with the wheat specialist or the corn and hog specialist or the grass farmer or the big and efficient poultry operator or the orchardist with from five thousand trees upward or the 100-cow dairy.

Actually the old-fashioned general farmer is attempting to

compete with all of these. While he may receive the same prices for his produce in the open market, he is paying the difference between his production costs and those of the efficient specialist in terms of money, hard work, a low living standard, and all too often, the ruin of his soil because he cannot afford to buy the fertilizer and the equipment to do a good job in apples, in poultry, in hogs, in cattle, in hay, corn, wheat, oats, etc., all at one time, in all of which fields he is attempting to compete. Labor is expensive in these times, whether it is paid for in cash or in terms of long hours and hard work by the farmer and his family.

I think the problem and its answer were expressed partially at least in a conversation which took place at Malabar between one of the men and a visiting friend. The conversation ran something like this:

Friend: "John, would you ever go back to general farming on your own?"

John: "No."

Friend: "Why? Weren't you doing all right?"

John: "Yes, much better than average, but probably in spending money not as well as here. And cash isn't the only answer."

Friend: "What do you mean by that?"

John: "I mean that when I was general farming on my own, I worked from six in the morning to ten at night. I had to harvest my crops the old-fashioned way, shocking the grain, picking the corn by hand and handling small grain two or three times before it came out the right end of an old-fashioned threshing machine. The only alternative was having the work custom done and almost never was I able to get the combine, the picker or the baler at exactly the right time. Nearly always I lost at one end or the other. And more than that, my wife often had to help me in a pinch and I don't like my wife driving a tractor or working in the field. Now she never sets foot outside her house to work excepting in the flower garden or to hang out the washing. I work from eight to six and not always that much and I'm better off."

The conversation brought out at least one aspect of the

reasons for the passing of the general farm—the aspect of hard work. But it revealed too the fact that any farmer who does not own *all* the mechanical equipment necessary to his job is always at a disadvantage no matter how much custom machinery there is available. Crops in a given region usually ripen at about the same time and that time, perhaps even on a single given day, is the moment when every farmer in the neighborhood wants the combine or the hay-baler. A week early or a week late may cause a loss not only of feed values but of actual dollars and cents.

The average pioneer family was a family of many children among whom sons were especially desirable, and the work done by the children at various steps of their existence was regarded as *free* work. Very often the children of a pioneer family, as they grew to manhood or womanhood, had little choice but to marry and set up farms within the limited community in which they were born. Today the pattern has greatly altered. The average farm family in prosperous agricultural America produces but three children and the work which they contribute can no longer be regarded as *free* work, since there are, in our highly complex civilization, great opportunities for them to earn good money. A hundred careers are open to the youngster of today when even fifty years ago, the local area at least offered very limited choices beyond the field of agriculture. Today agriculture must be attractive to young people not only as a way of living but it must open prospects of a life free from drudgery as well as economic rewards comparable to those of other crafts, trades, and professions. It is unlikely that the family-sized general farm can offer these prospects. It can offer neither a large gross income, nor freedom from drudgery, nor much prospect of a progress toward a higher standard of living.

None of this is meant as an argument against the existence of the family-sized farm, but only against that of the general farm. As I pointed out above, the size of agricultural income and profits are not determined by the amount of acreage. Many other elements enter into the picture—tax and land values, markets, specialized, efficiently-run operations, mechanization and many other things, which might perhaps be summed up as proper farm progress and proper land use.

At Malabar I get countless letters a year asking, "How much should we make per acre?" This is a question which is completely unanswerable because of all the elements listed above. Wheat farms on the low value, low-tax level of the great farms of the Southwest where the land is valuable *only* as wheat or grazing land, can make money most years on yields of wheat as low as ten bushels to the acre. The same yields upon the rich, well-watered valuable lands of the corn-belt country would be wholly ruinous.

I have one friend who on thirteen acres grossed in the year 1946 a total of $144,000 of which the greater part represented net profit. He was, however, a specialist, growing hothouse vegetables and truck produce. It is obvious that such profits can well support a high investment in machinery which in turn creates greater efficiency and lower costs of production.

I have another friend, operating a 160-acre farm of land reclaimed from the abandoned tax-delinquent level. Last year on the 160 acres he grossed $33,000 with a probable net of about $27,000. If he had been operating the same acreage as a general farm his gross income, even at the inflated prices of 1946, could not have been much more than seven or eight thousand dollars with a net of "spending money" amounting to about $1,000 to $1,500. He operates, however, as a specialist in fruit and hybrid seed corn. He operates with a high degree of efficiency in these two fields, with the most modern equipment and machinery which such a large income makes possible. He has a definite program with no labor peaks and no sitting idly about the stove in winter. His work day is short and his work easy. I know many farms of much larger acreage operated as general farms which do not have a fifth the net income of this efficient specialized unit.

In the picture of modern agriculture—the New Agriculture—in a complex, highly intricate and integrated national economy, the question of proper land use plays an important role, not only the proper land use of the individual farm, but of the county, the state and the nation. On a farm it means simply using the land according to the best, most profitable and often obvious use. We have tried to follow a proper land-use pattern. It has turned out profitably and seems to be justified both in production and in the great increase in capital value, based upon the Federal Land Bank appraisal of production per acre. Roughly the plan works out thus:

(1) We are in hill country with little or no level land. The soil is light but minerally rich. It is not land suited to corn but when properly handled grows the finest hay, grass silage, and pasture in the world. Many farms in our region were completely ruined in the past by trying to raise corn and hogs on hills. (2) The first step in achieving proper use of the land was doing away with the old, square fields and establishing an agriculture upon the contour *around* the hills rather than up and down them. It involved as well the establishment of wide strips kept in sod-meadow. Much steep land was put permanently into meadow and pasture. All these measures were designed to retain all rainfall and prevent all soil erosion. (3) One hundred and forty acres of rough and rocky ground, not even suitable to permanent pasture and already in timber, was put into efficient wood-lot management with all cattle fenced out and the seedlings allowed to grow into valuable timber. (4) A considerable acreage of steep land and low-lying land was put into permanent bluegrass pasture, limed, fertilized, clipped, and treated as a valuable crop with a high-carrying capacity of livestock. (5) A large acreage of less steep land was put into strip cropping given over to a rotation of hay, silage, and pasture production alternated with wheat and oats. (6) The fairly level land was worked intensively in a corn, oats, sweet clover rotation. (7) Gradually the corn acreage has been reduced and the whole area has become, outside the woodlots and permanent bluegrass pastures, a grass, small grain farm with the prospect of corn being eliminated altogether, putting the intensively farmed oats, corn, sweet clover area into grass and buying what corn we need from the flat prairie lands to the west of us where corn is a specialty. The flat-land Iowa farmer can produce corn more efficiently and more cheaply than we can, while we have the advantage over him in grass, hay silage, and pasture production so long as we do a good job of it.

The pattern of proper land use in the rich prairie country would bear little resemblance to our own. We are in grass and dairy country. That country is natural corn, hog and beef-feeding country. The great plains farmer needs another pattern of land use and the farmer in the Deep South, with its special problems, still another. The average, over-diversified general farm with a conventional four-year rotation is attempting to practice and compete with all these areas—and often many more.

We have moved steadily toward the pattern of the New Agriculture, toward efficiency and concentration of purpose and effort and direction. Our fields are mostly big fields, their size and shape determined largely by the contours of the land and the exigencies of danger from erosion and by the flexibility of use which electric fencing has brought to such agriculture. Although the program of grass-small grain farming has virtually eliminated the dangers of soil and rainfall loss by erosion, we still maintain many of the long strips laid out originally because they are very practical and easy to farm. Some of them run nearly a mile in length following contours and always on the level. For plowing, fitting, and harvesting, these long strips have great advantages with none of the frequent turnings, stops and diagonal dead furrows which come with the old square-field farming.

The pattern of our specialized, grass program was determined by soil, climate, topography, markets, labor costs, proper land use and many other factors inherent in the principles of a new agriculture under which the successful farmer must be, I think, part businessman who invests a dollar to make five dollars, part scientist who does not merely accept what the Department of Agriculture or the County Agent tells him to do but knows *why* the practice is good and *how* and *why* it works, and the specialist who concentrates on doing two or three jobs efficiently and well rather than a dozen or fifteen indifferently.

During the century or more in which our agriculture, depending always upon new and virgin soils in apparently limitless quantities, has been slipping backward and in the Middle West was often confined rigidly to the old pioneer, general-farm pattern, American industry has produced more telephones, more automobiles, more plumbing, more radios and more of everything at a lower cost than the industry of all the rest of the world put together. At the same time American industry has paid wages to its workers from 30 to 90

62

per cent higher than paid to industrial workers in any other country in the world. This great feat of abundance, of high wages and low prices, has been achieved through efficiency, through specialization, through assembly lines, mass production and high production per man-hour, per unit and per invested dollar.

The record of our agriculture until very recently has been moving in exactly the opposite direction of a declining yield per acre and per man-hour, and food costs which have been rising steadily since the Civil War. An efficient agriculture, specialized, mechanized, with proper land use and respect for the soil could produce much the same result in the field of food and fiber as industry has achieved in the field of industrial commodities. A good agriculture—the New Agriculture—could produce at the same time higher profits and rewards for its workers while lowering the costs of food. If we had an agriculture universally as good as that practiced by 10 per cent of our really efficient farmers it is probable that on a basis of increased production per man-hour and per acre the cost of food could be lowered as much as 30 per cent while the profits of the farmer increased by as much as 20 per cent, regardless of inflations or deflations. No such thing can come about so long as proper land use is ignored and so much of our agriculture still remains in the old pattern of the pioneer general farm.

Too many of our farmers, by far the great proportion, have fallen into the evil habit of expecting high prices rather than efficient and abundant production per acre and per man-hour to bring them prosperity, economic stability, or even a bare living. They have been content with waning production per acre. "What was good enough for grandpappy was good enough for me," failing to realize that increased production and efficiency mean lowered costs per unit and per man-hour and increased profits and *solid* incomes.

Considering the inflated prices of the war and immediate postwar years, every farmer should have made a small fortune, but this was not so. Many of them paid off mortgages and put some reserves in the bank. Government statistics showed a vast increase in gross farm income but like all statistics, which are not analyzed and qualified, these give a false picture. The net profits to the farmer represented only a fraction of the gross income just as the wages or salaries of other elements of our society do not in themselves represent net profits. The great discrepancy between gross and net agricultural income arose from a number of causes—rising prices of seed, fertilizer, labor, machinery and material costs when these things were available, but largely the increased costs of production lay in the widespread acreages of low yields and the plowing up of non-agricultural and essentially unproductive ground to raise emergency crops at high-price levels. Of course the biggest cost of the farmer could not be measured in dollars and cents; it lay in the drudgery and the long hours for which he received, unlike the industrial workers, neither overtime nor adequate or corresponding recompense in prices. In many senses the American farmer and his wife and particularly the good, productive farmer, next to the men and women on active duty, were the real heroes of the war.

In all of this picture the profits of the good farmer were notably higher than those of the mediocre or poor farmer on a corresponding acreage. This was so because he produced a much bigger gross and because that gross, owing to high yields per acre, cost him per ear of corn or quart of milk or dozen eggs, much less to produce in terms of actual labor and of money costs.

The relation between production and costs and profits, judging from our own practical experience can scarcely be overestimated. It shows up in farm operations, in a hundred small ways. It is quite clear, as was pointed out earlier, that in the case of two farms, side by side, on the same type of soil, the farmer producing a hundred bushels of corn per acre can produce an ear of corn or a bushel of corn approximately five times as cheaply on the same basis of taxes, interest, seed, and labor as the farmer raising twenty bushels to the acre.

The same holds true of pasture and grazing land. Our best permanent pasture, when we took over three of the farms, could at best carry about one cow or steer for every ten or twelve acres for a part of the summer. Today, while the base of taxes and interest has varied little, we are able to carry 1½ head per acre, and in seasons of good rainfall at times as many as two head to the acre throughout the summer.

On the pastures that were originally almost non-productive and needed ten or twelve acres to feed one cow or steer inadequately, we have raised production as much as ten to twelve times on the original base of capital and tax cost. Such a record speaks for itself in terms of pure economics.

One of the common errors, particularly of the old-fashioned general farmer, is the conviction that his money is made in the barn by his livestock because that is where the monthly milk or egg check comes from or the sausage money at butchering time. It is an easy error to fall into, but it is a serious error. The farmer makes his money in the fields, out of his soil and its yield per acre; the livestock, in whatever form, are merely machines which process the yields of the field. If these yields are small, the cost of the production shows up in the general picture, and it costs the farmer more to produce his eggs, meat, or milk. The barn profits are in direct ratio to the degree of yields in his fields. Inevitably these things go back to the soil, the productivity of the soil and the efficiency in working that soil and increasing its yields per acre while maintaining or even increasing its fertility. In other words it costs the farmer with yields of one ton per acre of hay approximately three times as much to produce a quart of milk as it does the farmer producing three to three and a half tons per acre of hay. Efficiency and intelligent feeding programs can lower production costs and increase profits in the barns and hen houses but the final determination of costs is based always upon the soil and its productivity per acre, whether it concerns the man who raises his own feed or whether it is the man who is forced to buy feed grown five hundred or a thousand miles away.

I am aware that the above arguments have raised a number of questions, principally the question of surpluses. If we had an agriculture comparable in production to that of the top European agricultural nations, what could we do with the surpluses?

As I wrote to my friend, the sergeant in Okinawa, I think the answer to that one is easy enough—simply that for centuries there have never been any surpluses of food in the world and very rarely have there been real surpluses of food in this country since its beginning. There can be no surpluses of food in a world where half the population suffers in times of peace from severe malnutrition and where at least 500 million people are born and die without ever having had enough to eat one day of their lives. There are no surpluses, particularly of high protein foods, in a nation such as this one where in normal times, 40 per cent of the population suffers for one reason or another from malnutrition. There are no surpluses of food; there is only abominable distribution and prices which are so high, especially in the realm of high protein foods, that great numbers find their consumption of such foods gravely limited by the contents of their pocketbooks.

High prices limit consumption and create surpluses, especially in the realm of quality and highly nutritious foods.

The war and the necessity for feeding a considerable part of the world in the immediate postwar years have proved quickly that in the world, even with the bumper crops produced in America, there was a great shortage rather than a surplus of food. The desperate need of immediate neighbors in Europe gave rise to an emergency distribution which quickly disproved the theory of surpluses. Even if Europe immediately regained the power of feeding itself according to former standards there would still be a shortage of food, especially of good food, throughout the world. If the war and postwar means of distribution were maintained, the United States, producing twice or more its record production, would still fail to produce enough food to meet the demands of world nutrition even on a low-grade diet of cereals.

Within the country distribution is almost as inefficient as upon a world scale. High prices, high protein foods such as meat, eggs, butter, milk, etc., are drawn irresistibly to the areas of concentrated populations and the higher-income levels because the prices of these things are high. Other factors raise the retail prices of all of them—such factors as the high overhead in taxes, land values, etc., in our monstrous overgrown cities, the virtually unregulated activities of the commission merchant who is often able to rig prices, holding them down to the producer, raising them to the consumer and sometimes causing a spread of as much as 75 per cent and more between the price paid the producer and the price paid by the consumer. There are endless and often unnecessary costs of refrigeration, transportation, etc., of which the notable example lies in those small towns within a radius of 200 miles of a great city—small towns which pay the big city commission merchant a cut, and pay shipping costs *into* the great city markets and *out* again on food grown originally at their very borders. All these things represent the minor idiocies of an economic civilization which considers itself mature, but again, while serious, they represent only a part of the picture. The fundamental is the high cost of food production which is inevitable under a poor or mediocre agriculture.

When agricultural prices decline sharply all farmers suffer curtailment of income but the productive, efficient farmer remains solvent and even perhaps modestly prosperous because the cost of his production is so much lower than that of the poor or mediocre farmer that he is still able to produce a profit margin. His gross income declines much less than the income of the unproductive farmer on the same acreage. The truth, of course, is that efficient production and reasonable and profitable prices and not scarcity and high prices is the answer to high standards of living, for the farmer as well as other elements of society.

Some readers might ask, "Supposing we produce twice as much food and agricultural products on half as much land, what would we do with the land that remained?"

At least a fourth or more of the agricultural land now under cultivation is not, properly speaking, agricultural land at all. It is not profitable to work and to make it so would cost far too great an expenditure of money. It may be too sandy, or too wet, or too dry, or it may be unsuitable and unprofitable for a dozen other reasons. Some thousands of American families today live upon such land where they lead lives not far removed from those of Chinese peasants at a level below that of the Central European peasant. The poor diet and the deficiencies of the soil itself handicap the health, vigor, and intelligence of these people. All of the same land could, under a universal system of proper land use, be put to forest and pasture production. Much of it would make excellent grazing country, and changed either to grazing or managed forestry would provide for the people living on that land a better

68

source of employment and a higher standard of living than they now possess.

It is an illusion, I believe, that a better, more efficient agriculture displaces agriculture workers and lowers the level of agricultural employment. A better agriculture of higher production actually opens new prospects for more profitable employment, especially in the field of processing carried on as a part of the farm program, for example, the production of cheese, butter, hams, sausage and a wide variety of other products which can be produced and sold locally or nationally from the farm itself. Only in vast single-crop areas, such as those devoted to cotton and wheat, does the element of mechanization as an element of efficiency, greatly reduce employment.

In our own experience, a better, more productive farm employs *more* people than the same land ever supported before—even in the days of big families—and at a much higher standard of living, one which includes plumbing, electricity, natural gas and the disappearance of all drudgery once associated with farm life for both the farmer and the farmer's wife. The truth is, of course, that no individual or no nation ever profited by poor, limited, and costly production of commodities of any kind.

Still another reader may ask, "But what became of the old sacred formula of crop rotation?"

I think that most modern agricultural authorities would agree that the long-established "three- or four-year rotation of crops" is not a necessity on any good and productive farm. The rotation was originally worked out for the old-fashioned general farm to prevent the descendants of the traditional pioneer farmer from working out their land completely by constant use of fields in openly cultivated row crops. In the traditional rotation, grass and green and barnyard manures were the backbone, as indeed they must be in any good farm program, specialized or otherwise, but in the conventional rotation of corn, oats or wheat, grass is neither an infallible nor a necessary procedure. Lime, green manures, and humus are the key to any well-managed agricultural enterprise. Barnyard manure is the best of all sources of fertilizer and humus but it cannot be produced in sufficient quantity to *maintain* the fertility of even a small farm and other means of maintaining and increasing the humus content of the soil have to be found.

The potato-growing specialist knows that he must turn back each year a certain amount of organic material along with commercial fertilizer or his yields will fall off and his plants become more and more subject to disease. The cotton and tobacco grower knows or should know this although, to the ruin of hundreds of thousands of acres of good soil, he does not always practice it. The single-crop wheat grower, except in the wheat specialty areas, has learned it the hard way. The successful potato specialist plows under each year a crop of green manure, usually rye. The good cotton and tobacco farmer alternates his crops with winter-growing legumes. The good wheat farmer in areas where there is too little rainfall to grow much but wheat has long since abandoned the use of the moldboard plow in favor of trash farming and has ceased to burn his straw.

In the whole of this picture there is probably little place for the old-fashioned general farm. The family-sized farm can certainly survive and upon a much more prosperous basis than in the past, but it must be upon a program which undertakes a definite project or a limited number of projects and carries them through efficiently and expertly.

The general, widely diversified, and self-sufficient program is, however, admirably suited to the small-scale enterprise of industrial, white-collar and middle-bracket-income citizens with a few acres in the suburbs or in the country itself. This category of small, largely self-sufficient holdings is increasing constantly in numbers and it provides not only a bulwark of security for the individual but a source of strength for the nation as well. A well-managed small place with vegetables, fruit trees, chickens, perhaps a pig or two and a cow provides not only a source of large saving in the family food budget, but it also is a source of health, recreation, outdoor life, and general contentment for the whole family.[1]

There is a revolution under way in American agriculture.

[1] *The Have-More Plan*, a booklet available from the author, Ed. Robinson of Noroton, Conn., sets forth the immense advantages of operating small family holdings.

It is a revolution of many facets, including soil conservation and better land use, of greater mechanization and greater efficiency, and also a growing understanding of what soil is as a source of production, prosperity, vigor, and health in plants, animals, and people. But there are as well economic pressures at work which are more powerful perhaps than the influence of education, and they are hostile to the old-fashioned pioneer pattern of general farming which is likely to impose low income, drudgery, inefficiency, and a lack of expertness.

The youngsters and the younger farmers are beginning to understand the operation of these pressures and it is likely that within another generation or two, the general farm, raising a little of this and a little of that, will have passed pretty well out of the picture and we shall begin to have an efficient and really abundant agriculture in which the farmer will be a combination of specialist, scientist, and businessman. We shall have better and more abundant food and agricultural commodities for industrial use at lower prices and higher profits for the good farmer.

It is also probable that in the meanwhile the city-dwelling housewife will weary of paying high prices caused by inefficient production and low yields per acre and the taxpayer will resist paying hundreds of millions a year for bribes, government-buying to support prices, price floors, subsidies, parity prices and other dodges to maintain in a mummified state a poor and unproductive agriculture and to pension the farmer who is not doing his job as well or as intelligently as he could. It is not a question of more and harder work. The better, the more productive and well-planned the farm, the less is the drudgery. It is much more a question of information, intelligence, and expertness. All of these things add up to abundance, to lower prices for food to the city dweller, and higher profits and a more solid economic base for the farmer.

# III: THE CYCLE OF A FARM POND

A useful contract with the earth places man not as
superior to nature but as a superior intelligence working in nature as a conscious and therefore as a responsible part in a plan of evolution, which is a continuing creation.

—Liberty Hyde Bailey, *The Holy Earth*

OF THE three ponds at Malabar, the low, shallow one at
the Fleming Place is the most productive of big fish. This is
so because it is the oldest and the richest in vegetation. It was
made out of an old ox-bow left when Switzer's Run was fool-
ishly straightened by the County Commissioners before we
came here. We raised the banks about two feet by a day's
work with hand shovels and thus raised the water level by
the same depth. It is fed by a big spring in the bottom which
has increased its flow by at least 100 per cent since we began
keeping the rainfall where it fell on our land, and by the flow
of an abandoned gas well which has turned into a first-rate
artesian well flowing hundreds of gallons a minute of ice-
cold water. Drainage from the neighboring barnyard during
heavy rain occasionally reaches the pond and fertilizes the
heavy vegetation in it. It is a comparatively shallow pond
with a gravel bottom long since stopped tight by layers of
decaying water vegetation.

The natural balance and cycle of this pond is very nearly
perfect. The population is made up of bass, bluegills, sunfish
and innumerable hybrid variations of the sunfish family which
occur in fish ponds. There is also a single large carp caught by
the children in Switzer's Run as a small fish and dumped into
the pond along with a miscellaneous assortment of min-

nows, shiners, suckers, etc. All but the carp have long since disappeared, devoured by the big bass. On the richness of the table set for him by nature beneath the surface of the water, the carp has grown to nearly three feet in length and must weigh in the neighborhood of thirty pounds. He is occasionally accompanied by a gigantic goldfish which seems to have for him a romantic attachment—a situation not unusual since carp and goldfish belong to the same family and in Lake Erie where huge goldfish, descended from a few which escaped from a pond in Cleveland years ago during flood times, are not uncommon and frequently breed with the big carp to create new crossbred strains puzzling of identification to the amateur and sometimes to the commercial fishermen who find them in their nets.

The goldfish also came into the Fleming pond through no design but through the zeal of the children who, six years ago, dumped into the pond a dozen fingerling-size goldfish bought at Woolworth's. On the rich diet of the pond they have grown to eighteen inches and more in length and to a weight of two or three pounds. They are very fat and lumbering and awkward beside the swift-moving streamlined bass and bluegills and have the appearance of red-gold galleons wallowing through the deep green-blue water moss and weeds. Some have the appearance of large luminous streamlined carp and others have long flowing tails and fins which trail behind them in the clear blue water like the veils of brides. Some have their red-gold scales variegated with silver. It is easy to see why the Japanese and Chinese long ago regarded goldfish as works of art, of high artistic value in their shallow ornamented pools, and made a science and an art of breeding them into fantastic almost artificial shapes and colors. A glimpse of these big, brilliantly colorful fish seen moving through the gently undulating weeds in the blue, clear water from the high bank of the Fleming pond gives the beholder the sudden delight that comes from the contemplation of an old Chinese painting or from the luminous beauty of Redon's flower pictures.

Neither the goldfish nor the great carp belong in a properly managed Ohio fish pond but all efforts to remove them have failed. The goldfish, fat and contented, will sometimes nose about a worm-baited hook but never take the worm. The great carp has refused all baits persistently and has even managed to escape the marksmanship of the boys who regularly attempt to shoot him with a twenty-two calibre rifle.

However, beyond consuming some of the food supply of the pond, neither goldfish nor carp do any serious harm. I am not at all sure that they are not an asset in the cycle of the pond and to the food supply of the big, small-mouthed bass. They have never succeeded in producing a single surviving descendant and there is consequently no way of knowing whether the romance of the great carp and his love-lorn accompanying goldfish has ever been fruitful. Each year the goldfish gather, after the fashion of carp, in a herd in the shallowest water and there thrash about in the ecstasy of reproduction for several days at a time. But apparently the big bass immediately devour the roe or any young goldfish which by chance have hatched out. Thus they continue —the great carp and his fleet of goldfish cousins—to lead, if not a sterile existence, a fruitless one, taking their place in the cycle of pond life and producing a perpetual supply of caviar for the bass.

I have seen literally acres of great carp spawning in the shallow waters of the big Pleasant Hill lake at the end of the farm in late May or June. In the late spring they gather from the deep holes of the Clear Fork and the deeper waters of the lake itself by some common and terrific urge and then move into the shallow waters where they indulge in a wild orgy of reproduction continuing for several days. At such times it is possible to walk in water up to one's knees among hundreds of thrashing, wallowing carp, which in their ecstasy pay little attention to one's presence—so little indeed that it is possible to knock them over with blows of a club. In Lake Erie at spawning time, the big carp put on a similar performance in the shallow waters along the beaches and boys amuse themselves by shooting at them with rifles.

The fresh-water shad which exist in great numbers in the waters of the lake and the Clear Fork have another way of spawning. They will gather in schools on the surface of fairly deep water and swarm and flash, jumping in and out of the water in the brilliant sunlight of June. They are prodigiously fecund and reproduce themselves by the hundred thousands and their offspring are devoured in great quantities by the big bass which fit into the cycle of life in the streams, ponds, and lakes of most of the Mississippi basin. So intent do the shad become during the season of breeding that you can swim among them while they continue their gyrations and silvery leaps above the surface of the clear, blue water.

There are no shad in our ponds but their place is taken in the pond cycle by the bluegills and sunfish which also reproduce themselves in prodigious numbers. Tom Langlois of the Ohio Fish Laboratories, one of the great authorities on mid-American fresh-water fish, tells me that not only are there many distinct and identifiable members of the sunfish family, but that they have an indiscriminate way of crossbreeding an infinite number of variations. Many of these are sterile, like the mule, and each year go through the fiercely compulsive process of breeding and laying eggs without producing anything. It appears also that the urge to breed overtakes them earlier in the season than it does the accepted and recognized members of the sunfish family. Very often they will pre-empt the available nesting grounds on shallow gravel beds in their fruitless and sterile efforts and fiercely fight off the fertile members of their tribe when these attempt a little later to find nesting places, a fact that can upset the regular cycle of pond life and food supply within the pond.

The mating habits of many fish and of most of the sunfish family in particular are fascinating to observe. In our ponds, they begin to nest about the end of May and all along the edges of the ponds in shallow waters, you will find them in great numbers beginning to clear away the mud or the decayed vegetation that cover the clean gravel which they like for nesting purposes.

The bass, the bluegills and the other members of the sunfish family all follow a similar urge and procedure. Each one will select, not without considerable fighting, a chosen site and then begin to clear off the silt or decayed vegetation that has settled over the gravel during the year. Each one will take a place above his selected site and without moving either backward or forward will set up a fluttering motion with his fins which in turn creates a current in the water that washes the gravel clean. This procedure sometimes requires a day or two of work. When the gravel has been washed clean and a slight depression of from one to two inches deep has been created (similar in appearance beneath the water to the nest of the killdeer plover which lays its eggs and hatches its young on a nest of gravel on the adjoining dry ground), the female will deposit her eggs in the nest and the male will swim over them and fertilize them. From then on the duty of guarding the nest becomes that of the male and until the young are hatched he will remain over the nest, moving his fins very gently, unless another fish of any species comes within an eighteen-inch radius of the center of the nest. Then he will attack furiously until the molesting fish is driven off. The bluegills and some varieties of sunfish build their nests in clusters side by side, each with a male fish fiercely guarding his own nest and darting angrily at his nearest neighbors if they attempt to cross the invisible line which guards his nursery from that of his neighbors.

I am not certain that the male fish is aware of the exact moment when the tiny fish he has fathered hatch, nor of how long the period of gestation is but overnight the whole pond will become infested with millions of tiny fish no bigger than a pin which move about in schools of thousands and promptly seek refuge in very shallow water or among the algae which by the time they have hatched covers large areas of the pond. There would seem to be some purpose in the presence of the algae as a protection for the tiny fish not only because its fabric makes it impossible for the big bass to swallow the young fish in a single sweeping gulp but because the larger fish find the algae itself distasteful and unpalatable. I have observed that even the smallest filament of algae attached by accident to a baited hook or fly will prevent the bigger fish from swallowing or striking at the bait.

I doubt that the male fish is aware of the moment when the young fry hatch out and flee the nest for the safety of the very shallow waters or of the webbed, clinging algae. I suspect that very often, driven by an urge which covers a comparatively fixed period well overlapping the period of gestation, the male fish often remains on guard long after the roe have hatched and fled the nest.

In certain parts of the pond which the fish have chosen

as nesting and spawning beds, the whole character of the pond bottom has changed over a period of years. On bottoms which once were clay and muddy, the clay-mud element has been entirely washed away by the motions of countless small fins season after season until they have become clean, gravel shelves, bars and beaches. If, as sometimes happens during the spawning season, which usually coincides with a season of rains and thundershowers, floodwaters cover the nests with a thin layer of silt, the male fish will immediately and frantically go to work washing away the deposit of silt to make the nests clean once more.

During the spawning season, the male becomes fierce and even the little male bluegill will stand by his particular nest and give battle to a stick or a finger thrust into the water near him. I have had my finger "bitten" by big male bass when I thrust my hand into the water above his nest. At other times when the fish are not nesting my mere presence on the bank or that shadow cast over the water will suffice to send them in a darting brilliant course into deeper water.

All of these elements play their part in the "balance" of a good fish pond. The algae and vegetation shelters and produces vast quantities of minute animal life upon which the fiercely fecund and reproductive small-mouthed, purse-lipped bluegills and sunfish largely feed along with the flies and insects which fall on the surface of the ponds during the long, hot, insect-breeding months on a fertile middle-western farm. In turn the small-mouthed sunfish produce millions of small fish which provide food for the big, predatory bass and trout and some of the larger-mouthed and predatory green sunfish.

Weather and flood conditions occasionally alter the nesting habits not only of fish but of marsh-nesting birds. During the disastrously wet spring and summer of 1947 the red-winged blackbirds provided a remarkable example of the effect of weather upon nesting habits. These lovely birds which normally nest among the sedge grass and bullrushes of marshes, creek banks and ponds, abandoned their usual habits and took to nesting on the high ground in the alfalfa fields. When I began mowing alfalfa in mid-June I started up considerable numbers of fledglings just old enough to fly and found several old abandoned nests set into clumps of alfalfa exactly as the birds normally set their nests in a clump of sedge or marsh grass. The fact raises again the old question of whether birds by some instinct are aware in advance of weather or the exact time of changing seasons. The migration time of many birds varies a great deal. In this case I do not know whether the birds anticipated the floods which later inundated their usual low-ground nesting places or whether they took to the higher ground because the whole of the spring had produced continuously flooding rains and abnormally high water. In the same season of disturbed and turbulent water in the ponds, the sunfish and bass did not breed and nest until five or six weeks later than usual. Whether they attempted to do so earlier at the normal time and found their efforts thwarted or whether their later nesting and breeding period produced the usual results I do not know. In that same summer, the red-winged blackbirds developed or at least exhibited habits that in my observation were new and strange. They appeared in great numbers, indeed in flocks, following the mower and gorging themselves on the leafhoppers which infested the alfalfa. Except at migrating time the red-winged blackbirds had generally flown about in pairs or occasionally appeared in groups of five or six all of the same sex. It scarcely seems possible that the birds through nesting on high ground suddenly and for the first time discovered the leafhoppers as a rich source of food supply. The occurrence, however, was one more proof of the benefit to the farmer of supplying adequate cover in fence rows or isolated patches of undergrowth and marshland for the bird population.

In the same season the killdeer plovers, which also nest on low ground along creeks made no apparent change in their nesting habits. They are among the most careless of nest-builders, taking no trouble at all beyond hollowing out a shallow nest on a bare spot of gravel or sand in a low pasture by a creek. Presumably the eggs and the young killdeer which were not yet old enough to leave the nest were destroyed by the floods. Like quail, however, the young of the killdeer are extremely precocious and leave the nest very early, running about on the sandbanks and on the short bluegrass pasture even before they are able to fly. The young of the red-winged blackbird, on the other hand, must be fully feathered and well grown before they are able to leave the nest. They live almost entirely in the air or by clinging to high bullrushes and weeds, rarely making excursions on the ground as walking birds.

The green sunfish is the broad general name in our part of the country for a group of fish with varying characteristics. Although they rarely attain a length of more than six inches, there is no fish which fights more gamely. Indeed, if their size is taken into consideration, I know of no fresh- or salt-water fish which puts up so valiant a fight. They are, so far as I have been able to discover, the only group of the minor sunfish which feed upon the young of other fish. I have observed them greedily pursuing young bass which is a little like the fox turning upon the hounds. Naturally they are equipped with much bigger mouths than the other minor sunfish and some of them actually resemble closely small bass in appearance. When they get out of balance in a pond or lake they may become a menace even to the predatory bass population. The green sunfish is altogether a very aggressive little fish and a gallant fighter which will provide good sport on a light flyrod.

All will take a worm from a hook and, of course, artificial flies, but at times it is difficult to take the bluegills or some of the varieties of sunfish because of the extreme smallness of their mouths. The bass, even the small-mouth which is the variety which inhabits our ponds, has an immense mouth and gullet, sometimes making up very nearly half his length. The great mouth and gullet permits him to swallow a good-sized sunfish at a single gulp. In the case of the Fleming pond, the bass provide an absolute check or block upon the increase of carp or goldfish by devouring their roe or their young very soon after they are hatched.

This process and control and the operation of a natural cycle and balance of life is observable not only in ponds but in the free, open, fresh-water streams. In almost any clear running stream with abundant vegetation throughout most of the Mississippi basin, the balance and life-cycle will include some carp and catfish as well as bass, crappies and other members of the sunfish, game fish family. If the stream becomes polluted either by sewage or siltation or is swept clean of vegetation by periodic floods, the balance is upset and the game fish will gradually disappear and the mud-loving fish will presently dominate in overwhelming numbers until gradually and finally only coarse mud-loving fish—carp, catfish, et al.—alone exist.

This has been the history of many once fine fishing streams and lakes in the Mississippi basin where either sewage pollution from cities or steadily increasing siltation coming from ignorantly and poorly managed farm lands gradually produce conditions which exterminate all the game fish and leave only the coarse fish and finally exterminate all stream life save turtles and frogs.

This is what happened to countless streams in the South which were once famous for good sport fishing. Increasing erosion has turned many of them at certain times of the year into what is little more than a mass of viscous, thin, slow-flowing mud in which all fish life becomes impossible.

For the sportsmen this gives the problem of soil and water conservation and reckless deforestation an important place in the scheme of things. In the past, stream after stream, pond after pond, and bay after bay in the bigger lakes which were once famous fishing grounds for sportsmen have been reduced, by incessant floods and siltation coming from bare, poorly farmed fields, to the category of coarse, mud-fish territory or of no fish at all. In Lake Erie even the commercial fishing business, representing millions of dollars a year, is being threatened by the pollution of the big industrial cities and the siltation of spawning beds in its shallower waters. On the other hand, in a few streams in limited areas where good soil, water, and forestry practices have come into existence, clean water and vegetation have come back into the streams, ponds, and lakes, and periodic floods have been largely eliminated with the result that in streams which only a few years ago had been reduced to the level of coarse-fish carp and catfish waters, the proper balance and cycle is being restored and the waters are becoming known again as fine places for game fishing.

In our own farm ponds every effort has been made to prevent siltation. The practice of proper forestry and soil conservation and a program of grass farming has reduced siltation virtually to zero, and after and even during the heaviest rainfall the excess water reaching at least two of the ponds is as clear as the rainwater itself. In one pond the water becomes discolored from the run-off of a neighborhing gravel lane which cannot be controlled, but the siltation amounts to little more than discoloration and is mostly very fine sand which settles quickly leaving the water clear and blue after a short time. Under these conditions the balance of aquatic life quickly establishes itself and the ponds rapidly become filled with too many fish, so that fishing becomes not only a pleasure but a duty, for unfished ponds existing under proper conditions need no stocking; on the contrary it is necessary to fish them constantly in order to keep down the population. Otherwise the population exceeds the food supply and the pond becomes filled with innumerable fish which are too small either for good sport or for food.

The pond on the Fleming Place has long since reached the point of ideal balance and cycle. If fished steadily it goes on producing quantities of big game fish providing both unlimited sport and "fish for supper" for every family on the farm as often as they want it. Because the pond is a fertile one filled with vegetation, it produces a constant supply of food for small fish and the small-mouthed sunfish which in turn provide food for the bass and the bigger fish. The cycle of production for sport and food is constant and prodigious despite the fact that the pond is little over an acre in size. Constant fishing is in itself a part of the cycle of abundance since the pond is land-locked and would quickly become overpopulated and the fish small and bony if a considerable poundage of fish were not removed from it annually.

The Fleming pond is an old pond. Those on the Anson and the Bailey Places are newer. The one on the Anson Place was constructed only seven years ago and the one on the Bailey Place only two years ago. In the Anson pond the perfect balance and cycle has not yet established itself. It is a deep pond with a comparatively small amount of shallow water. In the beginning no stocking was done, save the fish caught in other ponds or in neighboring streams and dumped into it. Two years ago about 500 fingerling rainbow trout were put in. The fish from local ponds and streams were largely bluegills and varieties of sunfish with a few suckers and minnows. Among them were a score and more of big small-mouth bass weighing from one to two pounds upward. These were taken out of the older Fleming pond which at the end of each summer is cleaned systematically by worm and hook fishing to eliminate the biggest fish which turn cannibal and devour not only the "food fish" within the pond cycle but also the young and half-grown bass.

Of all the fish put into the six-year-old pond on the Anson Place, the minnows and suckers very quickly were eliminated, either by being eaten or by going out of the outlet into the flowing streams which were much more their natural habitat than the still ponds. A heavy winter following the transplantation of the big bass kept the pond frozen over solidly and the lack of oxygen and sunlight was apparently too much for the bass for when the ice thawed in the spring all of them were floating dead on its surface. They never had a chance to nest or breed.

Fish ponds and even lakes of considerable size throughout Ohio suffered similar losses of the bass and some other fish during the same severe winter. Open streams did not suffer similar losses because the movement of the water kept them open wherever there were ripples. Ponds, of course, are not the natural or ideal habitat for the small-mouthed bass which prefers streams, varied by deep pools and swift flowing water over steep gradients. The fish for which the pond is a natural habitat suffered much less from the shortage of oxygen and sunlight.

As it turned out, this worked into the plan of control on the six-year-old Anson pond. Its waters ran to a depth of twenty feet and it was spring fed both at the inlet and from springs in the bottom and even in the hottest days of August the deeper water remained cold, at a temperature of about fifty degrees. This depth and temperature made it a possibility as a trout pond. Trout could never have survived in the old shallow Fleming pond which was too warm and which already contained a flourishing population of bass. We found long ago that trout and bass cannot exist indefinitely in the same waters; the bass inevitably exterminate the trout, perhaps because they have much bigger mouths and can out-swallow the trout both in number and size of fish. Therefore, the elimination of the big bass by a severe winter left the deep, cold, six-year-old Anson pond ready for stocking by trout, especially since the food supply of the smaller fecund sunfish of all varieties was already well established.

Rainbow or brown trout were chosen as the most likely to flourish in the Anson pond and eventually we put in the 500 fingerlings not more than three or four inches in length. During the first summer there was no evidence of them whatever. They were never seen at all, either alive or floating dead upon the surface, and I came to the disappointing conclusion that they had all left the pond through the open outlet. When spring came the following year there was still no evidence of the rainbows. None of them were seen either dead or alive or in the shallow waters where the sunfish could be watched nesting.

During the six years of the pond's existence, following the "amateur" stocking of native fish from neighboring ponds and streams, the fish population increased immensely until this spring it became evident that there were far too many fish and that we should have to go to "work" fishing them out. There were thousands of them, mostly too small for table use. When we went to work, we made a remarkable discovery. Among the scores of fish which we took out as rapidly as the hook struck the water, more than 99 per cent were of two varieties—either long-eared or green sunfish with some odd unidentifiable hybrids. There being no big predatory fish in the pond, we came to the conclusion that these two varieties had survived and dominated and because the green sunfish had the biggest mouths. They could swallow the other varieties of smaller, purse-mouthed sunfish like the bluegill, the punkinseed and even the long-eared sunfish. They had simply eaten the other fish out of existence, and themselves had no control placed upon them since the small-mouthed fish could not swallow them once they were above a certain size, even if they had been inclined to include other fish as legitimate articles of diet which, as a rule, the small-mouthed fish do not do.

In any case, we were made sharply aware of the vast population of green sunfish, which I suspect in our case, may have been a crossbred variety in that particular pond, for their mouths and gullets appear to be much larger than the ordinary green sunfish described and pictured in all books dealing with the fish of the Mississippi basin.

These voracious green sunfish, although they never attain much size even under favorable conditions and I have seen only a few that approached a pound in weight, make excellent sport with a flyrod. They take the fly with a rush and ounce for ounce put up a fiercer and longer fight than any trout or bass. That summer we did not look for sport in the Anson pond so much as to reduce the population of fish, so we used cane poles and worms to fish. Even with this steady tackle, I have seen the little fellows take a worm on the rush and bend the bamboo pole half way to double.

"Cleaning" a pond to reduce the fish population is a pleasurable procedure. Armed with cane pole and worms and with a big milk can at one's side we take fish after fish off the hook at half-minute intervals and throw them into the milk-can for transference to a new pond or at the neighboring streams, but there is not much real excitement in it. At times eight or ten of us will spend an evening simply "cleaning" a pond.

I began the "cleaning" process on the six-year-old Anson pond to cut down the population of green sunfish and I got my excitement, even with a bamboo pole and worm-baited hook, when after I had half-filled the milk can with fish, the bait was taken by a fish which behaved differently from the ones I had been catching. I brought him to the surface and the sight of his silvery speckled body gave me one of the thrills of a long fishing career. He was no sunfish. He was a rainbow trout, ten inches in length, one of the 500 I had put in a year earlier and bemoaned as lost. He was not only still in the pond but he had grown in the span of a year from three inches to ten. I raised him reverently from the water. I had hooked him through the cartilage around the mouth and he was unhurt. Reverently I threw him back into the pond to go on growing into a two or three pound big fellow who later on will make wonderful sport and wonderful eating.

And about every tenth fish we took out in the process of "cleaning" was a handsome, silvery, speckled fellow, one of the rainbow fingerlings we had put in a year earlier. Most of them were uninjured and were put back to grow some more.

It is clear what happened. The trout fingerlings stayed in the clear, cold, deep water and never appeared in the warm shallow water where the sunfish nested, frolicked and ate. They are still staying most of the time in the deep, cold water but now the fingerlings are big enough to go foraging into the shallow haunts of the sunfish, clearly in search of food which meant that they were after the young sunfish. The latter are now having competition from predatory fish with as big or bigger mouths than their own and it is probable that a balance and cycle like that between bass and sunfish in the older Fleming pond will establish itself between trout and sunfish in the six-year-old Anson pond. In the evenings we see the trout foraging on the surface for insects.

The vegetation and life growing in the algae of the pond are clearly already sufficient to support considerable population of food sunfish, enough to give the rainbow trout as fat a diet as the bass already have in the older Fleming pond. Whether the trout whose breeding habits are different from those of the bass-sunfish family will manage to reproduce themselves as rapidly as the bass have done in the Fleming pond or even at all, remains to be seen. I am hopeful. If they do, the productivity and balance of the newer pond will be established and we shall, in order to maintain it at the maximum level of food and sport, have to fish it regularly, a hardship any fisherman is willing to suffer when it means that he is getting fish from a pound to four or five pounds, all fighters whether they are big bluegills and sunfish or bass or rainbow trout.

The life cycle of fish is a subject of some dispute among scientists and to be sure, varies greatly with the species. Legend has it that there are carp in the moats and ponds of Fontainebleau and Chantilly which were there at the time of François Premier and guides point to the rings set in the snouts of the huge, mangy old carp with the statement that they were thus ringed two hundred years ago. All this may be true for certainly the carp are immensely old and very large. Recently a female sturgeon weighing 175 pounds was taken in Lake Erie and the press attributed to it an age of over a hundred years. This particular fish was a female and yielded many pounds of caviar at the time of the catch. It is a sad fact that the sturgeon population of the Great Lakes like that of many other fish, has been steadily decreasing as siltation, sewage, and industrial pollution has increased.

Growth and size of fish and perhaps their age is determined largely by food supply. A green sunfish in the controlled Fleming pond will reach what is apparent maximum size much more rapidly than in the six-year-old Anson pond where the population of its own kind, feeding upon its own diet, is much too great at present. In the Fleming pond where its food is abundant, a bass will reach a weight of three or four pounds in approximately the same number of years. The largest bass taken from the pond weighed a little over five pounds. I do not know its exact age. But because the Fleming pond is comparatively small and shallow it is possible to observe and check with a considerable degree of accuracy the age and growth of the fish. There always appears to be at least four sizes: (1) the newly hatched pin-sized fry. Those which survive apparently reach a length of three to four inches in one season. (2) The two-year-olds which at the end of the second season have grown from the four-inch length to a length of eight or more inches. (3) The three-year-old crop which runs a foot to eighteen inches. (4) Those fish of all sizes above eighteen inches which are the biggest ones and whose cannibalistic habits with regard to the five to eight inch bass lead us to clear them out of the pond at the end of each summer.

The newest of theories among fish experts is that if a pond or stream provides the proper conditions, and is not subject to violent periodic flooding, siltation or pollution and the food supply is adequate, there is no need for stocking and that, on the contrary, there is a need to fish the stream or pond constantly in order to control the population and secure bigger fish and better sport.

The Ohio State Conservation Commission, of which the author is a member, has opened several lakes and some streams where the food, and control conditions are right and pollution is virtually non-existent, to unrestricted fishing without season, size or bag limit, and the results tend to show over a short period of time that such wholesale fishing improves both the size and quality of the fish without diminishing the amount of the catch. Other states are making similar experiments and if the final results are in line with the early indication of the experiment it is likely that stocking fish in polluted or heavily silted streams where they cannot live or reproduce will be abandoned, together with bag and season restrictions, and the emphasis and expenditure of taxpayers' money will be diverted from expensive fish hatcheries and stocking programs to the cleaning up of streams and lakes and the establishment of conditions which permit and encourage almost unlimited fish populations which actually *demand* unrestricted fishing to keep their populations in control.

Among the great and beautiful artificial lakes created in the Tennessee Valley Authority area all restrictions as to season, bag and size limit have been removed. The result has been to create a veritable fisherman's paradise. The creation of proper conditions, clean water, vegetation, etc., has proven that legal rules on take, season, etc., are unnecessary and that actually the more fish taken the better the fishing becomes. This is both reasonable and scientific procedure since a single female bass will produce as many as a hundred thousand and upward of eggs which when fertilized become small fry. Sunfish, crappies and coarse fish reproduce themselves at an even more prodigious rate. Not long ago I happened along the shore of Pleasant Hill lake at the end of the farm when a Conservation Commission employee was dumping five thousand fingerling smallmouth bass into the lake. As he poured the bass into the lake he remarked cynically, "Each one of these fish cost a lot of money to produce and all this stocking is a lot of hooey. Maybe it makes some ignorant sportsmen feel they're getting something, but a couple of pairs of good bass could do the same job without any expense at all." The man was not a scientist. He was an unskilled laborer but he had learned a great deal of wisdom through observation. I am told that in Colorado where hatchery-raised trout are introduced into streams, the cost of each trout is about $4.75. This, of course, is paid out of the sportsman license fees which could be expended far more profitably in providing clean streams and proper habitat where the fish could reproduce themselves successfully by the million. The new belief that money expended upon clean streams and habitat is better spent than on hatcheries and stocking is growing among state fish and game commissions and sportsmen generally. The same theory is spreading to the realm of hatchery bred and stocked quail, pheasant, partridge, to raccoon "farms" and all fields of game conservation and propagation.

This is a revolutionary idea, but it is also a wise development in reason, science and common sense. If the streams and lakes of the country were cleaned of pollution and siltation and floods checked by proper agricultural and forestry methods, there would be fine fishing in unlimited quantity for the whole of the population which enjoys fishing. Certainly our own experience with both ponds and streams has proven that this is true and that fishing becomes not only a sport but at times a duty and occasionally a real job.

One of the most fascinating spectacles in the world is the fashion in which Nature herself will take over a naked, newly constructed pond and set to work to make it into an old fertile pond in which natural controls are set up throughout the whole cycle of its life.

We have had an opportunity during the past years to observe the process in the case of the new ponds constructed and particularly the one on the Bailey Place. The site chosen for this pond was the corner of a field which even in midsummer was too wet for use as cultivated ground. Nearby was a very fine, big spring and several smaller ones as a source of water. In two days' work with a big bull-dozer and scoop a pond was constructed of about three acres in size varying from under a foot to fourteen feet in depth. The shallow area is large and makes an ideal feeding and breeding ground for fish once aquatic life is fully established. The barrier was made by excavating the soil from the bottom of the pond and piling it up as a dam which also serves as a road way to and from adjoining fields.

Nearly seven weeks were required to fill the pond to its full depth for some of the water evaporated and much of it seeped through the bare, newly created bottom.

Watching the pond carefully, I observed a number of

things. The first life to appear was the native killdeer, accompanied now and then by a dozen or more of their cousins, the rare golden plover. They waded about, crying and fluttering apparently in delight over the shallow rising water. They did not appear to feed but simply to wade about screaming and flapping their wings. Then a few frogs appeared from the damp spots in the neighboring fields and numbers of water skaters and water beetles. In the water warmed by the sun a few thin strands of algae, possibly carried in on the feet of the killdeer and plovers, appeared and began to grow in long strands, like the green hair of mermaids, and presently as the frogs increased in number the smaller herons appeared, and at last the pair of great blue herons which has been with us winter and summer for six years and ranges the ponds and the shallows of the big lake at the end of the farm, acknowledged the existence of the new pond by visits to do a little frog hunting. What new life they brought to the pond clinging to their feet or in their excreta I do not know, but they too undoubtedly made their contribution to the growing, expanding life of the pond.

On the naked sides and on the newly constructed dam we put a layer of barnyard manure and sowed rye to bind the soil with its deep, widespreading fibrous roots and stop all erosion. In the manure there must have been millions of undigested seeds of ladino clover and other plants for there quickly grew up a carpet of vegetation which included ryegrass and bluegrass, white, sweet, red alsike and ladino clovers, and within a few weeks all danger of erosion or siltation from the naked soil surrounding the pond was eliminated. Even after a heavy rain the water remained clear. The apparent high rate of germination in the manure-sewn clover seeds could doubtless be traced back a season or two to the activities of thirty hives of bees which we keep on the farm to provide honey and pollenize the legumes. During all that first summer the level of the pond continued to rise and fall, varying according to the seepage in the pond bottom as it settled itself. By autumn there was a thick growth of algae over a considerable part of the surface. The winter came, the vegetation froze hard, the frogs and beetles disappeared, the killdeer and plover went south and the great blue herons abandoned visiting the pond for the richer, shallower, unfrozen waters of the big lake. Then the pond froze over and went dormant.

With the coming of spring, the ice melted and presently the crying of frogs and spring peepers were heard from along the shallow edges. The vegetation came back with a rush. Then in the shallows occurred the mating orgies of the hundreds of toads which appeared out of nowhere—accompanied by struggling and crying which put to rout the excesses of the Babylonians, and presently great strands of frog and toad spawn appeared in the shallow waters. In the same shallow waters the coarse hardy dock plants, submerged the summer before where they grew, thrust their tough heads up through the water and presently began to turn yellow and drown to slow death to be supplanted by the new growth of seedlings and water grasses brought in as seeds clinging to the feet of water birds. And the seepage problem seemed to have solved itself. The pond had settled, the weight of the water closing up the open places in the bottom. And the algae had done its part for with the coming of winter it had sunk to the bottom and laid a network of fine webbing over the whole of the pond bottom. The clay which had been squashy the season before so that when you waded into the pond you sank very nearly to your knees, became firm and hard under the weight of tons of water and remained only a little sticky on the top surface. What had once been a naked excavation walled in by a naked earthen dam had become within a year a watertight reservoir, its banks covered with protective vegetation, its shallow waters alive with vegetable and animal life.

The beetles and water skaters and water flies reappeared in vastly greater numbers and presently the shallow water was filled by millions of animated exclamation points that were tadpoles. And along the banks one came upon various kinds of water snakes which had discovered the new pond and taken up residence there to feed upon the young frogs and fish which their instinct told them would soon provide a rich source of food. But most curious of all, there appeared presently in a pond completely shut off from outside waters, among the myriad tadpoles, a few pin-sized fish. Where they came from I do not know unless the eggs became attached somehow to the feet of the plovers and herons as they waded over the nests of fish in the other ponds or in Switzer's Creek. They were, at the time, still too small to be identified as to species save through the use of magnifying glass or microscope. The eggs may have remained wet, the germ still living during the flight of the birds from one pond to another or from the creek to the shallows of the big lake at Pleasant Hill dam. Those who live near to water know that in the business of carrying on life, nature can be incredibly tough and resistant and overwhelming. As the summer progressed all of these small fry turned into varieties of sunfish indicating that their origin probably lay in neighboring ponds.

In the case of the frogs and tadpoles which appeared early during the second year of life in the pond, we were indeed overwhelmed. The tadpoles appeared by the thousands in the shallow waters and presently were turned into myriads of small frogs, mostly of the handsome green and black spotted leopard varieties, none of them too big to sit comfortably on a silver half dollar. As we walked along the banks they went into a panic and leaped into the water like flights of grasshoppers in a grasshopper year. One could understand easily the Old Testament plague of frogs brought upon Egypt in Moses' time. One could understand too why nature produced tiny frogs in such vast quantities for their behavior during panic was idiotic and made them an easy victim of any predator, snake, fish, or raccoon. As one approached, they went into a panic-stricken hysterical flight, some jumping into the water some away from the water. The truth was that the new pond, still partly undeveloped by nature and with no natural balance established, contained not yet enough enemies and predators to cope with the prodigious fecundity of the frogs which produced in the scheme of things thousands of frogs in order that a few score might survive. There were in the waters of the pond no bass or trout or pike which would have made short work of the hysterical young frogs which leaped into the open water, and not yet enough snakes, raccoons and herons to devour the more foolish of their numbers on land or in the very shallow waters.

It is easy to see how the frogs of the world, unhampered

by natural checks and predators, could soon increase to such numbers that they would overrun everything, fill the whole of the land, and leave no room for the rest of us.

The muskrats were certain to be the next settlers at the new pond. Always in the second year they make their appearance, coming up the narrow silver thread of overflow water in the moonlight from the marshes in the Jungle, a wild piece of wet land in the middle of the farm, and from the marshes about the big lake where they exist by the thousand. One rarely sees them save sometimes in the moonlight when the nose of a muskrat moves across the ponds leaving a long V-shaped wake behind it in the still, silvery waters. One rarely sees them but the evidence of their presence is all around the edges of the pond, in the holes they dig for dens in the banks, in the nibbled foliage of certain plants and in the runways they make along the edges of the streams that feed the ponds. Usually they migrate during the second winter of the life of a pond and once they are established they like the easy living and remain there. When their numbers exceed the food supply, the younger ones go back to the marshes about the big lakes which are a muskrat's paradise.

The ones which remain are an endless source of trouble. They devour the succulent roots of the water lilies and the bullrushes and the tender underwater shoots of the arrowleaf which we try to establish in a new pond, and they attack even the tubers of the irises in the flower garden only fifty feet from the house. Two years ago during a hard winter when the ponds were frozen over for three months they burrowed beneath a tree wistaria and ate off all its roots so that in the spring, it simply fell over, rootless and dead. They burrowed into the dams and threatened to destroy them until we discovered that twenty-four-inch chicken wire laid along the dam at the surface of the water, where they like to dig, prevented further burrowing. They are tough and shrewd and sly and prolific and no amount of trapping by the boys on the farm, who pick up a good many extra dollars that way during the winter, either intimidates or discourages them. Now and then one of the dogs catches a foolish young muskrat offside and ends his career, but the dogs do not serve as a sufficient check upon the fecundity of the water rodents. There are no more wolves in our country but there are an abundance of foxes which at night bark from the wooded ridge back and forth in the moonlight. Save for the dogs they are the only check upon the woodchucks and the muskrat and they get only the young and foolish ones. A big muskrat is too shrewd for a fox and a big, old woodchuck can outfight him. Without the dogs, the woodchuck would, like the frogs, eventually take us over.

It must be said, however, that one of the last things we should desire at Malabar is the total extermination of woodchucks. The holes they dig and their generous hospitality in sharing them with other animals make them a great asset in building game and wildlife populations. Their holes serve at all times, but particularly during the winter months, as shelter and refuge for rabbit, quail, possum, skunks, partridges and other animals and birds. Female raccoon, when natural tree dens are scarce or non-existent will house their litters in woodchuck holes. So valuable does the Ohio Conservation Commission consider the place of the woodchuck and the hole he digs in the whole cyclical balance of wildlife that in 1947 it established a closed season from March, when the woodchuck wakens to emerge from his hole, to August, by which time the young are able to take care of themselves. The ruling does not prevent a farmer from reducing the woodchuck population which gets out of control but it does put an end to the idotic and unsportsmanlike habits of some city dwellers who go into the countryside merely to use the woodchuck for target practice. Among emigrant Southerners, both white and colored, woodchuck is considered a delicacy.

Rarely have I seen a muskrat by daylight and then only when lying very still among the sedge grass and weeds, I have been so well hidden that he was unaware of my presence. His habit is to travel in the shallow water of a creek close to the bank and even though the water is clear he is difficult to notice or to see. The concealment arises less from his fantastically protective coloring than from the undulations of his wet shining body which are like the movements of the flowing water itself. He moves, half-swimming, half-walking with a flowing motion and only a sharp eye can detect his presence where there is any current at all.

Perhaps the most beautiful newcomers to the pond during the second summer were the dragonflies. They appeared in prodigious numbers, looking like gaudily painted miniature planes. At least three varieties were noticeable. One variety, the largest, was about three to four inches long, with purple-black body and with bars of black on the widespread transparent wings. Another smaller dragonfly came in various shades of green with deep emerald green wings. The third, smallest and most beautiful was a fragile dragonfly all of one color, an iridescent turquoise blue with body which appeared to be almost transparent as they hovered over the surface of the water. All three varieties spend the whole of their brief lives in frantically eating and breeding. They dart and hover over the shallow water, the floating algae and the water weeds, devouring hosts of tiny gnats, mosquitoes and other insects which deposit their eggs in the water where they hatch into larvae to feed the sunfish as well. The prodigious number of dragonflies over the new pond probably arose from the fact that the fish population has not yet become established to devour the larvae and act as a check upon the almost unlimited increase of insects.

The great numbers of hatching insects brought not only hordes of the delicate dragonflies, but wild, soaring flights of deep, iridescent blue and red swifts and barn swallows which each year build their neat mud nests on the beams of the big Bailey barn beside the pond. In the evenings they circle, hover and dive-bomb the newly hatched insects, dipping their tiny, swift wings into the water, sending up tiny jets of spray in the evening light.

Of course, within the depths of the new pond there came quickly into existence trillions of amoebae, rotifers and tiny plants and animals invisible to the naked eye which flourish in the warm shallow waters of ponds and in the form of fresh water plankton which makes up a large part of the food supply of the fish from the smallest pin-sized fry up through the larger sunfish. These animals and plants, seen under a microscope, reveal complicated and brilliantly beautiful patterns of life. Although invisible they comprise a vital part of the natural life-cycle of a pond. Doubtless they are carried there upon the feet of birds and muskrats or the damp skin of frogs and on the bellies of slithering water snakes from adjoining ponds and streams. Many already existed in the wet ground of the pond site. The Natural History Museum in New York City contains a truly wonderful exhibit of these organisms executed brilliantly in colored glass many thousands of times larger than life.

Nature has a million subtle ways of quickly converting a raw, new pond into an old pond, fertile and teeming with life, but in all our ponds we have helped her as much as possible to speed the rate of conversion. One thing which a good farmer quickly learns is that in fighting nature he will always be defeated but that in working with her, he can make remarkable and immensely profitable progress. Beside the barnyard manure and the seeding of the banks we have thrust young willow butts here and there along the banks and every three or four feet along the crest of the dam. Within two or three years the fast growing willows, the particularly beautiful and hardy, semi-weeping variety known as *Babylonica*, will grow twelve to fifteen feet and along the dam their roots create a solid mat which binds the earth together and makes it resistant to the waters of the most devastating cloudbursts. Along the edge they provide the shade which the big bass love and a resting place for insects which drop into the water and feed the hungry fish waiting below.

The Conservation Commissions of many states send out free to all farmers of the state bundles of shrubs and trees for planting around farm ponds. These hasten the efforts of nature to convert a new pond into an old one and provide food and shelter for small game. The bundles include native flowering wild crabapple, standing honeysuckle, fruit-bearing viburnums, hazelnuts, pines and many other shrubs and trees. These are now planted in the areas about the ponds and help to build up that balance and cycle in the pond and the area about it which is a part of any successful fish pond. The new ponds are treated with fertilizer along the edges in the shallow water to encourage the growing of vegetation which plays so large a part in the cycle of pond fertility and life. A little fertilizer—particularly phosphate— will increase the number and size of the fish enormously.[1]

[1] At Georgia State Agricultural College experiments with the fertilizing of fish ponds achieved an increase in fish production of up to five hundred pounds to the acre.

During the first summer of the Bailey pond's existence we transplanted to its borders a few roots of arrowleaf and some of the water plants already growing in the older ponds. It was a simple enough process, simply that of thrusting the roots into the soil in the shallow water. These took hold immediately and increased prodigiously during the summer, as much as many hundreds of times, joining the water and marsh vegetation already seeded there through visits of muskrats and water birds in providing shelter for all sorts of minute animal life as well as for the small fry which appeared mysteriously and those hatched out after the stocking of the new pond in the early spring with mature bass, bluegills, and sunfish from the older ponds.

By the end of the second summer the first evidence of balance had become apparent. The plague of small frogs and toads had leveled off to a normal population, the number of dragonflies diminished and the whole cycle of birth, life, death, and rebirth had begun to operate.

At the end of the third year the new pond on the Bailey Place already took on the aspect of the older ponds. The shallow water had been invaded by thick growths of arrowhead, bulrush, water lilies and a great variety of water grasses and subaqueous vegetation. Within the refuge they provide against the attacks of the bigger fish, the water snakes and birds, there appeared in due course of time literally thousands of young bluegills, sunfish and young bass up to three or four inches in length. The fingerlings of the pound-size blue gills and the big bass which will make the sport of tomorrow.

A week ago we began seriously the annual "cleaning" of the older ponds with bamboo poles, worms, and a couple of big milk cans, transferring fish wholesale from the fertile older ponds into the newer ones. The task becomes a sport in which all the farm takes part. The boys, the older men and even some of the women join in, and in the crowded ponds every cast means a strike, and one never knows what one will get—a bluegill, a bass or any one of the varieties of sunfish and sometimes in the Anson pond, a nice-sized trout. Only the trout are thrown back because we want to establish in the Anson pond that cycle of trout and sunfish based upon the bass and sunfish cycle which has proven itself so productive in the old Fleming pond.

Fish after fish, the catch is tossed into the milk cans, kept aerated by changing the water and pouring in fresh bucketfuls constantly from the pond. There is a wide range of beauty in the catch from the lovely deep sea-green of the bass and the silvery-spotted beauty of the trout, through the whole range of sunfish up to the iridescent, fantastic beauty of the long-eared type with his brilliant yellow belly, his stripes and changeable colors and the jet-black spot behind his gills.

Last night we sat among the willows along the old Fleming pond, fishing, nine of us, as the sun went down and a virgin crescent moon appeared as the sky changed from scarlet and gold to pale mauve to deep blue. The women sat in the grass shelling the glut of peas from the garden for canning and the quick freeze and the small children yelled with excitement each time they managed to hook and bring in a fish. We fished until it was too dark to see the bobber, and then set out with a flashlight to transfer the fish to the new ponds. There was at least thirty pounds of fish ranging in size from a few baby sunfish to a fine big bass of about four pounds which somehow had eluded us in "cleaning" the pond of big fellows the preceding autumn. And everyone had fresh fish for breakfast the next morning.

The farm pond is becoming rapidly not only a pleasure but a necessity. State Conservation Commissions are encouraging them. Ohio aids the individual farm without cost in their construction. Missouri plans to construct 200 thousand farm ponds during the next few years. They tend to catch and hold the precious rainfall on thousands of farms, to supply water for the livestock, swimming holes, and fish for the table. On our farm whenever a family wants fish for supper one has only to take a pole and a line and in a half hour or more get all the fish he wants.

But there are other advantages to farm ponds which are not wholly utilitarian. Our ponds are each one a spot of beauty, a small universe teeming with life. The big herons visit them and the lovely red-winged blackbirds build their nests in the rushes along the borders. They are the delight of the big fierce Toulouse geese and the tame mallards. They are the source of much music in the night from the peeping of new young frogs to the booming bass of the big Louisiana bullfrogs which we put in as tadpoles years ago and which now measure as much as eighteen to twenty inches when stretched out. In April their borders turn green and gold with the lush foliage and flowers of the marsh marigold, and later they are bordered with the blue of Siberian iris and the purple and gold of the native wild flags. At night the muskrats move across the surface in the moonlight and the raccoons and foxes and possum come down out of the thick woods to drink and catch unwary frogs, leaving the imprint of their small paws in the wet mud along the banks. And there are the scavenging mud-turtles and a few big destructive snapping-turtles which the mallards avoid by shrewdly never taking their young onto the ponds until they are well grown. And there are countless birds, the swifts and barn swallows which skim low over the ponds in the blue evenings, to catch the insects hatching from their depths, and the flocks of goldfinches which finally mate off and build their nests from the down of the purple thistles growing in the damp ground. And in spring and autumn there are the visits of the wild ducks which join our mallards and feast off the richness of the farm ponds and the neighboring fields for three or four weeks at a time. For a lonely farm a pond provides life and fascination.

Each year, spring and autumn, we have been accustomed to visits of wild ducks. Usually these were mallards and so-called shallow-water ducks, but with the establishment of the Bailey pond we began to receive visits from flocks of blue-bills and other deep-water ducks. We discovered presently that they were attracted by the tender shoots of the fast spreading arrowleaf, spending hours diving and burrowing for the young growth. Wherever they burrowed their bills left tiny holes in the mud bottom of the pond. Dessie and Al often sit on the veranda of the big, old Bailey house in the evening watching the life on the pond until darkness comes down, the swallows take to the barn and the muskrat and raccoons come out to haunt the reeds and the shallow water.

In a way, a farm pond is a symbol of life itself. It is a bright spot on any farm, a whole universe in which the laws of nature operate under the close and intimate gaze of the interested. One can find in farm ponds and along their borders almost everything. They change with the season, awakening from the frozen, silent sleep of winter, going into the beginning of spring and the fierce breeding life of early summer. They provide skating in winter and swimming in summer and good fishing for three seasons of the year. For the children they are a source of inexhaustible delight. And like the fishponds of the abbeys and castles of medieval Europe and the Dark Ages, when all the world fell apart in anarchy and disorder, they provide not only food for the table but peace for the soul and an understanding of man's relationship to the universe.

## IV:  MALABAR JOURNAL

### Winter  1944–1945

I return to farming with an ardor which I scarcely knew
in my youth.
    —Thomas Jefferson in a letter to George Washington

NOVEMBER 19: A long gap mostly spent in traveling. The
election is over and thank God we can live in peace again.
The first real news is beginning to come in from France.
Annie Chamay has had word that her husband who was
missing has turned up after having been twice seized by the
Boches and taken to Germany, once halfway to Lublin in
Poland. Twice he managed to escape and is now a Captain
in the Resistance Movement.

I have had a long letter from my French publisher, carried
by someone to England and posted there. He tells me that
he was able to turn over to the Underground and to French
soup kitchens a considerable sum in royalties belonging to
me. It was done through Denise Clairouin who came here in
1941 on a passport secured for her by one of the Underground working *inside* the Vichy government. I saw her and
gave her an order to my publisher to turn over the money
to the Underground. This he managed to do since the transac-
tion was between two French citizens. Otherwise, the money
would have been frozen or seized by the Germans who pro-
hibited the publication of my books after they took over
France. Long before that I was a proscribed writer in Nazi
Germany. Delamain writes me that Denise Clairouin was
finally caught and arrested and has disappeared.

Also heard again last week from Jean de Sourian who has

joined the American First Division as a liaison officer, how I do not know, as he is a French citizen. His mother is English and he speaks English perfectly. In any case he is, as an American soldier, allowed to write, and we have had much news from him. He and all his family lived during the war in a workingman's villa near his father's factory in order not to attract attention. He dared not go on the streets of Paris in the daytime for fear of being picked up by the Germans and shipped to Germany to work in a factory. This war has produced fantastic stories. It is remarkable the number of people who, like Denise Clairouin and Annie's mother-in-law, have simply disappeared.

The beef cattle are all in the barns as the pasture ran short owing to the drought. The dairy cattle are still out in the daytime feeding on rye and vetch and ladino. Fortunately it has remained warm.

Tonight it is raining—badly needed rain although the wheat never looked better to go into the winter. Just before I sat down to write, the dogs and I went out to put the cattle to bed in the big barn. It is one of the keenest of pleasures to see them looking fat and sleek standing in clean straw, their bellies full of silage and good mixed hay. There are about fifty big weaned beef calves in the feeding shed. I go out every night and put back the hay they throw out of the mangers while eating. Tonight they were so full that they simply nosed it over, making only a pretense at eating. They are a beautiful, uniform lot of blue-roans, sleek and black and hornless, save for a red maverich with horns for which we have never found any explanation save that he must be a throw-back. He has a faint wild look of Highland cattle and may have been the result of inbreeding which will often produce throw-backs.

Charley Kimmel, the Game Warden, and Fanny Copeland dropped in and stayed for Sunday noonday dinner. Charley, like myself, is interested in the new dam proposed at Lexington. It will help the industrial water supply of Mansfield and create a beautiful new lake four miles long on the upper Clear Fork. People are beginning to make sense about the water supply, but only, I think, after they have been scared into it.

Made two speeches on Conservation yesterday at York,

Pennsylvania, one to the women in the afternoon and another in the evening to a mixed audience of 1600 businessmen and farmers. It is remarkable how people are becoming interested in these things—a very hopeful sign. If we can overcome the evils, economic and social, which industry and great cities have brought us, we shall be making progress. That is the frightening element in the recent elections. A growing urban proletariat without economic security can wreck everything that America has been in the past and darken the whole of her future.

I have been reading Darwin's *Voyage of the Beagle*. It is the best escape literature I know, taking you completely out of the confusion and anxiety of the times in which we live. Darwin's books are filled with interesting observations which tie in with our own experiences in the crossbreeding of animals. In his day his great mind held intimations of discoveries which many scientists of today have not yet suspected.

DECEMBER 28: The house was filled all during the holidays with the children home and visitors coming and going—like my grandfather's house in the old days. Too many people for the small sitting-room so the fire burned every day in the big living room which became the center of life. Even in wartime there is plenty of everything, for all the thirty-five people on the farm.

Today we started curing the first of the winter-killed hams. The locker plant does a good job for a small price per ham. The flavor is good but not so good as our own home-cured stuff, and the consistency is altogether different. When baked, the home-cured ham is light and flaky. The locker plant injects the curing fluid into the ham, the way most commercial hams are produced today. It is one of those short cuts which doesn't add up in the end. Tom calls them "embalmed hams" which is as good a name as any.

The smokehouse is octagonal, on a plan worked out by Thomas Jefferson, and built of bricks from the house of General Cantwell, Henry Wallace's grandfather, one of the first houses in Mansfield, which was torn down a few years ago. General Cantwell came over the mountains early in the nineteenth century bringing with him all his household furniture and a big library.

It snowed again last night and today the roads were drifted so badly that we had to buck our way through in the big Buick to get to Mansfield where I had to make a speech at the Lumberman's Insurance Company Convention.

Anna Barretto and Jean Mixsell who were here for Christmas left yesterday and Dennis and Theo Heathcote arrived this morning for the New Year. Dennis is a lieutenant in the British Navy. Ellen had a party last night and twenty kids came down in a big moving van, the only kind of conveyance which could buck the blizzard and the drifting snow.

It was a great lark for the kids seated inside wrapped in blankets—like the old bobsleigh rides we used to have in my own childhood when the horses drew us to a country dinner and dance.

In wartime with all the obligations and traveling and speech-making it is difficult to keep any sort of regular journal. I wonder if the time will ever come again when life will be normal—whatever normal is. Perhaps it is better to ask if we shall ever have peace and leisure again. I doubt it. Sometimes it seems to me that we are in a period resembling the beginning of the disintegration of the Roman Empire, one of those periods when "civilization" having reached a peak, starts slipping back again out of sheer weariness and moral decadence through a kind of anarchy into a simplified primitive existence.

DECEMBER 29: This is indeed an "old-fashioned" winter. The whole valley lies buried deep in snow. Tonight there was a full moon coming up about five o'clock. While I helped Harry with the chores in the big barn, the light outside turned slowly a cold but brilliant blue, and the moon rising over the Bailey hill crowned by the single big oak, turned slowly pale yellow and then orange, then red and at last a cold brilliant silver color as the blue deepened in intensity into darkness. In the moonlight the wide valley turned white and glistening as the lights came out far down the valley in Kenneth's house and then Bob's and Harry's.

Inside the barn the blue-roan beef calves pushed their black muzzles into the troughs of silage, corn, and soybean meal, but they felt so well they kept backing off and running up and down kicking up their heels between mouthfuls. They are beautiful and sleek, putting on two or three pounds a day, all blue-roan or black, polled like their Angus sire, Blondy, with little clusters of black curls over their big black eyes. I like dairy cattle but my heart is always with the beef herd. There is something solid and satisfactory about them and I like their lazy, placid dispositions. The twenty-five blue-roan calves are my pets out of all the livestock, and the dogs have a jealousy toward them which the calves return. Gina and Folly are always trying to get in a sly nip at the black noses across the mangers when my back is turned, and if the dogs get into the feeding shed, the calves gang up on them.

I know no greater satisfaction than going out about midnight just before I go to bed to have a look at the cattle in the big barn. They stand or lie in the clean straw, dry and warm in their shaggy winter coats, the steaming breath curling up from the wet muzzles. When you turn on the lights the big sleek calves get up, stretch themselves and come toward you lowing gently. You throw an extra bale of alfalfa toward them and, they only nuzzle the hay and push it about because they are already filled up. It gives you a remarkable feeling of security and well-being, so rare in the world today.

With the deep snow, the rabbits have moved in close to the house again where they pick up the spilled corn from the cribs and what is left of the beans and oats put down for the turkeys and guinea fowl. But that doesn't satisfy them; they go to work on the roses and young fruit trees and shrubbery. In the morning the snow is covered with their tracks close to the house, just outside the door.

I don't like killing them but despite the abundance of red and gray fox they increase each year in such numbers that something has to be done to protect ourselves. The dogs, all six of them, have learned the trick of rushing out when I say, "Get the rabbits!" to drive them off. I had hoped that by sending out the dogs night after night, the rabbits would become frightened and stay out of the garden, but it seems to do no good. The timid creatures steal back as soon as the dogs are out of sight to begin nibbling again at shrubs and roses and fruit trees.

Today Tom shot two of them for his own house. When he went to pick them up he looked up and saw on the ridge above the house a big red fox sitting out of range of a shotgun watching him with interest and mockery. Foxes are the damnedest animals.

Harry is feeling very proud over his chicks. Out of 700 young pullets he has over 600 eggs a day for the last week and this despite the zero weather. Except for the fighting breeds, I haven't much feeling for chickens, but the two big poultry houses filled with healthy bright young pullets are a beautiful sight just now. Certainly Harry's success with them establishes some sort of a record.

106

Frank Lausche called this morning. He is the new governor. As I suspected in advance Ohio went against Roosevelt, but elected Frank, a Democrat, by 250,000 majority. It makes him one of the strongest men in the party. He has already appointed Frazier Reams and Jim Hoffman, two of his opponents in the Democratic primary, to his cabinet. Both excellent men and a wise move politically. I have suggested B. O. Skinner as Director of Agriculture, but his health may not be good enough for him to accept.

DECEMBER 30: I heard a fox barking tonight for the first time this season. It was a rare occurrence so early in the winter for ordinarily they bark and call to each other only in the mating season which is usually in February. Perhaps he was disturbed or lonely. The New Year is still two days away and the snow is deep on the ground.

Today just outside my door I noticed big purple stains on the snow looking as if someone had spilled indelible ink. On examination the stains turned out not to be ink at all but the juice from the fruits of the viburnum. With the deep snow the birds have come close to the house and are feeding on the viburnum, the hawthorn pips and the fruits of the Rugosa roses. It is the seeds they are after as they leave the pulp on the ground. A tiny bit of laburnum pulp dropped on the snow spreads into a great purple patch six or seven inches across.

The nightly chase after rabbits in the garden seems to be having little effect. Their tracks are everywhere. There are distinct runways and here and there circles where apparently they gather in groups. Last night when I went out with the dogs to drive them out of the garden they scattered off up the hill over the glistening snow in the brilliant moonlight toward the sandstone ridge, fanning out in all directions, fifteen or twenty of them. I'm afraid they've discovered that Boxers, having no nose and very poor sight, are not much of a menace as hunting dogs. They are big and heavy and crash their way through shrubbery and underbrush by sheer force of their great muscular strength. The sly fox lying behind a bush or a hummock, patient and cruel, is much more of a menace. I suspect that the presence of so many foxes drives the whole population of rabbits close to the house.

The foxes do keep away from the area frequented by the dogs, having lost at least two cubs to the Boxers.

Yesterday afternoon we were sitting in my office talking when Bob said, "Look!" I turned to where he was pointing and saw a handsome big red dog-fox moving along the hill on the other side of the ravine. He was taking his time and paused, suddenly stood still against the deep snow, and looked over his shoulder. Then, after a moment, he turned and moved on his way up through the trees to the crevices in the rocks. And then scarcely two hundred feet behind him appeared a shaggy, old farm dog, his nose to the ground, earnestly following the strong fox scent although all the time he was within easy sight of the fox. The pause and the gesture of the fox was exactly like that of a small boy thumbing his nose. By the time the old dog caught up with him, he was safe, deep in one of the lairs that dot the hillside, perhaps already asleep.

The calves bred by the Shorthorn bull from the blue-roan heifers are astonishing. Born only last May some of them will weigh five hundred pounds or more already. Three of them are too big to get into the creep, and if we make the opening any bigger, the cows can get through. With their shaggy winter coats they are magnificent, looking a little like Highland cattle save that they have no horns—a striking evidence of the great prepotence of the Angus blood of their grandfather. They are bigger boned than the Angus and more sturdily built. The crossbreeding experiment carried back to the Shorthorn has been so successful in producing quick quality feeders, we will cull out some of the purebred Shorthorn breeding cows and replace them with crossbred blue-roan heifers. If the results next year are as good, I should like to see the whole breeding stock made up of blue-roan cows. Curiously the best specimens among the calves are those which show white faces derived from some Hereford strain in the feeder heifers we brought in from the West and assumed from their appearance to be purebred Shorthorns.

The longer I work with livestock the more I become impressed with crossbred vigor. We never have lost a crossbred calf or had a sick one. Dr. Reed, Head of the Dairy Division, surprisingly agreed with me when we discussed breeding at Omaha at the Pasture, Forage and Livestock Convention.

He had much to say for crossbred dairy cows. We were both agreed that it was important for someone to keep the pure-bred strains so that we could have the strains to crossbreed. I have many friends who are in the purebred business—hogs, beef, and dairy cattle, and they regard our crossbreeding with horror. My friend Judge Hackney this year paid $25,000 for an Angus bull and Roger Black paid $22,000 for a Guernsey. I suppose if you're bitten by the purebred bug, nothing is so exciting as pedigrees. For myself, I get much more kick out of a big, healthy, hearty specimen regardless of its breeding. I have a suspicion that once you get into the purebred business you can't get out of it. Just now prices are tremendously high for purebreds but three or four years from now they may and probably will be low. I think in the long run we'll do better raising quick quality beef in quantity. The purebred fanatic always seems to me a little like the fox who lost his tail in Aesop's fable. He wants everybody to be in the same situation and so tries to make it fashionable. The more there are in the racket the more demand and the better the prices.

The barking fox made me think of the visit we had last summer from a pair of wildcats. The catamount, as the first settlers called him and the Southern hill people still call him, took up quarters in a big hollow beech on the edge of the ravine just opposite the house, about two hundred yards away at the same spot from which the fox barked last night. The first knowledge of his presence came when George called down from his room, "D'you hear that scream? What the Hell is it?" I opened the door of my room and was promptly treated to the most blood-curdling noise I have ever heard. The hair on my head and on the backs of the dogs beside me rose at the same time. Then the dogs rushed past me and across the little valley up the side of the ravine opposite, barking wildly all the way. Their barking had no effect on the catamount which kept up its weird, blood-curdling scream. But the scream had an effect on the dogs. It was a moonlight night and I could see them clearly. About fifty feet from the tree they checked their rush and their wild barking turned to whining and growling. Boxers are devils for fighting and are afraid of nothing but clearly the sound put the fear of God into them; and presently they returned to the house still disturbed, bristling, and growling.

Some nights the catamount took up a position on the other side of the hill behind Jim Pugh's cabin and treated him to the same kind of serenade. Jim took a rifle, an electric torch and his dog, a big Collie, a courageous dog and a good fighter, out to locate the beast. He never saw it although he heard the rustle of leaves as it scuttled away into the thick underbrush. His dog behaved in the same fashion as the Boxers. It rushed after the catamount but apparently did not attack it, returning indeed with his white ruff standing straight up around his neck, and whining in protest.

A man I met on the train in Texas told me he had spent his boyhood in the Kentucky hills and that the fox hunters there dreaded above everything to have their hounds corner a catamount. He said he had known a catamount to rip and slash fatally as many as three valuable foxhounds in a single encounter. Perhaps Jim's dog and mine had some intuitive knowledge of the beast's viciousness or perhaps they too were simply terrified by the supernatural cry of the "catty-mount." Once you have heard a catamount scream you understand why the catamount loomed large in the legends of the frontier life as a crafty, almost supernatural beast. The cry of the screech owl in a dark woods at night is blood-chilling but it is a lullaby compared to the noise made by that catamount.

None of us ever saw the beast. We missed no lambs although we did lose more pullets and ducks than the foxes usually took and we found the partly eaten carcass of a big Toulouse gander. The foxes never bother the big gray geese which seem quite able to take care of themselves with foxes or dogs. I think the catamount must have wandered in from the Pennsylvania mountains. It went away again as mysteriously as it came. I did not miss its blood-curdling moonlight serenades.

Now and then the farmers of the county have trouble with "wild dogs" which are nothing more or less than the pets left behind by the shiftless rural element in the process of moving from one place to another, from tenant farm to tenant farm or from farm into town to get a job that pays more money. Largely speaking, it is the element brought in from the Southern States in two waves of migration—the first in the early thirties when the farmers were seeking cheap labor and the second when high industrial wages brought an army of migrants northward. Both migrations have been failures in the agricultural areas and have raised countless economic, social, and racial problems.

One fact that has been overlooked in dealing with social, economic, and political problems not only inside this nation but among the planners for world peace and government, is that it is difficult and even dangerous to attempt applying a common formula to peoples or nations existing on widely different planes of living standards, education, social and political experience. The migration of the Southern hill people into this rich, literate, hard-working Ohio country has been an almost total failure. In the earlier, cheap farm-labor migration, induced and encouraged by the farmers themselves (just as the industrialists of the past century encouraged the migration of the poorer elements of Europe to force down the price of industrial labor), the whole movement failed because of the widely divergent standard of living, education, and social habits. One good Ohio farmhand could and would do as much work in a day as three to five "hill-billy" hands, and he had both initiative and energy which grew out of the richness of the very soil on which he was raised, and experience which grew out of the high-level farming typical of the Ohio country. With the Southern migration the Ohio farmer got a hand who, in most cases, was very near to useless at a cheap wage where a decent wage would have gotten him a good hand out of his own country, who in the end would have been far cheaper.

Most of the hill country families arrived in jalopies with little more than the clothes on their backs. The men "worked" until they had twenty-five dollars and then quit until the money was spent. A great many of them never went back to work at all, preferring by that time to crowd into the slums of the towns and cities and live on "the WPA." The few who remained in the rural areas took to squatter's shacks where they lived as pariahs with no contact with the other members of society and taking no part in the life of the community. Neighboring farmers missed eggs and chickens and tools, and in some areas it was impossible for a time to follow the age-old Ohio farmer's practice of leaving his machinery in the field lest in the morning he would find it stripped or gone al-

111

together. When I asked a couple of hill people why they took anything left loose, they looked at me in surprise and said, "Why, down in our country, if anything is left out in the field it means nobody wants it any longer and anybody can take it." Here lay the difference not in morals but of social and economic manners and customs.

The results of the earlier migration were disastrous. It failed to provide cheap labor for the farmer and it brought into his neighborhood a problem element which had never been there before. It had only complicated not only his problems but those of the individual county as a whole, for the larger part of the families on relief were among the southern migrants. Many of them remained on relief even into the war boom.

The families themselves did not benefit in any way. The men accepted lower wages, if they worked, than any Ohio farmhand would accept. They hated a life in which they were expected to put in at least eight hours a day of work. Their diet, in most cases, was not improved, partly through poverty and shiftlessness and partly because most of them stuck firmly to the old sow-belly—corn pone—turnip greens diet. The most that could be said was that at least the turnip greens, raised in the richer soil of Ohio, had in them some traces of the calcium and phosphorus which are essential to human growth, vigor, and intelligence.

Socially, men, women and children were outcasts. There was not even any place for them in the county churches which had played a large part in the lives of many of them "down south," and if there was, the church had none of the "shoutin', rollin'" religion which they relished. The first migration was in many respects not only a failure but a tragedy for all concerned. The best that can be said of it is that a few families, perhaps one in twenty-five, had the energy, vigor, intelligence and sense to better their conditions and acquire a better diet, a better education, and a more ambitious standard of living. A great many of them, desperately homesick, drifted back south to the poor, worn-out hill country from which they came, back to the one-room school, if it existed at all (there are some southern counties even today so poor that there are no schools), and back to the villages where they could sit happily on the steps of the crossroads store and "roll" and "shout" in the Baptist Church on Sunday.

New elements influenced the second, wartime migration. The first and by far the strongest was the pull of the fabulous wages in industrial plants which, by a grapevine that magnified the high wages into weekly fortunes, drew the poor Southern, rural and backwoods people into the North. The second, comparatively a small factor, was the effort of the federal authorities to bring in outside help for farmers in the rich Ohio country, harried by questionnaires and shortages both of labor and machinery. It, like the earlier migration on a cheap-labor basis, was doomed to failure, and it failed in record time. I was asked my advice by the federal authorities concerning the possibilities of a wholesale plan of importing hill families to work on Ohio farms and out of the earlier experience, gave a pessimistic answer. The only way the plan could work was to pick very carefully, through the aid of the county agents and the AAA, only the very best and hardworking families for the Ohio migration. I knew that importing the more shiftless southern elements was not only hopeless but would create serious problems for Ohio communities. I also suggested that any Southern families picked should be given a course of education to break them in advance to the exigencies and methods of an agriculture so different from that of the poor single-crop country from which most of them came.

An experiment was made by first bringing fifty carefully selected Southern hill country men for a course of six weeks at the Agricultural College of Ohio State University. With the first week, fourteen of the fifty, homesick, vanished to return to their southern hill farms. The others stuck it out and eventually were taken on by Ohio farmers and brought their families north. But even with this hand-picked, superficially trained element, the experiment failed as the earlier migration had failed. The men were indignant or sullen about the work expected of them and the new-fangled methods employed. The women felt strange in the new country, without a "proper" church and a general store. As often as not their children suffered at schools from the inevitable cruelty of other farm children who not only felt that the clothes and speech of the newcomers were strange but were aware of their sense of inferiority.

But migrations failed for the same reasons that nearly all the New Deal rural cooperatives failed. The cooperatives were a headlong, sentimental if commendable effort to change overnight the economic, social and even human backgrounds of thousands of unfortunate and handicapped people by crude transplantation onto another plane, without any preparation, physical, social or intellectual for what could only be an ordeal. Social reform by the scruff of the neck, through sentimental and superficial motives, is all too often dangerous and cruel and almost always chaotic and ineffective.

A parallel problem to that of the Southern hill whites has arisen among the Negro populations in some of the middle-sized industrial-agricultural towns of Ohio. Many of these towns, having been old stations on the pre-Civil War Underground Railroad, have large Negro populations, sometimes larger in proportion to the white population than many southern towns. The old Negro populations had been long established with their own churches, doctors, dentists, et al. They had lived side by side with the white populations and in most towns there was no question of segregated areas. Virtually all of the old Negro populations had high school educations and many of them were graduates of colleges and universities. They were an accepted and respected part of the population and very rarely was there any evidence of "Jim Crowism" anywhere in the community.

The trouble began when the industrial interests began importing cheap Negro labor from the Deep South. Few of the imported Negroes could read or write. Moral standards were abominably lax in comparison to those of the old established Negro population. Few of the newcomers had ever had more than a quarter in their pockets since they were born and were accustomed to being pushed off the sidewalk by the "poor white" population of the Deep South areas from which they came. In their new environment they were crowded together in shabby run-down housing quarters. But suddenly they had plenty of money—indeed, what, by their former standards, was affluence. They encountered no Jim Crowism and found that they had liberties in the old

Northern Underground Railroad towns the existence of which they had never suspected.

The result was that many of them ran hog-wild, got drunk on Saturday nights, carved one another up and in general became so obnoxious that police magistrates took what was illegal but what to many of them seemed the only solution—railroading the individual habitual bad actors back to the Southern area whence they came. Restaurants, beer saloons, theaters, means of transportation which had hitherto been frequented by the older Negro population were presently *closed* to all Negroes since it was impossible to distinguish between the old respected Negro population and the rowdy, arrogant, disorderly newcomers. The presence of the migrant Negroes was far more resented by the old Negro population than by any element in the white population, which rarely came into very close contact with it. Nearly three generations of adjustment, which in those old abolitionist towns had very nearly solved the "Negro problem," were upset and to a large degree nullified. The old Negro population in my own town at first made some sincere efforts toward providing recreation and education for the newcomers but grew discouraged and fell back into an attitude of apathy and resentment, and my town, like many another similar community suddenly found on its hands a "Negro problem" which had until the migration been nonexistent.

The fault was not fundamentally that of the Negro imported from the Deep South. It was the fault of the elements in our society which brought him suddenly out of one environment into another without the slightest degree of preparation. Many of the overnight Southern Negro migrants were scarcely above the level of an African savage, some of them considerably below the level of many an African native with a background of native tradition and primitive civilization. Overnight they were plunged into the midst of what to the average Deep South Negro must have seemed another world. At least it was another civilization—for such a gap separates the social and economic background of the average prosperous Ohio town from the backwoods communities of Louisiana, Mississippi and parts of other deep Southern States so that there seems to be little connection between the two.

The cure for all of these racial differences and ills is at base equal economic opportunity, education (in the case of the Southern Negro, and for the "poor white," better diet and better soil upon which that diet is grown), better ethics and finally the annihilation of ideas about the superiority of one race over another. Some day all races will commonly intermarry and when that day comes many of the problems plaguing us today will have disappeared. As a rule, the lower the economic and social status, the more intense the prejudice. You cannot cure Bilbo and Rankin of Mississippi until you have cured the poverty, ignorance and prejudices of the constituencies which they represent all too well.

All this is a long way from the problems of the wild dogs left behind by the constantly moving "poor whites" in our Ohio county yet it is all a part of the same thing.

The wretched, abandoned dogs take to the wooded hills and ravines and band together in packs to live off the poultry and ducks and sheep of the countryside, eventually to be shot by the dog warden or some irate farmer. The Boxers look on the farm as their property and God help any dog that comes on their land. They have killed two of the wild dogs, and a week ago Harry saw the comic spectacle of two foxhounds in headlong pursuit of a fox across the valley fields with the six Boxers hot on the trail of the foxhounds. Ruefully Harry told me two days later that he had seen in the county paper a reward of $25.00 apiece for the two foxhounds which had run away from their owner. But for the Boxers he might have captured them and the reward. When last seen they were going over the crest of the Bailey hill. The fox had long since escaped and the hounds were running hellbent to escape the Boxers.

DECEMBER 31: The last day of a year which can go without regrets so far as the world is concerned. I have had much to be thankful for in my personal life and the life of Malabar, most of all the great progress that has been made during the last year toward the goals which were set up in the beginning and I have been very lucky indeed in friendships far and wide.

There are times when I am very grateful for having spent so many years outside America, in Europe and the East, not

116

only because it helped me to understand the stupendous things going on in the world but because it has made America a new country to me, which I will never again take for granted as so many Americans do. Out of the countless letters I get from overseas, I gather that the experience of the war has made thousands of young Americans understand and appreciate this country as they could not have done without having seen something of the rest of the world. It seems to me that this country is inexhaustible in its variety and beauty and in the variety of its people. The Sinclair Lewis philosophy, like most of the thinking of the twenties, was superficial, especially in its assumption that Americans are standardized. A Texan and a Bostonian could scarcely be further apart and still belong to the same race and nationality.

Perhaps, most of all I am thankful for having been born in a country which, after an absence of twenty-five years spent all around the world, I found I would have chosen to be born in, if I had had the choice. Its woods, hills, streams, fields, and springs suit me. They have the fertile, half-wild, well-watered beauty which seems to me to include almost everything. I suppose everyone in the world feels that way about the country in which he was born, but the feeling is doubly important and sound after one has actually put it to the test against other countries and landscapes over most of the world.

Today it is raining instead of snowing, but the snow is so deep that the thawing rain has made little impression upon it. Very little rain is running off. It is being soaked up by the snow and carried on down into the earth. Sometimes the snow goes quickly and the streams turn to torrents, the water rushing off the land to create floods downstream. This time all the deep snow and the rainfall is being soaked up by the soil beneath, a good thing after the long, hot dry summer. The underground reservoir will need filling up after two dry years. Thus far the weather has been wonderful for the wheat and the meadow seedings. The ground beneath its deep cover of snow is scarcely frozen at all and is protected from the devastating heaving process caused by alternate freezing and thawing.

The deep snow has brought numbers of birds close in

around the house and the suet and grain box outside my window is covered all day long by a wide variety of them. I am very ignorant about wild birds, but in the next year or two I must repair the deficiency. It would add greatly to the pleasure of watching birds and understanding their actions. Heavy snows like this one often drive in rare birds, which in my ignorance, I do not recognize.

I do know the mourning doves which strangely do not migrate but stay with us all winter, and the jays and a variety of flickers and woodpeckers, and of course many of the migrating beauties like the Indigo bunting, the Baltimore oriole, the kingfishers, the goldfinch, and the shy and dazzling scarlet tanager which one sees only in the deepest part of the woods and the Jungle. And in winter the cardinal is very common when he comes in close to the house to feed. Our native Ohio birds can be surpassed in color and beauty only by the birds of India. One of the sights of the world is the assortment of brilliant-plumaged birds to be seen in Crawford Market in Bombay.

The sparrows are always with us of course, very close in about the house, for they seem to prefer people and bustle and sociability to solitude. They are noisy and thieving and at times when they build their big, shaggy, disreputable nests among the grapevines or in a roof gutter or behind the statue of Ganesh over the front door, I would like to be rid of them. Jane Francke, who is a great bird expert, says they drive away other more rare and timid birds but I do not find this so. She advocated shooting or poisoning them but that I cannot bring myself to do. It is true they drive shyer birds away from the feeding table but once they have had their fill they go away and the other birds take their turn. They never want for food because they are brassy and fearless and feed out of the corn cribs or on the barn floor and even inside the cattle-feeding sheds. In winter they sleep in the thick evergreens which are warm and dry and windless. In summer they like the grape arbors but I discouraged them last summer by turning water on them from the garden hose every evening. One little hen sparrow slept every night for three winters on a ledge inside the portico covering the front door. Even when you turned on the light she did not go away but watched you very quietly with bright little eyes.

This year she is gone. I am only afraid that Pete or one of the other big barn cats got her.

NEW YEAR'S DAY—January 1: The rain of yesterday has turned to thick snow which fell softly without wind and all the trees are white this morning. The roads are bad for when the temperature dropped below freezing, ice covered them. Now there is about four inches of fresh snow on top of the ice. Charley went off this morning to fetch Jennie Oaks to make the butter and has not come back. If he doesn't show up soon we shall have to send the tractor for him and his car.

Last night in bed I read Gertrude Stein's article about the liberation of the Haute Savoy country. It was a beautiful piece of vivid writing, as American as corn-meal mush. When Gertrude writes "straight" no one writing today is so able to transfer to a reader emotions and sensations of sound, smell, and touch. We knew Bilignin, the little town in the Ain where she and Alice B. Toklas spent the whole of the war, and have stayed in the house she writes about. All this gave the story a peculiar vividness. You could see the beautiful countryside and the towns all the way up to Chambéry.[1]

Gertrude's greatest quality as a writer and as a companion is her immense capacity for enjoyment of the moment. Each small experience is always new and exciting and filled with inner meaning. I do not know how old she is but she has been on this earth for a considerable time, yet there is no one I know who is younger. I have never met anyone whose mind is so stimulating. I think this is so because it is not really a cultivated mind but a naturally brilliant one. It is not like the minds of most of us, a derivative mind, formed by tradition, by culture, by the reading of books and daily papers and magazines. The thoughts which come from it are purely original, like the thoughts of a brilliant child. That is what makes her such stimulating company.

At the time of Munich, I remember Gertrude and Alice B. Toklas both said, "We worked very hard in the last war,

---

[1] Gertrude Stein died in 1947 at the American hospital in Neuilly. She and her friend Alice B. Toklas were among the closest friends of the Bromfield family.

bought an ambulance and hauled things and soldiers about. There is no excuse for this war which is coming. It was made by the stupidity and fear of men and we intend to take no notice of it."

That may be what Gertrude and Alice intended to do, by going off to their house in a remote part of France and staying there throughout the war, but they did not do it. It is clear from Gertrude's articles that they were in the midst of everything, making daily visits to neighboring towns, joining in the intense feeling of contempt for the Germans. And Gertrude had luck too for Bilignin is in the very area where the Maquis movement developed. She loves young men and the Maquis caught her imagination and affection. The radio broadcast and the articles were the first direct news we had had of Gertrude and Alice since March 1942. Then in a letter written just before Thanksgiving in 1941 she said, "Alice has finished putting up preserves. We have a turkey for Thanksgiving. The food situation is not too bad here." Evidently they were still trying to take no notice of the war. From the articles, it is clear they did not succeed.

I have not heard what became of their wonderful collection of pictures—Picassos, Braques, Picabias, etc., mostly given to Gertrude in the early days when she and her Brother Leo fought the battle for modern painting. All the pictures were in their flat in Paris in the rue Christine. It was a curious but beautiful house built in the seventeenth century by Queen Christina of Sweden. The Germans took a great many private collections, like that of the Robert de Rothschilds, but all the painters represented in Gertrude's collection belonged to the school which Schicklgruber designated as "degenerate art," so they may have been left intact, unless some shrewd and cynical German fell upon them and recognized their value.[2]

Alain and Elie de Rothschild are still prisoners in Germany. God help them! Elie was married by proxy to a girl in Provence. Yesterday I had the first news from the Herberts since I had a wild letter from Denise in Bordeaux at the time of

[2] The Stein collection remained intact and unnoticed during the war by the Germans. By her will the articles were left Alice B. Toklas or given to American museums.

the collapse of France, asking for help in getting a visa to America for herself and her mother. I did all I could but heard no more from them until yesterday. Monsieur Herbert died just on the eve of the war. Madame Herbert wrote of the battles in Grenoble between the Maquis and the Vichy Militia. She spent most of the war there. Denise had returned to Senlis. She wrote that Mademoiselle Julie Mancheron, the last of the three old-maid sisters who were our proprietairies, was dead. She must have been at least 95 years old. She remembered well the Franco-Prussian war and lived in a great, beautiful house in the Rue des Cordeliers, known as the Hotel Flamande, built in the sixteenth century by a rich Flemish cloth merchant who had come to Senlis to learn the linen industry.

She was the one who said, when I offered to pay the three old-maids three times what the place in Senlis was worth, "Monsieur, we could take your money but what would we do with it?" She had the wisdom that came of wars, of invasion, of a dozen inflations and deflations. Invaders could not carry off agricultural *land* and *land* was the only investment which remained sound during violent inflation. We leased the property for fifty years and in the twenty years we have held the lease, there has been invasion, occupation and two serious inflations, but the land is still there as solid, as valuable, as productive as ever.

All this news together with the letter from the Archbishop of Senlis and the little pamphlet telling day by day the progress of the liberation has brought back floods of memories of that beautiful and happy life in the Oise and of all the French people we love so much. We shall go back one day and see them all. It will be like opening a book which we have loved very much to reveal a chapter that pleased us. But the book itself is closed, like so much in Europe that was good and beautiful. France will be the least changed of all European countries for the quality of Frenchmen rises above occupation, destruction, politics, everything. It is, in all European culture, eternal. I think this is so because of the intelligence, the toughness, the *reason* of the Frenchman. All this makes for resilience in the face of change and disaster which no other country has ever displayed. My grandchildren and great-grandchildren will go to France and find there the same essence of France which I knew and which my great-grandfather found there.

JANUARY 20: Back again from California. It is extraordinary how bad weather can disrupt completely all our proud modern means of transportation—blocking cars, throwing trains off schedule, grounding planes, causing wrecks. On the day George and I left for California we spent two hours driving twelve miles from the farm to Mansfield. We tried road after road to find each one blocked either by snow or by other cars stuck and half-buried in the snow. On the high plain overlooking Mansfield, the wind and blowing snow were ferocious. I came to understand how people can be frozen to death and die quickly, scarcely knowing what happens to them. We took turns—Tom, George, Lieutenant-Commander Heathcote and myself—in digging snow from under the wheels of the big Buick with a borrowed shovel. It was impossible to work more than five minutes at a stretch; you could feel ears and face freezing. When the spinning wheels cut through the snow, they came down to ice and then it was necessary to put boards and branches under the wheels. At last we turned back and found an open road which led us all the way back to Lucas where we got onto Route 39 and managed to make the town.

About seven years ago a kind of Thomas Hardy tragedy took place on the high plain where we were blocked. A married woman and her lover started across it in an automobile in the midst of a similar blizzard on their way to a rendezvous in the lover's cabin. The whole story of what happened was never known, but it appeared that the car broke down and the lover, going off for aid, became lost in the blizzard. In any case his body was found days later beneath high drifts of snow in a ditch by the roadside. The following morning, farmers noticing the car half-drifted over, went to it and found inside the body of the woman, frozen to death. The tragedy was the first and only warning her husband had that his wife had been unfaithful to him.

Even after reaching Mansfield the fight with the blizzard was not over. A freight wreck at Massillon on the main line of the Pennsylvania had diverted all trains and the Heathcotes had to go to Crestline in a school bus hired by the railroad to take care of its passengers. The bus fought its way through ice and blizzard to arrive only just in time at Crestline. In the morning the Heathcotes wakened at the hour they should have been in the Pennsylvania Station in New York to find the train had gone no farther than Cleveland. They eventually arrived in New York twelve hours late.

George, Mary, and I went to the Prestons' for dinner to wait for the midnight train to Chicago and again, in the suburbs, were snowed in. Only the aid of Mayor Locke and the city snow plow rescued us and made it possible to reach the station. There we found that our train was five hours late, delayed by snow, ice, and wrecks.

Needless to say, it was odd to waken two days later among orange groves and green grass in bright sunlight in the San Bernardino Valley. I still like Ohio and even the wild Ohio climate better than California and for my money it is much healthier.

# V: GRASS, THE GREAT HEALER

*(A somewhat technical chapter for farmers principally although some others may be interested)*

Still, by rotation of crops you lighten your labor, only
Scruple not to enrich the dried up soil with dung
And scatter filthy ashes on fields that are exhausted
So too are the fields rested by a rotation of crops
And unploughed land in the meanwhile promises to re-
pay you.

*—The Georgics of Virgil*

IF WE had never heard of grass farming we should have become grass farmers simply through the evidence of our own senses—our eyes, our taste, even our sense of touch. The advantages showed up in the deepening color of the soil, in the miraculously increasing yields, in the evidence of the farm's account books, in the flavor and tenderness of the meat, in the sleekiness and shininess of the coats on our cattle, and the brightness of their eyes, even in the changing, ever-augmenting beauty of the landscape as grass and legumes healed over the old gullies, the poor spots in already poor fields, cleared the once muddy streams, brought life to dead or dying springs, and saved the rainfall which made the very trees more green and luxuriant in appearance.

We were always aware of the virtues of grass and of legumes and, generally speaking, our own experience paralleled that of other grass farmers and of the government and agricultural college and extension service experts. This single chapter reveals nothing that is not already known—that grass is a great healer and that an acre of good grass can be as profitable as the best acre of corn and far more profitable than three quarters of the acres given over to corn in the United States. This chapter is merely the record in concrete terms of what grass has done and is doing on approximately 900 acres of glaciated Ohio hill land, all of it at a low level of production only seven years ago and much of it abandoned farm land, of a level of production so low that it could not find a tenant or even bring a couple of dollars a year rent from neighbors.

In a sense, the full realization of the virtues of grass stole upon us. In the original plan we had set ourselves up on the pattern of the old-fashioned, general farm, raising something of everything, with a high degree of self-sufficiency. It included as many head of registered Guernseys, beef cattle, hogs and sheep as the place would carry without buying feed. The number was not many. It has been doubled five times in seven years and could be doubled again if it were possible at the moment to provide within economic reason more buildings to house the animals. To this steadily increasing production and carrying capacity grass has been the principal contributor.

As in the story of Kemper's Run our valley, once the virgin forest was cleared away, became largely a grass country. Our glaciated hills and even the remnants of the old pre-glacial plain raise, if handled properly, the finest hay and pasture forage in the world. In the old days of horse and buggy and of great beer-truck draft horses, timothy was the great crop. Once introduced in a natural grass country, it became virtually a weed and in some of our present-day operations, still is. For a long time, no fertilizer was necessary to raise bumper crops of timothy and unfortunately many a farm went on raising fields of it and exporting from the valley thousands of tons each year to the stables of the cities without ever returning anything to the land. The yields on some farms grew poorer and poorer until the fields produced more weeds than timothy and some of the farmers gave up altogether, lost their farms or became year by year tenants or fled to a miserable hand-to-mouth existence in the cities.

Then, with the automobile, the horse and buggy era died and with it the market for timothy hay, and the great corn and hog heresy came into the valley where it should never have been introduced. The old hillsides, once covered with grass or with grass and weeds, were plowed up and put to corn and the destruction went on at even a more rapid pace than before, for erosion was added to soil depletion and very rapidly the whole character of the valley changed for the worse until at last farm after farm became abandoned.

That is where we came in. We did not make the mistake of many a farmer taking over poor, worn-out land—that of overstocking and having to buy feed. We bought about the number of livestock the wornout farms could carry and went to work on the base—the only real base of all successful farm operations—the soil.

We knew what it needed. The first job was to stop the erosion. Then we added lime, which would bring us legumes and help to release the deep fertility of the rich subsoil and make available to a high degree the commercial fertilizers which we purchased to replenish the land. And finally, green stuff to plow in together with the barnyard manure produced in too small quantity. Naturally, green stuff meant first of all legumes, then grasses and other plants of all sorts—indeed almost anything that would bring bulk, decaying organic material, bacteria, fungi and moulds which retain moisture and aerate the soil. As the yields increased we would be able to carry more livestock and so produce more barnyard manure which, applied to the fields would bring still richer production which would in turn permit us to carry more livestock and soon, in brief, our job was to turn the economic wheel which had been running downhill on that particular land to rolling uphill. The fact, simply put, was that we had taken over several hundred acres of potentially rich land on which the soil was, after years of poor farming, literally "dead." Our job was to make that soil a "living" soil in which the potential fertility would once more become available.

During the first two or three years, the going was hard. What hay and pasture the worn-out fields produced was small in quantity and poor in quality. As a makeshift in order to get enough forage, we grew soybean hay. Grass silage was out of the question and so for three or four years we grew corn for silage, mixed with soybeans to get a higher protein content and a better feed for the cattle. We went to work at once on the permanent bluegrass pastures—those parts of

127

the farm which were too steep or too wet for steady cultivation by heavy machinery. These pastures got two tons apiece of limestone meal and 250 pounds of superphosphate, later replaced by the same amount of whole fertilizer 3-12-12 if put on in the spring; 0-12-12 when available if put on later in the year or in the autumn.

These last are formulas known to any farmer. For the sake of the uninitiated they designate the parts respectively of nitrogen, phosphorus and potassium, contained in the fertilizer. Nitrogen was omitted in late season applications as much of it would be lost during winter rains and snows. And in all permanent pastures once lime was applied, ladino clover (introduced by us) or the native white clover (which seeds itself and grows spontaneously where lime exists in sufficient quantity) supplied all the nitrogen necessary to stimulate a good growth of bluegrass.

In the secondary fields—that is, fields of considerable slope on which we could work heavy machinery, but which were still too steep to risk open cultivated crops like corn—we set up a program of small grains (wheat or oats) followed by hay and forage-grass mixtures kept in the field for at least three years before plowing and seeding again to wheat or oats.

Our flattish land (we have no really flat land) and the strips on the moderate slopes were put to hard work, producing corn, without the conventional short rotations, for feeding and for silage. The conventional short rotation is one year each of wheat or oats, corn and hay. Sometimes the hay period is extended to two years. It was introduced more than a generation ago by good agricultural experts who saw the rich "bread-basket" country going to pieces under a single-crop system of corn, corn, corn.

In this plan of hard-working the soil we were aware that recompense had to be made on a considerable scale if we were not to encounter the disaster of so many farmers who "corned" their land into decay and death and if we were to maintain even the miserable production which we inherited, let alone increase the fertility of the flattish fields. In this program too, grass played a large part, grass in the form of rye, seeded immediately after the corn, stover and all, had been removed for silage. The rye served two purposes—to cover

the field during the winter months of freezing and thawing so as to prevent water run-off and erosion, and to contribute a heavy residue of green stuff and roots to replenish and increase the originally lacking organic material, and the organic material burned up and destroyed by the open cultivation of corn and similar crops. But we knew that even a heavy crop of rye plowed in was not enough to make up for the losses incurred by the greedy corn which was carried off the fields, stalk, grain and all, to the silos. So each year on this hard-worked flattish land, we spread a heavy coat of barnyard manure on top of the green rye to be plowed in. In addition to all this two tons of lime was spread in the beginning and 250 pounds of 5-12-12 fertilizer was added to the field each year. In other words, we constantly put back not only as much as we took off in the form of fibre and grain, but *more*. In addition to the organic material contributed by the plowed-in rye, the green growth turned in at the height of about eighteen inches (the maximum balance of organic material with maximum nitrogen content) contributed considerable quantities of nitrogen to the fields.

The formula proved itself and paid off. An accurate record of one field treated thus, with a crop record of four years in corn, one in soybeans (pastured off) and one in oats, showed an increase of corn yields of from 30 baskets to over 75 baskets in a period of four years. Oats on the same field, after five years without rotation produced 75 bushels to the acre although our soils are too light to grow good oats.

On another farm which we rent from the Muskingum Conservancy similar gains have been recorded under a similarly unconventional treatment. This farm, without buildings, lies too far from the barns to permit us to haul barnyard manure to it often upon any reasonable basis of cost in time and labor. It has been kept in a two-year rotation of oats and corn, but only the grain is removed. All corn stover and oats straw is plowed back together with the annual fertilizer applications. The strongest factor in the fertility and productive gains on this farm is probably the plowing in every other year of a rank growth of sweet and mammoth clover. It is seeded every other year in oats and is plowed in the following spring, just before corn planting time, at the height of eighteen inches to two feet. The clovers contribute to the soil not only the organic material of roots and lush green growth but boundless nitrogen as well. Together with the rising production of this farm, the whole color and texture of the soil has changed. It has grown steadily darker and the texture is so loose and friable that in some years plowing and one passage over with the cultimulcher constitute the only fitting necessary to seed corn or oats. The yields of corn under this treatment rose from about 30 to a maximum of 90 baskets in five years.

Of course in the case of both the flattish fields and the Conservancy farm, grass or legumes (sweet and mammoth clover) played the great and perhaps the determining role in the record of increasing production. Without them, commercial fertilizer even in great quantities, would have achieved little. That is a fact we have proved over and over. To put it roughly and to say what will be said again and again in this book, we have found that commercial fertilizer is valuable to us and available to our crops in direct ratio to the amount of organic material and the moisture it absorbs and maintains in the soil. Most of the land we took over was devoid of organic material and more like cement than soil.

As the grass and green manure program progressed, the immense value of grass and legumes asserted itself in no uncertain terms over the whole of the 900 acres. After the first hard three years, fields which had been sickly began to burgeon into new life as lime and fertilizer brought rich legumes and a heavy growth of grass roots and tops. On those fields covered by grass, *no* rainfall and *no* topsoil was lost, nor was the organic material being burned out by open cultivated crops like corn.

In three or four fields, where original seedings of wheat or oats failed to produce yields that were worth harvesting, when plowed again after three years of rest and relaxation in grass and legumes, production jumped, to as high as 35 bushels of wheat and 50 bushels of oats.

In one field on the Bailey Place which we have operated for only four years, lime, grass, legumes, and barnyard manure jumped wheat production from under five bushels per acre when we took it over to 33 bushels after two years and to over 50 after four years of grass–wheat rotation.

The record of the field kept for a period of four years ending July, 1947, may be of interest to readers. It is this—

In the first year when we inherited the field already sowed to wheat, we did not even harvest the crop since it would not have been worth the time and labor expended. The field was limed in March of the first year and in the miserable wheat stand was seeded a rough mixture of legumes—sweet and mammoth, red, alsike and ladino clovers and alfalfa. The wheat itself was mowed down and left in the field, to reseed itself. The legume seeding came out in a spotty fashion, but with more legumes than we had hoped. There was a considerable growth of weeds. During the first summer, following the March seeding we made no attempt to harvest anything and the only operations were to spread over the field some of the "mine" of manure we found in the old barns and to clip the field three times, leaving the residue of weeds, legumes, and grass where it fell. Thus we got three growths instead of merely one to turn into the soil along with the barnyard manure when we plowed for wheat in the fall.

By this process we took *no* minerals from the field and got three growths of weeds, legumes and grass instead of one to turn back into the organically starved soil. Of this growth at least 95 per cent came out of sunlight, air, and water, and cost us nothing but the seed.

In the autumn of the second year we planted the field to wheat and the following July we harvested 33 bushels per acre. Into this plantation of wheat we put a seeding in March of the same year of alfalfa, brome grass, and ladino clover. The limestone we applied at the beginning, having broken down in two years, now made its effect evident and the legume seeding was fairly even and pretty good and came along beautifully. In the following year we cut two crops of good alfalfa ladino hay but the seeding was not good enough to suit us and that autumn we again plowed in the residue of legume growth and put the field to wheat. The same field which in 1943 had produced less than five bushels to the acre produced 53 bushels in 1947.

These gains appeared to us miraculous, considerably better than we had obtained in fields similarly treated on the other farms. After examination and investigation we came to the conclusion that the great quantities of organic material—weeds, grass, legumes, and barnyard manure—which we turned back into the soil had, together with the lime, simply released a great quantity of commercial fertilizer applied by the farmer ahead of us which was not available to his crops because the soil had been what could best be described as a mixture of cement and gravel with traces of acid.

This was one of the few fields which was ever taken out of circulation during the soil improvement process. On 90 per cent of our worn-out land we have raised a crop every year in order to pay taxes and interest *while* improving the soil, as indeed every farm should and sometimes must do. In the cases where we took a field out of production for a year and turned back into the soil whatever was raised upon it, the soil was in such poor condition that the harvest would scarcely have returned the cost of seed and fertilizer. Later on we discovered the great virtues of trash mulch seeding of alfalfa and ladino clover which gave us a good crop return without taking the field out of circulation even for a year.

We knew from earlier experience, that lime, legumes and abundant organic material did much to make the natural residual fertility as well as the purchased chemical fertilizer available to the plants, but in this case the gains in production were so great that the only reasonable explanation seemed to be that we had released the fertilizer purchased and put on the fields by our predecessor which had lain there unutilized because the acid soil was devoid of all organic materials and refused to absorb or maintain moisture from June onward.

Our experience with the Bailey Place was indeed almost fabulous. For at least two generations it had been known as "the thinnest farm between Newville and Little Washington," which meant virtually the poorest farm in Pleasant Valley. It was a farm of great natural beauty consisting partly of great hills and partly of rolling bottom land made up largely of glacial, gravel loam churned into great mounds by the waters of the melting second glacier. Here and there in the lower pastures there were smooth level terraces along the creek created by the same water action. At the big old brick house there was a magnificent spring with an ancient stone spring house containing great troughs chiseled out of

133

solid blocks and sandstone eight feet long and two feet thick where butter, milk and vegetables were kept cold and fresh in the icy spring water.

The farm had had a tragic history, so common in all parts of the nation, of absentee landlordism and yearly fly-by-night tenancy with both landlord and tenant squeezing whatever they could from the fields and putting nothing back. Our immediate predecessor had bought it in hopes of doing something with it and had at last given up hope and sold it to us at a loss.

We bought the Bailey Place with misgivings. We bought it because, despite apparently poor soil and weeds and sumach, it was a beautiful farm with a view from one hill, higher even than the Ferguson Place, which on a clear day looked into four counties—Ashland, Richland, Knox and Morrow. In *Pleasant Valley* I told many of the circumstances and related some of the surprising progress that we made in a brief period of ownership. Four years have passed since then and "the thinnest farm between Newville and Little Washington" produced in 1947 an average wheat production of 35 bushels to the acre despite the losses brought about by countless cloudbursts and windstorms. This production ranks high as against the state and national average production of less than 20 bushels to the acre. Some fields produced as high as 52 bushels to the acre.

The Bailey Place today raises, after four years, some of the finest alfalfa, brome grass, and ladino mixtures to be found anywhere in the United States, not only in quantity of yield but in high protein and mineral content. A pound of the alfalfa grown on the Bailey Place in 1946 and analyzed at the Battelle Institute,[1] was found to contain 6.5 per cent mineral content, two per cent and more higher than that contained in most alfalfa. And this from "the thinnest farm between Newville and Little Washington!"

[1] Battelle Institute is a heavily endowed and ably staffed institution devoted to all fields of metallurgical research. More and more, it has extended its activities into the field of soils and agriculture. This experiment and research is producing many scientific facts of great interest in the relationship between minerals and trace elements and their relationship to health in plants, animals, and people.

Lloyd Andrews, a good neighbor, who knew the Bailey Place all his life, found himself while searching for strayed heifers during the summer of 1946, in corn eight to ten feet high on the same fields which four years earlier had produced less than ten bushels per acre of nubbins with half the stalks bearing no ears at all.

In all the astonishing record of the Bailey Place no part was more astonishing than what happened on the Bailey hills on the north side of the highway. These were two great piles of glacial drift which for years had spoiled the view from the Big House by their barrenness. They had been "corned" out, pastured out and "sheeped" out over a period of three or four generations until they had become sterile eyesores in the green beauty of the valley. In spring and early summer, they raised a sickly yellow-green mass against the blue skies and by July they had turned red and brown from the masses of sorrel. By August they were an ugly faded brown with the burnt-out foliage of wire grass, poverty grass, and broom sedge. During the spring they provided a little sickly pasture for a few heads of livestock but after June 15 any cattle pastured there would have starved to death. Not only was there little or no foliage to be found but the existing acid soil plants provided little or no nutrition. Only on the peak of the highest hill, known as Mount Jeez, was there any green. There, against the skies was a patch of deep green bluegrass. It marked the spot where in hot weather the sheep, last product of run-down land, had gathered to profit by any breeze that stirred. During the years they pastured there, before the hills were abandoned altogether, they had gleaned what little fertility remained and carried it to the hilltop where they deposited it as manure minus the minerals they took off in the form of meat and wool. In midsummer the hill resembled a brown, sterile mountain capped by emerald-green snow.

Today in the fifth year of possession, the Bailey hills loom against the sky a deep emerald-green color from top to bottom. The green is the deep healthy green of alfalfa, brome grass, and ladino clover which yields three valuable cuttings a year of the finest quality forage—one for grass silage, one for high quality hay, and one for some of the most nutritious pasture to be found on the surface of the earth, a

135

forage on which cattle grow fat as if fed upon grain and from which cows come in smooth, sleek, and bright-eyed, dripping milk from their udders.

The miraculous transformation cost us about $20 per acre plus labor. In the first year of transformation we took off the once barren hills a value of at least $75 per acre in silage, hay, and pasture. In the second year, as the alfalfa, brome grass, and ladino thickened up, the value rose to well over $100 an acre. In other words, the procedure paid for itself more than three times over in one year, raising production from a level of about 25 cents to over $75 per acre. I know of no example so startling of the value of the New Agriculture which operates upon the principle of successful industry and business—that you *invest* a dollar plus knowledge and intelligence in order to make three or four or ten or fifteen dollars.

The process of restoration, which in essence was no more than unlocking the hidden natural fertility of these glacial hills, was simple enough. It was this—

Over the whole surface of the hills we spread two tons of lime per acre at a cost of $4.00 a ton. Once this was spread we began the process of killing the miserable, acid-soil vegetation—sorrel, poverty grass, broom sedge, sumach, and blackberry bushes which covered the hills. This we did by ripping up the vegetation with a Ferguson tractor and tiller, or field cultivator, going over the whole surface twice, the second time at right angles and at a depth of four to five inches. Once the hills were ripped up, the surface was disked twice and in the roughest spots, three times. This virtually killed the old vegetation and created an even surface for seeding with all the old trash left on the surface. We then drilled in 300 pounds of fertilizer, three parts nitrogen, 12 parts phosphorus and 12 parts potassium together with a seeding consisting of 9 pounds alfalfa, 5 pounds brome grass and one pound ladino clover. All of this was done in the dry weather of early spring—the windy season of March when the hills were exposed to the sweep of winds coming down the whole of Pleasant Valley.

When the heavy rains of April and May came along, the trash of dead roots, grass, and weeds left on the surface trapped every bit of rainfall. Because of the trash there was *no* erosion and *no* run-off water even on the steepest parts of the hill. To have clean-plowed the hill in the spring season would have invited and achieved a whole new crop of gullies and the loss of much valuable seed and fertilizer. The trash surface retained *all* moisture and the consequent germination was at the highest rate we had ever achieved. By late May, almost over night, the once sickly yellow hills had turned to a rich green color.

With the germination of the seeding came also a thick germination of the weed seeds that remained on the surface— sorrel, all the worthless grasses, wild carrot and other poorland pests. This crop of seedlings we actually turned to advantage by clipping the hills twice during the summer months. By this process we achieved not only two crops of badly needed surface organic material but laid down a fairly thick mulch over the whole surface of the hills which kept the soil moist and cool during the drought which came later the same year for six weeks during the months of August and September.

By October the seeding lay thick and vigorous across the surface of the hills. Against the blue October skies, the hills which once had been the worst eyesores of the valley were blanketed with what from the Big House appeared to be a mantle of deep green velvet. They also provided a heavy crop of October pasture.

In June of the next year, the miracle proved itself. Over the hills lay a crop of mixed legumes and grass hay so thick that at times it clogged the cutter bar of the power mower. The alfalfa and the ladino had made prodigious growth. The brome grass was in evidence but giving only one-tenth the production it would provide in three or four years. Perhaps the most startling of all was the appearance, especially in the wet, seepage spots, of quantities of red-top, a fine nutritious grass, and alsike clover which we had not seeded at all. Clearly the seed had been there all the time, distributed year after year by wind or birds, but until the lime and some fertilizer had been applied, the seedlings had never grown to maturity or even made enough growth to make their presence noticeable. There also appeared where it could gain a foothold thick, tight, creeping growths of native small white clover which had been there all the time but was never able to get a start until it had been given some help. The same was true of considerable amounts of red and mammoth clover which we did not include in the seeding. One thing which startled us was that the field of rich grass and legumes was completely weedless, stretching rich and green as far as one could see to the horizon. The weedless condition undoubtedly came from the clipping of the year before and from the fact that the ladino clover comes on so early and grows so rapidly that it chokes out all but the coarser weeds.

All this was achieved easily and at comparatively low expense on the "thinnest farm between Newville and Little Washington" on the barrenest, most sterile hills of that farm or indeed in the entire valley. I can think of no investment in these times which could show such vast returns. Yet at the very time we were cutting green forage of highly nutritious content off the Bailey hills at the rate of three tons per acre, the tenant a half mile down the road on fairly level, low-lying land was cutting half a ton or less per acre of weedy timothy hay that had little nutritive value, from fields which within three or four years more will not pay taxes and interest. In fact they do not pay taxes and interest now and no really serious tenant would touch the place.

That field and the farm of which it is a part are the result of the vicious, absentee-landlord, yearly-tenant system from which the Bailey Place had suffered for so long. I know of no sharper contrast between the old agriculture and the new—no contrast between an agriculture which wasted along in a worn-out pattern producing less each year at a constantly growing cost of production and an agriculture based upon maintenance of fertility, the realization that land is "capital," the most stable of all capital, and that farming is a business in which the farmer invests a dollar to make five dollars.

The deep green of the grass and legumes on the Bailey Place hills had other implications besides those of soil restoration and of increased income and production. The deep green against the horizon was plain for all to see but its importance ran through the whole economic structure of Malabar Farm and touched the lives of all the men, women, and children living there.

These hills were a part of the grass farming program, which meant not only a healed and restored earth but dollars and cents. They meant reduced labor and fertilizer costs and increased production and quality of meat, milk, butter, and cheese.

On Malabar there are four big silos to fill each year and at the beginning of the adventure it was necessary to grow corn and soybean hay to fill them. With poor yields per acre this was expensive feed in terms of labor, taxes, and interest, and the corn was each year contributing to erosion and the breaking down of the soil. Slowly as the rich grass and legumes came to flourish on our hills and slopes, we began to fill the silos with grass and legumes, and as we did so we discovered many things of great economic importance to us.

Briefly they were: (1) *That our costs on grass silage were approximately one-eighth the cost of corn silage in terms of seed and fertilizer and one-fifth in terms of labor.* This was so because a field well-seeded to a mixture of alfalfa, brome grass, and ladino could be left for a period of many years

139

without all the labor and seed and fertilizer costs involved each year in the cultivation of corn. We made most of the first lush June cutting into silage year after year. The immediate labor involved was slight. By July 1, all the silos were filled and sealed. There was no plowing, fitting, cultivating, and harvesting of corn with the burden of making silage in the early autumn when there was so much other work to be done. Year after year the only labor involved in the grass program was simply the harvesting of one cutting as silage and one as hay with the third rich cutting left to be pastured off. Rapidly the need disappeared for any supplementary summer pasture such as Sudan grass or the mixture of drilled corn and soybeans which we had once used and which in turn involved plowing, fitting, seeding, etc. Whenever in August or September, as in the case of drought, our regular pastures showed signs of running short we have only to open a gate and turn the herd into a new lush field of alfalfa, brome grass, and ladino.

The job of making grass silage with a field chopper is a simple one with no drudgery. The chopper mows the grass, drops it into a wagon whence it is blown into the silo. As we own no silage cutter Bob evolved an ingenious scheme for using the pick-up baler and the whole operation became simplicity itself. The process began with mowing the green hay and windrowing it in the same operation. In some cases the mixed hay was so heavy that the windrower attached to the mower would not handle it properly and a side-delivery rake, attached to the power mower, did the windrowing. From half an hour to an hour later, when the lush grass was wilted sufficiently, the pick-up baler passed along the windrow, picked it up, chopped it into neat bundles and pushed it across the platform onto the wagon attached. Of course, no bales were tied and any ten-year-old boy could build the load. At the silo the grass mass was simply pushed off into the silage cutter, no wrestling with twisted ropes of green hay. The operation as a rule keeps three or four wagons working constantly from the baler to the silo.

As to fertilizer, the expense of the grass fields amounted to four tons of lime per acre every twelve years and three hundred pounds of fertilizer broadcast by a home-built "spinner" every three or four years—an operation requiring only an hour or less for a ten-acre field. (We calculated that this amount represented about the quantity of minerals carried off the field and the farm in the form of meat, milk, cheese etc.) Poor or thin spots in any field or occasionally whole fields were treated with barnyard manure which returned both organic material and minerals to the soil. We have one field of alfalfa and brome grass which is still producing excellent yields of hay, silage, and pasture after eight years without plowing, fitting, or seeding. It is probable that with good treatment it will continue to yield good crops for at least another two to four years.

(2) *Two of the most expensive items of the livestock farmer's budget were eliminated: (a) Protein supplements in the form of expensive oil meals; (b) Nitrogen fertilizer.*

Nitrogen and protein are essentially the same thing and where legume and high-protein grasses are used as forage both exist in abundance, the protein in the forage and the nitrogen in the fields where it is fixed by the legumes out of the air and pumped into the soil in great quantities at no cost to us beyond the lime which makes it possible to grow the legumes. In the grass program we raise less and less corn each year, and it is possible that within another year or two we shall grow none at all and buy what corn we need. This is so because acre for acre, deducting costs of labor and fertilizer and the savings in feed supplements and nitrogen fertilizer, we can make more profit on an acre of good grass and legumes than 90 per cent of the corn and hog farmers make on corn. And with a reasonable use of lime and fertilizer we are constantly building our soils instead of tearing them down by row-crop cultivation and constant plowing.

In the grass-small grain program the principal grain acreage is in oats and wheat both of which serve as cover crops and protect the soil. The fine elaborate root system of these grain grasses also contributes great quantities of organic material to the soil and the straw used as bedding is worked through the cattle barns, enriched by animal manure and urine and returned to the fields. A good many farmers and some agronomists overlook the great contribution of organic material made to the soil by the root systems of most grasses and legumes, perhaps because they are invisible. In some cases green crops plowed in as green manure contribute more organic material from the roots than from the green growth which is visible. Certainly this is true in the case of rye grass. In Manitoba, fairly dry country, agronomists have traced out the fine root system of a single wheat plant and found that it virtually filled with its hair-like roots a cubic yard of earth. One plant of tufted mountain grass in Colorado was found to have 350 miles of fine hair-like roots. This is not true of "destructive" crops like corn and cotton which have comparatively coarse and limited root systems although corn, properly speaking, is a grass.

The wheat and oats, grown for various purposes and for the past five years at high prices, have been extremely valuable cash crops raised while seeding new meadows. Seedings of alfalfa, brome grass, ladino mixture are made in the grain plantations which themselves serve as cover crops. The oats is used as feed for young stock and milkers and the wheat is sold as a valuable cash crop directly out of the fields to the grain elevator. Neither crop is so depleting as corn and neither crop leaves the soil bare to the drying erosive effect of wind, sun, and rain except for the very short period from seeding to germination. Both through their elaborate root systems contribute great quantities of organic material.

The grass silage produces a high-protein feed; when well made it has a protein content as high as 10 to 20 per cent. Sun-dried hay, well made of the same grass legume mixture, also contains a very high-protein content so that in combination the problem of feeding is not one of more expensive oil meal and concentrate supplements but rather that of increasing the carbohydrate content of the diet to secure a better, more productive feed balance. Largely speaking, animals utilize both proteins and carbohydrates to the highest degree of benefit, if the two are in proper balance, provided the necessary minerals are present in the forage. On a high-protein grass and legume program, our problem at Malabar has become one of carbohydrate rather than protein supplement. Since the grass silage is made in June during uncertain weather there is no loss of nutrients through bad weather, for rain does not spoil silage as it may spoil hay. Most of our hay is made in the open field, sun-dried, during the more dependable weather of late July and in an ordinary year we have very little damage from weather.

Moreover, the combination provides a rich nutritional balance, the silage providing carotene and protein in quantity and the hay picking up certain vitamins of great importance through the sun-drying process. The full advantages of this are realized in the feeding methods used in the dairy barn. No feeding hours are maintained but the hay-racks and silage bins are kept filled around the clock. Since the cows are run loose in loafing pens and are not kept in stanchions, they are able to eat whenever they are hungry, and abundant green grass silage is maintained, a situation which is as near as possible to that of open, abundant pasture. Under this system when the dairy cows are brought in during the late autumn off green pasture there is no perceptible drop in production.

The loafing-shed system has in my opinion many advantages over the stanchion system. The risk of mastitis, udder, bone and joint injuries is greatly reduced. The cows, physically speaking, are certainly happier. The system also permits each cow to balance her own diet with regard to roughage, i.e., the amounts she consumes of both hay and silage. Two cows may each be giving 50 pounds of milk. One may consume twice as much dry hay as silage and the other twice as much silage as dry hay. If put into stanchions and "told what to eat" by being given equal amounts of hay and silage both will fall off in production. The milking cows are of course fed a mixture of ground oats and corn and obtain some carbohydrates from the ground corncob meal put in the silo at the rate of 100 pounds per ton of green silage. The corn meal also helps to keep the silage green and sweet although it is not absolutely necessary to make high quality silate. Minerals including some twenty trace elements are fed at the cow's choice from boxes placed beside the usual salt box.

One of the chief reasons for my liking the loafing-shed method of dairying is the quality of the manure produced in the loafing sheds. Being primarily the soil man on Malabar, I am especially interested in this aspect of dairying. In the loafing shed the manure is removed every six weeks or two months. Meanwhile two to three feet of fresh straw is spread in the loafing sheds once a day with a layer of sawdust put in once a week when possible to absorb liquids. Day by day the manure is trampled. No rain reaches it and all the liquids are preserved. During this process the count of benevolent bacteria in the manure increases by trillions and the straw and sawdust, by the time they are removed, are two-thirds of the way to becoming the finest of all fertilizers, both minerally and organically, plus the content of glandular animal secretions, hormones, and enzymes, which have undeniably an effect upon soil fertility and seed germination and exert a catalyzing effect in releasing and making available indigenous fertility.

Under the stanchion system little of such action takes place. Too often virtually all urine is wasted and the manure pile, even when covered, consists of a heap of dry raw straw interspersed with animal droppings. If the stanchion manure is removed to a covered shed with little or no moisture in it, the curing process (actually a kind of intensive composting involving the breaking down of carbon, cellulose, etc.) takes place slowly or does not take place at all. If the manure from stanchion barns is placed in the open the manure will lose valuable soil nutrients in great quantity through leaching. Most stanchion barn manure goes into the fields as a mixture of raw straw and droppings with most of the valuable liquids and the invaluable bacteria, fungi, and moulds, either missing or existing in small quantities. Raw straw, until it is broken down, is of very little value to the soil. For a certain period it may even be damaging in that through the operations of the nitrogen-carbon ratio, it actually robs the soil of nitrogen in the process of breaking down carbon and cellulose into decaying organic material. This breaking-down process is virtually accomplished in the loafing-shed type of operation before the manure goes to the field, and the manure feeds the soil rich supplies of nitrogen rather than robbing it of the same element.

I have seen many stanchion barns operated by city farmers or as show places with elaborate constructions to accomplish what is achieved easily and naturally in a loafing shed. These include tanks for catching urine and elaborate composting machinery. All of these, taken together, no doubt

144

produce a quality of manure somewhat approaching that of the loafing shed but the capital investment and operational costs are beyond the sound economic operations of the practical dairy farmer. Either he cannot afford them or the price of milk to the consumer must be raised enormously to cover these considerable items of expense.

Some states have laws forcing milk producers, on the dubious ground of sanitation, to keep cows in stanchions. In our own experience the cows in a well-managed loafing shed are not only healthier and more productive, but also cleaner. They are never milked *in the stable itself* but taken to a milking parlor at some distance which is always kept in excellent sanitary condition. The chances of dirt and infection are much less. The whole population of Malabar drinks the whole milk without pasteurization, straight from the milking parlor, thus losing none of the vitamins which can be destroyed by pasteurizing processes. Save in the case of careless or inefficient employees, the milk from a well-managed loafing shed-milking parlor establishment will always have a bacterial count much lower than that demanded by the law, and in most cases probably lower than that of most stanchion barns. In a well-managed loafing shed the cows will have a record of cleanliness as high as or higher than that of cows in open pastures. At the time of writing we have just come through a period of six months without a trace of mastitis in a milking herd of thirty-five cows. Even in the case of a heifer which injured her udder jumping over a watering trough infection failed to develop.

The laws demanding stanchion dairies smell of lobbies and private influence in legislation. There is also the question of a cow's comfort, always of importance to any livestock man who likes his animals, as well as production. I have seen some expensive, plushed-up stanchion barns which might well invite investigation by the Society for the Prevention of Cruelty to Animals.

I have often heard misgivings from corn-silage farmers regarding the difficulties of making good grass silage and of the possibilities of wholesale spoilage, but in our long, varied and extensive experience we have had no more spoilage than we have had with corn silage (at the top and sometimes near the doors). We have put up from time to time some odd mixtures such as vetch and rye (cut when the rye was in bloom), wheat and sweet clover (cut when the wheat was in the milk), and even sunflowers put in with corn, but none of these have proved difficult. We have made grass silage under all kinds of conditions, determined largely by weather, and always achieved good results. We have made it both with and without molasses or corncob meal, without or with water added and never suffered disastrous spoilage. To be sure, the greener it is when it comes out of the silo, the better the silage. Molasses will help greenness and so will the corncob meal for both act as preservatives, but the chief element is moisture content. If the grass going into the silo is too dry, the silage will heat and turn brown. It is still good feed but will have lost its carotene content and some other qualities. If it has too high a moisture content the effect will be more disastrous for an anaerobic action will take place which produces the kind of rotten silage found at the bottom of the silo at the end of the season. Our own test for moisture content is a simple and effective one. The grass and legumes are taken out of the windrow and put into the silo when they are at that point when a handful crushed together in the fist will remain a limp and wilted ball.

# VI: GRASS, THE GREAT HEALER
## (CONTINUED)

The general custom has been, first to raise a crop of Indian corn . . . which, according to the mode of cultivation, is a good preparation for wheat; then a crop of wheat; after which the ground is respited . . . and so on, alternately, without any dressing, till the land is exhausted; when it is turned out, without being sown with grass seeds, or any other method taken to restore it; and another piece is ruined in the same manner. No more cattle is raised than can be supported by lowland meadows, swamps etc. . . . Our lands were originally very good; but use, and abuse, have made them quite otherwise.

—George Washington in 1768

MUCH of the foregoing may seem a digression from the subject of the healing, restorative, and maintenance properties of grass farming. Actually even to the notes on the conversion of the straw of wheat and oats (both grasses) into high quality barnyard manure fertilizer are a part of the whole grass picture.

Fundamentally of course, while the grass program costs us one-fifth to one-eighth in labor and fertilizer as against corn, we are not only preserving the organic content of our soil and checking all erosion by grass farming, but are actually building up the fertility of the soil. Of course open cultivated crops like corn and cotton are constantly achieving the opposite results—those of creating erosion and of tearing down and burning up the organic content without which even commercial fertilizer at length becomes virtually unavailable and useless.

In our hill country the presence of abundant organic material in soil is the fundamental means of erosion check. It keeps the soil open and loose and as absorbent as blotting paper to rainfall, drinking up the water instead of turning it off a cement-like surface. In flat, drained land the depletion of organic material through persistent and unrelieved production of open-row crops, notably corn, arrives at what might be called the exactly opposite result. With the steady depletion of organic material in flat, drained land, the soil becomes more and more like cement and instead of turning off the water as in the case of erodible hill lands it refuses to give up the water and serves actually to cement the surface above the tiling that has been put in to drain it off.

In my own state, the drainage problem has become acute in the western and northwestern parts, as the native organic material has become depleted and no measures have been taken to replenish it. On some farms tiling which a generation or two ago functioned well in lines laid down a hundred feet apart is no longer adequate to drain the soil and today increased tiling, newly placed in lines only a rod (16½ feet) apart will no longer drain off adequately the surface water after a rainfall. During the heavy rains that afflicted Ohio throughout the spring and early summer of 1947 some whole farms in the western part of the state appeared for weeks more like lakes than fertile, productive fields. More than a million acres of what once was the richest flat land in Ohio were never plowed at all during the 1947 season owing to the failure of drainage, and an acreage of almost equal size was drowned out after planting. Certainly 40 per cent of the corn planted in the same area did not ripen because of planting delayed by faulty drainage resulting from the depletion of organic material through persistent and unrelieved corn farming.

Indeed over great areas of the United States, proper soil drainage has become as acute a problem as soil erosion and the Soil Conservation Service has recognized this fact by giving the problem increasing attention. In every case the waning efficiency of tile drainage has been traced to the steady depletion of organic material, and to the formation of invisible hardpan conditions caused largely by the same depletion.

In the flat lands with drainage problems, the grass farm-

148

ing program offers as great advantages and profits as in the hill country at Malabar, for grass and legumes instead of depleting organic material, maintain it and each time they are plowed in, serve to increase the organic content. The soil is kept open to air, to sunlight and to water which contribute 95 per cent and more of the growth of any plant, and the excess water is permitted to drain off to lower levels.

Recently we have had many visitors from the flat areas of western Ohio and Indiana. They have come primarily to learn what they can of profit from our grass farming program. All of them have come to understand, most of them by harsh experience, that year after year of corn, or even years of corn in conventional four-year rotation can be disastrous if more organic material than that provided by a four-year rotation is not introduced. In the minds of many of them, not only dairy farmers but beef feeders, has dawned the suspicion that they would make more money from an acre of grass than from an acre of corn while at the same time maintaining and increasing organic content of their land and preserving and increasing the efficiency of their soil drainage.

Their interest has given rise to a suspicion that grass farming is highly profitable not only to dairy farmers but to beef feeders as well. For my own taste, the best beef in the world comes from the lush pastures of Normandy and England where little or no grain feeding is practiced. The same is true of much of the beef coming from the Argentine, fattened wholly or almost wholly upon lush and minerally nutritious pasture. The minerally rich semi-arid ranges of the West and Southwest will produce frame and size and vigor in beef cattle but save for a few limited areas of rich, high mountain pasture, will not produce fat and finished beef. Nor will the average miserable, depleted weedy bluegrass pastures of the Middle West produce fat cattle, but at Malabar we have every evidence that livestock, from steers to lambs, will grow fat upon rich pasture properly cared for and treated as a crop and a valuable one. We and one of our neighbors working on the same lush grass program have sent lambs fed only on grass, without grain, to the Cleveland market and have had them bring top choice price, with the fact announced over the radio.

There are very few such pastures in existence today in the Middle West which is the great corn finishing cattle area. Beef feeding and to a great extent the feeding of hogs and other livestock is largely a process of stuffing corn, with or without sufficient protein supplements, into the animals. It is an expensive process, not only in its immediate effect of using costly feed and involving much labor but because corn, when not managed with great skill, is an exceedingly expensive crop in that rich area in terms of erosion, depletion, drainage and the general destruction of soil structure. Indeed, King Corn has in many respects been the curse of the Middle West as King Cotton has been the curse of the Deep South.

For many reasons it is impossible to overestimate the value of the legumes and most grasses as maintainers or restorers of worn out soils and builders of poor virgin soil. Very largely they are crops which need little or no organic material in order to flourish. A gravel bank or a soil like cement, with lime and a moderate amount of fertilizer applied, providing the subsoil is reasonably good, will produce good and increasingly productive crops of legumes and grasses and in the process, provide vast quantities of nitrogen, green manure and roots to build up the organic material without which no productive agriculture can long survive.

As topsoil builders their value is immense, since the building of topsoil is no more than the incorporation of masses of organic material into the raw subsoil. That is why the restoration of a deep topsoil upon any reasonably good subsoil is a much more rapid process than we have been taught in the past. Many neighbors and countless visitors have watched the process of Malabar over a period of years. The record of rapid rebuilding of topsoil from a base of good subsoil is there for all to see.

I know of no more striking example than the Long Field on the Anson Place. It is a field in which the subsoil is largely gravel loam with some outcrops of reddish clay heavily impregnated with iron. During the first year at Malabar, I plowed this field and found that the old topsoil had a maximum depth of three inches. Large areas of the field, perhaps as much as 60 per cent, had no topsoil whatever. The condition had come about through two causes: (1) erosion, (2) the old-fashioned farmer's fetish against plowing deeply

and bringing up the subsoil to convert into topsoil by the incorporation of organic material. The field had been limed, so the former owner told us, but it was clear almost at once that there was something wrong somewhere. Closer investigation revealed the fact that the field had, indeed, been limed but only to the amount of 500 pounds of ground limestone per acre, an amount so ludicrously small and so quickly used up by calcium-hungry plants and animals that it had little or no effect whatever.

Some years later in the autumn of 1946, I plowed up the same field for wheat, going slowly and forcing the plow as deeply as possible in order to turn up the minerally rich gravel loam subsoil, and although the plow reached an average depth of nine inches and sometimes as much as ten, it was very nearly impossible to find any traces of the subsoil. In other words a depth of at least 9 inches of topsoil had been restored in the short period of six and one-half years. Grass, legumes and barnyard manure had turned a trick for which nature, working slowly and unaided, would have needed thousands of years.

The history of the field is largely that of the topsoil building methods practiced on the whole acreage of Malabar—simply that of incorporating as much organic material as possible, as rapidly as possible, into the existing subsoil or completely depleted topsoils. In the Long Field the process was intensified. The record for the first four years was one of corn silage but each year when the corn was removed, the fields were seeded to rye as a cover crop and for late fall and early spring pasture. Each year during the winter months it was given a good coat of barnyard manure. It should be pointed out that, ravaged as we originally found the field, it was in far better condition than most of the land we took over.

During these four years the cattle, pasturing on the rye, spring and fall, contributed large amounts of liquid and solid manure. In the fifth year, when our grass silage program first began to operate in a small way and the same quantities of silage corn were no longer necessary, the field was sown to oats and produced a good yield. In the oats we sowed a mixture of rye grass and Korean lespedeza which came along well and provided a great amount of good late summer pasture. By November the lespedeza was gone but the rye grass had created a thick carpet of sod, as thick as the heaviest bluegrass but infinitely more valuable from the point of view of organic material because the rye grass puts out a prodigious system of fine roots in loose soils, especially during dry hot weather. During the winter the field was again given a coat of barnyard manure and in the following spring it was sowed to a summer pasture mixture of Sudan grass, millet, buckwheat, drilled corn, and hay soybeans. Nearly all of these, being legumes or grasses, made considerable contributions both of nitrogen and of organic material in the form of roots and the residue of plants and weeds left after the cattle were turned off, which was plowed in. Added to all of this, of course, were the droppings of the cattle during the period of pasturing together with the hormones, enzymes, bacteria, etc., about which we know so little but which have much to do with the creation of good soil and possibly of topsoil. Earthworms, whose population increased rapidly in ratio to the rapid increase of moisture, feed and organic material, undoubtedly made their contribution by the processes long ago described by Darwin. It was during the plowing up of the field for wheat that I made the discovery of the remarkably deepened topsoil.

This was our last planting of emergency summer pasture, for by the seventh year our grass program of alfalfa, brome grass, and ladino, was established so widely over the farm that there was always rich, abundant pasture available during the late summer and autumn months.

The history of that field was largely the history in varying degrees of the rest of the farm save that in the case of the Long Field repeated and intensive applications of barnyard manure had made weighty contributions. Basically, however, grass and legumes had done the job. The field gave about 50 bushels of wheat per acre and is now seeded to alfalfa, brome grass, and ladino and will remain in hay-silage-meadow-pasture production for at least four to five years with another two tons of limestone and 300 pounds per acre of 0-20-20 plus the droppings of the animals pasturing there during the late summer months.

It is true, of course, that all soils will not respond so quickly and favorably as our own to the topsoil creating process. Our soils are singularly well adapted to the process of restoration for two reasons: (1) Mostly they are gravelly, glacial-drift soils, very loose and workable and highly susceptible to the incorporation and mixing of green and barnyard manure. (2) The native mineral content of the subsoil is both high and well-balanced even to trace elements.

About 10 to 15 per cent of our land is a rich but heavy clay and with it the process of building topsoil is more difficult because the clay, more compact and gluey, is more difficult to mix with raw organic material and is likely to form lumps and pockets. Two tricks we have found effective in hastening the process of topsoil building in such clay land are: (1) Rough plowing in of organic material in the late autumn on fields where winter is not a serious erosion menace. During the winter, through the process of freezing and thawing, the hard gluey clay is broken down into fine particles which, like the loose gravel, loam soils, mixes easily with the organic material—roots, plants, manure, straw and trash—which is undergoing, through freezing and thawing, the same breaking-down process. (2) The process of literally *stuffing* the stubborn soil with organic material.

On some fields of clay structure in poor condition and almost wholly devoid of organic material, we have planted wheat two and even three years in succession. On these fields we have made spring seedings of hubam, a sweet clover which makes a prodigious growth in one season, flowers and dies. At harvest time the combine merely clipped the heads of the wheat leaving the straw standing, and as the summer progressed the fields produced heavy crops of sweet clover which, growing up in the straw, provided a really immense mass of material to be plowed into the clay soil in September for reseeding to wheat and the following year to hubam, again producing the huge bulk of green manure and trash to be incorporated in the stubborn clay within a short period. The process, together with lime and chemical fertilizer, produces rapidly increasing yields of wheat to pay taxes and interest and show a profit while the soil is being brought back to life and fertility. The wheat roots contribute much organic material and the rapidly growing deep roots of the hubam serve to break up the tough soil, and later to admit air and water while disintegrating at the same time *into* the soil structure itself. There is also a great contribution of nitrogen made by the leguminous hubam which is so great after the second year that nitrogen cannot be used as a fertilizer and actually must be omitted. The cost of the hubam seed runs about two dollars per acre—the best fertilizer, soil-restoring buy it is possible to make.

Within the last year we have put into use disk plows which do an even better job of *mixing* earth and organic material than that accomplished by moldboard plows adjusted to doing a rough job followed by disking. This is especially true when fall and winter plowing of heavy sods or weedy poor land is made in preparation for fitting and seeding in the spring. Owing to the rough fashion in which the disk plow turns over the soil there is no danger of erosion during the winter months. Snow, rainfall, freezing and thawing contribute enormously during the winter months to breaking down organic material involved, whether green or barnyard manures, and permits virtually the maximum degree of tilth and moisture for oats or grass-legume seedings in the spring. Curiously, the process appears to create better drainage in poorly drained spots on our clay gravel, perhaps because the loose rough soil permits the frost to penetrate more deeply into the subsoil and act in breaking up any hardpan which may have existed.

Beyond the winter plowing treatment for our small percentage of heavy clay land, we found very definitely that at least two other practices contributed toward restoration of this land and rapid increases in production. These were: (1) the use of a subsoiler, (2) the substitution of disk plow for moldboard plow on all heavy clay land.

One of the greatest problems with our clay land was clearly that of drainage. In fields which contained both clay and gravel loam soils, clay portions were frequently unworkable and unproductive because of wetness until days and sometimes weeks later than the surrounding gravel loam. In some cases the clay strip or patches never really drained and produced nothing but weeds and coarse wet-land grasses. This occurred even in fields on the tops and slopes of hills. The incorporation of heavy amounts of organic material helped superficially to make these clay areas tillable and productive but in the long run or in very heavy rainfall even this produced very little effect.

Close observation gave us the final clue to the trouble. On such strips and patches during a heavy rain the top nine or ten inches of soil into which we had pumped much organic material, drank up eagerly enough the first two or three hours of rain and then became completely saturated. After that, the water simply stood there, if the land was flat, or ran off, if it sloped. This clearly indicated that below the plowing level there was an impenetrable layer of earth, like a layer of asphalt, which blocked any drainage downward into the subsoil.

Investigation proved that this was true. A hundred years or more of plowing these clay areas had gradually produced a hardpan just below the plowing level which prevented *all* drainage or absorption of rainfall. Undoubtedly this land had been plowed and fitted again and again by our predecessors at Malabar when the well-drained gravel loam portions of the field were in prime condition but the clay portions were still much too wet. This fact, coupled with the vicious *pressing down* action of the moldboard plow which stays in the ground only through the violent pressure of the plow point

155

on the earth beneath, had created over the years the brick-like, impenetrable hardpan which turned the clay areas into undrained and undrainable bogs and cut off all production of valuable crops.

The use of the subsoiler—a big, curved steel hook or chisel, pulled by the tractor through these areas at a depth of from two to three feet—very nearly cured the condition almost immediately. Pulled through the earth on parallel lines from five to six feet apart the subsoiler broke up this hardpan and permitted the water to penetrate into the lower and more porous clay below and permitted the heavy rainfall to escape in a natural fashion. It also permitted plant roots to penetrate freely to deeper levels in search both of moisture and of nutrients. It was, of course, impossible to grow alfalfa or sweet clover on any of these areas until after the invisible hardpan was broken up. Once these vigorous deep-root legumes, which demand well-drained soil, were established, they in turn helped to maintain good drainage conditions by thrusting their deep vigorous roots down to a depth of five to six feet. The ripping up process followed by the deep-root growth of heavy legumes will undoubtedly keep this clay area open, friable and highly productive for many years to come, provided we do not put the moldboard plow back into these fields which are all on partly heavy clay soils. In such fields we will from now on use only disk plows which do not create a hardpan by pressure downward even on the heaviest clay soils.

The moldboard plow, plus the steady decline in organic material in the soils of all our flat land and heavy soil areas, has undoubtedly created the serious drainage problems which have increased steadily in many areas of heavy clay or gumbo soils to the point where even the most elaborate tileage systems have become futile and many thousands of acres of once rich, productive land have fallen out of production into the status of desert land. Each year thousands of acres in the rich flat lands of our own western and northwestern Ohio fall out of production because they can no longer be drained. I have seen, in southern Illinois and in Missouri whole fields which after a heavy rain resembled shallow lakes more than good agricultural land. The water simply remained there, held by the hidden, impenetrable hardpan until it was evaporated by wind and sun. One need not describe the effect upon the crops in such a field or the long range effect upon the prosperity of the individual farmer and the economy of the nation of these drowned and partly or wholly useless fields. In most cases the use of a subsoiler, an increase of organic material and the use of a disk plow rather than the moldboard plow would restore the land to high production within a period of two to three years.

Our experience with heavy clay soils and gravel loam soils existing side by side in the same fields has demonstrated once again that in a nation as vast as this one, with so many soils and climates, there is no general rule or any set of methods in agriculture which suits all soils and all conditions. Even on so small an area as Malabar we have found from hard experience, reinforced by a little intelligence, that there is no rule or set of rules which is efficient or effective under all conditions; and that applies to the use of moldboard plows, disk plows, disk and field cultivators or any other farm machinery. It applies likewise to rotations of which with us there is no fixed one; each field and area has its own rotation according to its topography, its type of soil, its location in relation to dairy and feeding barns and even the way it lies toward the sun. We have found conclusively that there are no over-all infallible rules governing agricultural practices. We use every method from trash mulching to the deepest kind of moldboard plowing according to conditions, purpose, and need. We even adjust the plows themselves to different sorts of plowing under different conditions and different topography.

All this is a part of proper land use and fits into our own philosophy that the good farmer is a man who knows as much as possible, never stops learning, and has the intelligence to apply his knowledge and information to the conditions and the program of his own piece of land. It is the kind of farmer we must have in the nation and in this world; it is the kind of farmer we will have inevitably because the other kind is certain to be liquidated economically, despite bribes, subsidies and price floors and their land will be taken over eventually by those who cherish it and can make it productive and maintain that productivity. In the world and even in this country, where there was once so much good land that we believed it inexhaustible both in fertility and in area, mankind, if he is to survive, cannot permit agricultural land to be owned and managed by the lazy, the indifferent and the ignorant.

As Dr. Hugh Bennett suggested recently in a memorable address at Princeton University, the time may not be so far away when in order to practice agriculture, a farmer will be required to have a certificate exactly as a lawyer or a doctor or an engineer must have today, in order to own or to cultivate the earth. Such a condition has already virtually arrived in England where food is so scarce that the poor and unproductive farmer cannot be tolerated if the people of the nation are to eat and survive. Such a measure will not be the result of any political ideology but of grim necessity.

In all but the trash mulch seedings made on the barren hills of the Bailey and Ferguson Places, where the sowing of any wheat, oats or corn crop could not have yielded back the original seed, the process at Malabar is to plow as deep and as roughly as possible. While this may appear to be a denial of the virtues of trash mulch farming and of Mr. Faulkner's ideas in *Plowman's Folly*, it is actually an extension of the whole theory since the process of deep and *rough* plowing merely carries the trash farming idea to a depth of nine to ten inches instead of merely scratching up the surface and leaving the trash on top. Actually the deep, rough plowing creates a kind of sheet composting since the plowing is usually followed, particularly in the case of corn ground, by heavy disking which incorporates all roots, tops, manures and trash *into* the soil instead of turning it over and burying it to be compressed by the weight of fitting implements into a thin layer of tightly compacted organic material, of little or no use and even perhaps a disadvantage to the immediately succeeding crop.

The process leaves soil and trash well mixed together to a depth of nine to ten inches, absorbs and holds moisture and in the process of disintegration produces stimulation to the bacteria, moulds, fungi, and worms which are so vital a part of any living, productive soil in which the mineral fertility is available to the plants. Actually the process converts and maintains our topsoil as a kind of perpetual compost heap in which we grow our crops.

During the disastrous flood rains of 1947 when cloudburst succeeded cloudburst for weeks, this sheet composting system demonstrated its great efficiency as a check upon erosion. On contoured slopes where there are sometimes on our land sudden dips and slopes, the soil, *mixed together* with great quantities of decaying organic material, kept the earth loose, open and absorbent of most of the water and run-off. Even in violent rains erosion was virtually checked. A handful of such soil appeared to be nearly 50 per cent in bulk of composition made up of rough, decaying organic material.

We plow as deeply as possible when plowing because of the high mineral content and the loose quality of all but our clay subsoil. We had hardly begun operations at Malabar before we discovered that perhaps our worst problem was the restoration of the mineral and organic content of the flattish areas where a so-called "topsoil" had escaped erosion. So badly had the existing topsoil been depleted by greedy farming that where a woodchuck dug a hole, the minerally rich subsoil which he brought up from ten to twelve feet below the surface actually acted as fertilizer on the *depleted top-soil and actually grew better, more vigorous crops than the surrounding topsoil.* The sight of a clump of extremely vigorous, deep green oats, corn, soybeans, or wheat in the midst of an otherwise mediocre or even sickly field invariably indicated a spot where the woodchucks had been at work. With this tip-off given us by the fat little burrowers, we set the plows as deeply as possible to bring up the subsoil and incorporate with it as rapidly as possible all the organic material possible.

Later on, continued experience led us to the heretical belief that we should have made more rapid progress in restoration if we had been able to scrape from the whole area of the farm the miserably depleted topsoil that remained and had gone directly to work on building new topsoil out of our minerally rich and well-balanced subsoil. It is largely a fact that in a period of eight years we have produced good productive soil directly from bare subsoil more rapidly than from the pitifully worn-out topsoil which we inherited. Since the many amounts of organic material introduced into both soils were approximately the same, the experience is a striking example of the mineral depletion and deficiencies of many of our old, still existing topsoils. The experience would certainly not be true in the case of all subsoils. At Malabar, we happened to be singularly fortunate in our subsoils as are all farmers in glacial moraine areas. Some subsoils are structurally and minerally so poor that once the topsoil is gone it is impossible to restore fertility by any method which is economically practical. Such land is fit only to be given back to pine forests or at best to be used as thin grazing land. All this is another evidence of the difficulty of making any *general* agricultural rules in a country with such an overwhelming range in types of soil, climate and rainfall as the United States.

Under the grass farming program now well-established at Malabar, it must be evident that most soils plowed for crops are heavy sods compounded of alfalfa, brome grass, and ladino clover. These when plowed up after several years produce prodigious amounts of organic material as well as a seed bed fairly well impregnated with nitrogen to a depth of six to seven inches by the shallow-rooted ladino and to a depth of many feet by the alfalfa. In cases where the plowed sod-soil is to be seeded for wheat, it is necessary to kill the alfalfa plants to prevent their rank growth the following year and consequent difficulties for the combine. In order to bury thoroughly and kill alfalfa without turning it over and burying it to the destruction of our sheet composting operations it was necessary to develop a special plowing technique which would leave the fresh plowed strips of sod in a rough vertical position and still cover the alfalfa. This was accomplished by skillful adjustment of the plows, the coulters and the jointers. This was found to be possible and effective, so that our rough-plowing sheet-compost methods could be retained while the alfalfa was buried and the whole field covered by two or three inches of clean earth as a seed bed for wheat. As a result many of our fields going from alfalfa sod into wheat have the appearance of an old-fashioned, clean-plowed field when actually beneath the surface they are as rough plowed as possible. The disk ploughs which cut the alfalfa roots have proved more effective than the moldboards in *killing* unwanted alfalfa. In the cases of two strips of wheat side by side on the same soil with the same seed and the same amounts of fertilizer, one strip rough-plowed and disked, produced as much as ten to twelve more bushels of wheat per acre than the strip which was "clean plowed" and fitted in the old-fashioned way. Needless to say, the rough-plowed strip had a much higher moisture content and was virtually immune to erosion either by wind or by water.

The absolute killing of the alfalfa is not necessary in the case of corn ground since the corn is not combined and alfalfa plants surviving here and there are no great disadvantage and possibly through nitrogen production, of some benefit.

Experiments have been made at the University of Illinois of growing corn with a rapidly growing grass and legume clover as a substitute for cultivation. While the experiments are not final, yields of 115 and 120 bushels have been obtained in successive years recently. This is, of course, far above the average yields in Illinois of below 45 bushels per acre for several years past. Such a method of growing corn would of course greatly reduce the damage caused by erosion and destruction of organic material arising from the existing methods of open cultivation. We have long cherished the idea of experimenting with corn in a sod of alfalfa and ladino clover. The plan is to cut strips through a heavy alfalfa, ladino sod with some implement like a rototiller which would "chew up" the strips of sod to a width of about six inches and then seed the corn in the chewed up strips. Any cultivation would be replaced by a mower which twice or three times during the growth of the corn would clip the alfalfa and ladino between the rows and leave it there for mulch. Such a process is an extremely reasonable one since it would eliminate all erosion and virtually all destruction of organic material. Also it would virtually eliminate weeds since the ladino grows so rapidly and persistently that it would choke out all annual weeds before they got a start. The process would also feed nitrogen heavily to the corn on the upper levels from the ladino and on the deeper levels from the alfalfa roots. The mulch of clippings would also conserve great quantities of moisture, together with ample nitrogen, so important to corn. We have not made the experiment because no suitable machinery exists and because we have not had time until recently from other arduous duties of soil restoration.

While it is scarcely possible to overestimate the soil restoring properties of the real grasses, the legumes remain the backbone of the process or of any grass farming program based upon the restoration of fertility and increased production. This is so because the legumes can grow, unlike many of the grasses, on land which is wholly devoid of the organic material that is vital to the growth of almost all other kinds of vegetation save the trees and the most worthless of weeds. Legumes will grow abundantly in bare subsoils of good or average quality and with good drainage where lime is present in sufficient quantities. At Malabar our best alfalfa and sweet clover grows upon bare gravel banks or in heavy clays, both minerally rich, but devoid of all topsoil or organic material. Once the deep-rooted legumes start growing, the incorporation of organic material and much nitrogen in the form of green manure becomes an easy matter and the creation of excellent topsoil is inevitable.

This is a direct contradiction to what farmers have generally been taught for a generation or more—that alfalfa is a plant which must be pampered, sown on carefully prepared ground, limed well in advance. We have found beyond dispute that alfalfa is not an aristocrat but a pioneer. So long as there is lime present, we have achieved really luxuriant crops of alfalfa, sweet clover, and ladino and alsike clover on the poorest land covered thinly only one year earlier with poverty grass, wire grass, goldenrod and broom sedge, and as I have pointed out earlier, the growth was stronger and healthier than that of alfalfa sown upon our little remaining *worn-out* topsoil. The experiments of Dr. A. L. Borst of the Soil Conservation Service at Zanesville, Ohio, with alfalfa as a poor-land crop also proved this point beyond argument. Out of 200 seedings made at the Zanesville station and on neighboring farms on subsoil of shale quality much poorer than our Malabar glacial subsoil only two failures were encountered. Dr. Borst has published the result of the experiment in a pamphlet issued by the Department of Agriculture. Our own experiments in the same field took place over virtually the same period as those of Dr. Borst and have been described at considerable length in *Pleasant Valley*. Both alfalfa and ladino have proved invaluable at Malabar not only as soil restorers but also as producers of rich forage and pasture on poor land during the building process. In our experience the only places where alfalfa, accompanied by lime, will not flourish is in poorly drained areas. While alfalfa roots will penetrate to prodigious depths in search of moisture it cannot survive "wet feet." In our experience even poor hill land is better for the production of long-standing, long-maintained alfalfa meadows than our lower, richer, moister land. Darwin in *The Voyage of the Beagle* describes his astonishment at finding in Chile on desert land great patches of succulent, deep green forage. He was told that it was a plant called *alfalifa*.

The deep-rooted legumes like sweet clover and alfalfa thrust sturdy roots to great depths, as great as the measured depth of 46 feet in Colorado. Fourteen- and fifteen-foot roots of alfalfa are commonplace at Malabar where the rainfall is much more abundant. At the Zanesville station Dr. Borst dug pits exposing nine- and ten-foot root systems penetrating even into the stiff gray shale underlying gravel loam deposits. These root systems tend to break up stiff soils and improved drainage. When the tops die as the plant is plowed under or killed, the sturdy roots, decaying, leave in the soil not only great quantities of nitrogen and highly available fertilizer in the form of phosphorus, potash, calcium and many of the trace elements, but leave small tunnels which admit both air and water deep into the soil. Moreover, legumes, both deep- and shallow-rooted, when sown in mixture with grasses, perpetually feed those grasses with a nitrogen supply drawn from the air at no cost to the farmer and serve to stimulate a rank growth of grass tops and roots so valuable both for forage and for building organic material and topsoil.

The healing properties of grass and legumes on poor or abused earth are like those of the white corpuscles of the blood in healing over wounds and burns on the human body. The value of grasses and legumes to the well-being and prosperity of the farmer and consequently to the nation as a whole in restoring the vast acreages of worn-out or poorly drained or eroded soils in all parts of the country is immense. The chain involves higher profits, reduced labor and fertilizer costs, increased purchasing power for the products of industry, lowered taxes and better food and diet for every citizen, whether the farmer or the city dweller who eats what the farmer grows.

On the day of writing this chapter I made a trip with three neighbors through three of our northeastern Ohio counties all based upon the Wooster silt loam which is minerally one of the finest soils in the world. We saw not one farm in ten producing a half of what it was capable. One in ten was falling into decay as the fields slipped nearer and nearer to the deadly line where they could no longer pay taxes and interest and became abandoned, a waste and a drain upon our economy. One out of ten had already fallen into this category.

Any or all of them could be brought back to a state of high fertility at a comparatively low investment of capital and a considerable investment of knowledge, experience, and brains. If I were a rich man, I could think of no investment of capital so profitable as the purchase and rehabilitation of these rundown or abandoned farms. Within a period of ten years, I would be certain of a 300 per cent gross increase of capital investment, a gain not based upon inflated prices but on the solid basis of Federal Land Bank appraisals—that of production per acre. It seems to me that too few people with reserves of capital and savings have seen the possibility of investment in basically sound but worn-out land in a world which is starving and in which there will never be in our time even a fourth of the food needed to feed it even on a modest diet. The population of the world is steadily increasing and the area of productive agricultural land and of production per acre has been constantly shrinking. The prices of food with increased efficiency of distribution are not likely to decline, short of a universal economic disaster and even then it should be remembered that people must eat even before they can satisfy the devastating urge to propagate new members of the human race which in turn must eat or perish. For this reason in times of disaster or vicious inflation good agricultural land always remains the soundest of all investment.

But beyond all that is the immense and fundamental creative joy and satisfaction which comes of making two grains grow where one has grown before, of seeing a whole landscape change from drabness and desert sterility to green and wonderful abundance. It is a joy which many a Jew, returning to his homeland in ravaged Palestine, has experienced in our time. There is perhaps no human satisfaction so profound. And there is the great contribution which the investor in such a project can make to the welfare and sound economy of the nation.

In most of our country grass, the great healer, and the legumes which flourish side by side with it, can turn the ebb tide of sterility into a rising surge of abundance and wealth and vigor. No sight is more tragic than a worn-out abandoned farm and none more beautiful than the prosperous home and barn surrounded by rich fields. And no sights present so vivid a symbolism in relation to our welfare and strength as a nation.

The experiences at Malabar have led all of us toward some new and, to many soil authorities, possibly some startling and revolutionary conclusions regarding the fertility of soils. Two noticeable conclusions have been forced upon our attention; even though we might have been ten times less observant and interested than we are, we could not have avoided them for the evidence has been thrust upon us again and again.

(1) That mineral balance plus nitrogen and indeed all the laws of balance in soil, which may be very nearly as absolute as those governing astronomy or physics or mathematics, have great bearing upon the health of plants, animals, and people and that in the case of plants a great bearing upon their resistance not only to disease but to the attacks of insects as well.

(2) That any good subsoil and notably our own good well-balanced minerally rich silt loam, possesses a fertility which, if managed properly, may be eternally available and very possibly inexhaustible. The problem is to make that hidden, locked-up fertility available to plant life, and available in sufficient quantities.

The case of balance in soils and the great and largely unexplored values of trace elements to plants, animals, and people has been explored with considerable thoroughness in the chapters "Gardening without Tears" and "of the Earth We Are Born and to the Earth We Return," so there is little need to go into it here any further than to observe that the subsoil at Malabar is not especially gratifying material to work with experimentally since it already possesses in its well-balanced glacial subsoil, from the evidence of the vegetation itself, a good supply of trace elements with the qualified exception of iodine. Our experiments have been most rewarding on the depleted topsoil which remained here and there on the farms at Malabar. The problem was actually to raise the *mineral* level and balance of the depleted topsoil to that of the virgin silt loam gravel-filled subsoil. In the vegetable and flower gardens we have been notably successful in raising the resistance of plants both to insects and disease and the campaign is being carried out elsewhere on the farm with similar, although less concentrated, results.

The second conclusion regarding the inexhaustibility of fertility in reasonably good subsoils can be explored a little further. In this book the reader will come across many times the phrase "universal law of fertility—the cycle of birth, growth, death, decay, and rebirth." It has been used again and again because it has played so large a part in the rehabilitation of the non-productive land at Malabar and because slowly, but again and again, the cycle has asserted its vital and unmistakable importance. In combination with the theory of balance of elements, that cycle has done the job of turning wholly unproductive, eroded fields into fields which produced more yields per acre than 90 per cent of the agricultural land in the United States.

It was not for the purpose of this book alone, that I have asserted again and again the mere fact of barrenness. Every neighbor knows the fields and every neighbor has watched the process across the fences that border the county and township roads. For two generations the Bailey Place had the sorry reputation of being the "thinnest farm between Newville and Little Washington." Four years of work upon it proved that its sorry reputation lacked truth and that fundamentally the whole of the Bailey Place was actually rich land, richer by far than most of the agricultural land in the United States. On it occurred a number of experiences which at first we could only regard in the light of miracles. The wiping out of gullies and of the loss of water and top-soil was quickly accomplished simply by engineering but the tremendous and rapid gains in fertility and yields seemed nothing short of miraculous.

There was the miracle of the Bailey hills, brown and red with sorrel and broom sedge and poverty grass, transformed within a year into thick, succulent emerald-green alfalfa, brome grass and ladino. There was the corn which changed in four years from sickly three-foot stalks bearing nubbins or nothing at all to a high level of production, and the miracle of the field that jumped in wheat production from 5 to 33 to 52 bushels yield per acre in four years, and the miracle of the grass which jumped from less than a ton per acre of weedy, wooden timothy to four and four and a half tons per acre of succulent legumes and brome grass. And on the Fleming Place, fields which once would not yield 15 bushels of oats per acre produced in the summer of 1947 over 80 bushels, although the soil is too light to be good oats ground. And the high field on the Ferguson Place, once a barren eroded field which in 1947 produced 60 bushels and better wheat per acre on that part of the field where the sub-soil was gravel loam. And the bluegrass pastures on the

Ferguson, Fleming and Bailey Places, not so long ago thin, burned-out, half starved, weedy pastures filled with iron weed and wild carrot which today are carrying on lush blue-grass and white clover twenty times and more the number of cattle they carried only five or six years ago.

When we began searching for the reasons for all of these things, often with the aid of scientists far more informed and qualified than ourselves, we came inevitably in every case, even in that of the pastures, back to the same and simple conclusion—that these gains had been made by restoring to the eroded, worn-out fields devoid of organic material and of mineral balance, that eternally fundamental cycle of birth, growth, death, decay and rebirth. By doing so we had made highly available the chemical fertilizer we put on the soil, unlocked the thin residue of fertilizer left by our predecessor which until then had been largely unavailable and in the case of the Bailey hills and the high Ferguson Place we had undoubtedly unlocked great stores of native *fertility* which until the cycle was re-established had long remained wholly locked and unavailable to all plant life. In other words, those farms were not really poor and worn-out farms at all. Except for the Anson Place, they had merely been farmed badly so that their native fertility, for various reasons, was no longer available to the crops.

There is nothing mysterious or magical about the process. It is available even to the poorest farmer. The pattern has long been in the possession of the Department of Agriculture and of the state colleges. The only mystery concerning it is why it has not been more widely used to restore millions and millions of acres of potentially good land which through ignorance and abuse has been going down hill since the first furrow was turned on virgin soil.

The theory of the inexhaustible fertility of basically good, sound, well-balanced subsoils may seem new, although Faulkner in his latest book *A Second Look* has dealt with it in some comments which are immensely stimulating. Sir Albert Howard, greatest of British soil men, with a knowledge of soils from the broad English counties to Indore and Ceylon, has moved steadily toward the conclusion which led him to believe that good soils should, to a large degree, take care of themselves and remain eternally fertile if properly handled. Dr. Bray of University of Illinois, certainly one of the finest living agronomists, has had intimations of the truth of the theory growing out of his experience. Certainly he believes strongly in the *balance* of soil. It is a theory which will never be supported or explored by the overspecialized or by those academic minds which believe that all that can possibly be discovered about agriculture has already been discovered, for it is a theory which in a sense, involves knowledge and curiosity in too many fields—biochemistry and bacteriology, chemistry, botany, biology, plant pathology and the scarcely touched mysteries of the place which moulds and fungi, animal hormones and secretions and many other things play in the universal cycle of health, fertility and production, not only in soils and plants but in animals and humans as well. It involves the pattern of the whole universe including the health and vigor and resistance of plants, animals and people and of the vigor and intelligence of people.

Needless to say, that is a vast and largely unexplored field and perhaps the truly intelligent and reasonably informed dirt farmer can make the greatest contribution of all as he has done so often in the past in the solution of agricultural problems. For he lives nearer to all these things than any scientific specialist and frequently understands infinitely more clearly the intricate interplay of *all* the elements involved. Therein lies the profound truth uttered by Confucius centuries ago and quoted in *Pleasant Valley* that "the best fertilizer on any farm is the footsteps of the farmer." Observation and intelligence in a farmer can sometimes outweigh in value countless tons of chemical fertilizer.

At Malabar it seems to us that the operation of these theories is a fairly simple one. The belief has come partly from observation, partly from experiment, partly by pragmatic methods. Like all farmers, we believe, above all else, what works. It is for the research people equipped with time and education and laboratories to find out why it works. But we have our own ideas, simple perhaps but deeply logical.

As has been stated before, we have at Malabar two broad categories of soil—about 85 per cent glacial drift gravel loam either in static deposits or that which has been worked about by the action of water, and about 15 per cent pre-glacial, heavy, but potentially rich, clay. In the glacial drift there are thousands of tons of stones ranging from minute fragments to glacial boulders weighing many tons. In the clay there is little gravel. These facts are important since the capacity of the gravel loam soil for *feeding* minerals to plant life and eventually to animals and people is probably much greater than the similar capacity of the clay. Also, as has been stated earlier in this chapter, it is much more difficult to incorporate organic material into the clay than into the loam gravel soil. These points have considerable value in the record of the two soils. While the same gains in fertility are achieved eventually in both types of soil, the results are achieved much more quickly on the loose, minerally rich gravel loam—indeed at least three times as quickly.

It is evident even to the most superficial observer that the accumulation of stones and rock fragments existing both in the gravel loam and the clay soils are constantly breaking down by the action of wind, heat, frost and water. Rocks and stones are the source of mineral fertility in *all* soils, which in essence are simply broken down stone and rock plus the organic material provided by the death and decay of vegetation and the mineral content of stems, leaves and tree trunks drawn from the disintegrating rocks and in the process converted into highly available organic form. In the broader sense, the rock and stone content of soil from the largest mountains to the finest pebble, are constantly feeding minerals to the soil both in the process of direct disintegration and by transmutation through various forms of vegetation. The important point in so far as fertility is concerned is whether these disintegrated or transmuted minerals are available to the plant life growing upon the soil.

Concerning this aspect certain things are well known and long established—that many minerals which could make a great contribution to fertility and production are simply not available to plants where there is an absence of calcium and that none at all are available in the total absence of moisture. It is also well known that organic material is a great absorber and conserver of moisture and is therefore vital to any soils upon which good crops may be grown. Organic material is also vital to the fertility even of land which must

170

be drained to be rid of too much water and land where unlimited supplies of water are available for irrigation. Plants vary greatly in their need and liking for moisture but none can wholly thrive, even to the lichen growing tightly against a granite boulder, unless some minute quantity of moisture and organic material is present. The lichen, once established on a rock, proceeds rapidly to provide its own organic material by the death and decay of its own leaves through which it has translated inorganic minerals into highly available organic forms.

Since calcium is a vital part of soil balance and of great importance save to a very narrow range of acid-liking or tolerating plants and trees, its place becomes of great importance in the process of unlocking fertility, partly because chemically it has a greater affinity for most minerals and trace elements than have iron and aluminum and snatches away the minerals and elements vital to health and growth of plants, animals and people from combinations with iron and aluminum in which they remained virtually locked up and unavailable. In combination with calcium all these minerals and elements exist in a form highly available to plant life and consequently to animals and to the people who feed upon the plants and upon the milk, eggs, and meat produced from it. (Most people and animals and plants living upon a sour land devoid of calcium have definite characteristics and display the symptoms of many mineral deficiencies, most of all, deficiency of the calcium essential to good bone structure, health and vigor.) On all definitely sour lands largely devoid of calcium the human stock shows inevitably a gradual deterioration in which in the course of time, individuals achieve definite general characteristics that set them apart from the peoples of more favored areas. The same is true of areas in which calcium and other minerals have become depleted. These facts are definitely responsible for the physique, characteristics and even in some degree the cultures of the so-called "poor whites," "hill-billies" and "okies" (all originating on poor soils or depleted ones).

Calcium then, is one of the keys to unlocking hidden and unavailable fertility. It is also the key to producing the high-protein nitrogen-producing legumes which also bring the organic material which plays so large a role in the whole cycle of birth, growth, death, decay and rebirth out of which all fertility and life are evolved and maintained.

Beyond these facts, which are established and well known, one enters a still mysterious and largely unexplored field having to do with the trace elements and their effect upon enzymes, hormones and the functioning of glands in animals and people, and the realm of bacteria and their actions and that of the fungi and the moulds from which those miraculous new anti-bodies, penicillin and streptomycin and others, have been or are being developed.

That these moulds and fungi contribute to the breaking down of minerals and their transmutation into availability to plants, animals and finally people is a fact that, in our experience at Malabar, cannot be overlooked since each day brings new evidence which we could not ignore if we chose. Sir Albert Howard's latest book *Soil and Health* has contributed perhaps more than any other authority to the establishment of the important place which moulds and fungi play in the foundation, restoration and maintenance of soil fertility. He makes the assertion that, together with the bacteria, they play an important role in the unlocking of inexhaustible fertility. Ed Faulkner with his enthusiastic, searching, speculating mind, has touched upon the power of bacteria, moulds and fungi to hasten the breaking down of all mineral material from boulders to tiny pebbles and their power to make the disintegrated minerals available to plants, animals and people.

None of these—bacteria, moulds and fungi—can exist without considerable degrees of moisture nor can they exist or multiply save by the presence in the soil of organic material in the process of death, decay and rebirth. Therefore organic material, in whatever form, becomes of vital importance to the productivity of any soil and particularly to the availability of the native minerals and elements in that soil and to the availability of chemical fertilizer applied to it. In addition to the fact that decaying organic material acts as host and food supply for bacteria, moulds, fungus, earthworms and other organisms which are intrinsic elements of all living and fertile soils, the organic material serves as well to check erosion and improve drainage and aeration. With calcium, organic material provides the key to that cycle of birth, growth, death, decay and rebirth which makes the mineral content of the soil, whatever it may be, available to the plants and consequently to animals and to people. When any segment of the cycle—moisture, bacteria, moulds, fungi, mineral balance, organic material or the calcium content—(which is perhaps the most valuable element in mineral balance—breaks down, the whole chain is broken and one by one the various links collapse, bringing about the rapidly declining production and eventual sterility which is characteristic of so much once good and still potentially good agricultural land in the United States and in the entire world.

Of course outside the circle lie other elements which contribute to a speeding up of the whole process of mineral availability or fertility, notably the residue of trace elements and the effect of the glandular secretions and bacteria from animals which contribute greatly to the cycle on soil where barnyard manure is used. As was pointed out in *Pleasant Valley* it would be possible to recreate synthetically and chemically the mineral content of a given amount of barnyard manure but the resulting mineral content would fall far short of achieving the same degree of fertility as the manure itself on a given plot of land, even if credit was allowed for the organic material contained in the manure. Somewhere there are mysterious elements which have not been sufficiently studied or understood. Nevertheless, while the content of barnyard manure is from all points of view, the best long-range fertilizer man can use, relatively excellent results in establishing the cycle of fertility and restoring or maintaining fertility can be obtained, as we know well at Malabar, by the use of green manures in which the animal element with its glandular contributions and its trillions of living bacteria are missing. And, repeating a statement which will be made again, all barnyard manures are not of the same content or value particularly on the mineral side. Poor land, deficient or depleted, or land where the mineral fertility is locked up in chemical combinations with other elements will produce poor manure, infinitely less rich in mineral content than the manure resulting from grain and forage off soil where there is an excess residue of minerals which the animals do not need or cannot utilize and which consequently is returned to the soil.

Since the publication of Darwin's book on the earthworm, few intelligent people have doubted the great contributions made by this lowly organism toward converting crude subsoil into rich and fertile topsoil of highly available mineral content. But the earthworm can exist and function only if the other links called "moisture" and "organic material" are present. Withdraw these and the earthworm together with bacteria, moulds and fungus all perish leaving the soil to become poor and unproductive, not because there is a shortage of mineral fertility but because this mineral fertility becomes unavailable to plant life. This condition has given much land in the United States a bad name—of being "worn-out," poor or unproductive—when a proper system of agriculture, based upon the eternal cycle, would prove it within a short time to be prodigiously fertile.

It is one of the errors of the earthworm fanatics that the planting of a few hundred earthworms in a sterile field devoid of organic material will restore the field to a high degree of fertility. Under such circumstances the planted earthworms will merely suffer from lack of moisture and eventually die from lack of organic material on which to feed. The presence of earthworms in a field where there is moisture and organic material in the process of death and decay will hasten greatly the process of unlocking and making available the natural richness of the soil but without moisture and

174

organic material they merely die out. Again the whole cycle fails because one or two links of the chain are missing. We have found at Malabar that the mere increase of organic material and consequently of moisture has brought in armies of earthworms which reproduce rapidly once the links are repaired and the cycle restored to operation. We have had bare dry banks converted into dark soil to a depth of five to eight inches in a few years merely by top dressing them with barnyard, and in particular with chicken, manure. Not only does the mulch of manure encourage and promote vegetative growth but it conserves the moisture vital to existence of the earthworm and provides decaying organic material to sustain it and give it the force to multiply rapidly. The spilled grain and mash present in chicken manure provides the earthworm with a particularly rich diet as the grain ferments and turns to sugar. Any fisherman knows that the best place to find earthworms in abundance is in or near an old manure pile.

Only one serious doubt remains with us regarding complete efficacy of the cycle of fertility and its ability to release from our own minerally rich soils a fertility available in sufficient quantities for the crops grown. We do not know whether, in the case of heavy yielding crops, the process of breaking down of minerals into availability is rapid enough to supply *all* the needs of plants growing in profusion.

*If* on a given square mile all wastes, even to human bodies after death, were returned directly to the soil, it is clear that that area would lose none of its mineral and comparatively little of its organic fertility, but on any farm these conditions do not hold. There is always the mineral drain represented by the eggs, milk, meat and bone, fruit, vegetables, etc., sold off a farm which to great extent is carried off eventually and in turn from cities in the form of sewage into the all consuming sea or buried in a lead coffin in a graveyard. If the soil, through the cycle of birth, growth, death and decay and rebirth can break down its content rapidly enough to replenish this drain, then commercial fertilizers on land possessing good, balanced subsoils would be unnecessary and the natural mineral fertility alone would suffice: but it is possible and probable that heavy yields drain off minerals more rapidly than the cycle breaks them down into availability. Under such conditions commercial fertilizer imported onto the farm becomes a necessity in order to maintain fertility and yields.

The opening of a gravel pit in the cemetery field revealed a whole new segment of information concerning what has been going on deep down in the "worn-out" soil of the lower fields on the Fleming and Bailey Places.

We needed gravel for the upkeep of the miles of lanes and barnyards; paying eight dollars a load to have it trucked in might have been a negligible item on some farms but it suited neither our budget nor our plan. Such precious gravel was clearly beyond the means of any but a millionaire farmer and we knew that somewhere beneath the surface of our own lower fields there must be deposits of gravel, clean enough for road building. It was Bob who did the prospecting. In his spare time, he began making borings with the posthole digger and wisely he turned to the cemetery field where, save in the lower end, there had been in the beginning no topsoil whatever. The field contained one edge of a sloping ridge which formed a rough semicircle extending through most of the bottom fields of the Bailey Place and Fleming farm where the revival of productivity in response to lime, legume and organic material had been sensational.

He chose the cemetery field for three reasons: (1) It lay hidden away where the possible unsightliness of a gravel pit would be least noticed in the general landscape. (2) It lay close to one of the principal lanes where gravel would be easily available for hauling. (3) There was every indication that the long, semicircular ridge had been produced thousands of years earlier by the action of waters rushing out from under the Second Glacier and that therefore the waters had probably done all the "washing" for us and we would be able to haul the clean gravel directly from the field to the lanes.

The prospecting was a brief affair. At about the fourth or fifth boring, he hit a beautiful mixture of clean sand and gravel and the Ford-Ferguson loader went to work.

It is necessary here, I think, to repeat the history of the cemetery field and of the particular ridge in which Bob made the boring. It had been originally a field from which all topsoil was eroded. By the use of lime and legumes plus a three-year period of "restoring" under pasture management it had, when seeded to wheat, produced thirty-seven bushels of wheat per acre. The seeding of alfalfa, brome grass and ladino (made in the wheat) immediately produced a great deal of grass silage, hay and pasture. The production along the ridge already described had been nothing short of prodigious and on the spot where Bob prospected, alfalfa left standing as a test was over three feet high. Moreover it consistently produced on that particular spot virtually the maximum quality of matured seed. These facts naturally aroused a passionate interest in discovering what miraculous process was taking place out of sight deep down in this subsoil.

The excavation was begun far down the edge of the slope that marked the ridge and the work of a day or two of digging produced a cross section of the subsoil to a depth of about twenty feet. Almost at once a large part of the story was revealed.

First of all, we discovered a great depth of stratified gravel and of sand so fine that it could serve as moulding sand. The layer of sand, although the season was dry, was saturated with water. The gravel was of all sizes from that of a pea to small boulders the size of a man's head and all of it smooth and rounded by the action of water which had been taking place for thousands of years. The gravel contained stones of a hundred different compositions, nearly all of them foreign to our country in preglacial times which indicated that they had been transported to our valley from regions perhaps as far north as the Hudson Bay country by the scraping action of the glacier, on the surface of the glacier or embedded in it. The stones ranged from iron through granite and flinty conglomerates to pieces of limestone so soft that it was possible to etch them with the fingernail. The gravel pit was indeed an amateur geologist's paradise. Practically every mineral, down to the minor trace elements, was represented.

Most of all, these stones were all in various stages of disintegration, according to their composition and hardness. The conglomerates, the limestone and even the granite, were rotting away slowly. The fact was that the gravel pit represented a depository of concentrated and diversified mineral fertilizer high in availability and virtually inexhaustible as

177

a source of plant, animal and human food. It was all there waiting to be utilized. Under the agricultural methods employed by our predecessors this mine of mineral wealth had simply become unavailable.

Originally the earth above had been covered by a thick hardwood forest with deep roots which fed upon the mine of minerals, carried them upward toward the sunlight and the air to translate them into organic form as wood fiber, leaves and blossoms; these—as they grew, withered and died—fell to the surface of the earth and over a period of millions of years formed a deep rich layer of mould and topsoil.

Then came the first pioneer who cut down the forest and burned the residue and planted seed in this rich layer of soil. The seed germinated and in the richness upon which it fed produced huge growths of crops other than trees—crops which fed the animals and people. The old, slow forest system of pumping up the mineral richness of the gravel pit and depositing it upon the surface of the earth was broken. The new crops were shallow-rooted and fed scarcely to the depth of the layer of rich topsoil. From the deep level there was no more replenishment and the farmer, blessed by the great natural richness, put nothing back either of minerals or of organic material into that comparatively thin, dark-colored top layer. And presently, after a couple of generations, the yield of crops and the mineral and vitamin content of them began to decline. But another process, even more destructive, was occurring at the same time. As the organic material of the ancient leafmould soil became oxidized and depleted under constant cultivation, the rain ceased to penetrate the earth and began to run off it, carrying away quantities of the rich topsoil down the neighboring creek into the Mississippi and Gulf of Mexico. A little was deposited on the more or less flat ground of that particular cemetery field below the gravel-impregnated ridge, but most of it was carried away altogether and lost, probably forever.

At least two disasters had occurred. The topsoil, formed by nature so slowly over millions of years, was carried away altogether down to the level of the raw soil and gravel. Or when the topsoil remained it was virtually depleted of all available minerals, especially of the calcium that nature had

178

provided as the great catalyzer to make the other minerals available.

Above the surface of that rich mine of mineral fertility the owner and then the tenant produced less and less until at last the fields became unwanted and deserted and the cemetery field became part of what was called a ruined and worn-out farm. And all the time deep down or even exposed at the surface of the eroded fields where it could be seen and touched lay thousands of dollars of virtually inexhaustible mineral fertilizer.

The deep section of earth exposed by the gravel pit showed us not only the great reserve which lay there beneath our feet but it showed us many things which had been taking place since we had gone to work on the cemetery field and which in turn had brought about the return of richness and fertility to a "worn-out" field.

To begin with, on the very surface of the soil which only eight years earlier had been bare gravel sparsely covered with poverty grass and sorrel, there appeared a comparatively thin layer three to four inches in depth of dark, rich, friable soil. It was made up of many things—of the roots and leaves which had been clipped and left there by mowing or had died in the course of the season's change to fall there and disintegrate; it represented the roots, stems and leaves which had been turned *into* the soil by the plow; it represented the droppings and the effect of the urine, hormones, and glandular secretions of the animals which had pastured over it for a period of three to four years; it represented the action of the nitrogen and the other factors, many of them still unknown, produced by the various varieties of legumes, red and white clover, alsike, ladino and sweet clover which had been seeded there, and the action of the finely ground limestone which had been spread there to make the existence of the legumes possible; and it represented, perhaps in minute quantities, soil blown from devastated prairies and grazing land, blown from hundreds of miles to the west by the prevailing winds. All this thin layer represented new topsoil created not by millions of years of action but by eight years of concentrated attention to natural methods.

Just beneath this thin layer could be seen the building process actually at work. Below the dark layer which extended downward in a fringed fashion, there lay a whole world of rootlets—the fine roots of the ladino, penetrating to a depth of seven or eight inches each covered with the tiny nodules of the nitrogen creating bacteria. Then below this the deeper mass of hairlike roots extending downward to a depth of more than two feet which represented the feeding system of the brome grass. These tiny rootlets, being fed with nitrogen by both ladino and alfalfa, penetrated deep into the richness of the disintegrating glacial gravel. In this area the formation of deep topsoil was in what might be termed the secondary stage. The individual stones of all sizes were crumbling rapidly and had begun to take on the appearance of topsoil in its earliest stages of development. Here as in the top shallow layer lay revealed the intricate tunneling of the earthworms which in the process of passing the plant materials and tiny fragments of stone through their bodies were darkening the mineral mass as they turned it into available plant food.

But most spectacular of all was the story told by the roots of the alfalfa. These extended downward to a depth of from twelve to fourteen feet into the slowly crumbling mass of sand and gravel. At the top, near the thin layer of topsoil they were coarse and thick as a thumb, spreading out at the surface in a crown of rankly growing stems and leaves. As they descended into the gravel they grew more slender, sending out all along the way small lateral roots covered with nitrogen producing nodules which extended horizontally on each side of the stem into the mineral riches of the gravel. Finally at a depth of twelve to fourteen feet the rootlets fanned out again in a network of hairlike rootlets penetrating in all directions. What we saw exposed was the whole system by which the alfalfa was tapping the deep mineral richness (as the roots of the primeval forest had once done) and bringing that richness upward to the sunlight and the air on the surface of the ground where it was deposited in highly available organic form. In other words the deep-rooted alfalfa and the deep-rooted sweet clover which preceded it had restored the ancient process by which these reserves of mineral fertility were tapped.

But there were other evidences as well of the remarkable

capacity of the alfalfa to convert the slowly disintegrating gravel into available fertility. In a kind of column surrounding each of the heavy alfalfa roots to a depth of two feet into the gravel and sand there was a casing of dark earth formed out of the surrounding gravel or descended from above along the course taken downward by the root. How this came about or what the process was by which this topsoil was forming about each root, I do not pretend to know. I only know that the result was there for all to see and that it explained a little the remarkable ability of deep-rooted legumes to create soil and make mineral fertility available.

One other happening had a special interest and in it a herd of yearling Guernsey heifers played a part. They were pasturing in the field when we opened the gravel pit and with the frisky, wide-eyed curiosity of young heifers they joined us to watch and would not go away. Presently one of them discovered the alfalfa roots that became dislodged and spread about as we worked. She picked up a root and began chewing on the coarse upper end near the crown. Then another and another followed her example until all of them were chewing on the alfalfa roots like children on lollipops. The roots were tough and required a lot of chewing before the heifers deemed them ready to tuck away for further use. They persisted and kept on getting in the way of the loader and truck in their eagerness to pick up the dislodged roots. This despite the fact that they were knee deep in rich alfalfa—brome grass—ladino pasture and had access to rich bluegrass and white clover as well as certain wild grasses and weeds in an adjoining bottom pasture. From then on whenever we worked the gravel pit the heifers were on hand to pick up the dislodged roots as if they were special delicacies.

I think the answer was that they found in the coarse tough roots a rich supply of minerals including a good many trace elements existing in a particularly concentrated form. These roots and crowns were of course exactly the part of the alfalfa which was turned *into* the soil to decay whenever we plowed down a sod; and of course in their great numbers actually provided not only quantities of mineral fertilizer brought up from deep down but also provided fertilizer almost immediately available in ideal form to succeeding crops—a fact which largely explains the immense revitalizing properties of both alfalfa and the sweet clovers on so-called "worn-out" land or even upon rich land.

While the gravel bed which we opened was clean washed and virtually devoid of clay or loam, the same remarkable mixture of small stones and boulders exists together with clay loam throughout all of our glacial drift soils at Malabar. Elsewhere in areas where the actions of water has not washed the gravel and sand quite clean the proportion of clay loam to gravel is, of course, much higher. Nevertheless, the same process was clearly taking place over the whole of the farm, even in the comparatively small area of pure yellow clay.

I know of no more vivid example, plainly evident to the eye, of the remarkable efficiency of lime, grass and legumes in rebuilding soils than was revealed to us from the moment we first opened the gravel pit. It illustrated as well the fact that once the cycle of birth, growth, death, decay and rebirth is established, fertility of all kinds, whether virgin and inherent in soils or applied in the form of commercial fertilizer or leached down to lower levels, becomes available once more and with it healthy and abundant crops became possible again.

At the moment we are endeavoring to discover the proper ratio between the amount of mineral fertility exported from the farm in the form of food to the amount of mineral fertility released each year through the cycle mentioned so many times. This is a ratio difficult to establish because of the intricacy in the operations of nature. When it is taken into account that a steer weighing eight hundred to a thousand pounds will remove approximately 100 pounds of calcium from the soil on which he is grown and that there are countless dairy cows which turn out fifty pounds upward of milk per day containing a high calcium content, it becomes evident that the drain on all minerals and on calcium in particular is considerable and may easily be out of ratio with the released, available, natural fertility of the land upon which the forage the animal consumes winter and summer is grown.

At Malabar we do not pretend to know absolutely about these things. We only know what has happened and what we have seen, and have made deductions accordingly. These observations have been included in this chapter, "Grass, the Great Healer," because grass and legumes and the lime which makes possible their growth and their abundance are perhaps the most important links in the whole of the cycle. Without the limestone and without the moisture, the soil maintenance, the great quantities of nitrogen and of organic material contributed by the grass and legumes, any soil will decline quickly to a condition in which erosion and either aridity or saturation, according to the topography and type of soil, become problems and the natural fertility becomes locked and unavailable to plants, animals and people. Conversely they are the means by which the whole cycle of fertility and its perpetuity may start again.

There are dead soils and living soils. The dead soils are those in which some link of the cycle has been broken and the whole process ceases to operate. They are the soils which produce poor plants, animals and people. The living soils, in which the cycle operates freely, produce plants, animals and people with physiques, intelligence, energy and initiative. As Dr. Jonathan Forman has pointed out—"We are very largely what we eat."

If we do not succeed in providing artificially or releasing by natural processes the varied minerals and elements vital to the existence of healthy, vigorous and intelligent people, we in this country shall become merely a people like the great bulk of Asiatic peoples who continue to *exist* and survive merely through the most brutal and ruthless biological operations of Darwinian law of survival of the fittest.

In all of this, the question of diet, so emphasized during the past two or three generations, becomes of secondary importance to the mineral and vitamin content of foods included in a given diet. In other words, the most carefully balanced diets in the world become ineffective if the materials included in those diets are deficient in minerals and vitamins. This mineral and vitamin content is determined by the quality of the soils on which the materials of the diet are grown. In other words, the finest, best balanced diet in the world, grown on some of the viciously depleted soils of the Deep South or even in some parts of the once fabulously rich Corn Belt, would have very little effect in raising the health, energy and intelligence of the people living on those soils.

Even the field of nutrition, appearing to the superficial observer to be far removed from grass and legumes, has in reality, a very close relation to grass and legumes, for grass and legumes play the key role in making available the mineral richness of the earth. The richest soils on the earth —the prairie corn belt and the vast midwestern plains, the black soil belts of Texas, the Ukraine, Mississippi and Alabama—are essentially grass and legume-made soils, existing primarily owing to the reserve of calcium in the form of disintegrated limestone or in a form transmuted through the cycle of birth, growth, death and decay into a high degree of organic availability. In a sense all of us go back to grass and legumes for our health, our vigor, our intelligence and indeed for our very existence. One has only to live in close contact and observation of their miraculous healing properties on worn-out and organically depleted soils to understand the part they have played in fertility and in man's growth and development since the beginning of time.

# VII: SOME MORE ANIMALS

> Brought four puppys, that is three dogs and a bitch
> distinguished by the following names viz. that with the
> most black spots Vulcan, the other black-spotted dog
> Searcher, the red-spotted dog Rover, and the red-spotted
> bitch Sweetlips.
>
> —George Washington's Farm Journal

SYLVESTER is a Guernsey bull. He is the biggest Guernsey
bull I have ever known and one of the handsomest. He is
also the biggest baby I have ever known.

He came to us from George von Penen who has a farm
near Kalamazoo, accompanied by a harem of thirty-four
lady friends, of all ages from six months to an old girl of
thirteen. At Malabar he found another twenty-seven ladies
awaiting him. From then on he occupied, as Lord and
Master, the big stall and bull pen in the dairy barn at the
Big House save for occasional periods when he was allowed
a holiday in lush pasture with the dairy cows and young
heifers.

On his arrival he was a young fellow, not quite two years
old and he continued to grow and put on weight and muscle
for almost another year, but from the first he revealed the
fact that there was a broad streak of ham actor in him.
He was always a *poseur* and as if aware of his own good
looks, he spent a great deal of time in the bull pen, striking
attitudes and showing his profile to anyone who would care
to stop and look at him. Occasionally, the plastic pose would
be interrupted by pawing and snorting and playing with the
big iron oil drum which was given him as a plaything.

I think he made up stories about the oil drum, converting

it most often into a rival when he would give it an unearthly drubbing. At times he would butt it up-hill on the slope of the bull pen. When it struck the wall of the barn it would rebound and start rolling downward back toward him. At just the right point he would give it another almighty butt so that it repeated the action. This game would go on for sometimes as long as an hour. It began, I think, as his own idea of fun and exercise but gradually like all his other actions it took a show-off form. The spectacle was exactly like that of a middle-aged businessman playing handball and showing anyone concerned or interested that he was just as young as he ever was. The larger the audience the more enjoyment Sylvester appeared to gain from his performance.

In the meanwhile he developed as well some of the characteristics of a spoiled Persian cat. Unlike most bulls he appeared to enjoy petting. Inside his stall, he would come and thrust his head over the edge of the barrier to be petted and talked to. I think it was the sound of my voice or Al's or Jim's he liked more than the petting. You'd say to him, "Well, how's the old stinker today?" and there would be a kind of answering deep rumble from his throat. And then "Want some attention, do you?" and again a rumble. The eyes which a moment before had been showing the whites in his performance in the role of the big, bad bull, would half-close with pleasure. Usually the petting and conversation was accompanied by a treat of some kind—a handful of grain or a fresh ear of sweetcorn or an apple. He knew perfectly well what "Do you want an apple?" meant. Also he clearly knew what we meant when we asked, "Want some attention, do you?"

Only one thing tempted him away from the pleasure of being petted and talked to and that was the presence of ladies who frequently took a timorous attitude toward him. The moment they would start back and, in a feminine way, cry out, "But aren't you afraid of that big brute?" all the ham in him would come to the surface and he would begin at once to arch his neck, to snort, show the whites of his eyes and to flex all the great muscles of his handsome neck. No ham actor, strutting through the lobby of the Hotel Astor, ever did such a job. Indeed, the performance was so impressive that I once had a letter from a lady visitor on her return home begging me "not to trust that ferocious bull" for a moment.

Of course I didn't trust him, nor did Al or Jim, because no sensible farmer ever trusts a bull. Many a farmer has been killed by a playful and friendly bull who wasn't ferocious at all but "simply didn't know his strength." Any farmer knows the playfulness of a bull calf and how he will put his head against you and push. A lot of calf remains in a lot of bulls after they are grown, only by that time the pushing is no fun any longer, at least for the farmer. Sylvester has a lot of play in him but I wouldn't want to play with him if I were sandwiched between the wall of his stall and his big head.

He carries his clowning, his hamming and his posing with him into the lush green ladino and bluegrass pasture. I think he realizes that here, in grass up to his knees the blue sky and the woods for a background, he is at his best, and certainly he is a handsome beast. As if he knew it, he plays the Lord to all the cows and heifers. When you first turn him out he does not, like many an eager, unwise male, run wildly to join the cows and heifers. Instead, he steps inside the gate and, striking a pose like the Bull Durham advertisement, lets out two or three ungodly bellows and waits. There is both lordliness and assurance in his manner and he has never had reason to change his tactics for within two or three minutes the silly cows and heifers all appear out of a clump of bushes or over a hill, high-tailing it toward him. Then for a while he paws and bellows and poses, permitting them to admire him.

He has an infallible instinct for those who are afraid of him and bullies them unmercifully. Only this autumn he discovered he could bully Jesse. Now Jesse, who is himself a character, is sixty-five and a man of all jobs with all the raciness and profanity of the Tennessee hills, and a word-by-mouth account of his encounter and feud with Sylvester cannot be set down here with any degree of literalness. Jesse and Sylvester occupied the same pasture while Jesse was engaged with the Ford tractor in ripping it up for reseeding and Sylvester took to leaving his harem and following Jesse about. So long as the tractor was moving it was all right but once it stopped, Sylvester closed in on him. I doubt that he meant any real harm but he knew he could rouse from Jesse a fine stream of Tennessee four letter words and he also knew that he could keep Jesse on the move. So for Jesse there was no peace. He had to keep on the move from the time he entered the field until he left. Two or three times, standing on the top of the hill, I have watched the comedy.

But worst of all, Sylvester wouldn't let Jesse get a drink at the spring. It was unseasonably hot October weather and Jesse got thirsty, but during the week he worked in the field he never once had a drink from the spring. Each time that Jesse turned the tractor in that direction Sylvester, as if divining his purpose, got there first. He even went further than that; when he tired of following Jesse about, he simply went back to the spring and lay down beside it. He knew perfectly well all the time that Jesse was scared of him.

But his behavior with Al and Jim and myself was quite different. If we encountered him in the field from the safety of the jeep or on the opposite side of the fence, he would begin his best Bull Durham performance. After you had watched with amusement for a time, all you needed to say was "Aw, Nutz! Come over here and get your head scratched!" And at once the snorting, the pawing and the eye-rolling stopped and he would walk over to the fence or the jeep and have his head rubbed like a pet calf.

Sylvester has never quite understood the jeep. He dislikes all machinery and puts on a terrific show whenever a truck or a tractor comes into the barnyard. I think trucks and tractors and jeeps puzzle him because he cannot figure out why Al and Jim and I can be his good friends on foot and then suddenly become part of a noisy chugging, Behemoth. In the pasture he will come up to the jeep and after his usual show-off performance, smell it, regard it from all sides, clearly and profoundly puzzled. He could of course demolish it if he chose and once or twice he has put his head against the radiator with every intention of doing so, but a single blast of the horn sets him back on his feet and back again into his chronic state of bewilderment.

His pasture behavior eventually resulted in a climax, however, when he went berserk and apparently decided that the

only sublimation of his dislike for machinery was to break it up. There came the day when Sylvester actually *attacked* two tractors and chased Jesse and Kenneth from the field. Both were small-sized Ford tractors and Sylvester, instead of merely following them about bellowing and pawing, actually went for them. With his tail high in the air, the whites of his eyes showing and with tremulous bellows he put his head under the back end of the field cultivator and lifted it off the ground. Jesse, seeing himself and the tractor rolling down the hill, jumped free and took to the woods. Flushed with his victory, Sylvester set out after Kenneth and repeated the performance with the same results. Then while Jesse and Kenneth watched from the safety of the woods on the opposite side of the fence, he put on a show of regal triumph, posing, arching his neck, pawing the earth and bellowing and at last when he felt he had shown off sufficiently, he turned and rushed up the hill and out of sight to rejoin his harem leaving Kenneth and Jesse to return sheepishly and rescue their tractors.

It is a pity that Sylvester could not hear Jesse's subsequent account of "The Battle of the Tractors." With each retelling it grew in detail and horror until Sylvester had attained the size of an African elephant and the ferocity of a sabre-toothed tiger. Fire came from his nostrils and sparks from his eyes. The tractor, in Jesse's later versions, was lifted in the air so high that he had to jump several feet to the ground, just in time to save himself. Indeed, Jesse's account of the Battle has reached such proportions that beside Sylvester, Paul Bunyan's Blue Ox was no more than a sucking calf.

Sylvester developed a lot of idiosyncrasies in his stall and bull pen. The one thing he cannot bear is lack of attention or being ignored. If you pass him without rubbing his nose or at least speaking to him, he will put down his head and pout and grumble like a small child. And at some period and for some reason no one has been able to divine, he took a dislike to the top bar of the gate to his bull pen. At first this was a plank which he proceeded to break in two. When it was replaced he broke the second one and when a steel pipe was substituted he proceeded to bend it and force it

190

out of position. Finally Al left the top bar off altogether and there remained only the lower bar less than three feet from the ground. Despite the fact that he could step over the remaining bar he has never attempted to do so nor made any effort to leave the pen, even though the cows pass him on their way from the milk parlor. It is useless to replace the top bar for he proceeds at once to smash or bend it. Apparently the top bar seems to present what psychiatrists refer to as "a psychological obstacle," which appears to be all that is necessary. Visitors, seeing him with nothing between him and the outside world, take alarm and say, "Aren't you afraid he'll get out?" He never does. Perhaps some day he will and we shall have to take other measures.

The day finally came however when Sylvester got his come-uppance and made a complete fool of himself. It was all his own doing and he was, I think, properly humiliated. For days afterward he became self-conscious and ashamed.

My first knowledge of his predicament came when I began to hear the most prodigious bellows coming from the dairy barn as I was working in my office. He has a good voice, Sylvester, and is never hesitant about using it, but on this occasion the bellows were more like those of a bull elephant ringing from hill to hill in the jungle. Realizing something terrific must be happening, I went toward the barn and as I reached the corner in sight of the bull pen, I discovered a spectacle which set me laughing so much that I could not act.

The head of the oil drum which Sylvester used in his version of handball had apparently rusted out and in some way he had got his head inside the drum where it became firmly stuck. Blind and helpless, he grew madder and madder, and the madder he got, the more he bawled, with variations basso profundo, tenor and even coloratura. No bull—not even the Bull of Bashan—ever bellowed louder.

It was no use trying to get the oil drum off without aid. It was really stuck over his horns. It finally took two of us half an hour to free Sylvester.

Once freed, he appeared momentarily dazed. Then he gave us both one of the most baleful looks I have ever received from an animal, grumbled once or twice, turned his back and went into his stall where he sulked the remainder of the day.

Since then, although I have not relaxed my caution, I feel that I have Sylvester under control. I need only say, "Remember the oil drum!" to cover him with confusion.

One of the most remarkable things about animals is the variety of their personalities and the fantastic tricks which, untaught, they will develop. To the average town dweller and even to some farmers all cows or hogs or horses appear to be alike and indistinguishable in characteristics and behavior, but nothing could be less true. A good stockman must have, it seems to me, three characteristics: (1) He must know and love his animals and divine the fact that they are sick or off their feed and what is the matter with them. (2) He must have a "feeling" for them so strong that he can virtually divine what they are thinking and what they are up to. (3) And in a broad sense he must treat them as companions.

The 4-H Club boy, showing his prize steer or lamb or hog in Kansas City or Chicago or Omaha or Cleveland, will know what I mean. Many a time I have seen a boy sound asleep in the clean straw of the cattle pen beside the prize steer which he will not leave, and twice at least I have seen tears in the eyes of a farm boy when the moment came to put the steer up for auction. Any good dairyman knows every cow in his herd and knows that each one of them is different in personality from all the others and that the understanding of this fact and treatment based upon it means money in the milk pail.

The forty-cow dairy at Malabar is located only a hundred feet from the Big House and I spend a good deal of time there so that I have come to know all the cows pretty well, although nowhere nearly so well as Al and Jim who milk and care for them. In some remarkable way, beyond my own powers, Al and Jim know by sight all the forty milking cows and the twenty odd which in rotation are dry and awaiting calves. They know them by name and personality and when the boys open the door of the loafing shed many of the cows will come forward at the calling of their names.

Because there are so many cows in the dairy as well as sixty or seventy-five new heifers each year which eventually pass through the milking parlor for a season before being shipped to the eastern milk sheds, the naming of them long ago became a problem which we solved by naming them for the women and children on the farm and for visiting friends. There are Mary and Dessi and Virginia and Martha and Gwenn, Hope and Allen and Anne and Fanny and so on. At times the custom leads to mirth and broad jokes: Al or Jim announces "Jenny freshened last night!" or "Wow! Did Fanny kick me in the behind tonight!" or "Myrtle has come in with six teats!"

There is Irene who will take on the milking machine peacefully until she is three-quarters milked and then begin to let fly with rabbit punches which could break your leg. And Essie, a big Holstein, who outdoes even the other Holsteins in her greed and will rattle her stanchion violently until she gets an extra handful of grain. And Mary and Martha and Jean who will follow you about to be petted. Each one is capable of her own set of tricks. Some will not have their heads touched and others will rumble and purr like cats when you sractch their ears. Jean, who clearly has a sense of rhythm, will chew her cud in time to the music from the milk parlor radio, alternating waltz time with rhumbas and fox trots. I think she takes pride in entertaining visitors with her performance, for she gives occasional backward glances (without losing a beat) at a sudden outburst of mirth at her performance.

But oddest of all performances was the feud which developed between Eileen and Mummy, the big female tiger cat who has staked out the feed room as her territory and does a first-rate job on the mice and rats who come to the milk parlor to feed off the spilled grain. Mummy was so named because of her extraordinary fecundity. In astrological realm she is probably what is known as the Universal Mother. Naturally she lives in close companionship with the dairy cows and, I believe, really knows them apart. Long ago she learned that by walking along the concrete ledge beyond the feed trough she would get some extra petting when the cows occasionally reached out and licked her coat as she passed. When this happens, she will stand quite still, arching her back and purring. It is a performance she carries out regularly at milking time, as much a rite as the milk which she receives twice a day.

All went well with the system until Eileen, a very big and greedy Holstein, took an unaccountable dislike to Mummy. I suspect Eileen felt that Mummy had designs on her allotment of grain but I do not know. In any case there came an evening when Mummy, walking along the ledge receiving the usual attentions from the cows, was seized by Eileen and given a good shaking. Al heard the catlike yowls of distress and discovered the astonishing sight of Mummy being shaken by Eileen. With her tail spread to balloonlike proportions and all four feet dangling in the air, Mummy was emitting outraged and furious squalls. For a moment Al was so paralyzed by laughter he could not rescue the indignant cat. A cat is the most dignified of all animals and no animal so resents a violation of its dignity. It was this violation, I think, which outraged Mummy far more than any harm she received by Eileen's astonishing un-cowlike behavior.

Twice more the incident was repeated, once in my sight, and by that time Mummy had had enough. She did not abandon her habit of parading the ledge behind the feed troughs. She simply gave it up while Eileen was in her stanchion being milked. As soon as Eileen was unlocked and released from her stanchion, Mummy resumed her promenade receiving with purring satisfaction the attentions of her bovine friends.

The life of cats about a farm is in itself worthy of a whole study. They come and go from one set of farm buildings to another, according, so far as I am able to make out, to the rise and fall of food supplies. No animal but a hog knows better how to take care of himself. We have a score of farm cats, fat and sleek and well fed on mice, rats and unwary sparrows, as well as on the milk from the dairy barn and the table scraps from the houses. In summer some of the big toms will take to the fields and thickets leading a sporting life and living off the countryside. More than once when mowing, I have started up out of the thick hay a big tom engaged in stalking field mice. I don't like it when they take young birds and chipmunks but there doesn't seem to be any way of controlling them and in the barns they are not only valuable but indispensable, prowling the rooms, the feed mows and the cattle stalls to keep down vermin. The number which "goes wild" in summer is small for they are well fed in the barns and find an easy living there and at the kitchen doors of the various houses.

Gilbert, the Tom turkey, is dead and Haile Selassie, the Karakul ram, has gone to live elsewhere. Gilbert, one of the minor heroes of *Pleasant Valley* was part of an experiment. He was a wild turkey brought in to cross with bronze turkey hens in the hope that we might produce crossbred hens that would display some sense in taking care of their poults. Our valley is natural wild turkey country and the early settlers of Ohio depended on wild turkey for a substantial part of their game diet, and it occurred to us that turkeys, like the guinea fowl and the fighting chickens, might well breed and reproduce on their own, living off the land in summer and on spilled grain and a little hand-strewn grain in winter. I had memories of my grandmother's turkey hens who would hatch out a dozen poults, take them on the countryside for the summer and return with them nearly grown by the first heavy frosts.

But no such thing happened. Man, by breeding turkeys to produce all breast or for quick fattening, seems to have bred out of the turkey hen the little sense she once had. Not only is the modern bronze market turkey unable to take care of her young, she cannot even take care of herself. She is just a plain damned fool. And even the crossbred offspring of Gilbert showed little more sense than their overbred mothers. The original flock of six went on living about the house as privileged guests until they died off one by one of old age. Gilbert got to be a nuisance for he liked people better than he liked his hens, and spent all his time strutting among them. At times his gobbling made conversation by daytime impossible just as at times the raucous squawking of the guinea fowl in the catalpa tree by the door of the Big House made life intolerable in the evening. The situation was not helped in any way when the parrot abovestairs in the children's rooms took to giving imitations of both

Gilbert and the guinea fowl which were even noisier than the originals.

The parrot was in himself a remarkable bird. Although he was with us until the children went off to school for good and his tyranny became unbearable, we never learned his sex. He never laid an egg but he was a confirmed man-hater and showed a great preference for the ladies. During all the years he was with us he never was locked in his cage but late at night he would enter it at what he thought was the proper time, go to bed, take his place on his perch and close his eyes. Occasionally he would make excursions from one of the children's rooms to another but he never made any attempt to escape. There were moments when all of us wished he would take it into his head to fly for the Jungle.

All the children are girls and Nanny shares their part of the house so that there were no men to speak of who could bother him until the girls began to grow up and have boy friends. Then, to put it in an unrefined way, all hell broke loose, and his persecutions could only be controlled by putting him inside the cage and throwing a cover over it. This failed to put him to sleep before the time he considered proper and from the darkness he continued to swear, mutter, and grumble until he fell asleep at last.

He was an exceedingly clever bird. No one ever attempted to teach him anything but he picked up plenty. Besides learning to imitate Gilbert, the gobbler, and the guinea fowl, he learned to whistle for the dogs and would spend hours at the window alternating shrill whistles, remarkable for their human quality, with sardonic and mocking chuckles. For three or four days after he began practicing the trick he had the dogs crazy but with their sharp hearing they soon learned that Thomas was a fraud and ignored him, I almost suspect, to his fury.

Then one day he began practicing on a new noise and for some time we were all baffled in our attempts to discover what the strange sounds he made were intended to imitate. There was no doubt that he was attempting something complex and difficult, as if a violin player were suddenly attempting to be a whole quartet, or a quartet a whole symphony. There would be a whole string of noises which

sounded like "gabble-gabble-gabble" with occasional shrill stretches which appeared to be music, interspersed without rhyme or reason by almost maniacal screeches. He would spend whole mornings practicing in his window directly over the main summer porch. Later, if not too hoarse, he would continue into the evening while we sat below. For a time, we thought that the noise was possibly a manifestation of parrot schizophrenia.

And then one night, after weeks of practice, the imitation took enough form to be recognizable. I might not have understood what it was meant to be save for the fact that, returning from the barn one night in the darkness, I found myself at a spot on the lawn at equal distance from the group of family and friends on the porch and from Thomas at his post in the window overhead. The people below were talking and laughing to the accompaniment of music from the radio inside the house, and upstairs in his window Thomas was practicing. From where I stood, the sounds came to me in about equal volume. And I understood—Thomas had been practicing for weeks to imitate the sounds of human conversation, laughter and radio music which rose night after night during the summer to his window.

When I reached the porch I said, "Would you all like to know what you sound like?" There was a silence and from abovestairs Thomas' imitation came out "gabble-gabble-gabble" with interludes of shrill music interspersed with insane giggles and maniacal chuckles. He had very nearly perfected it and it was good. What would have happened to him if he had been exposed to an average cocktail party I do not know. Very likely he would have burst apart in an explosion of flesh, bone, and feathers.

Where he came from I do not know. We bought him from one bird dealer who had bought him from another and his origins were lost in antiquity. We had only three clues to his past life—his hatred of men, his passion for toast soaked in coffee, and his habit of shrieking on occasion in an unmistakably feminine voice, "Shut up! Damn you, shut up!"

There came a time when Thomas' disagreeable and cantankerous personality became a strain, perhaps because he developed a habit of deliberately scattering the hulls of his sunflower seeds as far as he could over the whole of the room. I suspect that he enjoyed watching someone clean them up so that he could scatter a fresh lot.

In any case Thomas finally went too far when he began actually *attacking* any man who entered the room where he was. My novelist friend David deJong, on a visit at Malabar, told us that he had a way with parrots and he was sure that he would get on with Thomas. Despite protests and warnings he went upstairs to court the wicked bird. We had not long to wait for within three minutes David came down the stairs at full speed with Thomas clinging to his shoulders beating him frantically with his wings.

Shaken off, the evil bird remained strutting and chortling about the front hall until Nanny, clad only in her nightgown, appeared from abovestairs bearing his cage. Knowing his ways, she placed the cage on the floor and he immediately hopped on it and was carried back upstairs, chortling and leering back at us over his shoulder.

At times he was amusing but he was always a malicious bird without warmth or any humor save the most savage and bitter derision, and as he grew older and dirtier he became an untidy and shrewish burden like some malicious old man. We returned him to the bird store and the proprietor sold him to an elderly and very plain widow living alone. I think it unlikely that his antipathy to men is aroused very frequently and I am sure the widow has plenty of time to clean up after him. I suspect that both are now happier if indeed happiness or unhappiness ever played any part in Thomas' life.

The Karakul ram was named Haile Selassie because he bore, with his dark face, hooked-nose and drooping ears so striking a resemblance to the King of Kings, the Lion of Judah and the Emperor of Abyssinia.

Given to the children by Mrs. Grove Patterson as a tiny black lamb with tightly kinked, shiny black wool, he grew into an enormous ram with horns which curved twice round his drooping ears. Always he considered himself a member of the family and until he took to butting and hooking with his horns the guests and strangers (in the playful way he had) he ran free about the garden and the barnyard.

In *Pleasant Valley* I wrote of Haile Selassie and of his reception of the Commissar of Animal Husbandry from Moscow whom he butted through the front door of the Big House. The Commissar took it very well and in a mixture of French, German, and Russian, remarked, holding his posterior, "It made me feel that I was back again in Russia." There was perhaps something cryptic in the remark which we have never fully understood.

After that incident Haile was shut up in the paddock across the road where, with a Karakul and a Shropshire ewe, he led a fairly contented existence, like a Pasha with one Nubian and one Circassian bride. During this period he developed an inordinate appetite for chewing tobacco and cigarettes and would come running from any distance for one or the other. As I have never learned to chew tobacco without getting sick and Haile developed his tastes during the cigarette shortage occasioned by the war, his appetites

199

for tobacco became somewhat of a problem. This was especially true since the temptation to feed him tobacco was irresistible, as he stood with his forefeet on the bottom rail of the fence, his head peering over the top while he bleated for his tobacco. The problem was solved by saving all the cigarette ends and feeding them to Haile. Despite the warnings of the anti-cigarette league, he thrived on them.

The end came, as I have recounted elsewhere in the Journal, when he knocked down Nanny while she was innocently engaged in picking blackberries within his territory. As there were many children on the farm and many visiting children, we couldn't take the risk and so Haile and his harem went off to live with a neighbor who was embarking upon a joint poultry and Karakul lamb enterprise. I inquire after him occasionally and he seems to be enjoying himself.

Gilbert, the Tom turkey, who started all of this, died finally of old age. We found him dead one winter morning beside the pond. He was a venerable bird, who must have been ten or eleven years old at the time of his death. Although he was a nuisance at times with his gobbling, strutting and preening which kept interrupting conversations, we miss him. He was a bird of passionate likes and dislikes. If anyone teased him, the offense was never forgotten and Gilbert would attack his annoyer with claws and wings on sight and even pursue him down the drive. He had a special distaste for the driver of the bakery truck and used to follow the bakery truck all the way down the lane to the main road uttering a queer combination of angry and complaining cries.

His bronze wives all preceded him in death from one reason or another but he left behind a relic in the form of a white Holland turkey hen who was spontaneously known by the name of a much photographed dowager famous for her liking for Metropolitan Opera openings, her jewels, and for her wattled throat. She still lives about the house and has taken on "a companion" much younger than herself from whom she is inseparable. He arrived on the scene as a three-day-old chick, dyed a brilliant green, as an Easter gift. He quickly shed his dyed fluff and emerged as a handsome Leghorn rooster who got somehow the name of Tony. The fighting chickens would have no part of him and he attached himself to Gilbert's white Holland widow. They make a devoted but somehow ridiculous couple and Tony has defied all the rules of poultry husbandry by leading a natural out-of-door life and becoming the handsomest show rooster I have ever seen in or outside a poultry show.

There are plenty of other animals at Malabar like Jo, the Border Collie, who is scared to death of cows and Folly and Susie who are Boxers and so come of a race of watchdogs and fighters but who are excellent stock dogs and Tex, the handsome five-gaited Kentucky mare who was bred for the show-ring but has a passion and an unswerving instinct for rounding up cattle. And there are two Angus bulls called Junior and Pee-Wee.

As Ellen, the youngest daughter once put it, "The trouble with the animals on this farm is that they all think they're people."

## GOOD-BY TO A FRIEND

I had been fishing for three days among the islands of Lake Erie, escaping just ahead of a great equinoxial storm which shut the islands off from the mainland for three days. Friends drove me from Catawba down to the farm with the rising wind and the towering black clouds just behind us all the way. We won the race, driving up the long lane, between trees whipped by the wind, scattering showers of early falling leaves across the road. The Big House had never looked pleasanter nor the farm more green than in the sulphur-yellow light from the approaching storm. But in my heart there was always that uneasy misgiving which always troubles me when I return after an absence. At Malabar there are many people and animals of all ages and sizes and kinds which have a deep hold on my affections. And always there is a fear in my heart that, while I am away, something bad might have happened to one of them. It is the penalty, I suppose, for having affections and attachments. Life would be much simpler, I suppose, and the emotions less distressed if a man lived alone in a cave without either affections or attachments of any kind; but life would also be less warm and less rich and infinitely and painfully sterile.

Like all else, about which Emerson was so right in his clean, transcendental thinking, these things are a matter of compensation.

Always when I have been away I am almost sure to be greeted, as the car comes up the lane, by my wife and a troop of dogs. There were always Prince and Baby, Gina and Folly, the four Boxers, Dusky, the Cocker and Jo, the Border Collie. Once there had been the great and venerable Rex, the father of all the Boxers and little Patsy, the black and liver-colored Cocker, and Midge the Boxer pup, but they have been gone now for a long time, although the family talks of them as if they were still alive. It is always the dogs who give the signal of my approach and my wife, recognizing it, comes down the path from the house.

On that wild September evening, the arrival of the car was heralded by the rush of dogs, but almost at once I saw that two things were wrong. Prince was not with the dogs, leading them as he always did, and the door did not open and my wife did not appear. Instead it was Tom who came out of the kitchen across the lawn.

The old uneasiness rose again and then, as he unloaded the bags and fish, Tom was suddenly beside me and without even greeting me, he said, "Mr. B., Prince is dead!"

"Dead!" I asked, "What happened?"

"He was coughing badly and we sent him up to Doc's. He died during the night."

I knew now why my wife hadn't appeared. She couldn't face telling me because she knew about Prince and me. So Tom had been delegated and it was hard for him, so hard he didn't even accompany the news with the prelude of a greeting. I knew it was hard on him too because when my wife and I were away, Prince attached himself to Tom, following him everywhere all day long. Each morning when I wakened, Prince would get down from my bed, have his part of my breakfast and then go off to Tom in the kitchen to have his back brushed. Tom always used a whiskbroom. Animals and especially dogs are very conventional. The backbrushing was a regular ritual.

My friends expressed sorrow at the news and I was grateful but they couldn't know how I felt. I asked them in for a drink before they drove off to Columbus. My wife joined us and acted as if nothing at all had happened. We talked and my friends left, eager to continue their race against the oncoming storm.

When they had gone, my wife looked at me without speaking and I said, "I think I'll go and have a look at the farm before dark." She said, "I think that would be a good idea."

It was always Prince who went everywhere with me in the jeep. He loved it, partly I think, because it was open and he could catch every scent on the breeze as we drove and partly because in the jeep we went to the wildest parts of the farm where there were always squirrels and rabbits and woodchucks to chase. Now as I climbed in, Prince's brother Baby jumped quickly into the seat beside me.

I wasn't going to look over the farm. I was going to one place where all of us on the farm go instinctively when we are worried or depressed or something unhappy occurs to us. I was going to the pastures of the Ferguson Place which lie high above the valley just beneath the sky. It is a lonely place which has no buildings, a farm which is all forest and bluegrass, but it is not lonely. My wife knew where I was going.

Prince had slept on the foot of my bed since he was a fat puppy. Never once in the eight years of his life was he absent from his accustomed place. He spent twenty-four hours a day with me. If I moved across a room to another chair, he moved with me and lay down at my feet. People came to say that I did not own Prince: he owned me.

And now as I drove up the long, wild lane through the woods, his brother Baby was beside me and something curious happened. Halfway up the lane he leaped into my lap and began to lick my ear, exactly as Prince had done so many times when we set off alone together in the jeep—as if the pleasure was always too great to be borne. It was exactly as if Baby *knew*. Baby had always seemed a strange, self-contained dog, little given to demonstrations of affection of any kind. The sudden outburst was so violent that I laughed and said, "That's enough, Baby! Let me alone! I have to drive!" And he quieted down for a moment only to break out a little later with another wild and affectionate assault.

203

Boxers are big dogs and when they demonstrate their hearty affections the demonstrations can only be described as an assault.

We reached the high farm just as the clouds of a storm were blackening out the last rays of the setting sun. There on the green pasture the Holstein heifers and Pee-Wee, the bull, were grazing quietly, scarcely looking up as the jeep drove among them, and then, when I had turned off the motor and climbed out, followed by Baby, to lie on the grass, the cattle came up one or two at a time to stand there, very close, watching the two of us. Baby did what Prince had always done. He sat close to me, his back against my chest, to protect me from the peril of the docile heifers.

I don't know how long I lay there but the smell of the bluegrass and the friendliness of the heifers made the hurt seem a little less. This was a place where Prince had come with me countless times to sit in the evening looking down over the valley. It was all just the same. Despite the oncoming storm, the evening seemed quiet but for the wild beauty of the great black clouds touched at moments by the crimson and gold light of the setting sun. The thick woods shut out the rising wind and the only sound was the soft swishing, crunching sound made by the heifers and the bull as they ate their way along the bluegrass and white clover. Then there was a wild clap of thunder and another and another. I heard myself half-thinking, half-saying, "It's all right, kid! I'm coming back! Don't worry!" And I thought, "That's silly!" But somehow it made a difference.

It was what I always said to him when I went away on a trip. He always knew all the signs. He knew what a suitcase meant. He grew worried and miserable even if I put on store clothes to go into town for a few hours. So I'd always say, "It's all right, kid! I'm coming back! Don't worry!" And always when I came back I'd say after I'd recovered from the first affectionate assault of welcome, "You see, kid! It's all right! I told you I'd come back and I did." He came to understand it all and although the sight of store clothes or a suitcase never failed to depress him, understanding the situation and knowing I was not leaving forever made it all easier for him. On the occasions when I went away he never rushed to the door with me but stayed behind in my room till the car drove off.

Then as I lay there on the grass, Baby turned suddenly and again began licking my ear violently and quickly, and out of the threatening sky, the wild storm of the equinox broke. The heifers and Pee-Wee took to a sheltering thicket and Baby and I climbed back into the jeep to drive home down the wild, rough lane through a wild wind and a driving rain with flashes of lightning which illumined the very depths of the thick wood.

I know that much of what I am writing sounds sentimental and much of it is. And so I am a sentimentalist and so what? It is inevitable that anyone who likes and understands animals should be a sentimentalist. I think too that such people sometimes find in animals and especially dogs consolations and sympathy in time of hurt which no human, however close, can ever bring them. And there is much truth in the sentimentality about the animals, much which brings a special warmth and satisfaction in living and a clue to much that is a part of understanding and of God. Some people will perhaps not understand at all what I am writing about and others will know, instinctively and rightly.

All that night and for days afterward Prince was always with me in a way for, as when great friends die, one thinks of them almost constantly—they are indeed ever present in one's dreams. And so I thought a great deal about Prince, remembering all the small things about him and a hundred small incidents, good and bad. For he was a very human dog, neither wholly good or bad. He was willful and demanding in his love for me and very jealous. He fought with Baby and was even known to snip at Gina and Folly when they became too affectionate and intimate. Always in his mind, I was his special property.

He was a big and handsome dog, the child of Rex, a noble father, and Regina, a mother with an immense store of feminine wisdom, calm, and poise. Rex died four years ago and Regina is still alive going her calm way, wise and affectionate and pleasant as a good wife and mother should be. She brooks no nonsense from her children and grandchildren nor from her in-laws. Although she is quite an old lady she can quiet them all simply by making faces at them and she can make really ferocious and terrifying faces. Baby too is their child from a different litter from Prince. He was a year younger than Prince and no two dogs could be less alike, for Baby was always a clown and a ham actor. He holds long conversations in a variety of barks, whines, and growls. He taught himself to dive off the high platform at the pond and he cannot resist climbing into an empty wheelbarrow for a ride. He drinks Coca-Cola from a bottle and water straight from the faucet. He developed all these tricks and many more without ever being taught. He was always vain and comical but detached.

But Prince was different. Indeed he was different from any of the fifty or more dogs I have had in a lifetime. He was different because he was a Boxer and Boxers' owners will know what I mean by that—but he was a King, even among Boxers. Above all he was a good companion. To drive with him over the farm or to take him with me across the fields and woods was like having the company of a great friend who was intelligent and amusing. When I walked three or four miles, he would joyously run ten or fifteen, but in all his excursions he kept returning to me again and again to tell me what a beautiful morning it was or how he had treed a squirrel. And sometimes he would return with a woodchuck proudly, to show me, and would insist on carrying it all the way home. He was obedient too for when he uncovered a nest of young rabbits or as happened once or twice, came on a baby raccoon offside in the daylight, I needed only to say, "No, Prince!" and he would stand quite still, quivering with excitement, without touching the young animals.

And like all Boxers he was clever with his paws, using them with dexterity almost like hands. Most of the doors in the Big House have French door handles and these he turned easily, but he was very clever with round door knobs, using both paws to turn them. He went from room to room in the house and at the front door he would open the screen door and hold it open while he turned the knob of the inner door. Once his cleverness nearly caused disaster which might have ended in the death of himself and his wise old mother.

206

I had left them inside the car on a slope above the deep pond below the Big House, planning to return quickly but once inside the house a long-distance telephone call distracted me, and temporarily I forgot Prince and Gina, still waiting in the car. When at last I was free to return I stepped out of the house just in time to see the big car with the two dogs inside slipping down the steep slope toward the deep waters of the pond. It was the dogs I thought of and not the car. Running down the slope I arrived at the pond just in time to see the car slipping slowly beneath the surface. Fully dressed, I went into the water, dived, opened the car door and dragged them both out under water. They swam ashore, shook themselves and seemed unconcerned over what had happened. Indeed, I think Prince took it as a lark.

It did not take me long to divine what had happened. The car was heavy and the emergency brake never held it properly, so, on leaving them, I had put the car in second gear and turned the wheels against a nearby bank. Prince, left alone for so long, had grown impatient and tried to open the door to get out and find me. In doing so he had put one paw on the gearshift, pulling it out of second gear and turning the wheel at the same time away from the bank. The rest was easy—the car simply rolled into the pond.

It was Prince too who, on cold days, opened the doors of cars belonging to visitors and led the other dogs inside. He even closed the door after them in order to keep out draughts. Many a time, a visitor has left my office to discover that the car he had left empty and closed was now filled by four Boxers and a Cocker Spaniel.

He had the dignity and the nobility of his father, Rex, but with more sensitivity and intelligence, and this difference made him a sufferer, for he worried as I have never known any dog to worry. He worried about my going away and as soon as I returned, he would begin worrying lest I leave again. After the first roughhouse welcome on my return, he would be overcome again and again during the day by the realization that I had really come back after all, and at such moments he would leap from the floor into my lap and place both paws on my shoulders and lick my ear. Sometimes he would jump from the floor onto my big desk scattering ink and papers in his excitement. I couldn't punish him. How could you punish such a whole-hearted demonstration of affection?

His brother, Baby, the show-off, will talk and talk, very audibly to any circle of friends, but Prince rarely raised his voice. He would open his mouth and his lips would quiver but no sound would come forth, and then he would sigh as if he knew that no matter how hard he tried, he could never make with his dog's mouth the articulate sounds of speech that I was able to do, that he could never really talk to me, no matter how much we understood each other. At such times I would say, "It's all right, kid. I understand everything you say." And immediately he would be happy again.

It was a saying in the family that you couldn't talk confidentially in front of Prince because he understood everything you said, and indeed he appeared to understand perfectly all conversations or the plans made in his presence. He knew perfectly well how to wangle his way onto a sofa despite all rules to the contrary. He did it by degrees and insinuations, almost imperceptibly, until presently he was curled up on the fresh chintz as if that was where he belonged. Like all Boxers he hated draughts or cold floors.

Five or six dogs sleep in my bedroom. It is on the level of the garden with two doors which Prince opened easily, sometimes for himself and sometimes for the others. When the "coon huntin'" season opened, life at night in my bedroom was not placid and sleep was interrupted, for after midnight when the neighboring boys started running their hounds, the sound of baying drifted down from the ridge across the ravine and the dogs in my bedroom knew there were strangers on what they considered their territory. With a whoop and a halloo they were off, led by Prince, who opened the door. Then for an hour or two, all hell broke loose as the Boxers, with Dusky, the Cocker Spaniel trailing them, set out after the coon hounds, driving them out of the valley. Once the hounds were clear of the Boxers' land, the Boxers all returned with Prince leading to open the door for them to enter, to go back to their beds on chairs and sofas. Gina and Folly and Baby each had developed their own special ways of opening doors. Old Rex used to employ both teeth and paws. But none of them ever developed the proficiency of Prince. No door could withstand him and when he was with the others they always stood aside in deference to his particular skill.

If any other dog even approached the bed at night, he was in trouble at once. But for the period of my after lunch nap, he had made some sort of an arrangement with Folly. I do not know when or how it was made but it was one of perfect understanding. He never prevented her from joining me at nap time and never made any attempt to push her aside or to take his accustomed place. But at night it was different, the rug at the foot of my bed belonged to him.

That animals communicate and come to understandings, I have no doubt, for I have seen these things in operation too many times. I recall an afternoon when a group of visitors stopped at the lower garden with a strange Boxer in their car. It is always a risky thing to bring a strange dog in a car to Malabar for it is difficult to prevent the Boxers from removing half the paint from the car; so on this occasion I held Prince by the collar and told my friends to leave the car down on the road where it would be concealed, with the strange dog inside. Together we walked up the long hill and when we arrived at the house, where three or four empty cars were parked, the other Boxers rushed out to greet us. Then after a moment's exchange of communication they all began leaping at the windows of the empty parked cars, one after another, to discover which one contained a dog. Clearly and unmistakably Prince had spread the word.

When they found all the cars empty, they returned with disappointment to sit by us on the lawn, still convinced that there was a strange dog somewhere about. Then suddenly I noticed the hair begin to rise slowly on old Gina's back. She sniffed the wind and suddenly, followed by the others, all save Prince, she set off at top speed down the hill toward the hidden parked car. The odd thing was that Prince did not follow. I think it was because I had warned him to leave the strange dog in peace. He had told them there was a strange dog in a car on the farm but he did not tell them *where*.

In the mornings when I have breakfast in my office, each of the Boxers is given milk from a saucer. They have their own order of being served, apparently by arrangement among themselves. First Prince, as if this was his divine right as the leader and best friend of the boss, then old Gina, perhaps out of respect for her age, then Folly, the pretty, frivolous one and finally Baby, if he had not already gone out on the farm. The order never varied, nor was there any quarreling nor any attempt to return for a second helping.

Prince was a sociable dog and a great welcomer. Like all the Boxers, he loved picnics and parties and after the first uproar of barking had died away, he would welcome and say a few words to every member of the arriving party. Boxers are ferocious in appearance but they have the hearts of big babies. Sometimes the welcome to a small child would create more consternation than pleasure. Like all Boxers he was wonderful with children, and on the farm and among the visitors, there are many children of all sizes. Instinctively a Boxer will take care of children. I have seen little fellows on the farm pinch and ride and bedevil the Boxers and even take bones from them without coming to any harm. When the assaults become unendurable the Boxers will simply walk away out of reach without any loss of dignity.

On one occasion a small nephew of two years came to stay on the farm. He was one of those happy children with no fear of dogs and he moved in on the Boxers at once. He liked them all but he *adopted* Prince and Prince *adopted* him. The bond became so great that he even insisted upon having his afternoon nap with Prince. He would play with Prince for long periods of time, climbing on him and rolling over him. The friendship reached a climax and a test one summer afternoon while he was rolling on the lawn with the big dog. To the surprise of his mother and the rest of us, the boy was observed *biting* Prince's lip while the dog lay perfectly quietly with an expression not only of patience but of satisfaction.

He had many friends from all over the world and whenever or whereever I met them, they always asked, "How is Prince?" It was as if we belonged to each other and I know that when I was at home no one ever saw us separated, day or night. They asked about him as if he were one of the family. He liked people and remembered them when they returned, giving them a hospitable and friendly welcome.

During the three days I spent among the islands of the lake I should have enjoyed myself. I was among a dozen of my very best friends. We drank some and fished and played poker. We had an attractive and comfortable cottage and wonderful food. Yet, all the time I spent there I suffered from an unaccountable sense of depression and slept badly, an exceptional thing in my experience. I tried to believe that it was the weather with the approaching equinoctial storms, but never quite persuaded myself. By the third day the depression had taken the form of foreboding, of what I did not know. Like Dr. Carrell who was certainly no sentimentalist but a great and pure scientist, I believe that there are in the realms of intuition, of telepathy, of psychic communication things as remote from our understanding or knowledge as the knowledge of the physiology of man is remote from the most primitive savage. I *know* that in those three days, when for every reason I should have experienced a happy, care-free enjoyment in the open air and on the water, there was some force which dimmed the whole of the holiday and gradually assumed the proportions of menace and foreboding.

After returning with Baby through the storm from the high farm, I went to bed early and took a sleeping pill so that I wouldn't wake up and lie awake thinking about Prince. The place on the foot of the bed where he had always slept on an old green rug was empty for the first time since he had come there as a puppy.

Presently I fell asleep but twice during the night I was wakened despite the sleeping pill, once by the feeling of something stirring and pressing against my leg. The feeling was so real and so intense that I thought one of the other dogs had taken Prince's place. But when I sat up and reached down, there was nothing there.

After a long time I fell asleep again only to be wakened this time by the sound of scratching on the screen door. It was exactly the sound made by Prince when, in wet weather, the door stuck and he was forced to crook his paw against the grille covering the lower part of the door and give it an extra tug. I listened for a moment and then concluded one of the

211

other dogs had gone out and, without Prince to open the door for him, could not return. I put on the light and went to the door. The storm was over and the moon was shining high over the ravine. Outside the door there was nothing.

The two experiences were not imagined nor were they the result of drowsiness for each time I lay awake for a long time afterward. I do not know the explanation—save perhaps that no creature, in some ways even a human one, had ever been so close to me as Prince.

For weeks before he died he had seemed melancholy and looked a little thin but I thought only that it was the hot weather. Then two days before he died he began to cough violently and my wife sent him up to Doc Wadsworth's and thirty-six hours later he was dead of a hemorrhage which could not be stopped. He died of cancer of the lung and could only have lived a few weeks longer, perhaps in pain. If I could not have been with him myself I was glad that he was with Doc Wadsworth and his wife and sister-in-law for they feel as I do about animals and particularly about Boxers. When Doc comes to the farm, they all rush out and leap all over him. On two occasions they have knocked him flat with their joyous and affectionate welcome. I'm glad Doc was with him and gave him something to quiet the coughing and keep him asleep. But I wish I had been there to hold his head on my knee and say, "You see, kid! It's all right! I told you I'd come back!"

He's gone to join old Rex and the charming, frivolous little Boxer, Midge, who was like a ballet dancer, and little Patsy, the cocker who used to act as "sitter" for Old Gina whenever she had puppies, and Dash, the Don Juan of all Scotties. I have a feeling that I'll see them all some day and that as they rush down the path to welcome me with Prince in the lead, I'll be able to say to him, "You see, kid. I told you I'd come back and I did!"

The story perhaps would not be complete without relating the change in Baby in the days after Prince's death. Baby was, in one sense, an orphan. He was the one pup who survived in a litter of Gina's which she lost prematurely after she threw herself into the midst of a dog fight in a condition in which no lady can safely indulge in brawls. When her milk failed, Baby

was put on a bottle and brought up by Venetia Wills, from England, who was staying out the war with us. Despite the unfortunate circumstances of Baby's birth and upbringing he was always a stout and hearty dog and early took to farm life. Of all the dogs, he has always been the real farmer, spending most of his day in the fields riding on the machinery or following the plow. He is perfectly happy to follow the plow or mower round and round the field for hours, unlike his brother Prince who hated tractors and would leave me when I gave myself over to plowing. Unlike most Boxers, who dislike bad weather and hate rain, he has never minded either and in winter will sit in the snow looking down the road while the other dogs scratched at the door to be let in.

I have recounted earlier Baby's talents as a clown and a ham actor. His love for showing off frequently brought him into trouble with the other dogs, male and female, who detested the showing-off and when he began high diving would pounce on him to beat him up. He would certainly have been a great dog performer in vaudeville or a circus if he had ever had the opportunity. During the whole lifetime of Prince, I had thought of Baby as a peculiarly impersonal dog, egotistical and less affectionate than the others. It was only after Prince died that I discovered how badly I had misjudged him.

I discovered that he only appeared indifferent and egotistical because Prince, in his devotion to me and his jealousy, would not permit him to be otherwise. It was the ancient, classic case of the domination of the older brother. I know that whenever Baby tried to be friendly with me, a light of fury would come into Prince's eyes and a ferocious fight, sometimes damaging to tables, glassware and lamps would ensue. I did not, however, realize that Baby was really a frustrated dog and that all his tricks and showing-off were in a way merely a device to get attention and praise. He behaved exactly as a child behaves under the same circumstances, especially a child who seeks to attract notice away from a more favored brother or sister.

I do not know how much he understood immediately concerning the death of Prince, but he came presently to realize that Prince was no longer there to attack him when he entered the room where I was or if he tried to sit nearer to me in the jeep. For weeks after the death of Prince he never entered the house or my room save walking on tip-toe, his back arched and bristling, as if expecting attack. Gradually the old apprehension and complex began to disappear and his behavior became more normal. Then it was that I came to understand his troubles. I discovered that the big dog was perhaps the most affectionate of all the Boxers. He really didn't want to be a show-off. He only wanted attention and all the privileges Prince had had. He developed Prince's trick of jumping eagerly into my lap or on my desk. His whole character seemed to change. Instead of seeming to alternate between moodiness and showing-off, his temperament became even and happy. He still carries on his long conversations, conducted with a remarkable variety of rumbles, growls, barks, and whines; they are no longer complaints but outbursts of happiness. And gradually he became as inseparable from me as Prince had been.

One thing, however, did not change. He could not be induced by any kind of command or blandishment to take Prince's place on the rug at the foot of my bed. He would hold long conversations obviously in an effort to explain the situation to me but nothing would induce him to take the place of his brother. He clung always to the smallest chair which as a puppy he had chosen as his bed although he had long grown into a seventy pound dog whose head and stub-tail overhung both arms of the chair.

But he has become a happy dog with less and less inclination to do his tricks. He has moved into the place left by Prince which long ago had been occupied by their father, old Rex. He is Boss! There is a new puppy, out of Folly's latest litter, who is growing up—this time Baby's son. I hope to do better by both of them and prevent the frustrations that turned Baby ino an unhappy show-off. The thing that is most endearing about dogs, and especially about Boxers, is that each one has his own personality and that they are so profoundly like children.

# VIII: MALABAR JOURNAL

## Spring 1945

Have you become a farmer? Is it not pleasanter than to be shut up within 4 walls and delving eternally with a pen? . . . I have proscribed newspapers . . . my next reformation will be to allow neither pen, ink nor paper to be kept on the farm. When I have accomplished this I shall be in a fair way to indemnifying myself for the drudgery to which I have proved my life. If you are half as much delighted with the farm as I am, you bless your stars at your riddance from public cares.

—Thomas Jefferson in a letter to Henry Knox, Boston Book seller

MARCH 1: A long gap, but there seems no end to demands on time. The deep snow has gone and the spring came suddenly in two or three days with brilliant sun and a few showers. I hope it is here to stay. The suddenness put a quick end to sugar-making. Good maple syrup weather means cold freezing nights alternating with warm, sunny days. The nights have been mild, almost hot and all the sap has rushed up out of the ground into the high branches and twigs, swelling the buds and casting a faint cloud of pinkish green over the whole of the woods. While the sugar run lasted, the camp became as always the center of farm life. Even Ma had to clump through the mud with her cane. It brought back very old memories of her father's day. On Sundays neighbors and people from town kept coming and going all day. It was like a festival marking the wakening of the New Year. Certainly it is one of the most pleasurable ceremonies and in these times of sugar shortage it is good to have the storeroom full of maple syrup and honey.

Chris Hugert who has taken care of the bees for years gave it up this year to go permanently to live in New Mexico because of his health, and Sunday his cousins came to take over the job—a pair of big, hearty countrymen, very different from poor asthmatic Chris. They went over the hives and found that the bees in four of them were dead. It has been a hard winter for bees with the snow drifted high up around the hives and the temperature always close to zero with many blizzards. There seemed to be plenty of honey for them still to feed on. The shortage was in pollen but the quick turn to spring has brought out all the catkins and crocuses and all around them the air buzzes with the sound of wings.

I would like to care for the bees but it is one of the most complicated professions in the world. The person who thinks that all one has to do to have honey is to put up a couple of hives has much to learn. There is a book—a very thick one— called *The A.B.C. of Bees*, but to me it is more confusing than a book on advanced mathematics.

Today Kenneth, Bob, and I built fences between the lower blue-grass pasture and the cemetery field. It was a brilliant day and that corner of the farm is one of the loveliest spots— a kind of bowl with the big trees of the virgin forest on one side raising their top branches a hundred feet and more above the sugar camp. A spring stream wanders through the pasture with ox-bow ponds filled with young fish and bordered by water cress, marsh marigold, and skunk cabbage. The steep cemetery field is planted to wheat which has grown prodigiously in a few warm days and looks like a carpet of emerald green velvet. All the dogs—Prince, Baby, Gina, Susie, Folly, Kitchee and Smokey—played in the fields and chased squirrels and lay flat in the shallow water when they grew hot and tired. George Cook came down when the school bus dropped him off, his pockets filled with marbles, another sign of spring. Jim hauled manure out of the Fleming barn on to the small garden to make it ready for plowing. Charlie already has onions, lettuce, radishes and beets planted. Yesterday he was in a rage because Charlie Schrack's big red sows broke out, traveled down the creek and rooted up part of what he had done. I don't blame him.

The lower fish pond came to life today with a vengeance. It was filled with fingerling bass and the mud-turtles were scuttering about. I saw forty or fifty bass a foot to fifteen inches long. They are out scouting for nests in the shallow water covering the sand and gravel. The blue-gills have not yet made their appearance. Taking the giant bass out of the pond last year was a good idea. They are cannibals and were eating up all the young. The increase in the number of fish is very apparent this year. There are still some big ones to be cleaned out.

The dime-store goldfish the children dumped into the pond five years ago have grown monstrous in size and vivid in color. I saw several females today, enormous with roe. The goldfish never increase in number—still the huge, venerable brilliant-colored originals. On the edge of the pond the first red-winged blackbirds have appeared in numbers, looking for nesting sites on the hummocks of grass and among the cat-tails. The big gray Toulouse geese are fussing about on the islands making nests. I must take down a couple of straw bales tomorrow for them. I hope we shall have better luck this year with the goslings, now that we caught a giant snapping turtle offside in the pasture last summer. The geese can drive off the foxes but the snapping turtles get the goslings. Nor do the guinea fowl ever lose a single chick from the foxes. I think they put up such an ungodly racket they drive them off.

The upper pond at the Big House stayed frozen over all the winter and many of the fish died, from lack of oxygen and sunlight I suppose. When the ice melted there were several big dead bass, about four or five pounds each, a dozen blue-gills and a huge carp, about fifteen to sixteen pounds, the only one in the pond. The children caught him in the Clear Fork as a young fellow and dumped him in. I thought carp could survive almost anything, but apparently this is not so.

Louise Reese came to lunch today before leaving for Florida. She may stay there or she may come back. I hope she returns. She is a merry companion, a great fisherman and has done as much for hunting and fishing, soil conservation and forestry as anyone in the County. She is one of those who realizes that if you create proper and natural surroundings you will have all the fish and game any sportsman could wish. She is not the fish-hatchery, pheasant-hatchery kind of sportsman. We shall miss her. I know of no man who finds more delight in the fields and streams and forests than Louise.

MAY 14: Another long gap with abominable weather. Never can I remember a worse spring. The fantastically warm weather of March brought out everything—alfalfa, bluegrass, ladino, fruit blossoms, garden flowers. The alfalfa and ladino were frozen back. All the new growth on the grapes froze as if it had been scalded. What magnolias the rabbits did not girdle and kill, froze in full flower. Even the dogwood is pinched and frozen-looking and the wild crab blossoms singed and without the wonderful perfume they usually have. The bluegrass and the wheat have turned yellowish.

Added to all this were cold and torrential rains. By industry and luck we managed to plant 60 acres of oats which are flourishing although there has been too much rain and cold even for the oats which usually like that kind of weather. But we are much more fortunate than most for our well-drained glacial hill land permits us to plow in almost any kind of weather. Despite the awful season we are almost ready to plant sudan grass and soybeans when the frost is past. Even in this County only 25 per cent of the oats has been planted. In the flat country none is in the ground, and by the time the soil is dried enough to plow, it will be too late to put it in. This will have a serious effect on feed supplies for the condition is not confined to Ohio but in general all through the richest part of the country. I hope this is not the "bad year" agriculturists have been fearing. We have had enormous luck with weather during the war. A "bad year" would be disastrous and affect the history of the world for generations to come. We have never been so short of food and the needs for ourselves and all the rest of the world have never been so great.

Margaret Reed, who is always cheerful, pointed out that the late and violent freezes may do good by killing millions of insect pests which otherwise would have survived the mild snowy winter. Deep snow lay on the ground from December to March with the ground scarcely frozen—a condition which is usually followed by hordes of corn borers, chinch bugs, grasshoppers, aphids and other pests. The spittle bug has already been working on the alfalfa.

220

VE day has come and gone with few but the fools using the occasion as one of celebration. There is indeed very little to celebrate. Here we celebrated it by plowing all day—as good a way as I can think of. There is a particular delight in plowing this year especially in our bottom land in the Muskingum Conservancy. It is our only really flat land—two great fields, one of 90 acres and one of 70. Most of it is fine gravel loam that turns beautifully under the plow, but it was worn out by generations of hog-greedy farmers and very nearly abandoned until we rented it. To bring it back we have been practicing a rotation of corn, oats, and sweet clover. It was Bob's idea and a sound one for the land is too far from the barns to haul manure to it.

This year the "catch" of sweet and mammoth clover which followed liming is thick and lush and green—so beautiful that farmers came from all around to look at it. When you pull up a plant the roots are thick with nodules taking nitrogen from the air and fixing it in the worn-out soil. It is worth countless dollars per acre in expensive nitrogen fertilizer which we cannot buy today even if we could afford it. And the green tops plowed under will put back huge quantities of nitrogen and tons of the humus that the starved land needs so badly. No wonder that all of us look backward over the plow to watch the crumbling soil swallowing up all that richness. We came home at night with stiff necks and crooked backs from leaning over to watch.

We have been trying a lot of experiments with the big field—shallow plowing, deep plowing, burying all the green stuff and also setting the plows so that they do not completely bury it but set it on end mixing it *into* the earth. One strip we are Faulknerizing—chopping it all *into* the earth with "bush-and-bog" harrows which are really heavy, superdisks. It will be interesting to see what the results will be after the corn is planted. It is the sort of thing which makes farming a fascinating occupation and a "live" one.

Gradually we are becoming able to grow more and better corn on half the land. Perhaps presently we shall grow as much on a third of the land as we once did on all of it. Then we shall be approaching the goal of making every acre produce 100 per cent of potentiality without loss of fertility, perhaps even, as in parts of Europe, with a gradual increase. The sweet clover is doing it with its wonderful capacity for translating sun and air and water into nitrogen and organic material. One thing I noticed this year while looking backward over the plow was the great increase in the population of earthworms. That is a good sign.

The crows followed us as we plowed, unfortunately gobbling up some of the earthworm population. They are birds with scarcely a redeeming feature and in the Conservancy land they are a pest for it is surrounded by wild country and forest which gives them cover, where they gather in great colonies. Once the corn has begun to sprout they descend on the fields and tear it up grain by grain. We finally put an end to that by using something called Crow-tox applied to the corn before planting. It does not kill them but produces a burning sensation in their gullets and, being very shrewd birds, they soon connect the cause and effect and leave our fields alone. Clem Herring told me that he used to rid himself of them by using hen's eggs into which he had injected strychnine through a small hole at one end, sealing the hole afterward with paraffin. These he scattered about the fields. On several occasions he killed foxes instead of crows. Both are pests in our country and both are crafty and maddening. If you have a shotgun, they will come nowhere near you, but if you are unarmed, they become as bold as Moses.

While we were plowing the Conservancy land all seven dogs were with me and the crows tormented them all afternoon, descending quite near to them in a tantalizing way, only to leave the ground just as the maddened dogs came within a foot or two of them. They would chase the crows for an hour and then go down to the Clear Fork and throw themselves into the water, swimming about and lapping the clear, cold water greedily, and then return to the futile chase. They seemed to enjoy it although they got not so much as a crow feather as a reward.

The Clear Fork Valley is unbelievably beautiful with the steep wooded hills all about it, the lake mirroring the blue sky and the trees ranging in shade all the way from the black-green of the hemlock against the red sandstone cliffs through all the soft pastel shades of green, some of it pink and yellow and pale red. The young foliage of the red oaks is a deep pink so that it makes the tree appear as if it were covered with deep pink blossoms. The white dogwood and the pink wild crab grow all along the edge of the forest above the water, and through it all runs the wide thick carpet of pale emerald-green sweet clover, slowly turning to brown as the earth swallows it up behind the tractors that move across the field like shuttles on a gigantic loom. There is no smell quite so good as fresh-turned sweet earth, and all afternoon it was tinged with the vanilla-like smell of sweet clover being crushed by the moving wheels of the tractor.

Ma came with me and the dogs in the old Ford station wagon and sat there with her sewing all afternoon watching the plowing. She brought a gallon jug of fresh buttermilk which we kept cool in the running spring water and drank when we grew thirsty. It was buttermilk made of sweet cream with little flecks of golden bluegrass butter floating in it.

Once during the afternoon, I thought, "Paradise must be like this."

After supper we returned to the plowing and Harry and Naomi joined us with their three small children. Harry entertained them by carrying them in turn on his lap as he drove the tractor. In the old days they would have ridden on the fat back of a Percheron. It is remarkable how much children like machinery on a farm. One of our worst problems is to keep them off it. Even "Butch," George's nephew, and George Cook who are only seven have figured out how to drive a tractor and get aboard the moment you turn your back. They aren't afraid of tractors as they sometimes are of horses.

We stayed out until nearly dark—Jim, Kenneth, Harry and I—plowing, until a wild thunderstorm came up. We tried to beat it in a race back to the house but lost the race and came in drenched.

JUNE 6: May has whizzed by with some of the worst weather we have had in the history of Ohio. The freakish spring has been disastrous. The hot weather in March ruined the sugar run and brought out all the fruit trees into blossom, only to be slaughtered by the hard freeze of May and the frosts of early June. Added to the cold it has rained incessantly so that in the flat country—much of it the most fertile part of the Middle West—it has been impossible to plow. Thousands of acres of oats have never been planted and the land will probably be put into soybeans to add to the glut. Some corn land is still too wet to plow.

In such seasons I am thankful for our well-drained hills and glacial soil which can be worked almost any time. Owing to these advantages and Bob's good planning and organization we put in 90 acres of oats in March and have about 160 acres of corn planted and above ground. The wheat looks wonderful—almost like the fields in the Oise where the wheat, on land that has been farmed for a thousand years, lies even and level with scarcely room for another head. The wheat we pastured last autumn is better than the unpastured wheat. In our experience pasturing wheat does it no harm and in a cold, late spring such as this, pasturing does good by holding back the heading-out. In the unpastured fields some of the heads are not quite filled out at the bottom, owing to the cold. One year we even turned sheep on to the wheat without harming it.

There has been a long stream of visitors of all kinds— farmers, industrialists, government officials, foreigners, and friends. None of the bedrooms has been empty since March. Yesterday Lotsie and I finished the play. It is about a Pasadena woman who becomes a destructive monster through her addiction to spiritualistic seances. Ince who wants to produce the play with Arthur Hopkins arrived yesterday. Both

Lotsie and Ince are Hungarians and last night after dark we played with them what can only be described as Transylvanian bridge—very gay but erratic to put it mildly.

Charlie and I worked till dark putting in canteloupe and watermelon. It has been too wet and cold up to now. It is lucky that we did, for today it is raining again the kind of rain we should have had in May—warm, heavy showers.

P. T. Raman and Himat Sinhji, two Indian friends, spent a week end with us. Raman is perhaps India's most distinguished journalist and Himat Sinhji is a colonel in the Indian Army. He is the brother of the Maharajah of Jamnagar and in peacetime is largely responsible for the good administration of the state. Two more delightful and entertaining companions it would be hard to find. Roger and Helen Kyes and the Indians got together over the Ferguson machinery. Roger induced both of them to take a plow and tractor round one of the fields. Raman is no mechanic and Himat has never even driven a car, although he did not tell us until afterward. The tractor took them in hand and presently returned with each one, white-faced and terrified but safe.

We devised a plan for Himat's return home to his state. Instead of riding triumphantly on an elephant he would enter raised high in the air on the platform of the Ferguson apple picker.

Both Raman and Himat were impressed by the immense usefulness of the Ferguson tractor in India. A Ferguson tractor and implements in any Indian village could change the whole life of India, socially, economically, and even politically.

The visit gave birth to a plan which Himat is taking to General Auchinleck, Commander-in-Chief of the Indian Army, in London next week. The Indian soldier—so Himat says—is one of the best elements for promoting advances in India. He has traveled and learned to read and write and many of the men speak English and all speak Hindustani, the universal language in India. (The language problem with some twenty-seven languages, not dialects, is one of the countless complexities of India.) They have learned about machinery and most of them make excellent mechanics. Nearly all of them are *ryots*, coming from farms and villages.

Himat's plan is to set up a number of farms scattered over India based upon the plan set up at Malabar—cooperatives, financed by private capital as an investment. There is, as Himat says, almost unlimited capital available in India for such a purpose. The farms would be staffed by demobilized soldiers and their families and equipped with modern agricultural machinery. They would also have an educational function as "pilot" farms like those of the T.V.A. which could be visited by other farmers. It is a good idea which could have a great effect upon a huge agricultural country like India. Most people don't understand that 80 percent and more of India's population lives on farms and in villages. It is no good to plan industrial development in India without at the same time developing an agricultural program which will provide more food and better living standards and create purchasing power for the products of industry.

Export markets for manufactured goods, especially those of heavy industry are certain to go on shrinking as such countries as Russia, India, and China grow more self-sufficient. That is one of the facts that stands very much in the way of the reestablishment of the United Kingdom as a great and rich "processing" nation.

In New York, Colonel Robert Henriques and I talked at great length on this British question. He, like all Britishers, is alarmed about the future of the British Isles and like most Britishers he is not optimistic. He suggested a decentralization of the Empire and the Commonwealth of Nations in which there was a closer *federalized* relationship between the Dominions, Commonwealth and Colonies, and the mother country, with the Crown moving from one to another at periods of the year. It is the best solution I have yet heard suggested for Britain's troubles.

He also made, jestingly, a good solution for trade reciprocation—that Britishers acquire a taste for Rye and Bourbon whiskies and send Scotch in return for the many Americans who prefer it. He has learned to prefer American whiskies. I, myself, still prefer Scotch, so we should be doing all right.

JUNE 7: Back again from selling War Bonds in Indiana and New England. I know of no tougher work—beginning every

226

morning at nine o'clock with a municipal breakfast, then schools and colleges till noon when big lunch comes up. Then women's clubs and civic organizations all the afternoon and a big public dinner in the evening followed by a meeting of thousands in the largest available auditorium. Then a late train, rarely on time, to the next town. Thousands of people, dozens of speeches, handshaking by the hour, banquet food, sketchy train connections and not even five minutes rest all day. And worst of all perhaps is the doubt that maybe I'm selling something that may not turn out so well. The war *has* to be carried on and to carry it on money is necessary. But I'm not too confident about the future if enormous taxes, scarcities, and inflation continue. If I had not lived through two wars and watched the sagging economy of every country in Europe, I might be less concerned.

The weather continues to be abominable. Frost on June 6th and 7th with two or three days of terribly hot weather, followed by rain, rain, rain. There will be damned little corn "knee-high by the Fourth of July" this year. Our own may be but we are used to having it hip-high by that time. If it doesn't stop raining the weeds will be knee-high but not the corn. We have mowed ten acres of beautiful alfalfa-brome grass hay which has been rained on steadily for nearly a week. It is a total loss. The beef cattle may pick up some of it but it is really only fit for bedding.

In the flat country the corn is being drowned out and much of it is not yet planted. According to Director of Agriculture Hodson only about 30 per cent of the oats was planted in Ohio. On flat land even that is being drowned out. With the food shortage a reality and half the world starving, the prospects are grim. The Black Market is practicing wholesale. With little or no poultry in the market and people standing in line to buy two or three eggs or getting none at all, Black Marketers and even legitimate dealers are buying up laying hens, thin and tough, at three and three-fifty apiece. One farmer I know was offered $3500 cash for 100 skinny leghorn laying hens by a man who drove up in a truck ready to carry them off. These same poor hens will sell for five and six dollars apiece in city Black Markets.

The whole of the food situation was inevitable. The theories of administration economists could produce nothing but the present tragic shortages. It is impossible to regulate food production unless ceilings are placed upon every element concerned with food—the producer, the feeder, the processor, the distributor—and those ceilings must be adjusted at least monthly in order to keep pace with the value of the dollar which inflates in time of scarcity and easy money despite anything government bureaucracy can do. None of these things has been done and the result has been first gluts and lowered ceilings and checked production and then bitter scarcities. The end is not yet, nor is improvement in sight. Those of us who predicted the shortages and Black Markets two years ago, even so wise a man as Mr. Baruch, were mocked at by the "bright young men" who have today become discredited. Once price controls are lifted and supply and demand again operate, the public will forget shortages and Black Markets quickly enough. I am not so sure of prices; there is too much money in circulation.

Unfortunately the results of malnutrition arising from deficiencies of a protein diet are not immediately perceptible save in terms of lowered vitality and efficiency and an increase in absenteeism in factories. The results, however, linger long afterward in children and young people. The protein deficiencies of the First World War are still evident in the physique of mature Europeans of today. Some day people and government will come to realize that physically and in so far as diet is concerned, there is little difference between people and animals—except perhaps that animals have more sense. If you put before a hog all the ingredients of a perfect diet he will balance it perfectly himself, choosing something of this and something of that. If you did the same thing for many a city stenographer she would still lunch on an ice cream soda and a pickle. If you offered the "poor white" a perfectly balanced diet he would be likely to turn instead to his hominy, sow belly and turnip greens grown on worn-out soil, devoid of calcium, of potassium, of phosphorus—indeed of practically everything—and containing nothing to make either a strong or an intelligent or an energetic human being.

This winter we made a record in the laying house. Seven hundred leghorn pullets produced over six hundred eggs a day for six months. Even now after eight months of laying they have only fallen to around 500 at the lowest. There has been *no* cannibalism and no range paralysis.

The trace mineral feeding has great results here as elsewhere in the feeding of livestock. I am delighted to see the laying mash largely done away with, for it brought us about five different kinds of noxious weeds which we have never had before on the farm, among them quack grass. The seeds were distributed through those parts of the vegetable and flower gardens where only chicken manure was used. The check is absolute. There is no doubt as to where they came from.

JUNE 17: I mowed hay on the Ferguson Place until twilight. It was good clover and alfalfa mixture, so thick that it was hard to get the mower through it—a wonderful sight, some forty acres of it on the top of what was once a bare, bald hill where even the scanty weeds were sickly. I remember well the first time I saw that particular field—a gullied, bare cornfield unprotected during the whole of the winter and covered with a stubble of puny cornstalks. Today there is not a gully an inch deep on the whole of the Ferguson Place, or the whole of Malabar for that matter. It is a real hill farm worn-out and abandoned only five years ago. Today it is raising wonderful alfalfa and bluegrass and white-clover pasture that looks like a beautiful English lawn. In fact, after the pasture is mowed the whole place looks like a lovely park with the springs, the big trees, the cave and the waterfall where the water comes in trickles out of the overhanging sandstone. You can stand under one of the streams and drink the icy water merely by tilting your head and opening your mouth. Baby, one of the Boxers, has learned the trick and always drinks there. It is odd how all animals prefer cold, clean, *living* water if they can get it.

While I mowed this afternoon a whole army of fat, half-grown young rabbits kept coming out of the alfalfa ahead of the mower. There is something very engaging about them. During the morning I uncovered a woodchuck lair and as I came round the second time, I noticed something moving beneath the fresh mown hay. It was the young woodchuck himself returning home. Evidently I had caught him out and he was creeping back under cover of the hay. I stopped mowing until he was safely home again. In a week or two the alfalfa will be grown up again to give him cover. They are odd beasts, full of charm, always fat and always a little lazy. They seem to get all the water they need from the clover and the dew for many of them choose to dig their homes high on the hills away from water. On the other hand the marshes next to our corn land in the Conservancy are filled with woodchuck holes. Often enough, when the lake level rises they are flooded out and have to dig new homes on higher land.

Three times this spring I have had puzzling experiences with wild animals. Early in the year we found a woodchuck in the fork of a sapling a good ten feet above the ground. He lay there resting on his elbows, showing no alarm, not even stirring when I poked him with a stick to make certain he was not caught in the fork of the sapling. He seemed very sleepy. I do not know whether he had just come out of hibernation or had climbed the tree to die in peace. The next day he was gone. I have never before heard of a woodchuck with tree-climbing habits. In June, I encountered another woodchuck in the middle of the road below the Big House. He showed no inclination to run away and when I turned the old Ford slowly toward him, he held his ground and gnashed his teeth at me. At last I drove off leaving him there but when I returned later the same day he was lying dead in the road, the victim of some driver, more bloodthirsty than I.

Yesterday in the Bailey barnyard I came on a young rabbit feeding on the spilled corn from the old crib we tore down. He showed no fear and paid no attention to me, except to move away about ten feet. As I moved toward him he kept just out of reach stopping and turning now and then to regard me without fear but with curiosity. I talked to him for a time and he seemed to like the sound of my voice. I went away and he returned to the scattered corn. Fortunately the dogs were not along.

The only time they do not go with me is when I go out with the power mower. They have learned that the mower means long hours of boredom and heat for them while I go round and round a hay field. And I think they don't like it because they cannot *ride* on the tractor.

Evening on the Ferguson Place has a beauty that is almost unbearable. The whole farm lies against the sky with a view of thirty miles across Pleasant Hill lake and a panorama of hills and valleys, woodland, and farms. It is like the lake country of England on a much bigger scale. Last night Anne went for a walk just before dinner and was caught in a wild thunderstorm. When she did not return I took the power mower and went up to the Ferguson Place, thinking she might have gone to the cave to collect some of the fungi and the pre-glacial moss and primitive plants that grow there. The cave lies at the head of a wild, deep ravine and there is always danger of falling. When there was no sign of her I stayed up there and mowed pasture.

The whole place was wet and green after the thunderstorm. Even the light seemed green and while I mowed, the shadows in the valley turned blue and the mist began to rise from the soaked earth into the air, chilled by the storm and the heavy hail that had fallen in the northern part of the County. On the top of the hill the shadows of the trees grew longer and longer and bluer and bluer across the emerald green of the bluegrass and clover. Presently the cattle came up to the top of the hill, their favorite feeding spot in the evening when the air begins to cool. In the heat of the day they stay deep in the bottom of the ravine in the shade of the great trees where a spring stream and the damp sandstone keeps the air too cool and moist for flies. Indeed the whole Ferguson Place is a kind of paradise for cattle with the deepwooded ravine, the cold water, the springs, the bluegrass and white clover and when that grows short in August the whole of a field of knee-deep alfalfa and ladino to replace it.

Few things are more pleasant than to sit watching the herd. The big white bull is a docile fellow who pays you no attention. At first the cows and calves will gather round you to study you for a while. If you sit quite still and the dogs are not along, they will come quite close and nuzzle you, and then, presently, they will go away again to eat lazily. But the young calves stay around, skittering off in mock alarm if you make a sudden movement, only to return in a little while to watch you like children daring each other to come closer and closer. As you lie on your back in the thick blue-

231

grass looking up at the sky you can hear all about you the "whisk-crunch" as they eat their way across the meadow.

The herd seems to lead a very ordered existence, always remaining together and the cows feeding their calves at prescribed hours—morning and evening. During the day they will put all the calves together in a kind of kindergarten well hidden in a copse while the herd goes roaming. If you stumble upon the kindergarten, the calves will lie quite still at first but if you disturb them at all, they will set up a bellowing and are answered at once by the mother even if they are a mile away on the opposite side of the big pasture. The calves will high-tail for their mothers who come running anxiously from the opposite direction.

The other herd, of Shorthorn cows on the Bailey Place are ruled by Blondy, the patriarchal coal black Angus bull. He takes his paternal responsibilities more seriously than the white bull, Elmer, and will always stay behind to guard the kindergarten although he is never alone but accompanied by two or three of the cows on watch. I do not know how he selected the honored ladies-in-waiting. I wish I did.

Just at dark Anne appeared, flushed from the long climb up the hill through the woods to tell me she had been found. She had gone up the road toward Hastings and stopped in at the Areharts when the storm broke. She "visited" after the storm and forgot all about dinner. She stayed with me for a while clearing fallen branches out of the path of the mower. The dogs came with her and were glad to see me but disappointed at the sight of the mower. When Anne left they did their best to make me return home, too, barking and jumping and carrying on generally. Prince came back twice after Anne started down the hill and finally gave up and went home with her.

Finally, while I mowed, a blue-wet darkness came down and the valleys and woods and farms faded out first into a blue mist and then into blackness, starred with the distant lights of farmhouses and the comets of moving light made by cars on the roads far below, I turned on the tractor lights and kept on mowing and the whole herd found a new curiosity in the lights. The calves frisked round and round me as I mowed and even the cows would stand in front of me staring at the lights until the last moment. When I yelled at them they would frisk off kicking their heels high in the air, their udders bouncing about ludicrously, giving that "rabbit-punch" kick which can break your leg if you come into contact with it. Altogether they enjoyed the evening, I think, as much as I did.

About ten-thirty I gave it up and set out for home down the steep, rocky lane that goes through a tunnel of woods bordered by ferns and laced with wild grapevines. All the way down I had an eerie feeling that I was being watched by the eyes of wild things—foxes and raccoons and mice and owls. Once, near Jim Pugh's cabin the lights caught a pair of green, phosphorescent eyes that may have been one of the cata-mounts that live on the hill opposite the Big House. Or it may only have been a fox or a raccoon. In any case the goose pimples rose all over me and my hair stood on end like the hair of a dog.

Smokey and Baby stayed at the house last night instead of going down to the barracks to sleep with the boys who have come to work on the farm during the summer. Usually they spend the day following Charlie who feeds them or following me while I am plowing or working in the fields. With Charlie and me both away they were lost and deserted my room for the company of the boys. Prince still slept in my room with Dusky, the Cocker. Both Gina and Folly were at Dr. Wadsworth's—Folly to be bred. Gina not to be. While Charlie and I were away Prince, Baby and Smokey fought incessantly, once knocking Ma out of her chair on to the lawn.

Boxers are strange dogs. They have no tramp habits and will not go fifty yards from the house unless they have human company. They are affectionate but never groveling. In fact, I sometimes find myself groveling to them, especially to Baby, who is a clown and a ham actor, but still possessed some-how of an immense dignity and indifference. If you do any-thing foolish or unworthy, they know it and do not hesitate to let you know.

This year the boys are living in a Quonset Hut given us by the company which manufactures them to discover farm uses for them. The four boys working on the farm, Eddie who is working in the big garden, and Jim and Bob Cook all live there—Army fashion. It is cool and airy. There is a weird assortment of beds, ranging from army cots to brass and iron beds. Nowadays you have to take what you can get. Most of the boys come from Cleveland but Craven comes from St. Louis and Eddie from Tiffin, Ohio. It is remarkable how well they turn out, considering the fact that we have seen them at most only once before and some of them not at all. There has never been one we had to send away. Two or three times we have had boys who didn't work out very well at first but always they developed into good responsible workers. Most of the older ones have gone into the Service as they reached the age of eighteen. Without them we should have to curtail farming operations or shut down altogether. They help with hay-making, straw-baling, fence-building, lime-spreading, and corn-cultivating. It is a good summer life.

With mechanization they don't go to work until eight o'clock and are finished at six with all the long summer evenings free. There is swimming, fishing and riding. What they like best is tinkering with the old cars and motors in the farm repair shed. They turn out some mechanical monsters, made up of parts drawn from a half dozen old cars, but they seem to run somehow.

Jimmy Caddick, who has graduated as a veteran to the position of foreman, bought Johnny's and Dave's old jalopy when they went into the Army. It is a 1930 Ford with flags and foxtails flying, painted bright yellow. Jimmy is, like Johnny and Dave, a remarkable fellow—conscientious and capable as a grown man, with a wonderful sense of humor. Like the other boys he came here in summer to keep in training for football but in the end he and all the others decided to take up agriculture, in one form or another. I think it is because they find here how fascinating and how profitable agriculture can be but most of all they like the life and the deep satisfaction of soil and animals and trees and wild life. Bob is largely responsible for this interest for he seems to make everything on the farm take on an added zest. The boys have a real sense of *participation* in what is a fascinating job of restoration and soil management. That is also the reason why all of us get on so well together. It is not a question of hired labor or of merely working for a living. Everything that happens is I think charged with interest and a sense of achievement and satisfaction. Emma, Tom's wife, cooks for the boys. They eat at the miller's house, where Ceely Rose murdered her whole family, and do their own washing in Bob's basement with Virginia's washing machine.

When the war is over and we can buy or build what we need, we shall probably take on fifteen or twenty boys instead of five of six. The waiting list is already far beyond our capacity to handle. Vane Close has two boys from Cleveland helping him this summer. They come over frequently on Sunday and in the evening. The kids like all the machinery and seem to prefer the life to that of a vacation in a summer camp. Also they earn money which most of them put away for college. Meanwhile they have contributed mightily to the food supply in wartime.

The week end was terrific. The four Texans came back with us from the Cincinnati conservation meeting sponsored by the Junior Chamber of Commerce. Also Roy and Marie Ballinger. So the house was full. The Texans are Victor Schoffelmayer, agricultural editor of the Dallas *Morning News* who, with Mr. Dealey and his son, the owners, make up a strong force for good agriculture in the whole of Texas and among the best in the whole of the United States; Dave Reed, R. C. Schmid and Gilbert Wilson. Reed is a big oil operator and owns hundreds of thousands of acres in Texas. Schmid, born in Switzerland, is his manager and Gilbert Wilson is the man who invented the sweet potato dehydrating process which has played a large part in the war effort. All four are filled with Texas gusto and the week end was gay and filled with laughs. Schoffelmayer is the most serious of the lot and a fine musician as well. He lured Reed and Schmid up here to convert them to better uses of the huge agricultural holdings owned by Reed. Schmid is a dynamo, and Wilson the slow drawling kind of Texan, who couldn't keep up with the volatile Schmid but when he found an opening in the conversation scored heavily. Reed has about as much gusto as I've ever encountered. Nobody is more charming or better company than the Ballingers.

On Saturday night Billy Foster and his band came up from Delaware for the annual square dance before the big barn is filled with hay. Bob, Kenneth, Harry and the boys spent two days cleaning the big mows and arranging bales of straw as seats all around the edges. We furnish the music and the soft drinks and everybody brings box lunches. Each year the dance gets bigger. This year there were about seven hundred, mostly from Richland and the neighboring counties, but there were people from all over the state. The boys acted as traffic policemen and had a Ferguson tractor on duty to haul those who got stuck out of the mud. I think everybody had a good time. The party lasted until well after midnight and then broke up into other parties—one at Jim Pugh's cabin and one in the Big House with Billy Foster, his band and friends, having a couple of drinks for the road. There is no better square-dance band in the world and no better caller than Billy Foster. I think the prize for dancing went to Jeff and his wife. They are sixty or over but he can throw her high in the air on the turns. It is odd how much square dancing done with gusto resembles modern jitterbugging—the same zest for pure dancing without much sex thrown in.

# IX: MALTHUS WAS RIGHT

Beef, mutton, and pork, shred pies of the best,
Pig, veal, goose and capon, and turkey well drest,
Cheese, apples and nuts, jolly carols to hear,
As then in the country is counted good cheer.
                                        —Thomas Tusser

LONG ago Liberty Hyde Bailey, the Dean of one of the world's greatest agricultural colleges at Cornell University, wrote "The farmer was the first man and he will be the last man."

He had in mind the eternal and classic relationship of Man to the Earth and his ultimate dependence upon the earth. He also had in mind the fact that man first began his upward climb toward civilization when he began to till the soil, and the fact that, at periods in history when civilization falls apart, as it seems on the verge of doing today, when food becomes man's major preoccupation, the land, even the fortified farm, provides man's ultimate security.

Since Dean Bailey wrote these words, much has happened in the world to emphasize their immense significance. Perhaps, despite the breadth of the Dean's great vision, much has happened which was beyond his calculations at the time he wrote.

First among these happenings is the fact—not merely the threat—of world famine, caused largely by war, devastation, droughts and dislocations of distribution. The fact of famine has brought to public attention much information regarding food which hitherto was either unavailable or overlooked, especially in this country where abundance of food has, in the past, always been the rule and where people either did not know or believe or consider the fact that at least two-

237

thirds of the world's population suffered, even before the second World War, from serious malnutrition and that at least a fourth to a fifth of the world's population lives perpetually at a starvation level; being born and dying without having enough to eat for a single day in their lives.

A little over a century ago there died in England a man about whose theories controversy raged among philosophers, intellectuals, economists, and sociologists throughout the greater part of his lifetime. His name was Thomas Robert Malthus and he was no fool. He was educated at Oxford University with a distinguished scholastic record and later became a practical and efficient administrator of the affairs of the British East India company. His ideas stimulated the thinking of Darwin and Huxley but for nearly a century he was, in many circles, the object of mockery and derision. He is known to history as the originator of the Malthusian Theory—that one day, not too far distant from this time, the population of the world would outstrip its available food supply. Explicitly, Malthus claimed that population, when unchecked by artificial means, increases in geometric ratio while substance only increases in mathematical ratio, and that population always increases up to the limit of the means of subsistence. He contended that population is prevented from increasing beyond these limits only by the positive checks of war, famine, pestilence and by the influence of misery and vice.[1]

In popular thought and in the case of many distinguished thinkers, the theories of Malthus were discredited or derided during the whole of the nineteenth century. However, shortly after the beginning of the twentieth century, a few isolated scientists and thinkers began to see that the theories of Malthus, so well documented and clearly thought out, were not so fantastic as they were held to be in the nineteenth century. Even the *Encyclopedia Britannica* in its recent editions notes that "since the European war of 1914–18,

[1] It is interesting to note that the father of Malthus was a friend and one of the executors of Jean Jacques Rousseau. He was also a friend and shared the beliefs of Godwin and Condorcet, with which his son differed. Out of the controversy between father and son grew the first pamphlet written by Malthus which became the basis of the Malthusian Theory.

however, the spectre of overpopulation has returned and
Malthus is coming into his own again."

I think most of us, even the man whose primary interests
are the sport page and the comics, is willing to agree today
that Thomas Robert Malthus had something. The bitter truth
is that we are having our noses rubbed in the Malthusian
theory. It has become clear that the population of the world
has outstripped the means of its subsistence or at least approached a balance so precarious that a drought or a dislocation of transportation in any part of the world can today
produce famine over large areas. It is also true that some
millions of people, particularly in Asia, suffer all their lives
from *slow* famine and die by the millions in non-famine years
either of actual starvation or of the weakness and diseases
arising from severe malnutrition. Even in the United States,
in city slums and worn-out agricultural areas, some thousands, perhaps hundreds of thousands, of people suffer from
severe malnutrition approaching slow starvation.

Probably Malthus was right in his main premise, but many elements have arisen which prove him to have been even more right than he knew. He died before the industrial revolution was in full swing and out of it grew many factors which he failed to foresee. During the nineteenth century, it was claimed, for example, that Malthus failed to foresee the astonishing development of transport and colonization which increased so enormously the area from which foodstuffs and raw materials could be drawn. In a sense the increase of colonization and means of transport only proved the rightness of Malthus' Theory, for the industrial revolution and colonization simply served to increase the population of the world more than five times since Malthus' own lifetime. In other words, as new lands opened up they quickly filled up with populations largely to the limits of subsistence and as increasing means of transport developed, certain areas, depending upon food imported from the outside, actually filled up far beyond their independent means of subsistence.

This is the fact which we face today and the principal reason why certain vast areas, dependent upon food from outside sources, are immediately subject to real famine the moment there is a dislocation of supply, transport, or distribution. The recent famine in Bengal where nearly two million people died when Burmese rice supplies were shut off was a perfect example, and it must be remembered that some millions of Bengalese even in normal times live continuously and perilously close to the borders of starvation.

Malthus did not foresee directly the quick and enormous increase in world population, nor did he take into consideration certain other elements which have developed or become understood since his day. He has been credited with stimulating Darwin's thought and with being partly responsible for Darwin's development of the theory of selective breeding and the survival of the fittest. Yet Malthus failed to understand that countries like India and China, with large populations living perpetually near to the line of starvation, had under Darwin's theory gradually *bred out* the weak and the unfit, so that each succeeding generation became increasingly tough and fit and more able to survive famine and disease. Consequently deaths, either in infancy or later in life caused by malnutrition, became in each generation fewer and fewer. In other words, in these broad cases the checking effects upon populations of misery, vice etc., were partly nullified by the breeding out of the weaker and more unfit elements. Both the so-called "Untouchables" and the Tamils of South India are notable examples of a toughness and a resistence to disease, starvation and malnutrition which permits them to survive somehow when, under similar conditions, western peoples, accustomed to better diet and a softer life, would quickly succumb. The average Chinese coolie is also a notable example of *bred up* resistance through the gradual elimination of the weaker stock.

At the same time that in the East the age-old process of survival of the fittest was in operation, the West, with its better diets and softer living, was keeping alive a much higher percentage of the weak and unfit to breed and thus increase populations. Also through advances in science the West was keeping alive countless numbers of weak and unfit who, under *natural* or at least under *primitive* circumstances would not have survived to increase the population still further. By increasing the span of life of the average person by many years science is steadily adding to already great populations many millions more mouths to be fed in each generation. More recently the discovery and effective use of penicillin, streptomycin and other various sulfa drugs had already done much to cure or eliminate the evil effects of venereal disease in the direction of sterility or the procreation of weak individuals who previously had small chance to survive to maturity and the breeding age. In other words, with the means of checking the natural effects of venereal disease, countless children will be born and survive who in the past would not have been born at all or would through weakness have quickly succumbed. All of these "artificial" conditions have served more and more to nullify the effects of the natural checks on populations operating through disease and vice. These effects Malthus had considered beneficent in so far as the creation of excess populations was concerned. Very largely they have disappeared, at least in the western world.

And in Malthus' time, the rule that as living standards decline, the birth rate increases was not fully understood, as indeed it is not fully understood even today. In every country in the world the highest birth rate is at the lower economic levels and consequently in the levels where food and diet are limited. This element together with the Darwinian element of survival of the fittest, possibly accounts for an increase in population of approximately ten millions a year in a country like India which already is unable to feed its more than 400 million population.

Malthus, it must be said, placed no faith in continence as a means of checking populations and in this he was probably right. Birth-control methods of every sort appear to operate effectively only within the limits of the minority population living upon the higher economic levels. There would appear to be a natural law operating which, as living standards decline, the survival of the individual is imperiled, especially through malnutrition and the weakness and disease arising from it. There then occurs a kind of frenzy of breeding and reproduction in order to carry on the species. This law is understood by all livestock breeders who know that with a fat bull or a fat cow fed upon a rich diet, the rate of fecundity is much lower than with thinner animals.

All of these elements Malthus either partly overlooked or did not foresee, yet they have all hastened the development of the very conditions he predicted.

According to Department of Agriculture figures, the ratio of all possible agricultural land in the world, available for producing food under any existing methods of agriculture, is about two acres per person. Under this ratio, even if every individual in the world had his proportionate share of food, the world would still be unable to feed itself on any but a near-starvation diet of cereals. Under such a hypothetical division of food, high-protein animal foods such as meat, dairy and poultry products would have largely to be abandoned and we should all have to live upon a meager diet of rice, wheat, gram, barley, etc., relieved only by wild game or the high-protein foods available from the sea.

Such a diet is a fact in India, China, and Japan where population has for a long time far exceeded food production based on the diet to which Americans or even inhabitants of Europe are accustomed. This is so because it requires about seven pounds of grain to produce one pound of meat, a ratio which holds largely in the production of milk, eggs, cheese, and other high-protein foods. In other words

the people of the Far East live largely upon a diet of rice, relieved by occasional vegetables and fish, because they are compelled to if they are to survive. In such areas only the rich know the luxury of meat, poultry, and dairy products, because the price of these things through their scarcity or the high cost of their production is far beyond the incomes of 95 per cent of the population. Actually in this country we are beginning to approach the fringes of such a condition with declining agricultural production over large areas and a population increasing at the rate of over one million a year.

In addition to the declining ratio of agricultural land to population, another serious element which Malthus touched upon but did not develop, perhaps because of the vast agriculturally virgin colonial world opening up in his time, is the declining agricultural production *per acre* over most of the world's area. In very few areas in the world—notably France, Holland, Belgium, Denmark, Japan and parts of India—is there an agriculture of maximum maintained production of potentiality per acre. Elsewhere over vast areas the production per acre has been declining steadily from the time it was put under cultivation. This is particularly so in these newer areas which were largely counted upon to feed the world—the United States, Australia, the Argentine, Canada and even countries as new as South Africa and Venezuela. In these countries both the area of good agricultural lands and the production per acre are declining and have been, largely speaking, since they were first colonized. This is so because of the devastation caused by wind and water erosion and by poor, destructive and inefficient agriculture. Some once richly productive areas like that of North Africa (once the granary of the Roman Empire), the valleys of the Tigris and the Euphrates and vast areas of India and China have ceased to grow even sufficient food for the population of the immediate areas or have been turned virtually into desert regions. A similar process is in progress over large portions of the new "colonial" areas which opponents of Malthus claimed would nullify the operation of his theory. Already one-fourth of the good agricultural land of this nation has been destroyed by erosion and a poor agriculture and all but approximately 10 per cent of what remains is in the process of more or less rapid destruction by

244

floods, wind, and water erosion and by an agriculture which depletes the soil and lowers production per acre through a constant process of taking off more than is put back. Meanwhile the population of the United States continues to increase. This is exactly the process experienced by India and China in the past. The only fundamental difference is that it is occurring much more rapidly in this country than it did in India or China.

The declining production *per acre* (and it has been declining steadily since the first furrow was turned in this country, despite juggled statistics and arguments of politicians, economists and government bureau officials) is serious in the economic sense as well as in the sense of food production. By mathematical formula, the less food produced per acre, the more the cost of production is increased. This fact lies behind the rising cost of food for the last two generations. It lies largely behind the demands for higher and higher wages as the cost of living, of which food is the basic item, increases. It is also largely responsible for the "creeping inflation" which has been in progress during at least two generations and which becomes steadily more apparent as the population increases and the production per acre of food declines and the costs of production increase. As the costs, particularly of high-protein foods, increase through growing scarcities, lowered production *per acre,* and increased cost of production per bushel of corn and wheat, and consequently per egg or quart of milk or pound of meat, the prices of these foods rise higher and higher and restrict more and more the markets for them as the citizens of the lower economic levels are forced to forego high-protein animal foods, and eat meat, eggs, butter, etc., fewer and fewer times a week. This is what was meant by the statement made above that we are in the first stages of approaching, through declining food production and increasing population, the dietary standards of India, China, and Japan.

During the recent war, the farmers of the nation set up a series of record food productions, but never in any country at any time was food produced at so high a cost because the production per acre was so low and the cost of production, consequently, so high. The fact, more than any other, accounts for the introduction of subsidies, price controls, etc., and even the constant battle of the farm bloc for re-adjusted parity prices and steadily rising prices for farm commodities. It lies largely at the root of the inefficacy of money raises in wages. Food costs rise steadily because of declining production and increasing production costs per acre. Rises in industrial wages do not compensate since inevitably they are passed on to manufactured commodities which in turn increase costs for farmers and consequently costs of his economic survival and of production, and im-peril the living standards of all. It is this fundamental fact which renders all stop-gap remedies in terms of money rather than by production and abundance utterly futile, as India and China found out long before the days of farm blocs and labor unions and planned economies.

The effort of this world to stave off widespread famine is actually the first effort that has been made by the world or by this nation to divide up properly the available food supply of the world. It has become abundantly apparent that the United States cannot possibly "feed the world"; it can-not possibly even help adequately to feed the famine areas on a bare subsistence diet and still preserve the levels of diet and high-protein food consumption to which it has long been accustomed. To put it very simply, we cannot feed grain to animals at the ratio of seven pounds of grain to one pound of meat, poultry or dairy products, and still have enough left over to ship great quantities of grain to millions of starving people. We cannot possibly ship meat, poultry, butter, eggs, and dried milk to feed these people because we ourselves are already suffering periodic or more or less per-manent shortages of all of these things. It becomes clear that if world food is properly distributed per capita of population, if famine is to be wholly checked, either now or in the future, it must be upon a basis of *cereal* diet with wild game and fish as very largely the only variation. The fact is that we are much nearer to the realization of the Malthusian Theory than we think, and we shall understand this fact even more clearly as the shortages in high-protein animal foods, born of our effort to feed a large part of the world with grain, become more evident during the coming years. At the time of writing, the government is making "loans" of wheat, already assigned to starving nations, back to flour and feed mills to provide bread for the home population and to provide cereal feed to produce high-protein animal products at the ratio of seven pounds of grain to produce one of meat.

There still remain methods by which food production in the world may be increased, waste eliminated, and distribution better managed, which include "technological" methods by which food supplies can be increased through "artificial" means and do not directly employ the soil.

The food supply of the world as a whole could possibly be increased by a higher degree of agricultural mechanization, by the checking of soil destruction caused almost universally by erosion and poor agriculture, and by the restoration of ruined or half-ruined soil where restoration is possible in reasonable economic terms.

Most of the world's agriculture is extremely inefficient since it is dependent upon animal and sometimes upon human power. Not only does this fact have a lowering effect upon actual production but makes agriculture under such conditions acutely subject to losses from weather conditions, seasons, and the element of time itself.

Actually food production could be increased in this country as much as 50 per cent per acre through a better and more efficient agriculture. Dr. Walter Lowdermilk of the United States Department of Agriculture and one of the world's great authorities on soil, estimates that if this nation had an agriculture as efficient and productive as that of France, Holland, Denmark or Belgium, or of 10 per cent of our own farm operators, our farmers could easily feed a population of 250 million people at existing levels of diet upon the agricultural acreage now under cultivation. Actually we are experiencing shortages of certain high-protein foods and higher and higher prices which limit consumption, while trying to feed a population of only 140 million.

There also remain in this country and in other parts of the world certain areas which through drainage or irrigation could be converted into agriculturally productive land. These

248

areas however are insignificant in relation to the areas already under cultivation or the areas already destroyed by erosion and poor agricultural practices. The fact is that the great virgin "colonial" areas counted upon by the nineteenth century opponents of Malthus to refute his theory, have been very largely filled up by populations which consume their total food production. It must be remembered too that conditions of soil, or more especially of climate, permit certain of these "colonial" areas to produce only certain kinds of food, sometimes extremely perishable—and consequently difficult or impossible to distribute upon a world basis.

Although no actual figures are available, the waste of foodstuffs especially in America is obviously colossal. The waste of food thrown into garbage cans by shiftless housewives annually would probably feed many millions of people. But more vast quantities of food are permitted to deteriorate or spoil on farms themselves because distribution is faulty or wholly inadequate. Crops are plowed under and weevils and rats destroy or devour millions of bushels of grain every year. No figures upon the deterioration or destruction of carelessly stored wheat in our "ever normal granaries" have ever been published, but the loss was in the past enormous and may again be in the future. There is also an immense loss of food caused by the finagling of middlemen to run down the prices to the farmer, so that annually thousands of tons of food are destroyed which never reach the public market because price rigging has forced down prices to the producer which do not merit the harvesting of his crops.

This loss and many of the other losses and wastes represent largely a failure of distribution and are partly responsible for the high prices, often contrived artifically, which limit purchase and consumption. This failure of distribution in the country, state, nation and world and the high production costs arising from a low production per acre, are very largely responsible for the "surpluses" of which politicians and farm blocs profess such an unholy terror.

It is abundantly evident that in a world where at least two-thirds of the population suffer from malnutrition and hundreds of millions live at a starvation level, *there are no surpluses*. Nor can there be any surpluses in a nation such as this in which 40 per cent of the population in ordinary times suffer from malnutrition. There is only poor distribution and the high prices caused by an unproductive agriculture which limit consumption of high-protein foods. Increasing wages or incomes in terms of money do not cure these conditions since all prices, including those of farm commodities, inevitably follow in the upward movement and nullify money increases. The only *real* raise in wages and incomes can be accomplished by making the dollar buy more and that in turn can be achieved only by a more efficient and productive agriculture which lowers production costs and by better distribution. The fact remains that "surpluses" of food in this modern world is a grotesque and tragic myth.

Finally, the world food supply *may* be increased by the production of concentrated foods only indirectly related to soil. I mean by that, high-protein foods or food pellets produced through the processing of wood and other crude products of the earth into food both for people and for livestock. Considerable progress has been made in this direction, especially in Germany and the Scandinavian countries during the last war but as yet on no scale large enough to affect profoundly the problem of feeding the population of the world. The science of hydroponics (the culture of plants in minerally saturated solutions) has not yet proven economically feasible because of costs and because such culture is limited by the comparatively small range of vegetables which can be successfully cultivated under such conditions. Also there are doubts concerning the full nutrition value of plants grown outside the range of the natural processes taking place in living soil.

There are means of increasing food production, and there are also means of improving distribution and of preventing waste, high prices, and artificially created "surpluses"; and there is still a comparatively small amount of agricultural land which can still be made available for food production.

All of these things can help but none of them nor all of them taken together can effectively refute the growing evidence of the soundness of the Malthusian Theory in a world where the population is steadily increasing and the agricultural production per acre is constantly declining. Even the man in the street who never heard of Thomas Robert Malthus is feeling the pinch, if not in his stomach at least in his pocket-book.

It is a little terrifying to consider that at this time the population of the world is increasing at the rate of twenty-five people a minute. That makes agriculture and a good agriculture seem more important than it has ever been in all the long history of the world.

# X:  THE STORY OF KEMPER'S RUN

Oh, universe, what thou wishest, I wish.
                                    —Marcus Aurelius

THIS is the story of a creek called Kemper's Run.

It runs along the middle of a valley that lies wide and flat between the cracked and slowly disintegrating shoulders of a pre-glacial sandstone canyon about two million years old. The first great glacier, acting like a gigantic bulldozer, filled up the canyon with scrapings of rock and earth pushed before it all the way down from Northern Canada. The second great glacier came to a slow stop about on the line of the filled-in canyon and started melting, leaving behind as it slowly withdrew northward great heaps of mounds of glacial drift.

This residue, made up of gravel and loam, was rich stuff and presently there sprang up on it the finest hard-wood forest in the world—a forest of oak, chestnut, maple, ash, beech, and hickory. For a million or more years these trees shed their leaves, grew, and died, fell, and returned their substance to the earth in the form of an incredibly black and rich topsoil. This topsoil, covered by virgin hard-wood forest, was what the first trappers and settlers found when they came into the valley.

During all that time Kemper's Run wound its way through the bottom of the rich valley between the ancient shoulders of the pre-glacial canyon. It was a crystal clear stream, here and there bordered by marshes filled with game—mink and beaver, bears and deer, muskrat and otter, wild duck and geese, flocks of carrier pigeons that darkened the sky, and thousands of other birds. The creek was fed by springs gushing out of the hillsides and the sandstone rock that bordered the valley and its clear waters were filled with cress and other vegetation. Now and then after torrential rains lasting two or three days, there were floodwaters which raised the height of its flow a foot or two, but the floodwaters were clear and never of a violence to tear out the vegetation in the stream which fed and gave shelter to myriads of bass and crappies and bluegills and sunfish.

The valley was a paradise for the Indians who lived in the country. They grew corn and squash and beans on the rich lowlands that bordered the marshy land and there were unlimited supplies of game from the woods, and fish and crayfish in the clear water of the little stream. That is a fair and accurate picture of the valley when the first settlers came into it about the beginning of the nineteenth century.

They claimed the rich, glacial, forested land in sections of 640 acres. The bottom land went first and then the gently sloping hills on each side and finally the top land, and as rapidly as they could the settlers began clearing away the forests, heaping the tree trunks of oak, beech, ash, maple, chestnut, and hickory in great piles and burned what they did not need for building barns and houses. They were eager to get at that deep, black, rich topsoil laid down on top of the minerally rich, deep, glacial drift. The grain and the cattle they could grow were urgently needed by a nation at the beginning of the great industrial revolution with a population rapidly growing not only from the steadily increasing birthrate but by hundreds of thousands of newcomers from old, oppressed Europe where there were too many people and not enough land.

That was the beginning.

I first remember the valley about 45 years ago when I went there fishing with my father at the age of five, about a century after the first settlers had come in. I knew it intimately for that next ten years through fishing, hunting, camping, and friendship with most of the valley people. At that time it was still a beautiful valley and still fairly productive. There were still lots of fish in the creek although their numbers and size were diminished. The marshes still existed on the borders of the bottom farm lands. There were deep holes in the creek that provided both swimming and big fish.

There were three old mills with big millponds that held back the water and made breeding places for fish. It was the best hay and pasture country in the world and the farmers were making big incomes from the timothy hay they grew on the slopes of the glacial drift cleared of the forest. Every year they shipped out thousands of tons to feed the draft horses, the carriage horses, and the saddle horses which existed by the millions everywhere in the country.

There wasn't much corn grown there—only enough to feed the few hogs—and the hills and the bottom lands grew hay or pasture or wheat and oats planted largely to get the land back into meadow seedings. About 40 per cent of the forest land remained although it was pretty badly cut over and coming back with second growth. There wasn't much erosion and very few floods and even those weren't big enough to flood the bottom lands or carry out the mill dams. There wasn't much chance for the water to rush across naked fields carrying off topsoil because most of the fields were covered by sod in pasture or meadow.

But the land was being "farmed out." Few of the farms in the valley put back enough to recompense for the tons of fertility in the form of minerals which each year were carried off out of the valley into the cities in the form of timothy hay. Some of the farmers even dumped the manure out of their stables into the creek itself to be rid of it. Some regarded the creek as a great asset for that reason—it was an easy way of *getting rid* of manure. But already on some of the hilltops and higher slopes, the soil wouldn't any longer grow timothy either in quantity or quality, and those farms began to go to pieces. They didn't produce enough, and roofs began to leak, buildings to go without paint. Taxes became delinquent, and fences began to rot down or rust out without replacement. On the high land there were already abandoned farms with broken windows, sagging roofs and fields overgrown with weeds.

About that time, when I was fifteen years old, I left the valley and I did not see it again for twenty-five years.

When I came back to that country I found it terribly changed and when I went to fish the familiar creek, I found it perhaps had changed the most. The mill dams had been carried away by floods and the millponds had vanished, silted up with mud, and gone were the big holes that had provided both swimming and big fish. There wasn't a pool anywhere with more than two or three feet of water. The vegetation had gone out of the creek bed and virtually the only fish were minnows and carp and bullheads—tough, coarse inferior fish which could survive flood and silt and drought, and in the woods and hillsides and bottoms the game had begun to move out as they will do when a countryside grows poor.

What had happened in these twenty-five years of absence was simple enough. First the soil, being farmed out, grew less and less hay per acre per year and then the automobile came along and replaced the horse and the market for timothy hay, so easy to grow, so easy to harvest long ago on the once rich land, had shrunk along with the price and demand. Some of the farmers gave up and moved out, leaving the farms either to a locust horde of fly-by-night tenants or to solitude and desolation, producing nothing, supporting and feeding no one, often paying no taxes.

As the market for hay declined other farmers had looked west and had seen on the flat lands of the prairie country that the farmers there were growing rich by raising corn and hogs and they said, without thought or knowledge, or wisdom, "If they can do it, we can." And so they ploughed up the grass and meadow land and even the pastures of that rolling, hilly country and planted corn. They planted corn in rows, running more often than not up and down slopes and hills, and every time it rained each furrow between the standing corn became a miniature gully, carrying off the precious rainfall as rapidly as possible and bearing with it the good topsoil that remained and the fertilizer the farmer had bought out of his diminishing hard-earned income.

In winter after the corn was harvested the fields were left bare for the freezing and thawing and heavy rains of winter to disintegrate the soil and sweep it away. And rapidly the corn ate up the residue of organic material left in the soil by long years of hay and pasture growing, and as the organic material went out and ceased to soak up the rainfall, the soil became more and more like cement, turning off the water instead of soaking it up and the little gullies became big gullies until sometimes whole fields had to be abandoned.

As more and more land was turned into corn and the pasture and meadows produced less and less, the farmers took to turning livestock into the woods and woodlots to graze. The cattle destroyed the new forest seedlings and came in at the end of the season with ribs showing because ferns and forest seedlings will not fatten cattle or even make them grow. And where too few big trees remained, even the woodlots began to develop gullies that channeled the water quickly off, leaving the bigger trees to die slowly from the top down.

Each year the fields produced a little less per acre, and presently more farms went out of circulation or fell to the possession of the banks which didn't want them. The banks wanted the deposits, the loans, the interest of prosperous, productive farms; they did not want the worn out, weedy fields which produced nothing. Many a farm had become unsalable, even for ten dollars on the courthouse steps at sheriff's sale.

What happened to Kemper's Run which had once been a clear flowing stream with its millponds, its deep holes, its game fish? It became a monstrosity and a menace, flooding badly after each thunderstorm, filled with silt and devoid of vegetation, inhabited only by minnows and mud fish. As the land grew less productive the farmers crowded in on the marshland to turn it to some use and they began to ditch and drain it and they told the local authorities that they could never accomplish their purpose unless the floods from the bare, higher land were controlled and the stream bed deepened and straightened so that there would be "fall" for their ditches and drainage tiles.

So Kemper's Run was straightened and deepened. They brought in machinery which cut brutally through the marshlands in a straight line down the center of the valley. They cut down the protecting willows along the banks and destroyed the deep holes and what remained of the silt-filled millponds. They created a deep ditch through bare gravel which channeled the floodwater from the bare fields as rapidly as possible downstream to damage fields and cities and farms all the way across the United States to the mouth of the Mississippi. And all of it did no good; it did only damage; and Kemper's Run with its willows, its swimming holes, its game fishing had been murdered.

The big ditch did no good because within a year or two it was silted up again with the millions of tons of topsoil that came off the bare eroding cornfields, and within a short time the "fall" for drainage ditches and tiles was gone again and the mouths of the tiles buried beneath layers of topsoil, fertilizer, and mud from the sloping fields that bordered Kemper's Run. The farmers didn't ask to have the stream dredged again for they had discovered the hard way after paying thousands of dollars in special assessments that you couldn't use these marshy lands even after they were ditched and tiled. The water in the water-logged soil was seepage water from the hill country all around and no amount of drainage would make it possible to get into it early enough in the spring to plant corn that would ripen. If you planted wheat, it was drowned out in winter despite all the tiles and ditches.

So a community had murdered a beautiful stream only to fill it again in a year or two with the silt off its own fields. All the thousands of dollars of taxpayers' money and special assessments had been spent only to create more damage not only in the valley and to the stream itself but to people living hundreds of miles away along the great rivers which were fed by Kemper's Run and a thousand other small flooding streams like it. And everywhere in the nation taxpayers were paying more and more taxes for levees and dams to check at the mouth of the Mississippi the floods of Kemper's Run and streams like it which man himself had turned from valuable assets into terrible liabilities. And all the time the farms that bordered Kemper's Run were producing less and less real wealth for the nation, borrowing and depositing less money, paying less and less taxes. It was the spectacle of a country devouring itself. The final chapter of the story of Kemper's Run is more cheerful than the rest of it.

I have lived near Kemper's Run for close to ten years, and I have seen it slowly return to its old state, the way I knew it as a small boy. It has been slowly finding its old level again, curving and winding through bottom pastures and marshland. The deep holes where the big bass used to lie beneath the tree roots are coming back. The cress is beginning to grow again in water which is once again clear and free of silt. There are deep holes with bass and bluegills and crappies and sunfish and the mud-loving fish have almost disappeared. The willows are growing again in spots along the banks and for two years there have been no floods at all, save during the disastrous spring of 1947. Bottom pastures which only a few years ago were flooded a dozen times a year to a depth of two or three feet have been flooded once in the last two years. The springs that feed the creek have begun to flow again as they used to flow long ago, all the year round, regardless of drought. Old dried-up, half-forgotten springs are coming back to life and beginning to flow.

How did this come about? It came about because the farmers in the valley learned the hard way. They had to give up and get out like the farmers who once lived on the abandoned farms that lay high on the shoulders of the valley, or they had to mend their ways. The abandoned farms have been, ironically, friends of Kemper's Run for their fields are no longer left bare to erosion in the process of being farmed out. Their fields are covered with weeds and poverty grass, and forest seedlings are moving across them to reclaim them less than six generations after the forest was cut down by the first settlers. No water runs off those abandoned fields. Most of the good precious topsoil has long since disappeared from them down Kemper's Run into the distant Gulf of Mexico, but nature has begun to build it back, now that man has left her in peace. When the rain falls it stays where it falls, sinking into the ground to feed wells and springs in the valley below. Even near the abandoned hilltops springs have begun to flow again for the first time in a hundred years.

And today as you drive up the valley you see few fields of corn with furrows running up and down hill and virtually no fields left bare all through the terrible, destructive winter rains. They are covered with a kind protective blanket of wheat or rye. And where corn is grown it is mostly on the contour, *around* the hill rather than up and down it. Along the hillside lie wide green strips of meadow sod that catch and hold all the rain and any topsoil that shifts. And instead of the old timothy hay that helped to ruin the valley there grows alfalfa and red clover and ladino and everywhere piles of lime dot the hillsides waiting for the spreader. Each year one sees rich fields of healing meadow and pasture spreading along the hillsides.

It isn't only Kemper's Run which has changed but the look of the whole countryside itself. Houses and barns and fences are painted and prosperous again, and skinny cattle no longer pasture on the young green seedlings in the woods and woodlots. Millions of young trees are growing up into good sound timber that the nation needs so badly.

But here and there in the valley there remains a farmer who still believes that "what was good enough for grandpappy is good enough for me." He leaves his fields bare and cheats on fertilizer and pastures his skinny cattle in the woods and plants his corn up and down the slopes. And each year he raises less and less per acre. Each year it costs him more and more to produce a bushel of grain because he produces less and less per acre. High prices can't help him because he produces so little per acre that the first major decline in prices will wipe him out, one more victim of the school of agriculture which *fights* nature. In less than another generation there will be no more of his kind remaining. They are the last representatives of the army which carried on a furious rape and assault upon our good land. They are defeated because no man ever yet won a victory by *fighting* nature and the laws of nature.

Most of them in the valley learned the hard way, the greatest of all lessons—that by working *with* nature man can be prosperous and even rich and happy and healthy. Fighting or cheating her, man is always defeated, poverty-stricken, bitter and miserable, and eventually is destroyed himself. I have lived long enough to have seen three phases in the history of the valley and I have lived long enough to have seen Kemper's Run murdered and come back to life again to what it once had been, a clear, bright stream with fishing and swimming and cress and mint-bordered pools with clear, cold water all the year round for the cattle in the bottom pastures. I have seen the game fish return and the game birds and animals come back to a valley which they had almost deserted during the evil days. And on the hillsides the farmers are raising better crops and better livestock than have been raised on those slopes for the past fifty years. It all goes together. It's simply a question of working with nature. Work with her and she gives back health and abundance and prosperity.

The story of Kemper's Run is the story of a single creek, but it is the story too of land, of prosperity, of good hunting and fishing, of health throughout all the nation. The story of its rebirth for farmer, for sportsman, for the city dweller in search of peace and recreation, for the country banks and the nation which need its prosperity and its wealth is a simple one. Through the knowledge which man has developed, the farmers of the valley are restoring the conditions that existed when the whole valley was a paradise for the Indian hunter and fisherman. Game fish, quail, mink, rabbit, muskrat, and raccoon are coming back in abundance, and so are the yields of hay, wheat, corn, and the health, the prosperity of the farmer, of his fields and his livestock. It is an easy business and a profitable one. It takes a little time but it has made the difference between life and death in the little valley drained by Kemper's Run.

# XI:  GARDENING WITHOUT TEARS

Nature imposed these laws, a covenant everlasting
On different parts of the earth right from the earliest
days
                                        —Virgil, *The Georgics*

BY COMPARISON with some of the preceding chapters this is
a sunny and agreeable one. It is the record of experiments
which succeeded and of that curious and intensely pleasurable satisfaction and excitement which is born when a theory
turns out to have been right.

The story begins on a sunny, brilliant day eight years ago
during that false spring which so often comes in March to
the midwest, bringing with it the awakening of all country
life and the anticipation of the warm, rich, growing months
of summer. All too often in our country this gay, false
spring brings disaster in its trail by encouraging growth and
blossoms which are killed when winter returns for a farewell
visit in moody April.

The scene was a piece of bottom land that we had fenced
out for a central vegetable garden from the adjoining pasture
through which wanders Switzer's Creek. The size of the
area was a little over an acre. Although the time was early
March, the day was so bright and warm that we worked
with our shirts off.

The tractor and plow had made three or four rounds of the
plot, rolling over the weedy bluegrass and white-clover sod
and turning up the black soil, when a car stopped along the
road and a neighbor stepped out and came toward us. He
was an old man, a friend of my father's, with gray thinning

hair and hands calloused with hard work. He was a good farmer who had taken good care of his land in a time and in a neighborhood where this had never, since pioneer days, been the rule. He kept plenty of livestock and hauled out his manure and bought fertilizer to replenish the losses which had occurred even before he was born. He had even applied lime to his soil, an act which had led him to be regarded by some as a revolutionary and a fool. One problem he had never been able to solve was the gullying which every heavy rainfall brought to his fields. I knew that for all our long acquaintance and the fact that I came from the county, he regarded us working at Malabar as upstarts. We had deliberately chosen to buy along with a fairly good farm two other farms which were considered worn out and useless, which most farmers believed could never be brought back. There were rumors of new-fangled and disturbing ideas being brought into the valley. At Malabar we were all younger men who thought that we knew more than he had learned in all his lifetime of farming the hard way.

He was, perhaps, typical of a good many good farmers of his generation, men who loved their land, who worked long hours, who very often did everything the hard way. In fact, like many another elderly farmer he believed that in agriculture hard work, whether necessary or not, was the only way to success. In his heart he mistrusted the new-fangled ideas because some of them achieved startling results so easily.

My father's old friend came over to us and leaned on the fence and at first the conversation was about the weather and the way the wheat looked after the long winter and about the Guernsey herd we had just bought. I could see all the time the shadow of mockery in his eyes. Here were some young squirts who were going to spend a lot of money and rip up some worn-out land and then after spending a great deal of money, give up, defeated in the end. He had seen a lot of "city farmers" go the same way.

And then he looked down at the stripes of black soil and green turf and found what he was looking for. A twinkle came into his blue eyes and he said, "Is that all the better you fellers can plow?" I knew what was in his mind. If he'd been plowing the patch, he'd have turned the sod all the way over and buried it completely without so much as a blade of grass showing. That was what was called "good, clean plowing," a thing for a farmer to be proud of.

The twinkle in his eyes irritated me and I said, "We're doing it that way on purpose." And he looked at me with a fishy eye as if saying "Oh, yeah!"

"Sure," I said. "We're trying to mix the sod into the soil without burying it."

And then I stopped for I understood that in order to really explain what we were trying to do, it would have required a whole lecture on a lot of things such as trash farming and organic material and rainfall absorption and erosion and all the things which belonged to the New Agriculture. There wouldn't have been time if I spent the rest of the afternoon, and we wanted to get on with the job of plowing and fitting for the soil was turning over just right, mellow and crumbling and begging for the harrow.

And then the old farmer said, "That sure ought to make a good garden. That's virgin soil—never been plowed since the forest was cut off and the cattle have been manuring it for 130 years. It's been gettin' better all that time."

I looked at him to see whether he was serious or whether he was merely attempting to trick us into believing the soil was better than it really was. But very clearly he was in earnest and perfectly honest. That was what the farmers of the old pattern really believed—that pasture took care of itself.

So then I broke down and said, "It isn't virgin soil even though a plow has never touched it and it isn't very good soil. It's worn-out soil."

He looked at me with astonishment, "How can that be? A plow has never touched it!"

So I took the time off. I said, "It's simple enough. I don't know how many cattle and sheep have pastured on that field for a hundred and thirty years but everyone of them took off more than he put back. They took it off in bone and meat and milk and wool and nearly all of it was carried off the place or eventually to some other field. They put back in droppings about a fifth of what they consumed and as the minerals grew depleted, the cows gave less milk and the steers put on weight less rapidly. Why, one steer alone will carry off a pasture like that around one hundred pounds of calcium in his bones by the time he weighs eight hundred to a thousand pounds. That's been going on for a hundred and thirty years, Herman. Figure it out!"

A puzzled look came into his eyes and after a moment he said, "I never thought of it like that."

I said, "You know this pasture, Herman, better than I do. You've lived near it all your life. Is it as good as you remember it as a boy? Aren't there a lot more weeds than there were then? Hasn't it fed less cattle every year?"

"Well, yes. It's full of thistles and iron weed now. It didn't used to be when I was a boy."

"Sure. It's worn out—that pasture just like that field over there that's been corned to death. Sure, the soil looked black enough but it isn't very good soil. There's a lot missing from it."

Then Herman changed the subject and pretty soon he went away. He was still thinking.

The idea of that garden and what I wanted to do with it had come to me a long time before. It was born out of many things I had seen done elsewhere in the world, out of things I had read and learned, out of my own experience with soil. But most of all on my return to my own country it had seemed strange that in a comparatively new country like my own, there should be so many plagues and blights and insect pests. I hadn't encountered them in Europe. In all the years I had farmed or gardened in the rich country of northern France we had never used a dust or an insecticide or a spray against either disease or insect pests. Why should there be so many plagues and insects here at home? Why was the market swamped each year with new forms of poisons to protect our apples or celery, our cabbage, our string beans, indeed, all the range of fruits and vegetables that are consumed by the American people? Some residue of these poisons must somehow reach all of us. Certainly they could be harmful. Could it be that they were in part at least responsible for the increasing toll of heart disease, of glandular derangements, of cancer. The average city dweller was absorbing all these poisons in however minute quantities

266

along with the chlorine and other chemicals used to disinfect the drinking water polluted by his own sewage.

And behind that thought lay another. All these sprays and dusts, poisons and chemicals were perhaps no more than patent medicines. They were merely used to cure and protect plants which had too little resistance, which were, in fact, already sick or because of weakness subject to the attack of whatever blight or disease or insect appeared. Why could you not raise plants healthy enough to resist these plagues? And why were they weak and unhealthy?—probably because of the soil in which they grew. Perhaps the truth was that most American soils were depleted soils or minerally un-balanced soils even in the beginning. Could not vegetables grown in a balanced soil created especially for them prove completely or almost wholly resistant? I knew well enough whatever any observant gardener knows—that in a row of plants the sickly ones were those which disease and insects always attacked first.

What seemed to me the answer was *preventive* medicine rather than *patent* medicine.

We were setting up Malabar Farm to cure and restore old eroded worn-out land. Why should we not do the same thing in this patch of garden where we could work intensively and set up the pattern to be used eventually over a thousand acres?

So that was what we were doing when Herman leaned over the fence and talked about the "virgin" soil we were plowing up. We were making a beginning on almost the only level acre out of a thousand.

The beginning occurred eight years ago and for the last three years there have been no patent medicines used in that garden, no dusts, no sprays, no insecticides and, save in the bad year of 1947, there has been no need for them. The vegetables and berries grew in a balanced, complete soil, prob-ably better even than the good, well-mineralized glacial loam of the region when it was still virgin. They grew naturally under the principles of the New Agriculture and their quality and flavor is unquestionably superior to most of the sprayed and dusted vegetables found in the city markets.

The process and the formula was neither difficult, expensive, nor complicated. The New Agriculture is largely based upon them. They had the backing of research and science and we tried a few wrinkles of our own. The principle beneath the experiment was that of utilizing all available knowledge regarding soils and of working *with* Nature rather than *against* her as so many farmers in the old pattern had always done, battling their way at last into defeat.

To begin with we had quantities of barnyard manure to supply organic material and a great many minerals as well as the animal secretions of which not much is known. It was not the best barnyard manure because it still came off poor soil and the animals producing it had to claim for their growth and milk most of the inadequate mineral supply that came from the depleted fields. What was left over to be passed through their bodies could not be much. But there was always plenty of nitrogen in it of which vegetables, particularly leafy vegetables like spinach and rhubarb and cabbage, have need in great quantities.

I knew the virtues of barnyard manure in making healthy plants and I observed among other things that old farm gardens which had been manured and cultivated year after year in the same spot raised healthy vegetables which rarely if ever fell victims of disease or insects. This was so, very likely because for years the fertility and the minerals from the fields of the farm had been carried in through the manure and concentrated upon the small area of the garden. That soil had been fed constantly and the mineral balance had been maintained at the expense of the outlying fields which like our pasture had gradually become depleted.

So each year for seven years manure was plowed *into* that garden—not plowed under but *into* the soil as I had observed French gardeners who are the best in the world mixing it *into* their soils. A Frenchman never spreads his manure or trash over the soil he is working and then turns it *under*. He spades across his garden and then puts in a layer of manure or trash *vertically*, then spades another row with another vertical layer of trash and manure and so on until he is finished. In the same fashion we plowed and fitted that garden, mixing the manure and the trash left over from the year before *into* the earth.

We knew that while the soil of the old pasture was rich in organic material, it was *old* organic material, so old indeed that much of it was carbonized and had long since passed beyond that cycle of life, growth, death, and rebirth which is essentially a part of all living soil. There had been very little new organic material in the process of decay laid down on that pasture land for many generations. Each year it was pastured close to the ground and as it grew less productive it was more and more over-pastured. The bulk of the organic material we plowed up was at least a hundred years old. It no longer provided a feeding ground for bacteria, moulds, fungi, or earthworms which are essential to any cubic foot of earth which contains the pattern of the universe. In a sense even that unplowed "virgin" pasture land was "dead" soil. The manure and the trash plowed *into* the soil restored the constant cycle of both death and rebirth and restored a feeding ground for the moulds, bacteria and other complex organisms which must be a part of any living soil.

We knew too that the "virgin" soil needed calcium and potassium and phosphorus, and in order to restore these elements in proper quantity and in quickly available form, we used commercial hydrated lime and commercial fertilizer and continued to use the commercial fertilizer each year. In the fourth year when the vegetables showed a vigor which indicated that the balance of these major elements with the increased *living* organic material was fairly well established, we began the application of trace elements. We applied on one half of the garden a mixture of boron, manganese, magnesium, copper, cobalt and iron and on the other half a new fertilizer made upon a base of coal baked together with calcium, phosphate rock, and with nitrogen added. It contained through the dolomitic base of the calcium and the phosphate rock a wide range of trace elements existing in quantities small but apparently sufficient, since the effects it produced were as good and perhaps better than those obtained in the mixture in which the exact formula and amounts of minerals were known. This may have been so because in the baking process all the minerals were reduced to a highly available form and their action was observable at once.

Until the fourth year sprays and insecticides were used of

necessity notably against squash bugs and cabbage worms, bean beetles and against mosaic blight on the celery, but in the fifth year there appeared to be a perceptible change and a marked diminution in the attacks both of insects and disease. The celery was sprayed once with Bordeaux mixture and insecticides were used only once upon the squash, cucumbers, beans, cabbage and broccoli. In the fifth and sixth years no insecticides or "patent medicines" in any form were necessary and in the seventh year the garden was virtually free of all insects and disease. The record has continued.

The only exception came in the bad year of 1947 when three times the garden was drowned out by heavy rains and three times replanted. For days at a time the area lay under water. What plants survived were sick plants, weakened by root rot and lack of oxygen. The abnormal soaking moisture of the season upset all results, especially the special experiments we were making with trace elements and soil balance as a control for potato bugs. Only one thing was proven—that any sick, weakened or undernourished plant was immediately subject to vicious attack by both disease and insects. The old diseases and notably the mosaic blight returned to the celery and Mexican bean beetles which we had not seen for three years reappeared in numbers. Squash bugs which, although visible in numbers during years immediately past, had not attacked the vines, reappeared and this year voraciously ate the yellowing sickened plants even to the stems.

Perhaps most remarkable of all was the fact that insect pests were actually visible at times each year although they showed little or no inclination to attack the plants. The eggs of squash bugs hatched on the leaves in full sight but no bug attacked a leaf or blossom unless it was weakened by some injury. A bruised leaf or vine weakened by the attack of a form of nematode on root and stem were quickly covered by an army of bugs arriving from nowhere. Even the nematodes, living in the soil rather than above it, decreased in the number of their attacks with each successive year. Four varieties of squash—acorn, butternut, green and yellow hubbard—were grown. The record of all was the same. Eventually even the nematodes ceased their attacks.

Cabbage worms appeared in small numbers to attack the

early leaves and then vanished after creating small damage. The same record was true of bean beetles. They appeared during the first few days of bean growth while the young plants still fed upon the stored food of the seed bean and then disappeared as the roots penetrated the balanced soil and the minerals and notably the trace elements became available. The cucumbers normally subject to all sorts of ills, were completely free of disease or insects for the whole of the three successive years. Although cabbage worms made early transitory attacks upon cabbage, they did not touch either the broccoli, the Brussels sprouts or the cauliflower, all cousins of the cabbage. As in the case of injured or weakened squash vines, the only cabbage subject to persistent attacks from worms were five heads out of some two hundred which grew near the entrance to the garden where the earth around them suffered continual trampling and packing which retarded their growth. The record of the cantaloupe was one of freedom from insects. The subterranean nematodes attacked them here and there, although with steadily decreasing violence.

Peppers, eggplant, lettuce and the whole range of root vegetables were completely free of disease or insects save for the radishes and turnips which suffered sporadic attacks from the nematodes.

Perhaps most remarkable of all was the complete freedom from blight, diseases, or worms of the tomatoes. In the summer of 1946 tomatoes through the East and part of the Middle West suffered a new kind of blight which devastated gardens and the fields of the commercial growers, but no trace of the blight appeared in our garden. In the preceding years, a plague of gray aphids in our area destroyed most of the tomato plants in an early stage of growth. In some cases the whole planting of tomatoes had to be replaced. Not one aphid appeared within the borders of our garden. In the same year tomato vines growing in the fields nearby were badly cut by tomato worms but none paid the garden even a passing visit. It is worth notice that the greatest victims of the tomato blight and the aphids were the victory gardens established upon depleted vacant lots or agricultural field land. In many cases the entire plantations of tomatoes were

272

destroyed. The old, long-established, annually manured gardens of the farmers' wives remained immune to both blight and aphids.

Mosaic blight on celery is a universal pest and one feared by commercial growers. During the first four years we were forced to use Bordeaux mixture in order to produce clean celery but during the last three years, although signs of the blight appeared on the older outer leaves, the inner leaves of the new growth remained completely free of blight with no dusting or spraying. Each successive year the traces of Mosaic blight have grown fainter and it is possible that during the coming summer they may disappear completely.

The increasingly fine quality of the vegetables both in size and excellence of flavor followed the line of increasing freedom from disease and insects. This was especially notable in the cases of squash, cabbage, eggplant, broccoli and all the range of greens from escarole through romaine to iceberg and leaf lettuce. After the fourth year the cracking and the uneven ripening in tomatoes disappeared completely, probably owing to the presence of manganese. For the same reason split stems in celery were no longer to be found.

During the summer of 1946 we harvested broccoli worthy of a horticultural show from successive growths on the same plants from June 25 through the summer. As late as November 18, we had broccoli *au gratin* for dinner from plants set out on May 4. But the most fantastic of the results of good and balanced soils occurred with the cabbage during the summer of 1945 and again during 1946. After the heads of early cabbage had been cut the stems were left standing because they had become enveloped by a luxuriant growth of acorn squash planted in the next row. As every gardener knows, tiny heads usually no bigger than Brussels sprouts, will appear along cabbage stems left standing after the main head has been cut off. In this case the stems were completely covered by squash vines and what had happened to them remained unnoticed until a frost killed the vines about the middle of September. Then was the miracle revealed. On nineteen of the twenty-five old cabbage stems appeared new heads growing from the side of the stem—good, solid heads as large as and in some cases larger than the original heads harvested during late June and early July from the same plants. Eight of the stems bore twin heads and three stems carried three heavy heads apiece. The six remaining stems of the twenty-five each carried smaller, still undeveloped heads which with a longer season might have grown into fully matured cabbages.

Two other elements undoubtedly contributed something to the results obtained in the vegetable garden. One was the use in occasional irrigation of water which came from an old farm pond, with a heavy population of bass and bluegills, which received in times of heavy rains the run-off water from a neighboring barnyard. The richness of the pond and the trillions of tiny aquatic organisms spread over the garden actually turned the water into a solution of weak fertilizer with a very nearly perfect mineral balance. Also, the pond being comparatively shallow, the temperature of the water approximated that of the air.

The second element which contributed much was the practice of mulching used for nearly all of the vegetables. Newly set-out plants were mulched at once and onion and carrot seedlings as soon as they had had a first weeding and were large enough. The mulch kept the earth moist and looser than if it had been cultivated throughout the hot weather. It also promoted the growth of bacteria and the increase of earthworms which did a little cultivating and aerating of their own. Mulching also suppressed all but a few coarse weeds which were easily pulled up and added to the mulch and it reduced the necessity for irrigation by three quarters.

Casual observation revealed another process for which the mulch was responsible. After a few days there began to appear beneath the mulch and on the surface in the upper layer of the soil a whole world of fungi and moulds. On lifting up the mulch they were evident everywhere, white or grayish-white against the dark earth. Even with the slightest observation their purpose became clearly evident; they were attacking the dead mulch above and converting it rapidly into organic material and making the minerals contained in the mulch available to the *living* plants growing *in* the mulch. Strands of one kind of grayish fungus, which grew in a lacelike pattern, attached themselves to the decaying mulch and penetrated into the soil itself. Closer examination revealed the apparent fact that strands of the fungus seemed actually to be attached to the hairlike roots of the living plants, both on the surface and beneath the earth as if actually they were transmitting to the living plants the minerals and elements breaking down in the mulch itself and actually feeding them.[1]

And of course whenever the mulch was lifted there were earthworms to be found, feeding upon the decaying mulch material, taking it in at one end of their long slippery bodies and passing it out the other as digested, rich and highly available plant food. The holes they made in their progress through the soil left it open to aeration and the penetration of rainfall.

Actually what we observed in examining the mulched garden closely was the process by which soil restores itself, makes both chemical fertilizer and the minerals and elements already existing in the soil and dead vegetation highly available to the living plants, growing in the mulch. All the elements were there—moisture, bacteria, fungi, beneficent acids and earthworms. It was the eternal pattern of the universe—birth, growth, death, decay, and rebirth without which no soils can be productive, healthy, and consistently fertile.

The mulches used varied with the vegetable mulched. To avoid an excess of nitrogen which would drive tomatoes into tropical growth, small yields and late ripening, ordinary wheat or oat straw was used, which through the action of the carbon-nitrogen ratio, actually controlled and reduced the amount of nitrogen in the rich soil by absorbing the nitrogen and feeding the bacteria, fungi, and moulds which took part in the process of its own decay. Straw was also used upon root crops in order to check the nitrogen and prevent the vegetable from going "all to tops." On all leafy crops, the lettuces, cabbage, celery, etc., where quantities of nitrogen were beneficial to growth, alfalfa hay and old pea vines were used. These, being highly nitrogenous took no nitrogen from the

[1] Sir Albert Howard devotes many pages in his recent book, *Soil and Health*, to this macro-micronutrient process of feeding. The book also contains some fascinating photographs of this process in action, showing the attachment of long filaments of fungus to hairlike roots of the plants.

soil and perhaps added a little as they decayed. The same nitrogenous mulches were used also upon the greedy fast growing squashes.

Nitrogen, indeed, proved the most difficult of all elements to control, especially since the nitrogen needs of vegetables vary considerably and too much or too little nitrogen will affect yields and quality.

One striking example of the relation of nitrogen balance occurred during 1946 in the case of the celery. Six large rows existed and Eddie Melick, the Ohio State Agricultural College student who was in charge, was mulching it with alfalfa when, after mulching five rows, he ran out of the supply. On the sixth row he substituted straw with what turned out to be a devastating effect but which proved another instance of what happens to plants when the balance of their nutrition is upset.

The results came quickly within two weeks. The five rows mulched with the nitrogenous alfalfa grew rapidly and vigorously and were a rich dark green in color and almost wholly free from blight. The sixth row rapidly turned a yellowish green and was attacked by Mosaic blight which spread more and more rapidly as the nitrogen deficiency and the unbalance of soil diet increased. Actually the straw with its high carbon-cellulose content was robbing the celery of nitrogen while the decaying, rich protein-nitrogenous alfalfa on the adjoining rows was actually feeding the nitrogen-greedy celery. A few handfuls of sulphate of ammonia in solution with water, a highly available form of nitrogen, applied on half of the yellowish blighted celery caused the new growth of the leaves to be as dark and healthy a green as the foliage on the adjoining rows and on the new growth no Mosaic blight appeared.

Research has established various blights as virus diseases and has tended to prove, if not proved, that the virus is not only the lowest form of life, an organic thing, part animal, part vegetable, but that perhaps further research will discover in the life and character of viruses the very secret of the origins of life itself.

Immunity to some disease created through inoculation and the corrective effects of antibiotics like penicillin and streptomycin in the case of disease are both well established, but no research has yet determined why balanced *health* should establish resistance and even immunity to disease in plants, animals and people. In all of these fields of research there lie immense possibilities, revolutionary not only in the field of medicine and plant pathology, but in the field of life itself and the principles which determine the facts of life as well as the facts of decay, illness, and death. It is not only that in a cubic foot of good, living soil lies the pattern of the universe but that there may lie within it the key to that force which animates all living, growing things and establishes the difference between them and that which is inanimate and dead.

The answer will be found not by one man alone but by many men and women working together in countless fields, using in their research one part observation, one part instinct, one part information and two parts hard work, for that is the pattern of all real and truly profitable research. Perhaps, as in the case of Darwin, the instinctive and inspirational part is the most important of all, the spark which may illumine the still undiscovered and unknown element which makes rebirth and life out of death and decay.

What is happening in that garden where intensive treatment was possible is spreading out at a slower rate in concentric waves over the whole of a thousand acres. The cattle and poultry in barns and in the fields are getting forage which contains the nourishment it should contain and the results show up in freedom from disease, in greater milk production, in more rapidly growing beef, in shinier coats, in breedability, in stronger and more numerous offspring, in freedom from the old infections which originally plagued us upon the worn-out soils and pastures.

We have had evidence of the same growing health and resistance in field crops.

In the beginning we had chemical soil tests made of all the fields and all of them where any topsoil remained showed what we already knew—that the topsoil had been hopelessly robbed until in most fields there remained in the wasted topsoil little if any calcium, phosphorus, potassium or nitrogen. The tests did not show what we already knew—that much of what remained was hopelessly locked up in that same soil with iron and aluminum and unavailable to the vegetation growing in the soil. For a good many people the result of these tests might have proved discouraging but we were banking on two things—the knowledge we possessed of how to create a new and balanced fertile soil and the knowledge that so much of our subsoil was of a glacial type known as Wooster silt loam, a richly mineralized soil which was a composite of all the scraped up soil pushed ahead of the second great glacier from the country perhaps hundreds of miles north of us and deposited in our valley with the melting of the glacier. Also the subsoil was the most sympathetic and workable subsoil in the world—a gravel-loam mixture which drained well and absorbed organic material as rapidly as any soil on earth.

For a long time we have abandoned soil tests not because they fail to be valuable but because plants and vegetation themselves tell a much more accurate story than any chemical or laboratory test. Plants exhibit symptoms of malnutrition or lack of mineral balance in their diet in exactly the same fashion as animals or people.

I have related in *Pleasant Valley* the striking example of soybeans screaming out a deficiency of available potassium during the first year of our experiments. I repeat it here because of its significance. In that first year we were short of good hay and seeded a twelve-acre field to Wilson soybeans. The field was one of the more level ones where a good deal of worn-out topsoil remained. The seed germinated and from the beginning the beans had a sickly, yellowish appearance with brown spotted leaves save for about twenty or twenty-five spots, perfectly circular in shape and about fifteen feet in diameter. Within the circumference of these circles the beans from the very beginning grew deep-green and rank. The symptoms of the sickly beans pointed to a grave deficiency of potassium but the explanation of the rank-growing, healthy areas came to us only after much thinking. Then it dawned upon me out of the blue one day. The answer was that a long time earlier, perhaps as much as a hundred years ago when the forest had been cleared off that field, the branches and even good timber had been heaped together in piles and burned. The ash residue, rich in highly available potash, had been so great on these particular circular spots that the earth was still rich in potash after three or four generations of poor and greedy agriculture.

No soil test was needed to show the deficiency of available potassium in that field. In the summer of 1945, five years later, when we were still raising Wilson beans in the same field in the rows of corn to cut for silage, the beans grew rankly to a height in some cases of four to five feet, dark green in color, perfectly healthy, and even growing with the corn, heavily productive of seed. In the five years the potash deficiency of the field has been corrected and mineral balance in the worn-out topsoil well on the way to correction. Nevertheless, the polka-dot pattern still persisted faintly in the alfalfa which covered the same field in 1947.

Deficiency of potassium is almost universal throughout the country. I have seen all the symptoms in most of the states and in hundreds of counties, east, west, north and south. It has a close connection with the legend among farmers that oats and wheat and other small grains lodge or "go down" because there is too much nitrogen in the soil. We have found the reason of lodging small grain to be not an excess of nitrogen but a deficiency of potash in the balance of elements. The nitrogen, it is true, produces a rank growth but the potash produces the strength of stalk which can support the rank growth but the potash produces the strength of stalk which can support the rank growth and contributes something to the yield of grain. Potash is linked closely to organic material and the deficiency of *living* organic material in the agricultural areas of the United States is probably our greatest soil deficiency and one which is increasing. In some areas, notably again in the Deep South, there is very often no organic material at all, either dead or alive, in the soil. Available potash is closely linked in particular with barnyard manure.

Last year we took seventy-five bushels of oats to the acre off one field without any *lodging* whatever. We have two fields of wheat in which I am confident we shall harvest sixty bushels or more and without lodging. In France where the average yield of wheat is about sixty bushels to the acre I have never seen a field of fallen wheat. Yields of seventy-five and even eighty bushels per acre are fairly common without lodging. Our own national average is less than twenty bushels to the acre.

The story of symptoms, weaknesses and deficiencies, disease and insects carries over into alfalfa. As the years have passed,

279

Malabar has become more and more a grass farm and today we are raising corn, our only open cultivated crop upon the flat land bottom farm we rent from the Muskingum Conservancy or upon those strips so contoured that they are, even on the sides of hills, virtually level. We have had experience with alfalfa under almost all soil conditions and all weather conditions within the range of our climate. We have grown it on worn-out topsoil, on glacial drift, on alluvial bottom land and on the heavy clay where fragments of the prehistoric pre-glacial plain still jut above the level of the superimposed glacial drift. Soils and variations of soil created both by the vast action of nature and by the puny and sometimes destructive hand of man have provided one of the most fascinating aspects of the whole adventure.

No plant, save perhaps corn or tobacco, will scream its deficiencies more noisily than alfalfa. With us, it has told us again and again exactly what are the deficiencies of the soil in which it grows. In some fields it has even told us the particular spots in fields which were weak in lime, in potash, in boron. The one thing it has told us beyond all argument is that when the plants have developed roots, during the third and sometimes the second year, deep enough to penetrate down into the glacial drift, it finds there in the gravel loam, churned up a million years ago, what is very nearly a perfectly balanced mineral diet.

We were, at Malabar, among the pioneers of alfalfa as a poor-land crop, seeding in the spring directly upon the worn-out topsoil immediately after applications of two and later four tons of limestone meal and 300 pounds of mixed fertilizer, 5-12-12 per acre when available. Part of the seedings have been made in wheat or oats in fields where the fertility was still high enough to make seedings of small grains profitable or even possible. On hopelessly poor or eroded fields we have seeded it directly without plowing on a trash mulched surface. The record of alfalfa as a poor land crop producing hay, silage and good pasture on what a year earlier was useless land has been notably successful. As a barometer to soil deficiencies the alfalfa has served another important function, for by its symptoms it has told us what was missing in our remaining worn-out topsoils and almost exactly where the mineral unbalance lay.

Alfalfa will show a potassium deficiency in brown spots on its leaves and a deficiency of boron, one of the trace minerals virtually essential to the growth of healthy alfalfa, by yellowish spots. It will tell you of phosphorus by the quality and amount and perhaps even by the "set" of seeds. Without lime it will not grow at all. And so our alfalfa told us a story regarding our soils that was more accurate than any soil test for it told us not only what the soils needed but the degree to which the minerals already existing in the soil were locked up or available.

During the first year and through most of the second year, alfalfa seeded upon our worn-out topsoils showed acute symptoms of potassium and boron deficiencies. Lime did not enter in for we make no alfalfa seedings without first making a generous application of lime. Once the root has passed through the depleted topsoil and penetrated into the virgin glacial drift, a revolution takes place in the appearance of the plants. They become vigorous, dark-green and free from the brown and yellow symptoms of deficiency and from then on produce quantities of first quality hay, silage and pasture. Not only does the alfalfa find the minerals which it needs in the deep glacial subsoil but it very likely finds amounts of fertilizer applied to open-row crops by preceding farmers which has leached down long ago into the subsoil.

One fact in this connection is notable. It is that during the first and well into the second year of seeding our best alfalfa grows upon those slopes and hillocks where before our time *all* topsoil had been washed away. In other words, for the first year and until the rapidly growing alfalfa roots penetrate beneath the depleted, unbalanced *topsoil* that topsoil in our country is actually a *handicap* to the plants because of its past depletion by the action of man.

But there is another aspect of great interest which fits directly into the theory of preventive medicine in plants and in their immunity to insects when their mineral nutrition is sufficiently balanced and abundant to make them healthy and vigorous.

Most farmers will tell you that the leaf-hopper, the worst insect pest of alfalfa in our region, causes the brown and yellow spots on alfalfa. Our own experience and our own careful observations have shown us that the brown and yellow deficiency spots do not come *after* the attack by leaf-hoppers but *before* the insects appear, and that they attack the plants because they are already sick and weakened by deficiencies and an *un*balance among the elements. There is every evidence by observation to support the belief that they attack the brown and yellow spotted alfalfa *because* it is already weak and sick from deficiencies. There is no question that the number of leaf-hoppers to be found in first- and second-year seedings on worn-out topsoil is many, many times greater than in the older seedings where the roots have penetrated deeply and found the proper mineral balance and are therefore green, vigorous and resistant.

By accident we achieved incontestable evidence that the leaf-hoppers will attack by preference the sickly plant. In one field containing a long curving bank of glacial drift from which all the topsoil had vanished, we fitted the field which had been in alfalfa during four years for reseeding to wheat. On the flatter portions of the field we plowed the land, but on the long bank of the exposed glacial drift we put aside the plow and tore up the whole surface of the bank with tiller and disk. We did this because we did not want to risk further erosion upon a bank where we were trying to build up topsoil. With a trash-mulch surface we believed, and rightly, that on that steep bank we should have neither any erosion nor any water loss. When the field had been fitted we seeded the whole to wheat, but found almost immediately that all the work with tiller and disk on the bank had not killed the alfalfa growing there. The old roots and stems developed very quickly a new and vigorous growth. The tilling and disking appeared only to have stimulated most of it. In the following summer the alfalfa growth on the bank was so lush and vigorous that it made impossible the combining of the wheat.

Meanwhile, a fresh seeding of alfalfa, ladino, and brome grass had been made on the flat areas of the field as well as on the exposed alfalfa-infested bank. The germination was excellent but as we expected from experience, the new seedlings exhibited the usual brown and yellow spots betraying deficiencies in the topsoil of potassium and boron which had not yet been wholly corrected. Therefore we had in the same field deep-rooted alfalfa, green and vigorous and new alfalfa

282

seedlings still shallow-rooted which were sickly and displayed the symptoms of nutritional deficiencies as clearly as animals or people show them.

About the middle of the summer the leaft-hoppers appeared in hordes and in that particular field they attacked *only* the sickly plants and *avoided* the vigorous ones. On the new alfalfa there were millions of leaf-hoppers. On the green and vigorous alfalfa growing on the bank in the very midst of the field it was virtually impossible to find a leaf-hopper. The results of the accidental experiment with leaf-hoppers were noticed by many hundreds of agricultural-minded visitors during the summer of 1945.

It might be contended that the leaf-hoppers rejected the older, deeper-rooted plants because they were *tougher*, except for our experience in another field on the Ferguson Place which we keep in a rotation of one year wheat and three to four years alfalfa or alfalfa, brome grass, ladino mixture. The field is of peculiar geological structure, part of it being glacial drift (Wooster silt loam) and the rest of the heavy yellow clay which was a fragment of the ancient worn-down preglacial Plain. The clay is heavy and fairly rich but lacking in the mineral balance of the glaciated part of the field. Here the leaf-hopper story was equally striking. The alfalfa growing on the glacial soil was from the first year onward rich, green, and healthy. There was little worn-out topsoil left and its roots penetrated almost directly into the well-drained gravel-loam soil. On the clay portion of the field the alfalfa showed symptoms of deficiencies throughout the three years of its existence and never attained the health of that growing on the well-balanced glacial soil. When the leaf-hoppers came they remained in myriads on the sickly alfalfa in the clay portion of the field and scarcely bothered the healthy alfalfa growing in the glacial soil.

In this case the whole field of alfalfa was seeded at the same time and was of the same age throughout its growth, but the alfalfa on the minerally unbalanced clay (which also suffered from poor drainage in comparison with the glacial soil) remained deficient and sickly and subject to attack by leaf-hoppers throughout the whole of its existence.

This same field exhibited a curious behavior in the matter

of "heaving" as well. The winter of 1945–46 was an especially bad winter with constant freezing and thawing. On the clay side of the field a third of the alfalfa "heaved" out and on the glaciated, gravel portion not a single plant was loosened or lost. We have found a close relationship between organic material and the "heaving" of alfalfa or any very deep-rooted legume. In soils with abundant organic material "heaving" is scarcely in evidence at all, even in bad, open winters. On soils deficient in organic material heaving is generally prevalent. The clay portion of the field just mentioned was far behind the glaciated material in organic content, chiefly because, although both portions of the field were treated alike from the organic point of view, it required about three times as long to incorporate the material into the tough heavy clay as it required in the loose gravel-silt-loam and therefore the clay, as compared with the glacial loam, was still out of organic balance.[2] It is also true that the native textures of soils have a considerable effect upon heaving of deep-rooted plants under the process of freezing and thawing. Gravel-loam soils, being infinitely more flexible than heavy clays, expand and contract with a minimum of disturbance to roots.

What has been written of alfalfa has been largely true of the well-known clovers—sweet, red, alsike and mammoth. It has also been true of the invaluable ladino, although the ladino, being a trailing clover and not rooting more than five or six inches in depth, was rarely able to reach the rich, glacial subsoil below the worn-out topsoil. It flourished, however, on banks where all topsoil was eroded away and showed an immense response to lime, phosphorus and potassium which increased its yields by as much as 200 to 300 per cent.

The reason for the comparative immunity of plants grown upon well-drained, well-balanced soil to disease and insects I do not attempt to explain. The whole story still lies in the vast realm of things we have not yet investigated sufficiently, in

[2] The best available book I know on mineral nutrition in crops and the symptoms of deficiencies is *Hunger Signs in Crops*, published by the American Fertilizer Association, Washington, D.C. It contains many colored plates which help even an amateur to recognize the symptoms of unbalance and malnutrition in plant life.

the vast field of soil, minerals, health, and preventive medicine. It is a job and a fascinating one for men with time for patient research. I only know that the results set down above are the result of careful observation. The process has been partly experimental, partly pragmatic. I do know that where we put into practice the discoveries we made by observation the results obtained were uniformly effective and that they have been seen by many hundreds of people including practical farmers, commercial vegetable growers, agronomists and experts of grasses and legumes.

There are, to be sure, other elements besides malnutrition such as poor drainage or a poor fitting of a field which can make sickly plants and therefore plants subject to disease and the attack of insects. It is also true that insects in "plague" proportions, coming in from outside areas—insects such as the locust and the ordinary potato bug, might not show the same antipathy for healthy, vigorous plants, although our experience with leaf-hoppers of "plague" proportions indicates that they, at least, will avoid the healthy vigorous plants. Gradually, all the land at Malabar is achieving a good mineral and organic balance and it is possible that within a comparatively short space of time, all our crops and especially our alfalfa, will be in the rich, vigorous, self-protecting category. It will then be interesting to see whether the leaf-hoppers pass us over entirely and go on to neighboring fields where the legumes are suffering from deficiencies.

Insofar as the garden is concerned, I am convinced that preventive medicine is more effective than patent medicine and for three years no one at Malabar has eaten sulphur or arsenic or rotenone or D.D.T., or any other poison contained in the dusts and sprays which are the patent medicines of the plant world. I also believe that the people and the animals on the farm are getting their minerals and vitamins through the food they eat rather than in pills and capsules taken to cure poor eyesight, tendencies to colds or "that tired feeling." I know that the animals at least have shown a remarkable response in health and vigor and breedability.

All of the evidence and the speculations set down here come largely within the realm of the scientifically unknown and undetermined in a field of research which is already having its effect upon the whole aspect of health and even upon the philosophies of dentists and doctors. It is a rich field and research may lead us still deeper into the revolution which is taking place in the field of agriculture and of vigorous health.

In all of this our observations and experiments have led us toward the belief that the laws of a maintained and productive agriculture are largely based upon balance and upon laws very nearly as absolute as those of mathematics or physics. The balances appear to be three. (1) Between minerals and organic materials. (2) Among the major elements—nitrogen, phosphorus, potassium and calcium. (3) Between the major elements and the so-called trace elements—boron, cobalt, manganese, copper, magnesium and a score of others.

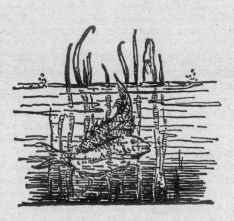

# XII: MALABAR JOURNAL

## Summer (1) 1945

The proper caretaking of the earth lies not alone in maintaining its fertility or in safeguarding its products. The lines of beauty that appeal to the eye and the charm that satisfies the five senses are in our keeping. . . . To put the best expression of any landscape into the consciousness of one's day's work is more to be desired than much riches. . . . The farmer does not have full command of his situation until the landscape is a part of his farming.

—Liberty Hyde Bailey, *The Holy Earth*

JULY 7: One hundred and twenty farmers from Morrow County came up a week ago with their wives and children to spend the day going over the farm, field by field, under the direction of Hecker of the Soil Conservation Service. They were mostly members of the recently founded Soil Conservation District and much interested in the results of our pasture treatment, in the brome grass, alfalfa, ladino mixture and many other things.

There is no doubt but that on our soils *whole* fertilizer, 5-12-12, gets better results in pasture restoration than simply superphosphates. The calcium and phosphorus are essential of course, but the nitrogen is immensely important in starting the growth of legume seedlings until they can set up their own nitrogen manufacturing plants, and the potassium deficiencies of soil everywhere in the country are much greater than are realized or understood. We have got tremendous yields of pasture on hilltops where only two years before were bare, eroded bald spots. I think *whole* fertilizer is the answer.

A couple of weeks ago I made a triangular trip from here to Indianapolis to Cincinnati and home again. It was a trip through some of the richest agricultural country in the world, yet nearly all the permanent pastures I saw were thin, weedy, and sickly, producing on the whole a tenth or even a hundredth of the pasture it should have produced. It is extraordinary that so many farmers fail to realize the value of good pasture. This is, of course, especially true of dairy and livestock farmers.

We regard a good bluegrass and white-clover permanent pasture as a valuable crop and the bookkeeping figures show that this is easily true.

The pasture policy in American agriculture in the past has been generally in line with the whole soil mining philosophy of the American farmer. Permanent pasture has always been the field which was too steep or too wet for row-crop cultivation, or the field which was abandoned and given over to pasture because it was worn out. Pastures were supposed to take care of themselves, with the result that most pasture has grown steadily meaner and poorer and weedier year after year, and its carrying capacity both in number of livestock head and in quality of beef and milk production has grown less and less each year.

The old economic problem which lies at the root of so many of the ills connected with our agricultural prosperity and living costs, is that of using constantly more and more acres to produce less and less food. Few farmers ever calculate the millions of tons of calcium, phosphorus, and potassium which have been carried off to market from our grazing land in the bone, flesh, and milk of cattle, sheep, and hogs over the period in which our land has been grazed. Only a feeble effort has ever been made to return any of this to pasture lands. One of the magical exhibits we are able to show is the result of applications of lime and whole fertilizer to pasture together with the mowing process which lays down year after year a deeper layer of protective organic mulch.

Two or three years ago some of our neighbors were of the opinion that we were using too much fertilizer and wasting it. Some of them have come round to our way of thinking after seeing the results both in pasture and in crop fields. Alfalfa and especially sweet clover were considered difficult crops in our part of Ohio and their use very nearly abandoned after many trials. I think we have been able to show pretty conclusively that both crops—perhaps the most valuable a farmer can raise—are difficult only because of the mineral deficiencies of eroded and worn-out soils. Once we adopted the policy of increasing the amount of whole fertilizer used on wheat or oats in which seedings were made or in direct trash-farmed seedings, there has not been even the faintest difficulty with getting very nearly 100 per cent successful seedings. The clue, of course, lay always under the eyes of all of us—that sweet clover and alfalfa in our country attains a rank weed-like growth along roadsides and in fencerows where the minerals are not eroded, leached-out or farmed-out.

The business of soil conservation, of checking run-off water and erosion is becoming generally accepted and is being more and more widely practiced. The next stage is soil *restoration*—the restoration of *both* organic materials and minerals. Until all this is understood and practiced our American agriculture will continue to be wasteful and extravagant. Our food costs will continue to mount and the farmer's margin of profit to decrease. We are headed toward fruit or cereal rather than a meat diet and eventually in the last resort toward the low-living standard and wretched diet of the Indians and Chinese.

JULY 12: Sunday six farmers came from York, Pennsylvania, to spend the day going over the farm. Joan Fontaine and the Hutchinsons came over from South Bend for the week end. Also twenty-five members of an amateur photographers club came down from Cleveland to spend the day photographing. This country, with its streams and forests and pastures and cattle, is certainly photogenic.

On Tuesday we went to Detroit where I saw the new Ferguson, Inc., picture in the "Prosperity from the Ground Up" series showing the relation of agriculture as our fundamental industry to the rest of our national economy. The picture is the second of a series and part of a national campaign to give greater emphasis on agriculture and enlist the interest and cooperation of labor, industry, bankers, and city folk generally—a very important job and being well done.

The next day in Battle Creek where there are four thousand

or more boys who have suffered amputations as a result of the War, I spent the day talking to them about agriculture and the revolution which has taken place in methods and machinery. A very high percentage are farm boys and there is a remarkable number without farm background who want to take up farming. Very few of them are looking simply for employment. Most of them want independence—the kind that comes from operating a small business, or a service station of some kind, or a piece of land. The new machinery, which takes virtually all the drudgery and heavy work out of farming, is a God-send to boys like these, especially the Ferguson stuff which requires no more skill or strength than is needed for driving an automobile.

I talked twice in auditoriums, once at Percy Jones Hospital and once at Fort Custer where the convalescents are. Both were good-sized audiences and listened with remarkable attention and concentration, with many intelligent questions. Afterward I talked to a good many individuals and later visited two wards filled with boys paralyzed by spinal injuries. They were the most tragic of all. Yet the spirit of nearly all of them was extraordinary and made me feel very humble.

It was a long day and a hard one, what with wanting to do so much more for them than could be done and feeling bitterness and hatred for the men who made war and such tragic mutilations possible. And then about four o'clock Colonel James, head of the hospital, said to me, "There is a great favor you could do for me. There is a boy here who is a quadruple amputee. He only arrived here a couple of days ago and I think he'd like to talk to you."

I knew what he meant. He was using technical language but he meant a "basket case." He said the boy was the only case in this war.

I felt sick and said, "You'd better ask him first if he wants to talk with me. Sometimes they don't want to talk at first. If he wants to I'll be glad to talk to him."

"He's a remarkable fellow," the Colonel said. "He and his wife want to go into chicken farming and he'd like to talk to you about it."

The Colonel couldn't be a better man for the difficult job he has as head of the amputee hospital. He has a warm pleasant personality and an air of great casualness, which is so reassuring and so right. He went away and in a little time Lieutenant Kerrigan came back and said the boy wanted very much to talk to me.

I think the hardest thing I ever did was to go into that hospital room but as soon as I crossed the threshold everything was all right and easy and casual because the man himelf made it so. He was Master Sergeant Hensel. I don't know what I expected but in any case it was a surprise. He was lying on the bed with scarcely anything over him because of his fever and the heat. He had a dark, intelligent, and sensitive face, with a high forehead and bright blue eyes, and as he turned toward me he made everything all right, by the way he looked at me. There was no sense of strain at all, no bitterness in him.

We talked for nearly an hour about chickens and farming. His wife was with him, a remarkable girl about twenty-three or four from a Kentucky hill family with some Cherokee Indian blood and great dark eyes. I told him everything I knew and boasted of the record made by seven hundred of our pullets who had laid over six hundred eggs a day for nearly six months. I told Hensel about Harry who, Bob says, becomes a chicken himself when he enters the poultry house to take care of the hens. When I told Hensel that he laughed, but the courage of that laugh, the reason, and acceptance of it made me want to cry.

The sergeant and his wife will be all right. They love each other and they're planning for the future. He'll have two artificial legs and two artificial arms and learn to use them efficiently because he's that kind of a guy. The hour I spent with him was one of the greatest experiences I have ever had. I went out at last stronger and wiser than when I went into that room. All the weariness was gone out of me and I was filled with humbleness. When I said, "When you're up and about you and your wife must come and spend a few days at the farm. Harry can tell you all there is to know about chickens," the sergeant replied. "That's an invitation that will be accepted. You can count on that."

The Army sent out his story to all the newspapers the same day—a wise course, I think, to put an end to all the stupid, sinister and sometimes malicious rumors about "basket cases." Sergeant Hensel is the only one from the battlefield, of this World War.

When the press asked if they might take his picture he grinned and said, "Of course, a picture of me would be good propaganda against another war."

He was brought up in an orphanage and married before he went away to war. His wife whose name is Jewell—a good name for her—had the news of his injuries in a letter written for him by one of the nurses before he arrived. She came at once to the hospital and is staying with him. General Marshall has called twice to ask after him and to see that he gets the best of attention.

He got his injuries when he stepped on a Japanese mine at Okinawa—not an ordinary mine for the Japs had buried a heavy charge of TNT beneath it in order to do greater damage to the tanks, the service in which Hensel was Master Sergeant. Certainly, I shall never forget him and the dignity with which he made everything all right for everyone in the room.[1]

Dined before leaving for Detroit with W. H. Vanderploeg of the Kellogg Company and Emory W. Morris, head of the Kellogg Foundation. The Foundation is conducting at the Kellogg farms together with Michigan State College some remarkable long-range experiments concerning the relation of minerals in the soil to the health of plants, animals, and humans. Have arranged to visit the farm in September with Bob and go into the whole thing in detail. They are certainly on the right track. As Huge Bennett says, "Poor soil makes poor people and poor people make poor soil worse."

JULY 13: It was good to be home again. I think sometimes that the farm is becoming an obsession to the exclusion of all else; which is bad, but there is in it so deep and so fundamental a satisfaction which is difficult to control.

I have come to the conclusion that of all farm implements the mower is the greatest and most important. Certainly it is in our hilly country where hay and pasture are

[1] A popular fund raised for Sergeant Hensel provided him with cash to set up a poultry farm in Georgia where he and his wife are now established.

of so much importance. We keep a mower on one tractor all through the summer to cut hay and mow pasture and weeds on fallowed ground. On the Bailey Place where the soil had been reduced almost to the texture of cement, a year or two of fallowing in legumes with lime, mowing the legumes and letting them lie on the surface to mulch the hard ground, retain moisture, and finally to be mixed in the soil, has increased production in a year or two by as much as five hundred to a thousand per cent.

All the way to Battle Creek and back I saw not one blue-grass pasture a tenth as productive as our own at this mid-summer period of the year. Nearly all were burned out, dormant, weedy, and dry while our own pastures are green and almost lush. Lime, whole fertilizer, and mowing which lays down a constantly increasing layer of humus mulch and preserves the moisture, have done the trick. Some day all live-stock farmers will understand that pasture is one of their most valuable crops and do something about it.

This afternoon while I was mowing on fallow ground, I flushed a whole family of baby rabbits and their mother. They could not have been more than a couple of weeks old and too young to know how to save themselves. They just hopped about in aimless circles. The dogs—Gina and Folly—were with me and behaved very well. At my command they simply stood still, trembling, and let the rabbits hop away into the thick oats of an adjoining field.

The pheasants seem to be increasing in the valley fields, away from the foxes which haunt the hills. I flushed two families yesterday. And despite the snow of the winter, the quail are more abundant than usual. They seem to be everywhere and very tame. It may be that they are attracted to our fields by the abundance and by the presence of minerals that have been restored to the land.

Last night Bob ran down a fox with his car in the lane leading up to Jim Pugh's cabin. The legislature has now declared an open season on foxes and permits County Commissioners to offer bounties. Foxes have become a serious menace to other game as well as to poultry. Last summer they took more than a hundred of Walter Berry's pullets on range in broad daylight and when we mowed the hay in the field next to his, we found it littered with the feathers of

young leghorn pullets. With all the crevices and caves and thick cover in this country they are very difficult to exterminate.

Tonight Bob and I drove to the Conservancy fields to look at the corn. I have seen no better field anywhere in the Middle West, even in Indiana or Illinois. It is a deep, luscious green, even and solid over the whole 80-acre field, with the leaves extravagantly ruffled. If we have enough rain it should bring in a hundred baskets to the acre, easily. No matter how worried or depressed you may be, a sight like that drives away all depression.

Bryce Browning, Secretary of the Conservancy, is coming tomorrow with six farmers from Tuscaroras County and a young soldier is coming up from Dayton to look over the place and get some advice about setting up as a farmer.

FRIDAY THE 13TH: What a day! The farmers turned out to be twelve instead of six. We spent three hours going over the fields. I was very proud of the appearance of the crops and animals. We are going to save out a couple of thin, gullied acres on the Bailey Place as a museum piece of what the farm looked like when we took over.

Noble Crane came up from Columbus to go over the "Prosperity from the Ground Up" plan which aims to bring farmers, industry, and labor into closer and more friendly relations. Also to restore the farmer to that position of authority and dignity which was largely lost in the madhouse industrial scramble of the past fifty years.

Two American Field Service boys on leave drove down from Cleveland—one back from Burma, the other from Africa. The boys certainly get around nowadays. Pete, our former dairyman, sent a picture of himself yesterday taken in the garden of our house in France!

Just after lunch a taxi drove up with a strange woman in it. Wishing to keep the taxi to take Noble Crane back to Mansfield I went out and asked, "Are you keeping the taxi?" To which she replied, "Oh, no! I've come to stay a few weeks. I had a lot of troubles and thought I might get them straightened out if I stayed with you a while."

She returned with the taxi; and a large suitcase obviously packed for a long stay. We've had some other screwballs from time to time. The old man who arrived with all his baggage to make his home with us, the old woman who wanted to stay for a time because she felt I could help her commune with her dead husband whom she saw from time to time "through the cleft in the Rock of Ages." Almost every week there are two or three in addition to about twenty or thirty letters from crackpots of one sort or another, either filled with obscene abuse or containing thirty or forty pages of the one and only plan to save our economic system and humanity. A good many of them are nebulous versions of "the Common Man" philosophy. Sometimes I think we produce more nuts per acre in this country than any country in the world.

After the unexpected visitor left, another lady, younger, all dressed up and wearing high-heeled shoes appeared coming up the road. She had hitch-hiked from Mansfield and wanted to know how to write. Of course there isn't any recipe except to have something to say and to learn how to say it. Nearly always the people who want to "know how to write" want to be writers not because they like writing or have anything to say but because they think it's a free and easy life with a lot of money—which it isn't, God knows! But it's a poor basis on which to build any success. As Henry Ford once said to me, "Most successful people want to do something passionately. They know what they want to do and stick to it. The money takes care of itself. Usually you can't keep the rewards of money or recognition away."

The longer I live the more it seems to me that most people never get on as far as they should because they never make up their minds what they want to do and never stick to it. They're always looking for "breaks" and always suspecting others of double-crossing them. The energy spent in trying to take advantage of a "pull" and "breaks," if spent directly, would carry them a great deal farther. The person who is just "looking for a job" never gets very far, either materially or in living satisfaction. I suspect this is the group Henry Wallace refers to as "The Common Man."

After supper mowed all the near-by marshy ground out by the "Stoll Field." There is about three acres of it, fairly weedy, but very moist all through the hottest weather. Am certain it can be turned into the best ladino-alsike pasture for the dairy cows.

I like the natural names that places acquire in the country. "The Stoll Field" has its name from an eccentric Pennsylvania Dutchman who built a cabin there about a hundred years ago. Of course the various farms are known as the Anson Place, the Bailey Place, the Fleming Place, and the hilltop farm is "Up Ferguson Way." Then there is the "Cemetery Field," the "Bottom Pasture" and the "Lower Bottom," the "Bailey Hill," and the "Hog-lot Field."

A kind stranger enlightened me the other day by letter concerning the curious name of "Steam Corners" bestowed long ago on one of our crossroad villages. It appears that after the first county roads were laid out bisecting each other at right angles, small settlements grew up at each intersection. The first buildings were usually placed on the four corners and among them was the first steam sawmill in the countryside. The crossroads became known as "Steam Corner" later corrupted to the plural.

I still haven't been able to run to ground the origin of the curious name of "Pinhook" another crossroads near us.

Among other things the day was marred by two heroic dog fights both staged within five minutes involving five dogs on one side and seven on the other. Prince, Baby, Gina, Folly, Smokey, Susie and Dusky were all with me when I stopped at Harry's house to inspect the improvements he was making. Laddie, his big St. Bernard, came running out, followed by Sandy, the Border Collie who has ten new pups, Penny, Harry's Boxer, and the St. Bernard pup.

It was a real brawl with all the ladies joining in a hair-pulling match—six Boxers and a Spaniel on one side, two St. Bernards and a Border Collie and a Boxer on the other. We just managed to separate them and lock the Heller's dogs in the house when one of the children opened a door at the back of the house and all of them came galloping out to renew the battle. The big St. Bernard seemed to have been the chief casualty. Prince got hold of his big floppy ears and wouldn't let go.

After two years we are still "mining" the manure out of the Bailey barn and barnyard. We can use it to advantage in restoring the bare Bailey Hill to fertility. I doubt that it has seen manure of any kind, green or barnyard for at least twenty-five years, perhaps never.

I suspect from the sounds that the field mouse which haunts Mary's and my bedrooms has built a nest inside the radio beside my bed. The dog doesn't seem to mind so I don't. He is a pretty little fellow with very bright eyes and enormous ears and sits up like a kangaroo.

Harry and Jimmy are amassing a small fortune by working the haybaler on custom service on Sundays and during the long summer evenings in the neighbors' fields. The arrangement satisfies everybody—ten cents a bale, split fifty-fifty with the farm for the use of the baler—and the neighbors, terribly short of help and machinery, are getting their hay in. They work as a team and have arrived at a high state of efficiency, Harry pushing the wires and Jimmy tying. It is a comical sight to see them crossing a rich hayfield with the baler running about fifteen miles an hour tossing off bales like a carp spawning. They made twenty dollars apiece last Sunday. Harry wants money to buy a new car and Jimmy, who is seventeen and foreman of the boys, is saving up to buy a farm. It is fairly light work and, except for the dust, one of the most pleasurable jobs on the farm.

Observation: When some silly woman asks Mary, "But don't you get lonely on a farm?" Mary answers, "Spend a day there some time and see how lonely it is!"

JULY 14: French Independence Day! Good Lord! What has happened to the world since that last Bastille Day we all spent in Senlis in 1938?

The rain broke early this morning. Thunder woke me about daylight and I couldn't get to sleep again for waiting for the sound of rain. Oddly enough, despite all the long downpour of the spring, we needed rain badly for the corn and the bluegrass pasture. Only ten days ago it seemed that not a day could pass without rain. Every time we cut hay it rained. Then days of summer heat accompanied by hot winds which did the most damage. They simply suck the moisture out of the ground by the thousand gallons. That's what rarely happens in central or northern Europe. There is none of the violence of climate which is typical of all the United States even in temperate, well-watered Ohio. In Europe, if it rains, the water stays with you, coming down gently and rarely followed by great heat or hot winds. We are likely to get our summer rains in violent downpours coming in a flood. Much of it runs off if the soil hasn't enough organic material in it to soak up the flood or if fields are left bare. The sun and wind soak up what remains. Because of the intensive campaign to increase the humus content of our soil, we suffer much less from the sun and wind than most farmers, but we still have a long way to go to raise the content to the level of the good Amish and Mennonite farmers over in Holmes County.

It rained all day—good rain—slow, soaking rain like that of northern France save for an occasional half hour of flooding downpour, when the heavens seemed to open and hurl down buckets of water. At the end of the day our own brooks were still running clear which is something of which to be proud.

The odd thing was that for two hours or more after the rain began all the birds kept up a chorus of singing as if in gratitude.

At noon Bob and I drove down to the Conservancy to watch the rain falling on the corn. I have just come back from a trip through Indiana, Ohio, and Michigan, and our eighty acres of corn, all in one field, is the prettiest piece of corn I have seen anywhere—deep green in color with the leaves ruffled along the edges with the vigor of growth. And these fields never get any barnyard manure, since they lie too far from the barns. It is organic material—mostly sweet clover—and the wise use of mineral elements. The stand is perfectly even, with scarcely a gap in any of the rows. As far as you can see it is all of an even height, texture, and color. I took Ma down again in the evening to look at it. The sight gave her the same satisfaction it gave Bob and me. Warm rain falling on strong, healthy, even corn is one of the most satisfactory of sights.

In the evening I walked out over the fields to feel the soaked ground under my feet and smell the odors arising from the warm, wet earth in pasture, alfalfa, corn, and oat fields. Even the dogs seemed to enjoy the experience, barking and playing wildly. And the horses came up around me, even Tex who usually plays coy and hard to get. Down by the bridge I came upon Kenneth Cook and George, his eight-year-old son. They were doing the same thing, walking out across the moist growing fields. We sat for a long time on the bridge talking or just sitting silently enjoying the evening after the rain.

Harry is worried because the cow-tester says he has got to quit testing because he hasn't enough support in the county. Harry, rightly, is proud of the records of some of the cows, and especially of the heifers. He wants to keep up the tests.

The three of us—Harry, the cow-tester, and myself—talked for a long time about the problems of farmers, particularly in this county where I was born. Too many of them have reverted to subsistence level and only a handful of the original families which once operated rich farms still survive as good farmers. They are the ones who have been intelligent and kept up with progress and *reform* in agriculture. I emphasize the word "reform" because in the past American agriculture, on the whole, has been so bad that a revolution was necessary for its eventual survival at all. Those who do not choose to go along with the revolution are doomed. A good many have already been eliminated and the remainder will be liquidated, not by firing squads but by economic circumstances, within the next generation.

Farming as a "way of life" is at the same time a romantic and a sound institution for the nation as a whole, but it has to be more than that. Nowadays and in the future it will have to be a scientific, well-managed business as well—no matter whether it is intensive farming on five acres or farming on thousands of acres. At the moment farming as a "way of life" seems on the way out because too few farmers will change their ways.

Here in our hill country, potentially the finest cattle, forage, grazing country in the world, you see farmers plowing up the hills to raise corn and hogs, in emulation of hog farmers in the prairie states—simply because "hog and corn farmers get rich." They too could get rich if they used their land properly and well for cattle and sheep and dairy products. Instead they try to raise quantities of hogs in hill

300

country and gradually either lose their farms or sink to subsistence level by destroying the very soil which is their
capital.

On the other hand in the flat, once-rich land in the northern part of the county, the record is little better. You have
only to drive along the road to see what is being done—
crops today in which no farmer could take price considering
the good soil and good conditions with which that part of the
county was once favored, bare fields in winter, bluegrass
pastures which in midsummer are bare and dry as an asphalt
pavement save for the encroaching weeds and thorn bushes.
All that land was once worth $200 to $300 an acre in
average times. Very little of it has anything like that value
today.

We talked of one case which all three of us know, a
monumental example of short-sightedness. Usually dairy
farmers are prosperous and far-sighted and fairly open to
new ideas, because they have to be. This fellow, a dairy
farmer, was fairly prosperous but only about fifty per cent as
prosperous as he should be. With two hundred acres he
milked about thirty cows but the work was done entirely by
his wife and himself. They are middle-aged but they look
fifteen years older and in another fifteen years will be worn
out. His barn is badly arranged so that it takes a third more
time than is necessary to do the chores. His fields produce
not more than sixty per cent of potentiality, which is high as
farms go, and his pastures (the base of his summer production) not more than thirty per cent of potentiality. That the
standard is so high comes only from the fact that a big
herd of dairy cattle produces much manure and manure
has to be hauled into the fields if only to get it out of the
way. A few years ago an oil well was drilled on his land
quite near the barns. The drills struck a rich vein of artesian
water and stopped drilling. They offered to leave the well
flowing if the farmer would pay for the casing. He refused,
saying he'd "be damned if he'd pay for any casing." The
casing was pulled. The sides of the well collapsed and it
stopped flowing. For the past few years the farmer has been
hauling water all through the winter for his livestock. Perhaps it has occurred to him since that the labor spent in

hauling water for just one season would have paid for all that casing. I do not know. I doubt sometimes, that farmers like him think at all.

Recently he bought another 160 acres which adjoined his farm. When asked why he did it, he said, "Because it lays nice, joins me and I want to increase production." It had never occurred to him that he could have increased his crop production by at least forty per cent and his pasture production by seventy per cent by managing the land he already owned as well as he could. Instead he will try, by cutting the corners on labor and fertilizer expenditure, to farm 360 acres less well than he is farming the original 200. Whatever he produces will cost him more per pound, per gallon or per bushel not only in money and in land values, but it will mean that he and his wife lead a more and more inhuman existence and work themselves more quickly into the grave. It never occurred to him that there is much less work and much more profit in raising 100 bushels per acre on one acre than 100 bushels on two and a half acres which is about the ratio between the potentiality of his good, flat-lying land, and the production which he is actually achieving. In other words in his expanded, inefficient, unintelligent set-up he will be spending in labor, in taxes, in fertilizer, in seed, in gasoline, oil, and wear and tear, for a bushel of corn two and one half times what he should to produce the same amount of farm produce.

Fundamentally the situation of this man lies at the root of many of our agricultural economic ills and affects seriously and adversely our whole economic structure. As I have suggested too many times in this book we are farming in this country an average of five acres to produce what one acre should. This increases the cost of food to the consumer by approximately five times and reduces the profit of the farmer proportionately. There are, of course, other elements entering into the vast and complicated problem of how to maintain a sound and profitable agriculture but a much improved agriculture is the fundamental answer.

The case of the farmer under discussion is largely typical. Without knowing it, he is headed toward ruin *through* expansion instead of farming the land he already had to the utmost of its potentiality. It is the farmers in this group who

302

are headed for liquidation as many like them were liquidated during the Great Depression. He is farming as a "way of life," not as an intelligent, well-planned operation, in which he will be secure in bad as well as in good times. When bad times come he will have to borrow money or go out of business altogether. He is following that tragic rule, "What is good enough for my father and grandfather is good enough for me!"

Subsidies, parities and all the other formulas proposed on the one side by the New Deal and on the other by the absentee landowners of the Farm Bloc are not the answer. All these things only tend to support and *encourage* a poor and unproductive agriculture. The answer is a better and more efficient agriculture, greater production on fewer acres, longer production costs and cheaper, more abundant food, with greater profit margins for the farmer himself.

Some of our neighbors accused us a few years ago of using chemical fertilizer wastefully because we put on fifty to one hundred pounds more per acre than was the custom. The local habit was to use just enough to carry through a crop of oats, wheat, or corn to maturity, with none at all on pastures. Some of them have begun to change and to understand that the extra fifty or hundred pounds not only paid for itself about twenty times over but left a residue to replenish the elements farmed or leached out of the topsoil itself. This second benefit has shown up in a gradually increasing fertility which must be calculated in the steadily mounting production. Topsoil in itself is not the answer to the millennium. Much of it in the United States is so devoid of organic material and of minerals that it is little more productive and sometimes actually less so than the minerally unexhausted subsoil which lies beneath it.

JULY 21: Finished mowing the hog-lot field. It is much bigger than it looks—an irregular field cut out of the forest sloping southeast. The moon is in the first quarter but very bright and I kept mowing with the lights on the tractor until the field was finished. It is rough hay in which the cursed timothy crowded out most of the alfalfa and clover. The beef calves picked up what they could and we are mowing the rest to leave it on the ground as mulch and to be worked into the soil for wheat ground in the fall. It will be pretty well rotted by then and presently will make good humus.

The system of mowing and leaving weeds and hay on the ground is much better than the old-fashioned system of fallowing which merely left the ground bare for a year to give it a rest. If hay or even weeds are allowed to grow and are mowed down twice a summer and left to rot and be plowed in, nothing is lost minerally from the soil for everything is left in the field and there is all the growth above ground and also the root system below which is a gain, taken from the air and sunlight. Agronomists estimate that only five per cent less of roots and stalk and leaves comes out of the soil itself—all the rest from sunlight and air. The gain through the mowing system is immense and will raise yields on some of our poor fields as much as 500 per cent within a year. On the Bailey Place where Kenneth is combining wheat, it is yielding about 35 bushels to the acre on ground which only two years ago yielded not more than five and was not even worth combining. The mowing system plus mixed legumes, barnyard manure, and lime did the trick. Not a bad yield considering the fact that the average yield for the nation is only 20 bushels. The Conservancy wheat and that on the Fleming Place will yield easily 40 to 45 bushels.

While I mowed, the fireflies came up out of the grass almost in swarms as the cutter bar passed through it. Because the year has been so wet there are millions of them. They hung over the field, glittering in the moonlight as the mist came up over the damp ground of the lower pasture. Gina and Folly stayed with me fixing most of their attention on the woodchuck holes I uncovered while mowing.

Later Bob came up to advise me to give up and go to bed. We talked a long time about the farm. He fusses and worries because each day is not perfection itself. I told him that in the last six months I had been over a large part of Ohio, Indiana, and Michigan and had seen no farm that looked as well as ours—no better wheat, no corn as far along or as vigorous, and no comparable bluegrass pasture. Of course, in a wet year like this the flat-country people are at a disadvantage except on pasture.

Pierre Sauvegeot and Mme. Lucienne Erville left today after three days. They have been at the San Francisco Conference representing the French Ministry of Agriculture and stopped here to see what was being done and to discuss the whole problem of soil in relation to health, vigor, and intelligence—a subject in which Sauvegeot is an expert.

He is very sound, save when he turns mystical. I reproached him for this. Every good farmer is a mystic at heart and a religious man, but a good farmer's mysticism and faith are founded upon the base of the earth itself, and so very different from what to me is that implausible mysticism of the detached spirit. I am Protestant enough and Anglo-Saxon enough to demand concrete results. This is where I am forced to part company with many who practice the mysticism of debased Hinduism. The mystic who retires into contemplation seems to me an egotist, futile, and slightly ridiculous.

Sauvegeot gave me an account of the two strange interviews he had with Henry Wallace and later showed me a copy of a letter he had written Wallace before the interview. Wallace has much the quality of the mystic without base—the same grandiose looseness of phrase, the same absence of logic, the same simplicity (which in Wallace used to be genuine) and that same voluptuous indulgence in a vague, amorphous idealism. Some mystics wallow in it up to the ears.

Sauvegeot, in his peculiar kind of mysticism, indulges himself in all sorts of vague plans for a return to nature and a new agriculture which ignores wholly the immense political and economic complexity of the world in which we live. He would have us, in a world of machines and its teeming ill-fed millions, return to a kind of medieval and mystical agriculture, which, aside from being economically impossible, would leave four-fifths of the world to starve. There is much that is good in his philosophy but it needs both integration and some relation to reality and the practical aspects of the earth. The interview between him and Wallace must have been strange indeed—double-talk in a fog. One element which Sauvegeot did not know and which I explained to him was Wallace's rumored earlier and unfortunate experiences with the Crystal Gazers, which threatened his political career and has made him acutely suspicious of any mystic. Wallace may succeed politically one day, but only under the circumstances which produced Hitler. That might happen here!

Madame Erville is Russian by blood, Belgian by citizenship. She is intelligent and well-informed and worked in the Underground during the whole of the War.

We got away from agriculture in the evenings and had a lot of good talk about Gertrude Stein, Edith Wharton, the Royal Tylers, André Germaine, Bernard Fäy, Pierre de Lanux, Leni Reifenstal and all the bad melodrama of the period in Europe between wars.

Rose and Ernie Necker were also here for three days. They spent three years in the prison camp of Santo Tomas at Manila. They went to Manila with the Mackay Radio Company and were caught there. Some of the stories were hair-raising. All those in the camp were being slowly starved to death and plans were under way to remove all the men between fifteen and sixty-five and liquidate them, when the flying tank column arrived in time and rescued them. The column was far-outnumbered but the Japs failed to find it out in time. Rose who normally weighs 130 pounds, weighed only 80 when they were freed and Ernie lost fifty pounds. They still have what Rose calls "Blanks" when they forget what they are talking about. They take it all humorously with a great deal of spirit and common sense. They left today to meet in New York my nephew Johnny Mauger who is here after 35 missions as engineer of a B-29 over Japan. Johnny, who stayed here on his way through from San Francisco, had some terrific stories and photographs. The whole experience has greatly subdued him. He was with one of the first B-29 Squadrons before the Iwo Jima landing fields were established and the losses were heavier than we have yet been told.

The Klats drove down from Cleveland for lunch with Sir Sultan Chinoy. Klat is former director of the General Motors interests in Bombay. Sir Sultan is a former Mayor of Bombay and is here with the Indian Industrial Commission at the San Francisco Conference. He is a Moslem and a charming man. We talked a lot about Indian friends—that great character, the Dowager Maharani of Baroda, Indira Cooch-Behar, her daughter, and the Frank Kerrs, the Raschild Baigs and a lot of others. All the talk made me very homesick for India again. Sir Sultan and Frank Kerr both have farms and racing stables at Poona.

JULY 31: Went to Columbus yesterday to attend the second joint meeting of agriculture and industry called by the Farm Bureau and the State Chamber of Commerce. It was a good meeting attended by leading men of the Chamber, the State University and agriculture and much more was accomplished than at the first meeting when there was much beating around the bush and all the effort and talk ended only in a high-fallutin' and innocuous resolution about everybody being for cooperation and employment and prosperity, of course!

The second meeting began in the same way but after lunch we broke down and got to brass tacks. Until then everybody had talked in high-sounding statistics (promptly twisted to prove whatever you wanted to prove). Sometimes the businessmen and the Farm Bloc can be as cockeyed as the New Dealers in their manipulation of statistics, using them as a cloud in which to protect themselves when hard pressed as a squid uses ink to escape from pursuers. Something broke down the accumulation of rubbish and nearly everyone present began to make sense and talk about fundamentals with the result that for the first time the meeting became interesting and there appeared some possibility of really achieving something more than a set of windy, bromidic, and high-sounding resolutions. When things came out in the open it appeared that nearly everyone present believed that the answer to postwar security and prosperity lay in abundance, greater production, and low prices, yet agriculture, labor, and industry, all working as segments and encouraged by the New Deal elements which still remain in government, are really working all the time for scarcity and high prices.

The only one who really dissented was the economist of the United States Chamber of Commerce who defended the shocking cotton subsidies. No doubt he was forced to this position as representative of cotton interests. But the fact remains that one day the rest of the country will rebel against paying taxes to subsidize the execrable agriculture of the South and the absentee landlordism which is so largely responsible for the cotton subsidy, the appalling, greedy and destructive agriculture and the frightful social, economic and educational conditions of the Deep South.

Once an acre of good land would raise two bales of cotton but for a long time now it has required as high as five acres of worn-out land to produce one bale. In other words the cost of a bale of cotton is increased in labor, fertilizer (if any), taxes and seed about ten times what it should be under a sound agriculture and the taxpayer in other parts of the nation is forced to pay a fat subsidy in order to permit the cotton growers to go on farming ignorantly and wastefully, raising a crop for which there is no market in the world at the present cost of production. A sound, diversified agriculture plus efficient mechanization with one-fifth of the area now devoted to cotton could produce as much cotton as is being produced today in the South, at costs which would make cotton a profitable crop without subsidy. Yet the absentee-landlord, sharecropper, tenant-farmer system goes on producing less and less cotton each year at higher and higher costs and the taxpayer pays up each year (most of us being unaware of the fact) to preserve a foolish destructive system and a rising cost of production.

Our glacial hill country is coming into its own again this year. Our crops look better and are yielding more than any I have seen on the flat prairie country. The cold, delayed, wet spring held back planting and the late rains flooded flat country fields long after our crops were well along. What interests me in all this is that on some of our land where the war shortages have not prevented us from going ahead we are raising better crops on our hills than most of the flat prairie country. We can do this every year, regardless of wet, late seasons, for our gravel-loam soil drains well and can be worked at almost any time. But the interesting economic fact is that our land, after the money and labor spent on restoring it, has cost us only seventy dollars or under an acre. It was worn out but potentially good agricultural land which with proper treatment and agricultural methods is producing as much as flat land costing $200 an acre and more, so that on our capital investment we are getting about three times as much return.

The average wheat production in the United States is 20 bushels per acre. This year our *average* on a dozen fields good and bad in various stages of restoration has been close to thirty bushels. The average corn production of the richest middle-west area is 43 bushels. We shall not make less than 75 bushels on some of our land and near to a hundred on other fields. All of these facts seem to me to be arguments *for better agriculture* as the answer to the woes of the average farmer, better agriculture on less land with less labor, taxes, seed, and fertilizer expenses. The margin between the seventy dollar cost per acre of our land and the $200 an acre cost of the better agriculture land allows a lot of money to be spent in mechanization and making our agriculture more efficient and productive. Yet the average farmer when he wants to increase production rarely does a better job of farming the land he already owns; he goes out and buys a couple hundred more acres which together with his earlier holdings he farms less well and at greater cost.

These are fundamentals but not many politicians consider them. It is easier to vote subsidies and bribes to satisfy the short-sighted slovenly farmer or the absentee landlord who must be "saved" every time there is a depression. At times it seems to me that we as a nation deliberately support and *encourage* poor and costly agriculture.

AUGUST 4: Mowed all day while the boys got in the rest of the hay from the big Bailey field. It is an old seeding of alfalfa and brome grass in which some red clover and a little timothy and some wild grasses and weeds have seeded themselves—more like a Swiss meadow than a single-crop, American hay field. It is the prettiest hay I have seen in a long while, as green in the mow as in the fields and as green as any artificially dried hay. The weather, of course, was perfect with a hot sun that tanned even my tough hide a deeper brown and with a cool drying wind out of the north. The dairy cows will relish it more and do better on it than on any crop of pure alfalfa or clover. Experiments at Roehampton in England showed that beef cattle on mixed "meadow" pasture put on many pounds a month more weight than cattle fed the best, pure, one-crop pasture.

It is remarkable how well the Shorthorn herd does on the poor weedy Bailey pastures, very nearly as well as the blue-roan herd on the rich, improved Ferguson pastures. Up there the blue roans have not only the advantage of good lush pasture but of *mixed* pastures as well.

Heard from Lord Portsmouth today. He plans to come here for a visit after a trip to his brother's ranch in Wyoming. He has 30 thousand acres in England and is at the head of the sound movement to revive and improve the agriculture of Britain, neglected during the century and more of her industrial ascendancy. Now that is over and the question of *feeding* England becomes vital again—more indeed than ever before in her history. Portsmouth, born Oliver Wallop, grew up on a Wyoming ranch and married an American wife. Much that we have done here in revitalizing soil and raising production should be of value for the soil problems of much of agricultural England are similar to our own. England must produce 100 per cent of potential capacity of her soil without losing fertility. And even such a high level of production will not feed her population.

Yesterday while I mowed I was accompanied by scores of barn swallows which swept over and around me catching the insects driven out of the heavy alfalfa by the mower. Sometimes they brushed my head and I could feel the rush of air from their wings. I know of no bird of which I am fonder. They build dozens of nests each year on the big hand-hewn rafters of the old barns, very close up against the upper floors with scarcely room to enter the nest. They are, partly at least, responsible for the total lack of mosquitos at Malabar. The fish in the ponds, the frogs and toads, and the good drainage all do their part.

While I was mowing yesterday near the Jungle there suddenly appeared out of the thick wild undergrowth a small figure clad only in pants and galoshes. It was Herbie, the boy Harry and Naomi have taken to raise with their own children. He is about ten years old with slanting eyes and a curious fey look in them. No one seems to know quite where he came from. He had the name of "bad boy." He isn't. All he needed was someone like Harry or Naomi who like animals and birds and all natural things.

As soon as he came out of the Jungle he began to babble.

He said, "I seen a big frog" and "all the little fish nibbled at my legs." He had been swimming at the hole in Switzer's Creek surrounded by a wild thick, growth of trees, brambles, skunk cabbage and rushes. His eyes were shining and the words wouldn't come fast enough in his eagerness to tell me all the wonders he had seen on that bright, clear morning in Pleasant Valley. A moment later Naomi and three small children came out of the thicket. They too had been swimming. Before they came here they had lived—the children since they were born—in a big industrial city and at first they were *afraid* of the country, but they are getting used to it now and loving it and discovering that in the country there is never a dull moment, but a whole universe filled with light and air and water and living things.

Harry wants now to get the children a pony. They go up to Vane Close's place with him when he takes the baler up to help Vane with his haymaking and Vane, who likes animals too, has a lot of horses and ponies—why, I do not know—which they ride. I discussed with Harry the question of whether he could afford a pony but to Harry that didn't seem to matter. When he took on two St. Bernards I raised the same question but Harry said, "The kids have a lot more fun out of the dogs than out of a new set of clothes." That, it seemed to me, is real wisdom.

All the children have changed a lot since they came here —not only have they grown plump and gained color but they have lost the furtive, frightened look which they had acquired in the city. They spend a large part of the day paddling in the brook that flows from the big Bailey spring, out of the solid rock, its banks green with mint and willows, its course clogged with watercress—a little better than the dingy, sooty background hung with washing in the city. And they have a big swing hanging from one of the limbs of one of the big cut-leaf maples that surround the big Bailey house and red sandstone rocks covered with ferns and wild columbine to climb over. But most of all, they love all the animals. One can't help speculating how different their lives and characters will be through having escaped from the city.

The farm is full of children as it should be. Butch and Patti, George's nephew and niece, aged nine and twelve spend all summer here and hate going back to Long Island when school opens in the autumn. The other day Butch said, "There's never enough time here. Back home I have to think up things to do. I don't want to go to bed at ten o'clock here. There's always so many things left over that I haven't done." He is small, very freckled and a great friend of Charlie's whose room he shares. He won't come into the big dining room but insists on eating in the small dining room with Charlie and the boys. He wants to be one of the "men" on the farm.

Emma, Tom's wife, has taken on the job of cooking for the boys who work here during the summer. Fortunately she loves it and the boys love her. It gives her quite an income as she is paid by the head. She is a marvelous cook as is well known in the Big House where in a crisis she helps out. It is remarkable how so many people can get on so well in a small community which is almost like a village. Perhaps it is because the lazy ones, the gossips, the trouble-makers have finally been sifted out and because everybody is really interested in the job that is being done. Certainly no more widely assorted group of personalities and backgrounds has ever been brought together. Fortunately everybody speaks of Malabar as "our place."

George, Mayo Bogart, Hope and Mac all left yesterday for the East for a couple of days. The house gets to be more and more of a hotel with people going and coming.

AUGUST 5: Haile Selassie, the big Karakul ram, left today. He had become obstreperous and dangerous to the kids on the place and to visiting kids, not because he was bad-tempered but because he was too playful and didn't realize how much harm he could do with his big horns. The other evening he attacked Nanny while she was picking blackberries with the children and knocked her down three times cutting her leg badly. His butting didn't matter so much but he has the Karakul's bad habit of *hooking* with his horns. I hated to see him go. He is a handsome, rowdy character with a great addiction to tobacco, but he has gone to a good home over near Mifflin Lake where he will be a pet which is what he wants to be.

We have had two days of annoying weather of the kind

which in England is called "blight" weather, neither sun nor rain but overcast with a high temperature and now and then a few spitting drops of rain. It spoils haymaking and does neither corn nor pasture any good. We have twelve acres of good clover and alfalfa hay down which will be spoiled if the weather continues. I wouldn't mind a good soaking rain that would help the corn and pasture. We have enough hay to afford losing what is on the ground. However, all of it is on land that goes into wheat this fall so if it spoils, it would not hurt the soil to plow it in.

Last night (Sunday) Nanny arranged a picnic for the boys up on the Ferguson Place and finally everybody on the farm ended up there coming up the hill on foot or on tractors.

The drawing power of the wild, deserted farm with no dwellings or barns is extraordinary. Everybody loves it—high against the sky overlooking three counties. We built big fires and burned up a lot more of the fallen branches, old fence posts and rubbish that always clutters a run-down abandoned farm. We have been five years at off moments clearing up the Ferguson Place and the job is at last nearly done. I must say Nanny and Anne did most of the work while I ran the mower over about five acres of pasture. The kids enjoyed themselves and Betty Pugh came up from the cabin to join them. It was a cloudy evening with all the farms in the valley far below and among the woods on the opposite side all misty and blue like the trees and houses in a French landscape.

We saved two big old chestnuts killed years ago by the blight for it was evident that the hollows of both, one of them upright and one prostrate, were filled with animal life. At the foot of one lay four black-snake eggs empty with a small hole where the baby snakes had emerged. Most of us rode up the rough road through the forest on a hay wagon hitched behind a tractor and we picnicked alongside the giant dead chestnuts where every now and then a turn in the breeze brought to us the pungent, musky odor of the raccoons who were inside the old, dead trees hiding and listening to the hub-bub outside their house. It is a very solitary place and they are rarely disturbed from one year's end to another.

Afterward when it grew dark we all came to the Big House—men, women and children—where we sat very late gossiping and talking about farming at Malabar and the world over. It was one of the pleasantest of evenings.

Harry joined us later in his work clothes with his hair slicked down to make up for the fact that he was the only one in work clothes but myself. He had been baling all day for a neighbor over near Perrysville and came back enthusiastic over the cooperation he had received. The farmer had even windrowed the hay so that the heavy baler could *go across* the steep hillsides instead of up and down them. Such cooperation as Harry observed, is rare. Handling heavy balers and combines in our hilly country is a ticklish and dangerous business. Saturday night on one of our own fields on which I know every variation of the level of the land the baler got out of hand and started waltzing down a hillside temporarily out of control. It is not a nice feeling.

The picnic was a kind of consolation for the boys to whom I had refused permission to ride the horses up to Vane Close's farm three miles away. Only Sandy claimed to know anything about riding and neither Tex nor Tony are horses to be left in the hands of inexperienced riders. On Friday, Tony even gave Hope, who can handle most horses, a bad time, and Tex is always unpredictable and wicked. She knows the minute someone mounts her how much she can get away with and will go the limit. She is a beautiful mare very vain and domineering with great intelligence and a prankish sense of humor. Last year a French cavalry officer went out on her to ride with Hope, who was on Tony. After dark Hope came back along with the news that the Captain couldn't make Tex come home. I drove in the car about a mile up the Hastings Road to find the Captain patiently waiting for Tex to feel like coming home. He had tried everything he knew but none of it was any good. I turned over the car to him and when I mounted her, she went off home gentle as a lamb. The exploit was no credit to me; it was merely that for some reason she had taken a dislike to the Captain.

AUGUST 6: The testimony of Laval at the trial of Petain is full of interest, though to date less sensational than might have been expected, perhaps because he is playing the old shrewd Laval game, currying favor with both sides, seeming plausible and twisting every issue. One thing is certain, he would still be in Spain instead of occupying a common cell in Paris if the Tories had won the recent elections. Too many of them were afraid that if brought to trial he would "sing." To date he has only touched the fringes of the nefarious and complicated negotiations of the Tory Government with Hitler and Mussolini in the years just preceding the war. One thing he has made clear—that the shameful Hoare-Laval agreement at the time of the Abyssinian War was *not* made independently and *without* the knowledge of Baldwin, Chamberlain and other members of the Tory Cabinet, although Baldwin and the Tories, when caught in the fury of popular reaction claimed that the negotiations were undertaken by Samuel Hoare, on his own, without the knowledge of the Cabinet—a stupid and unbelievable falsehood at the time, and like John Simon's deceit and doublecrossing of our own State Department at the time of the Manchurian incident, one of the countless reasons for the lack of faith in the honesty and wisdom of the Tory leaders and for their overwhelming defeat in the recent elections.

One of the remarkable things about the reactionary mind (and one of the things which always checks its success in politics) is the smugness and the capacity for underestimating the intelligence and powers of integration in other elements of society.

There should be much information coming from the "War Criminal" trials if they ever take place. It is clear that certain elements in Great Britain have struggled to prevent them and very nearly succeeded. None of those being brought to trial are men of great honor or faith and will undoubtedly "sing" in order to save themselves. What Ribbentrop has to say should be the most interesting. I remember when all London was divided between the Ribbentrop and non-Ribbentrop factions who scarcely spoke to each other. He always gave me the impression of being a slimy skunk and a cheap wine salesman.

What has become of Lord Derby and the Londonderrys who took him up? Since the beginning of the war both seem to have been extinguished. Seven years ago I lunched with Thelma Cazalet at a party given in honor of Londonderry. His place at the table was vacant because through an ironic mistake his book decrying charges of Nazi aggression and "proving" how nice the German people were had come out that very day—the day the "peaceful" Nazis marched in and took Austria.

The pictures of Laval at the Petain trial are appalling. I have never seen a more ravaged or evil face. Perhaps it is that evil may in the end turn and devour its creator. I never saw Laval but once and that on the occasion of a luncheon, given by Jesse Straus while he was American Ambassador, to celebrate the announcement of the *fiancailles* of Laval's daughter José to René de Chambrun. He gave the impression of an oily, physically unclean *maquereau* from a small seaport town. He had a homely knack of telling a provincial comic story well. The shrewdness seems to have been of the sort which takes everything and gives nothing—a tactic which in the end always defeats itself. It is doubtful if today he has a single friend in all of France.

But all of this was only a part of the incredibly bad melodrama which was the history of Europe between the two wars. When you attempt to write it as fiction, it becomes sensational and cheap and unbelievable and unreal—the Cianos, Carol and Lupescu, Hitler and all his gang, the King of England and Mrs. Simpson, Abetz and his spies and collaborationists, Corinne Luchaire. By the way, where is Abetz? He was a little Ribbentrop although more attractive and more of a gentleman.

Poor Petain emerges more as an old fool than as a traitor, although fools can often be more dangerous than deliberately evil men. But the old man was a fool all his life, even at Verdun where he was given a credit which belonged to Nivelle. It seems to me that most of those who seek to defend him are also fools. I remember when he and Madame Petain were treated as sacred white elephants by the more stupid, snobbish, and foolish elements of Paris society. He was always a very dull old man and always a defeatist and through a large part of his life the victim and tool of forces shrewder, and more malignant than himself.

AUGUST 8: Great excitement when the Fred Herring's huge scoop arrived to begin work on the ponds below the old house on the Bailey Place. All the farm down to the dogs and the smallest children were on hand to watch the operations. The big caterpillar and scoop can move 12,000 cubic yards of earth in eight hours. It proved too big for the construction of the little pond next to the house which had to be abandoned until a smaller bulldozer undertakes it. The engineer underestimated the flow of water from the Bailey spring, one of the biggest in the state, and the water got ahead of him and bogged down the 14-ton bulldozer.

Everybody spent the day watching the big scoop excavating and building the dam for the big pond across the road by the barn. Whatever work went on consisted of combining or baling straw in the fields surrounding the pond site so that all could watch the progress. Something very profound in the human soul is touched by all that has to do with water. It is akin to the old Biblical feeling for springs and pools and oases. The pond will provide nearly three acres of cold, clear spring water on land which has always been marshy and difficult. It is exactly beside the turnpike and once the trees and shrubbery grow up about it, I think others besides ourselves will enjoy it.

All the kids had to take turns riding with the driver on the big caterpillar.

# XIII: THE ORGANIC-CHEMICAL FERTILIZER FEUD

I do not believe that anyone really knows very much about farming.

—Wheeler McMillen

In Darmstadt in 1803 there was born to a small shopkeeper a son called Justus Liebig, who as a boy played about in his father's shop among the colors he mixed and sold. In the course of years the playing took a serious form and by the time he was fifteen when he took a job as apprentice in an apothecary shop, his mind was made up. He would be a chemist. He went to the University of Bonn and eventually became a professor of chemistry. He might have gone on for the rest of his life sitting in a chair and expounding the chemical knowledge known up to that time as complete, ultimate and final, as many a professor has done before and since his time, but in Liebig there was a spark. From the earliest days in his father's paint shop, he wanted always to extend the walls of scientific knowledge further and further, to penetrate into the jungle of the still unknown which many of his academic contemporaries regarded with timidity and doubt. He was at times unorthodox. He speculated upon things which other professors regarded as already settled beyond dispute. Eventually he became one of the world's greatest scientists and he brought to world agriculture a revolution. He was the creator of the principle of chemical fertilizer.

Today, in line with the overspecialization which has become one of the great weaknesses of our educational and cultural system, Liebig is commonly regarded and treated as a specialist;

but Liebig, like all great men of science, was much more than that. His interests, like those of the great men of the Renaissance, ran into many fields. He was an expert pathologist and physiologist, something of a physicist and even a philosopher. He possessed a keen interest and curiosity not only concerning the immediate field for which he became known, but concerning the universe in most of its manifestations. He did not believe that chemistry alone was the universal key to the explanation of the cosmos. He was a man tinged by mysticism, by wonder, by a sense of his own insignificance, and by a flame which kept him exploring and exploring. He learned *both* by experiment and by careful observation.

The same individuals who will tell you that Liebig was only a chemist are likely to tell you that Liebig discovered all there was to know about soil and that in his creation of chemical fertilizer he solved the problems of agriculture and food supply for the rest of eternity. It is a statement, or more often an insinuation, which disproves itself in the record of continuing declining yields, with or without fertilizer alone, on most of our agricultural land. Liebig himself would have been the first to mock them for he understood as a man of broad culture and knowledge that the content, implications, and potentialities of a cubic foot of soil reach far beyond the realms of purely inorganic chemistry.

From Liebig there stemmed a whole school of false disciples (or rather narrow and limited fellows), which included the manufacturers and vendors of commercial fertilizer, the overspecialized, limited teachers and experts who believe and preach that *in*organic chemistry holds the key to the universe and that with the creation of chemical fertilizer the problems of agricultural production were ended. When any experiment is made beyond the narrow range of their special field, whenever any speculation is made beyond the limited realm of inorganic chemistry, the cry "unscientific" is raised. To Liebig, as to all great scientists, nothing was unscientific which might hide even a smoldering spark of truth that needed fanning into a flame of revelation. Liebig would have been the first to disavow these followers.

I recently had a conversation with a soil "expert" who dominated the teaching on soils in one of our leading states.

He had never heard of enzymes, of streptomycin and its relation to fertile soils and to disease, and had only the most shadowy knowledge concerning trace elements. His knowledge, philosophy, and teaching seemed to have come to an end with crop rotations and the plentiful use of chemical fertilizer. It is a good rule but it seems to me that in agriculture we have advanced far beyond that stage.

On the other hand there has grown up during the past generation another school of thought, as fanatic as the pure specialist, inorganic chemists are limited and academic. They are the people who believe passionately that all chemical fertilizer is poison and that in decaying and decayed organic material alone lies the salvation of the agriculture and of the world. They are perhaps a shade nearer the truth than the men who believe the "Liebig formula" for chemical fertilizer marked the end of all agricultural knowledge. There are, however, very serious limitations to the purely organic school for a number of reasons, economic as well as purely agricultural.

What is set down here is the result primarily of observation —observation of what plainly exists, observation made in the profound belief that a reasonably wise, intelligent and observant person, provided with a reasonable degree of education, can learn as much regarding soil from his own land as from any agricultural college, and observation made concerning theories and experiments by which we have sought to push the realm of agricultural knowledge a little further into the unknown. Like most farmers we believe at Malabar what we see. We accept the truth of what *works*, not only in the short run, which may sometimes lead to illusion, but in the long run as well. It is quite possible to secure an immediate stimulated *and* simulated fertility which may be bought at heavy cost and cause in the end only deterioration. That is one of the traps into which have fallen the pure advocates of chemical fertilizer as the farmer's salvation.

In our own experience the answer lies somewhere between the two extreme schools of chemical and organic absolutism. The more we have worked with the soil, the more it has become clear to us that fertile soil, its composition and its fertility, are regulated, as in all natural law, by something approaching closely a mathematical formula. With relation

321

to the inorganic-organic controversy, the fight between the extreme advocates of chemical fertilizer and the extreme advocates of organic material, we have found that the value of chemical fertilizers and their inability to cause actual damage runs in direct ratio to the amount of organic material present in the soil. In other words, chemical fertilizer will be of very little immediate or even ultimate value upon soils virtually devoid of organic material and of great immediate value upon soils high in organic content. The capacity of chemical fertilizer to "burn out" crops or to destroy bacteria, earthworms and other living organisms in the soil is determined very largely by the amount of organic material present and of the moisture content which accompanies its presence in the soil.

This is so, very largely, because of moisture which has so much to do with the dilution and the availability of chemical fertilizer as well as the check upon its "burning out" potentialities. Nothing—not even the engineering aspects of soil conservation principles—is so effective in trapping and holding rainfall and moisture as organic material in every stage of decay from the surface trash which covers the great wheat fields of the Southwest, which entraps *all* rainfall, and prevents erosion either by wind or water, down to the finest decayed humus.

The early virgin soils eroded less easily than the soils of today because of the presence in them of great quantities of organic material accumulated in all its forms from a humus so ancient that it was virtually carbonized to the living roots, leaves and stalks turned under by the first plowing. Our agriculture on rich virgin soils went ahead greedily producing without regard either to depletion of mineral or of organic materials. As the organic materials gradually became exhausted the *erodability* of the soil increased in exact ratio. Devastating erosion did not appear all at once in our agriculture. It *crept up* on our farmers as the organic material became gradually but steadily depleted. This was possibly the reason that so little general notice was taken of the approaching disaster until it had already arrived. At the same time as the mineral content of the soil became depleted, the plant and particularly the root growth of all crops became less and

322

less vigorous and contributed steadily less and less to the already declining total of organic material. As this process continued the rate of erosion increased by leaps and bounds, particularly in those southern areas where the higher temperature, longer hot seasons and the *artificial* stimulus of almost universal open crop cultivation "burned up" organic material much more rapidly than in the more temperate areas. Until very recently much of the agriculture of the middle-western Corn Belt was no better or more intelligent than the devastating agriculture which has reduced millions of acres of good land in the southern states close to the status of desert land. The corn-belt farmer has simply been luckier, in that his land is newer, his topsoil deeper in many areas, and his climate kinder to organic material. Fortunately with the awful example of the Deep South and even of certain middle-western areas under their eyes, the *good* farmers of the Corn Belt are developing a new, more careful and more profitable agriculture which takes into consideration the elements mentioned above.

We have had countless examples of this relationship between organic material and chemical fertilizer and also between moisture and chemical fertilizer. On the whole the use of chemical fertilizer in reasonable quantities (sufficient to maintain and feed the current crops and leave a residue to build up mineral reserves in the depleted soils) has shown no evidence of harm to living organisms so long as there was sufficient decaying organic material in the soil to absorb the rainfall and to feed these organisms. In field after field where we have increased organic material as rapidly as possible the living organisms and particularly the earthworm population have *increased* rapidly in spite of the annual use of from 200 to 250 pounds to the acre of commercial fertilizer.

The earthworm itself is a good gauge of *living* agricultural production but like the pure organic fanatics in their claims, the advocates of the earthworm have made extravagant claims concerning its virtues and abilities which do not measure up to fact. The earthworm, as Darwin pointed out long ago, benefits soil in many ways—by aerating it, by creating better drainage, by consuming fresh organic material and translating it into highly available plant food, by slowly translating subsoil into topsoil, even by possible breaking down of the minerals which pass through its tiny body into other forms much more available to plants. All of this is true, but the earthworm is subject to two immensely limiting factors. The earthworm must have a considerable degree of moisture in order to live at all and he must have decaying organic material upon which to feed. The need and the quantity needed undoubtedly vary somewhat as to the variety of worm, as does the degree of moisture necessary to keep him alive.

In the vegetable garden described in the chapter "Gardening without Tears" the relationship of the earthworm population to organic material and chemical fertilizer showed interesting results. On that small area, processes practiced elsewhere on the farm existed on a greatly intensified scale. Chemical fertilizer has been used every year along with barnyard manure, crop residue and considerable quantities of decaying organic material in the form of alfalfa, pea vines and common straw used as mulch. On the first plowing of the depleted, overgrazed pasture land that was utilized by the garden, not more than a score of earthworms were turned up by the plow. They were all of one variety, large, dark red, and fleshy. Today, after seven years of soil building, the worm population has increased many hundreds, perhaps thousands of times. A spade thrust into the soil almost anywhere will turn up three or four earthworms, and in addition to the original, single variety, there are many kinds of worms. In a sense the garden was an earthworm paradise in which a mulch, usually of high protein vegetation, was constantly in some stage of decay under conditions of moisture beneath the mulch which were ideal for the worms. My friend, Walter Pretzer, a first class hothouse vegetable grower and truck gardener, who uses considerable quantities of chemical fertilizer and of necessity maintains in his soils a high degree of organic material, complains that the earthworm population is so great that one large and voracious type of worm attacks and drags below ground *living* and sturdy celery plants.

I have heard extreme earthworm fanatics say that it was possible to remake barren soil devoid of organic material merely by introducing a colony of earthworms into a field of such soil. This, of course, represents the ardor of a crank and is a preposterous claim, for the earthworm under such conditions will simply die of starvation and during the hot months would perish from lack of moisture even at considerable depths in soil devoid of organic material and therefore incapable of absorbing or preserving moisture. We have found, even in the most depleted fields that once the organic content was restored there was no need to import earthworms. With proper food and moisture conditions they appear out of nowhere and continue to increase their numbers infinitesimally so long as conditions are right. There is no doubt that they contribute much over a period of years to the life and fertility of soil but they are only a part of the whole picture and if conditions are unbalanced in any one of a number of ways, they will not flourish.

Perhaps the most striking example of the effect of organic material upon fertility and its capacity to *release* chemical fertilizer and even native minerals by entrapping water and preserving moisture content occurred in the lower fields of the Bailey Place. These fields, uneven in contour, lay in the valley and had been farmed to the borders of death while the fields lying on the hills had been mercifully abandoned to the weeds, goldenrod, wild aster, broom sedge, poverty grass and wire grass which would grow in the eroded, worn-out topsoil that remained. Actually the lower fields possessed little if any more productive capacity than the grown-over abandoned hill fields. They were still worked because they were easier to work and lay nearer the barn. Actually in most of the area there was no organic material whatever in the soil. It had never been limed and the soil could best be described as a kind of cement with traces of chemical fertilizer acids, for our predecessor was one of those who believed that chemical fertilizer was all that was necessary to a good agriculture.

In many places in this book I have used the phrase "productive capacity" rather than the word "fertility" for we discovered beyond all dispute that over the whole area at Malabar all the fields were low in "productive capacity" but not in "fertility." All of the subsoil, even that wholly devoid of topsoil, was fantastically fertile but was not productive owing largely to lack of lime and of organic material, and to poor farming methods. In our experience fertility and actual productive capacity are quite different. Soils may have a high degree of potential fertility which are actually producing little or nothing because that fertility has not been made available to plants. That is where the universal cycle described in the chapter on grass becomes vital to any good and permanent agriculture.

Corn, year after year had been planted up and down the slopes and when heavy summer rains fell on the hot soil, the first great drop sealed up the surface and turned the water off exactly like water falling on a pile of cement. The whole lower area was a network of gullies ranging in depth from a few inches to six and more feet. When we took possession of the farm we did not bother with soil tests for we were aware that the soil probably needed everything, most of all lime and organic material. As it turned out the soil was minerally far richer than we believed, richer indeed than the soil on the other farms which had appeared to be in better condition.

As rapidly as possible we spread two tons to the acre of limestone meal over those lower fields. We seeded a mixture of legumes and we set up contours and strips in order to hold the rainfall "artificially" by engineering until we had increased the organic content sufficiently for the soil to trap and hold the water by itself. Also we spread over the fields a mine of manure which took us nearly two years to get out of the barn and barnyard.

In the season before we took over those fields the corn yield on stalks three or four feet high could not have been more than ten bushels to the acre. The wheat which we inherited was not worth combining the following season; we simply mowed it and left it in the field to increase the organic content.

In the third year of our possession, we took off the same fields corn yields varying from a minimum of sixty baskets to a maximum of ninety on some of the strips. From the same land where the original wheat yields would scarcely have returned the seed we harvested thirty-five bushels to the acre.

No one was more astonished than ourselves by the extraordinary jump in production within so short a period of time. We had expected out of our past experience approximately half that gain by using the same methods. The contouring and stripcropping had held the water in place. The lime had contributed much and made possible the growth of legumes for nitrogen and green manure (curiously the sweet clover, most avid of all legumes for lime, flourished most). And the quantities of barnyard manure had contributed considerable organic material and some minerals. But investigation showed a surprising thing—that actually from a mineral point of view neither the apparently worn-out topsoil nor the exposed subsoil was anywhere near as depleted minerally as we had supposed. Actually, the topsoil was rich in fertilizer which had never been available to the crops of our predecessor because of the lack of lime, of organic material, of moisture, of bacteria and of the whole combination of elements which goes to make up a living soil. As near as we were able to judge, the liming, the content of water and the intensive application of organic material had probably released about three years of chemical fertilizer applied by our predecessor but unavailable to the crops he grew, especially after the beginning of July when the soil simply became dry and hard as cement. In this case the immense value of organic material with its countless effects established beyond doubt its great virtues.

In the succeeding two years the process of increasing the organic content of those fields has continued with remarkable results. In the beginning we could not risk the danger of erosion on strips and contours more than seventy-five feet in width running around the slopes with rows as nearly level as possible. Even on such narrow strips (bordered by water-absorbing sod) there were difficulties with run-off water during the first year or two and whole networks of tiny gullies appeared after each heavy rain. As the organic material was increased, however, the soil began to drink up the rainfall and it was possible to increase the width of open cultivated strips to 150 feet without danger of any loss of soil or water. Rapidly, by the intensive use of barnyard manure, rye, legumes and other forms of green manure, by deep rough plowing which does not bury the green manures but incorporates them *into* the soil, by disking and leaving the surface open rather than *sealed* to rainfall, the soil is rapidly reaching that stage in which the pioneer knew it when there was sufficient organic material present to prevent virtually *all* run-off water and loss of soil. When that point is reached, and it already has been in certain parts of the area, it would be possible to do away altogether with strips and contours and still experience little or no loss of soil and water.

Whether sufficient organic material would serve eventually as a *complete* check to soil and water loss on steep hillsides, I do not know. I do know, however, that among the Amish farmers of Holmes County in Ohio, yields of 100 to 125 bushels of corn to the acre are grown without soil or water loss on hillsides steeper than any we have under cultivation. But the Amish farmer has always guarded his organic material jealously and it is possible that today the fields of many an Amish farmer contain *more* organic material in the constant process of decay than the original virgin soil.

The fanatic advocates of the organic material school will tell you that worn-out depleted soil can be restored without the use of any chemical fertilizer, and to some extent this is true. They fall into error, however, when they assert that vegetation grown upon utterly depleted soil of a seriously deficient virgin soil can produce out of the air quantities of calcium, potassium, phosphorus, trace elements or even substantial quantities of nitrogen for return to the earth. In the first place none of these elements save nitrogen can be produced by any amount of the composting of vegetation grown upon soils where they do not exist. The possibilities of improving worn-out topsoil by composting vegetation grown upon that soil are largely determined by the richness and mineral variety and balance of the subsoil to which deep-rooted plants or earthworms have access. It is possible to restore worn-out topsoil through such deep-rooted, luxuriant, legumes as sweet clover and alfalfa for these plants which feed deep in the subsoil will bring constantly to the surface in the form of roots, leaves and stems, considerable quantities of minerals which they find deep down below the subsoil.

If these roots, leaves and stems are composted and returned to the topsoil or merely plowed or disked *into* the topsoil, they will contribute a supply of minerals drawn from the subsoil which will display at once a remarkably replenishing effect. Moreover they will contribute large quantities of nitrogen which they have drawn out of the air itself into root and

328

branch or have fixed in highly available form in the nodules on the roots. However, they will be able to "pump up" from the subsoil to the topsoil *only* the minerals which they find there. And it should be observed that without the application of lime in one form or another on seriously depleted or naturally sour soils, it will be virtually impossible to grow either alfalfa or sweet clover, the two most valuable of soil restoring legumes. We have found indications that they will "pump up" not only the native minerals existing in the virgin subsoil but also considerable quantities of chemical fertilizer which in areas of fairly heavy rainfall and light soils will have leached down to a depth below the reach of plow, disk or tiller. Not to be overlooked is the whole range of trace elements which deep-rooted plants may find at considerable depths and bring to the surface both as soil ingredients and as food for livestock where these minor elements play a great role in health, growth, vigor, and resistance.

The same inability to contribute minerals to the soil where few or none exist holds true as well of barnyard manure from animals fed on the vegetation grown on that same poor soil. Indeed, the barnyard manure will actually contribute less under such conditions for there will be in the barnyard manure the loss of minerals which are snatched greedily by the desperate needs of the animals to create bone, meat, and milk, etc. As has been pointed out in the garden chapter, poor soils make poor barnyard manure just as they make poor plants, animals, and people. The principal and most valuable contributions of poor soil manures will be not minerals but the bacteria, enzymes, hormones and glandular secretions which we know from experience at Malabar exert a considerable influence upon germination of seed and in other ways about which very little is known. Also the contribution to organic content of manure, either from good or bad land, is of great importance.

While the use of organic material grown on poor soils to restore those soils can be accomplished, provided the subsoil is of reasonable mineral richness, it is a slow process. Depending on the work of the earthworm, the value of which has never been accurately determined, to do the work is also a slow process. Both processes are indeed too slow to be of much value to the average farmer who, in the process of restoring worn-out land, must produce crops each year to pay interest, taxes and the costs of restoration. He does not have and cannot borrow enough money to carry himself along while waiting for green vegetation and earthworms and composts to restore the missing minerals necessary to the fertility which will and must eventually finance him.

At Malabar, except in the case of the most severe depletion, a crop has been grown every year on every field while the business of soil restoration was in progress. No process was employed which was not within the economic possibilities of any farmer able to secure a loan from a government agency. Not only could he afford to borrow the money necessary to restore the organic and mineral lacks of his worn-out soil. He could not afford not to do so.

In all of this it becomes clear that there is a distinct need for chemical fertilizer which provides the missing elements in considerable quantity and in a high degree of availability provided conditions are right both to grow crops and to provide in vigorous quantities the green manures so valuable in restoring the organic material which in turn is so vital an element in making the fertilizer itself available to the succeeding vegetation. It is a kind of complex pattern, circular in design, in which one element of the pattern contributes to another and vice versa. The more perfectly the balance is established—the organic material contributing to the availability of the fertilizer and the fertilizer contributing to vigorous growth of green manure—the more rapid will be the process of restoration and increase in fertility.

At Malabar we have not only been fortunate in setting in operation such a cycle but we have benefited as well by having beneath our feet one of the finest balanced subsoils in the world. It is light, glacial drift soil known as Wooster silt loam which contains at least a little of almost every mineral and trace mineral. This constitutes a valuable mine upon which the deep-rooted legumes may operate. Undoubtedly they find there as well considerable quantities of minerals derived from chemical fertilizers used in the past which have leached down through the light gravel loam.

In all of this the fact should not be overlooked that such

330

vigorously growing legumes as alfalfa and sweet clover are greedy of certain minerals, notably potassium, phosphorus, boron and manganese and that these in any process which harvests the growth and removes it from the soil may in time deplete the soil even to a considerable depth. Calcium will also eventually become exhausted at least near the surface, and, like the other minerals, will need replacement from time to time.

Yields of alfalfa which were enormous on virgin soils in certain areas in the western states have, after a period of a few years, shown a rapid decline as the vegetation was removed at the rate of five to eight cuttings a year and shipped out of the area without any effort at replacing the minerals which were "pumped up" into the vegetation and removed from the soil in large quantities. In our own gravel loam it is doubtful if the deep mineral richness of the constantly disintegrating mixed gravel could be depleted even by centuries of growing deep-rooted plants. The question is whether the disintegration of the mixed gravel proceeds rapidly enough to make available each year *enough* mineral nutrition to support the deep-rooted vegetation. That is a point which we have not yet determined.

The more reasonable advocates of organic material will assert that there are "natural" ways of replenishing minerals which do not involve chemical fertilizer. They point to ground limestone as a "natural" means of restoring calcium and phosphate rock as a means of restoring phosphorus, but in the cases of both of these the time element and the necessity for producing quick income again enters into the problem of the average farmer. The process of the "breaking down" of both limestone and phosphate rock to that point where considerable quantities are available to plants is a comparatively slow one. In the case of dolomitic limestone we find that, although some of the calcium is available after the "breaking down" effects of the first winter season, we do not achieve maximum results from it until the third year and only when it becomes thoroughly incorporated in the soil and well broken down by the action of weather, soil acids, etc. In order to get immediate action, such as to provide a quick and vigorous crop of sweet clover, we have on occasion used hydrated lime. The results were immediate and highly satisfactory but the hy-

331

drated lime was more expensive, it leaches down and out too quickly in our light soils and it is dusty and difficult to handle.

The "breaking down" action of phosphate rock is perhaps an even slower process and in the case of deficient or worn-out soils the more quickly available chemical superphosphates become necessary if one is to raise crops which will contribute quickly toward paying taxes and interest and operating expenses. The superphosphates not only make phosphorus available more or less immediately but also leaves a certain residue of phosphorus behind after each application so that slowly a reserve is built up in the worn-out soil. Once that reserve is sufficient we at Malabar shall perhaps abandon the use of chemical phosphorus compounds and use only the "natural" rock phosphate, which if used in sufficient quantity will supply phosphorus gradually over a period of years through a slow disintegration.

In the long run both limestone and rock phosphates are to be preferred over "treated" forms for in our own experience in all fields of agriculture the natural way, whenever it is possible, has proven in the long run the best way. It should be remembered too that both dolomitic limestone and rock phosphate contain a number of trace minerals of great and still largely unexplored value to plants, animals, and people. These, of course, are at present, missing from the formulas of nearly all commercial fertilizers which are largely "chemically pure."

It would be possible of course by the wise and abundant use of ground limestone and rock phosphate to build over a period of years out of any reasonably friable soil, a soil as vigorous, productive and balanced as the *original* soil of Kentucky bluegrass regions. It should be remembered that the high quality of that soil does not rest alone upon the presence originally of calcium and phosphorus alone. These are of immense importance but so too are the trace elements found in combination with both limestone and phosphate rock in their natural state. These do not exist except in minute and accidental quantities in most commercial chemical fertilizers and then only by accident and not by design. One or two fertilizer manufacturers have recently taken the revolutionary step of mixing trace elements—boron, manganese, magnesium, cobalt, etc.—with their chemical fertilizers but the value of this measure is still scarcely recognized. However this procedure will become largely universal as more is discovered concerning fertility, nutrition and resistance to disease.

Unquestionably the best fertilizer we have discovered in our intensive garden experiments is a commercial product which is a combination of natural and chemical fertilizer. The process, a patented one, utilized a base of limestone, coal and rock phosphate baked together at high temperatures which reduces the elements contained in all three to a highly available form. To this base is added potassium and nitrogen in highly available chemical combinations. We have used this fertilizer in every kind of test including flower pots and window boxes, lawns, vegetable and flower gardens, open fields, depleted topsoils and on subsoils absolutely devoid of organic material. In each case the results have been remarkable not only in abundant production but in healthy and vigorous growth of all vegetation and general resistance to disease and insects. The presence of trace elements coming from the baked limestone and rock phosphate and the quick availability of the mixture as plant food have no doubt contributed much to its efficiency as a fertilizer. There are other advantages, notably that there is no waste material contained in the fertilizer; none of the very nearly useless cement-like bases contained in many commercial chemical fertilizers of low formulas, which add greatly to the shipping costs is present. In other words it is *all* fertilizer. At present the company possessing the formula is unhappily in difficulties and none is at the moment in the process of manufacture. When available it was marketed under the trade name of *Soilex*.

It is reasonable to say that in meeting the needs of the modern farmer and of the "New Agriculture," the big producers of chemical fertilizer are as far behind the times as were the agricultural machinery manufacturers a few years ago. Progress has been made by the Tennessee Valley Authority in its program of high analysis fertilizer and by certain packing-house producers and one or two producers of chemical fertilizers, but by far the greater amount of chemical fertilizers now on the market are what might be called "primitive direct action" stuff produced and shipped at too high a cost for a sound and good agriculture.

The program advocated by both the Department of Agricul-

333

ture and the Farm Bureau of setting up fertilizer factories in all parts of the country to produce fertilizers of high analysis cheaply at low distribution costs to the farmer is one of great importance to farmer as well as consumer in raising the farmers' profits and reducing the cost of food to the city consumer. Properly managed it can serve as well to augment the quality and the mineral and vitamin content of the food produced. Chemical fertilizer is still too expensive and long range shipping costs and the presence of great amounts of "filler" contribute greatly to that expense. There is by no means enough fertilizer produced today in this country to meet the needs of our depleted soils and much progress is delayed by the high costs of production, shipping and profits.

In the production of quantities of organic material for incorporation in the soil, lime is, of course, the keystone for it permits the farmer to raise the whole range of leguminous plants which in turn provide him with valuable organic material in the form of green manures to incorporate into his soil. These legumes also produce for the farmer great quantities of pure nitrogen, which produced in chemical combinations, is the most expensive of fertilizing elements. The deep-rooted legumes also provide the "pumping up" action upon minerals both native and leached downward from the subsoil into the topsoil. Once lime is applied to worn-out soil, the legumes flourish and the restoration of organic material and fertility and the increase in the availability of applied chemical fertilizers and native fertility all work rapidly in a logical, natural cycle to restore fertility, increase yields and cut production costs.

Barnyard manure is of great value but minerally speaking, as has been pointed out above, poor soil produces poor manure and indeed no farm operating profitably or even with a balanced budget can cover the whole of its acreage each year with barnyard manure. Even if it were able to do so there would still be a drain upon its mineral reserves created by the amount of minerals carried off the farm to market in the very products of the animals which consume the forage of the farm, i.e., bone, meat, milk, eggs, etc.

In our opinion it is impossible to restore or even to maintain the fertility of a farm by the use *alone* of the barnyard manure it produces. In order to do so it would be necessary to carry so many livestock that it would be in turn necessary to buy large quantities of feed from elsewhere in order to support the animal and to bring sufficient replacing minerals onto the farm, in the form of feed. Barnyard manure manufactured out of *bought* feed is the most expensive of fertilizers, as many a city farmer has ruefully discovered.

In all of this there is no derogation of the magical qualities of barnyard manure. It is merely that no farm can sustain its mineral balance through the use of barnyard manure alone, except by importing large quantities of feed and forage—a process, which economically, is unworkable for any but the most highly specialized dairy and poultry farms.

Two striking almost exaggerated examples of the agricultural methods which have ruined so many millions of acres of our good land come to mind. There was a time when in our hill country a good-sized stream running through a farm barnyard was considered an asset and commanded an augmentation of price since it permitted the farmer to rid himself of the barnyard manure by simply throwing it into the stream to be carried away. In parts of the worn-out South a man who wasted time spreading manure on his fields was regarded as crazy or at least eccentric. The commonest use for manure was as "binder" on the sticky, red mud roads.

I repeat here an old saying re-quoted out of *Pleasant Valley* which is the product of ancient wisdom among good farmers. "A farmer can make big money by raising both hogs and feed. He can break even or make a little money by raising the feed and buying the hogs or by raising the hogs and buying the feed. But he will go broke if he buys both hogs and feed."

At Malabar we avoided the error in the beliefs of many city and some dirt farmers that the only way to raise the level of fertility is by the purchase and feeding of large quantities of livestock. In the beginning we stocked the worn-out farms we took over with as much livestock as they could feed and then went to work with lime, fertilizer and green manures in the fields, using the manure produced in the barns to the best possible advantage where it was needed most. By working in this fashion we increased steadily the yields and quality of feed and forage in the fields and this in turn permitted us to carry more and more livestock and to produce more and more manure to return to the fields both as organic material and mineral replenishment. Under such a plan we have increased the number of livestock the farms could carry without buying feed or forage by approximately 800 per cent. The number could be increased still further but for shortage of housing and inability during the war and postwar years of finding good workmen and building materials.

When we first took over the farms that now comprise Malabar two of them had reached the end of the road. The wheel had run completely down and they were abandoned. On the other two the wheel was rapidly running down. In other words, each year the fields produced less so that the farmer was compelled to carry less livestock which produced less manure which reduced the yields from the fields still further and so on until at last it became impossible to pay taxes and interest and the farm was abandoned. By the process of going to work on the *fields* with minerals, green manure and fertilizer, we have raised each year more feed, which enabled us to carry more livestock which produced more manure which contributed to greater yields. The wheel has been turning faster and faster uphill instead of slower and slower downhill and we still have a considerable distance to go before we arrive at maximum potential production of both crops and livestock. Moreover it should not be overlooked that not only the quantity but the *quality* of manure was greatly increased as the mineral content of the soil was raised and the animals, instead of snatching at all available minerals for their nourishment as these passed through their bodies, found an excess of minerals in their feed and returned a considerable quantity of minerals to the soil in the highly available form of manure. The feeding of trace elements directly to animals as well as incorporating them in the soil has also led to a similar process whereby any excess of trace elements was returned to the fields in manure.

One other process employed at Malabar for the rapid incorporation of large quantities of organic materials to depleted land may be of interest to others faced by the same problem. It was a process which in one way took advantage of nature and in another was no more than working with nature in the principle upon which the whole of the new agriculture is founded. We profited by a rule which not enough farmers understand—that by working with nature it is possible to obtain great quantities of organic material and of expensive nitrogen at little or no cost at all. At the root of the process lies the law that less than 10 per cent of the growth of *any* plant, even the most greedy, comes from the minerals of the soil itself. All the rest comes out of sunlight, air and water.

With this in mind we employed a process by which we obtained from two to three times as much green manure in a single season as we had done in the past. The process was simple; it was simply that of clipping the legumes and even weeds used for green manures with a power-mower three times during a single season, each time acquiring a new growth of vegetation which was left on the field. This was done only on those fields where the fertility was so low that any attempt to raise a crop during the first season would have been foolish since there would have been small likelihood of even a bare return of fertilizer, tax, seed and labor expenses. Thus we achieved instead of one crop *three* crops of vegetation to be used as green manures to replenish organic material.

Of course the most valuable of green manures lies within the range of the legumes and of these alfalfa and sweet clover are the most valuable because of their high nitrogen fixing properties, deep roots and lush growth. The problem was to obtain a growth of legumes on poor soil, freshly limed. By making mixed seedings of alfalfa, sweet clover, red clover, mammoth clover, ladino and alsike (all legumes), we achieved in most cases a good germination and a fairly rank growth. Surprisingly, the sweet clover, one of the trickiest of legumes, had the best results, perhaps because in fertilizing the seeding, despite the fact that all the legumes included were actually nitrogen producers, we included nitrogen. This nursed along the young legume seedlings to that point where they began to manufacture their own nitrogen supply. Some credit must go also to the fine mineral quality of our deep subsoil into which the rapidly growing roots of the rank growing sweet clover and alfalfa penetrated to find, beneath the worn-out topsoil a good and balanced food supply. Of course, alfalfa, sweet clover and ladino clover—all new to our soils—were inoculated with their own bacteria.

The use of nitrogen in fertilizing legume seedings even on our best fields has proved profitable for the reasons stated above. In 1946 a poor season for seedings, our own seedings ranged from 100 to 80 per cent perfect; this in a year when at least three quarters of the seedings in our area were plowed under as failures. We attribute our success primarily to the application of a "booster" dose of fertilizer made at the time of seeding and to the nitrogen included in that fertilizer which fed the seedlings during a difficult period of spring drought. It is also likely that the higher organic content of our fields over those plowed up by the neighbors also made a valuable contribution in the form of retained moisture.

Until quite recently there was a firm legend in our area that sweet clover could not be grown successfully even after the application of lime. In view of the fact that sweet clover grew rankly along the roadsides where the soil was still "virgin" and had been impregnated with lime from the stone used in surfacing the road, there seemed no basis for the legend. It did, indeed, prove false, for once the soil had received a sufficient application of lime and the seeding itself had received an extra boost of fertilizer including nitrogen, we raised sweet clover in rank abundance. Where seedings are made in spring oats the seedings have the benefit of the fertilizer applied to the oats and also of a better seed bed than when made in winter wheat. On one farm the rotation of corn-oats-sweet clover is used with no barnyard manure, the sweet clover seeding is made in the oats and plowed in the following spring. Every other year a luxuriant crop of sweet clover is produced. Recently some agronomists have advocated the use of nitrogen on mature alfalfa, although we have never found this necessary in our soils. Possibly the main reason for the legend about sweet clover was the fact that most farmers in our area used too little lime. On fields which they claimed had been limed, we discovered that they had used not more than 500 pounds, and sometimes as little as 200 pounds per acre. These small amounts, breaking down slowly, had little or no effect.

In the operations of growing three crops instead of one for

green manure, certain plants and certain legumes make much greater second and third growth than others. Alfalfa is, of course, the queen of producers although mammoth clover, red clover and biennial sweet clover will make considerable growth if the first cutting is made early enough, before the flowering is advanced. Ladino clover is, in our experience, a great producer on any soil, however poor, with or without lime, although its yields will be increased approximately three to four times by use of lime and phosphorus. It will yield in our northern Ohio climate as many as six to seven cuttings and the equivalent in pasture in one season. The disadvantages are that, being shallow rooted, it does not reach into the subsoil, is therefore subject to the effects of drought and produces much less bulk of organic material both in root, stem and foliage than the coarser legumes.

Of all pasture plants ladino is the unrivaled queen, under conditions of well-distributed rainfall, both in the field of production and of protein content. In our experience only three things affect its tremendous high quality production: (1) Severe drought. (2) Over-grazing by sheep. (3) Invasion after a period of years by bluegrass, a process which falls into the natural white clover-bluegrass cycle of our area. Despite its shallow roots ladino produces prodigious amounts of nitrogen in the top four or five inches of soil. This encourages the bluegrass which grows with almost incredible lushness once it starts to invade a ladino pasture. For the benefit of those unfamiliar with the plant, it is a super-giant member of the white-clover family, growing under favorable conditions 3 to 4 inches higher than White Dutch. Following the habits of the white-clover family, it is a creeping plant which sends down roots at each joint. These joints in turn become plants which in turn send out new shoots which follow the creeping plant which sends down roots at each joint. These joints in turn become plants which in turn send out new shoots which follow the creeping multiplication process. We have found that a single plant will within two years carpet an area forty inches in diameter. One greenhouse experiment with a single seed of ladino has produced in two years a circular carpet of ladino thirty-six feet in diameter. It is especially valuable for covering the soil of fresh cuts or bare subsoil where, seeded in a mulch, it will quickly carpet the area, to be followed later by a spontaneous growth of native grasses. Lime and fertilizer will promote the speed and vigor of the growth. Ladino seed has been considered expensive but actually it is not, for the seeds are small and a pound contains about three times the number of seeds as a pound of sweet clover or ordinary red clover. This together with its rapidly spreading habits reduces greatly the number of pounds necessary for a seeding as compared to most other legumes. For a straight ladino seeding we use only three pounds per acre. Such a seeding made in March with good summer-rainfall conditions produces a heavy pasture by the end of August. In our original mixed seedings consisting of 5 pounds of brome or orchard grass, eight pounds of alfalfa and one pound of ladino, we have reduced the ladino to a half pound per acre because its rapid, vigorous growth choked out some of the slower growing alfalfa and grass seedlings. In such a seeding the ladino eventually creeps in around the alfalfa plants and tufts of brome grass, covering any accidental bare spots so that by the second year a moderately good seeding becomes thickened into a 100 per cent stand. The ladino also adds tremendously to the protein content of the hay or silage cut from such a mixed seeding. Of course the cuttings of ladino contain no stems and no woody material but only leaves and blossom. Owing to its rank and rapid growth in the early spring it chokes out weed seedlings, thus giving us meadows that are beautifully clean mixtures of alfalfa, brome grass and ladino.

In all of this it is, I think, evident that none of us at Malabar Farm are fanatic advocates either of the chemical fertilizer or the organic school. It is, of course, possible to use so much fertilizer that its chemical action will destroy the growth and life of the bacteria, fungi, moulds, earthworms, and other life which are all essential to productive soil and good agriculture even when considerable quantities of organic material and of the moisture which accompanies it are present. We have never used more than 300 pounds per acre, and that only upon the poorest soils where meadow-pasture seedings were made on a trash-mulch surface. For grain crops or grass seedings on good soil or top dressings of pastures and long established meadows, we have found that 250 pounds per acre are about the right amount to secure good crops at a sound economic cost without long range deleterious effects. Of course all chemical fertilizer, even small amounts used upon cement-like soils devoid of organic material and bacteria, moulds, fungi, etc., and incapable of holding moisture will be of little use and can actually cause damage by the "burning out" of plants.

Out of experience we have found simply that the whole dispute between the two schools resolves itself into a question of *balance*, as indeed does all else in agriculture, in nutrition and indeed in life itself. We have found that chemical fertilizer is valuable and available in exact ratio to the amount of organic material (in all stages of decay and assimilation) present in the soil, and we have found that the restoration of poor soils by the use alone of organic materials (either green or barnyard manures composted or uncomposted) grown upon these poor depleted soils is a process too slow, economically speaking, to be undertaken by any farmer who is not willing or able to undertake financial losses over a considerable period of years.

I believe that both sides in the controversy should recognize what from our experience seems to be fact. The chemical fertilizer producers would be commercially shrewd to advocate, indeed to propagandize, the increasing use of all manures, barnyard and green, since the organic material they contribute makes the chemical product infinitely more available and valuable to their customers and consequently serves actually to increase its use. On the other hand, the organic people would do well to recognize the economic necessity of quickly available minerals in chemical fertilizer and not lead inexperienced agricultural novices into the belief that they can profitably and quickly restore poor or depleted soil by the use of organic material alone.

A letter from an organic fanatic illustrates perfectly the economic fallacy of the purely organic school. It stated, "We are very proud of the results we have obtained in purely organic farming. This year after seven years we have raised wheat production to 20 bushels per acre." In the better, high value agricultural lands in the United States 20 bushels per acre of wheat will scarcely pay taxes and interest on the investment. No farmer in the Middle West can afford a wheat yield of 20 bushels although in some of the great semi-arid wheat areas where land and tax values are very low, and efficient mass production is the rule, it is possible at fair prices to make money on much smaller yields per acre. At Malabar in 1947 our wheat yields, including the poorest lands in the process of restoration, averaged 35 bushels to the acre. Some fields yielded over 60 bushels, largely owing to the balanced use of organic material and chemical fertilizer and to the general grass farming program in which alfalfa, brome grass and ladino sods are plowed for wheat production. This represents increases in yields on some farms of as much as 500 per cent after seven years of the restoration process employing *both* chemical fertilizers and organic materials in balance. On the Bailey farm, in a period of only four years, yields jumped from under 10 bushels to 33 bushels in two years and to 52 bushels in four years. The process and details were dealt with in the chapter "Grass, the Great Healer."

# XIV: OUT OF THE EARTH WE ARE BORN
# AND
# TO THE EARTH WE RETURN

> We have assumed that there is no obligation to an
> inanimate thing, as we consider the earth to be; but man
> should respect the conditions in which he is placed;
> the earth yields the living creature; man is a living
> creature; science constantly narrows the gulf between
> the animate and the inanimate, between the organized
> and the unorganized; evolution derives the creatures
> from the earth; the creation is one creation. I must ac-
> cept all or reject all.
>                    —Liberty Hyde Bailey, *The Holy Earth*

THERE is a new movement going on in medicine and in
agriculture which may lead to the most important developments with regard to the health, vigor, longevity, and general
future of the human race. It is a movement away from
patent medicines and toward preventing disease, a movement
which plans to lock the stable *before* instead of after the
horse is stolen. Put very simply it is a movement to create
health and resistance to disease in plants, animals, and
humans, rather than to attempt to cure the ills and diseases
after they have developed by the use of sprays, dusts, injec-
tions, and other patent medicines. The principle follows,
generally speaking, the centuries-old custom existing in China
of paying the physician only during the periods when the
patient is in good health and of cutting off his payments
during the period when the patient is ill.

In the past the relation between agriculture, medicine,
and even surgery was regarded as a fairly remote one. In

the beginning the doctor was a witch or a warlock concocting brews of herbs, "eye of a newt and horn of toad" and the surgeon was a barber engaged in bone-setting or blood-letting as a sideline. To some extent these traditional backgrounds determined the general philosophy of surgery and of medicine until well into the middle of the nineteenth century when the improved microscope and rapidly intensifying research revealed the phenomena of bacteria and microbes and their relation to plant, animal, and human life, health, and vigor. There followed immediately great advances in medicine based upon bacteriology, immunization, inoculation, etc. Somewhat later the science of endocrinology (the relation of glands to human health and behavior) revealed new aspects of human illness and health, and recently there has begun a new movement of advance based upon such antibodies as penicillin and streptomycin. The evolution of the doctor and surgeon from the realms of magic and witch-doctoring, like the development of bankers from the level of pawnbroking is, in terms of historical time, a comparatively recent development. I mention this fact merely as a measure of comparison in relation to the antiquity of the profession of agriculture.

From the middle of the nineteenth century surgery has been making tremendous advances away from the old barber-surgeon tradition, largely in relation to the nervous system and along the lines of what might roughly be called surgical engineering and technology. These advances have dealt with new ways of operating upon human organs and setting shattered bones. Medicine has been making similar advances away from witch-doctoring and patent medicines and toward fundamental foundational good health and resistance to disease. Continuing research has led medicine into new paths and almost imperceptibly into wholly new fields—notably into the relationship between soils and health and between the minor trace elements existing in soils in relation to the health of plants, animals, and humans, and in the relation of these things to glandular functioning.

Much of this research is only partially complete in a purely scientific sense, but the rush of discovery in the agricultural, medical, and biological fields seems to indicate that we are on the way to or in the midst of a whole new concept of understanding and of a new philosophy of health which is based upon preventative rather than corrective medicine. Much of the research has uncovered wholly new facts, and some of it has confirmed and explained the efficacy of many medicinal and agricultural "superstitions," long practiced by peasants in all parts of the world simply because they "worked."

In the broadest sense such facts as the necessity for calcium and phosphorus in the growth and functioning of the human body have long been known. It was known that a shortage of calcium affects the blood count, the structure of the bony frame, as well as the condition of both mother and infant in the case of pregnancy. It was also known that phosphorus is necessary for the very existence of the human race. However, it has been widely recognized only recently that the shortage or near-absence of these major elements from wornout soils can affect whole areas, and affect the growth, health, and intelligence of the people living upon soils originally deficient or badly depleted of these minerals.

Again only recently has it been recognized that all vegetables of one kind or all milk do not contain the same or even similar amounts of vitamins or minerals and the vitamin and mineral content of one head of lettuce grown upon rich, minerally well-balanced soils may be 75 per cent greater than the content of a head of lettuce of similar appearance grown upon poor or depleted soils, or muck soils consisting principally of nitrogen and carbon content. Finally it has been scientifically proved that the difference between the two heads of lettuce will have an appreciable effect over a considerable period upon the health, intelligence and even the character of the people consuming them.

Selective Service records during the recent war in one Southern State where the soil has been badly leached and depleted by a century and a half of poor agriculture, showed a rejection record of nearly 75 per cent of the young men as hopelessly unfit physically. In the State of Colorado, a comparatively new state not yet subject to the devastating effects of a bad agriculture and not subject to the leaching and eroding effects of steady and violent rains, the record was exactly the reverse.

The effects of minerally depleted or unbalanced soils upon

cattle is by now well established. In certain areas of Florida and Louisiana one can see cattle walking about in grass knee-deep with their ribs and hipbones showing while on the ranges of New Mexico and Arizona and West Texas where a superficial glance reveals scarcely any vegetation at all, cattle look sleek, healthy and well-fed. The difference is one of the mineral content of the vegetation, in the first case highly deficient in balance regardless of its luxuriant appearance, and in the other, highly balanced and minerally nutritious though apparently scrubby. In other states there are areas where original calcium deficiencies or depletions are so great that the backs and legs of cattle fed upon the local forage will break when they attempt to rise. The people in these same areas suffer eventually from the same deficiencies and other evil results extending not only into the realm of health and resistance to disease but even into the realms of intelligence and mentality.

In the realm of the so-called minor trace elements, it is rapidly becoming a recognized fact that deficiencies of these elements in soil and consequently in vegetation may produce derangements of health resistance, vitality, intelligence, and in particular of the functioning of glands. The trace elements include notably iodine, fluorine, manganese, magnesium, baron, cobalt, copper, zinc, sulphur and many other minerals. Most soils save those of marine or glacial drift origin are likely to be deficient in some or many of them. Probably few soils contain every one of them in sufficient quantities. They need to be present only in small, even minute, quantities as small as a handful or less to the acre, yet, their presence or absence has in some cases definite, and in others suspected, effects upon the determination of characteristics, of health and vigor of plants and animals, and upon the health, vigor and intelligence and even character of the people living within a given area upon given soils and feeding upon the products of those soils.

Two of the simplest examples of the effect of these trace elements upon health and growth are so long and so well-established as to be classic. One is the relation of iodine to the thyroid gland. Soils deficient in iodine coincide exactly with the so-called "goitre belts" where large segments of the population are subject to a thyroid malfunction which affects

character, vigor, intelligence, and longevity. In many such cases the absorption into the system of only a few drops of iodine during a lifetime would have prevented the malfunction of the thyroid gland and consequently the development of goitre.

The effect of the absence or presence of fluorine in soils upon teeth structure and decay has been established nearly as long as the need for abundant calcium in teeth and bone structure. As in the case of iodine and the thyroid gland, only minute quantities of fluorine are necessary for the structure, growth, and preservation of good teeth. Experiments are now being conducted in certain areas in which quantities of fluorine are added to the drinking water in an effort to produce sound and healthy teeth in the oncoming generation. Deaf Smith County, Texas, has gained world fame as an area in which teeth decay is below the level of a fraction of one per cent. The answer has proved to be an abundance in the soil of the major element calcium in combination with minute quantities of fluorine.

The latest research in relation to the dread leukemia, a malady related to cancer, has shown that a definite connection exists between the coincidence of the disease and a deficiency of zinc in almost infinitesimal quantities. At one time there existed in specific areas over the United States, notably in Florida, Michigan and the New England states, an illness known by a variety of names such as "salt sickness," "droop neck" etc. Only a little more than a decade ago it was discovered that the disease, the symptoms of which were exactly the same among both people and cattle in these specific areas, was a form of anemia resulting in gradual physical decline and loss of appetite, and in the case of cattle frequently in a literal process of self-starvation. During the last generation it was discovered that the disease occurred only in areas completely deficient in cobalt. Once this element was added to the soils upon which the food of both cattle and people was grown, the disease completely vanished.

Experiments with manganese and dairy cattle tend to prove that its presence in feed has a definite effect as a control and protection against the feared and destructive Bang's disease, which in humans takes the form of undulant or Malta fever. Many progressive farmers and livestock feeders have taken to feeding mixtures of trace elements directly to

348

their livestock, and others are arriving at the same results in a slower but more natural and certain method by applying the elements directly to the soil whence they eventually reach the animals by being absorbed out of the soil into the grain and vegetation upon which the animals or poultry feed.

The relation of trace elements to Bang's disease (Brucell abortus) in cattle and hogs and to range paralysis in chickens, was forced upon our observation both in cattle barns and poultry houses. While, as was shown in the chapter "Grass, the Great Healer" it is probable that most trace elements exist in our glacial soil and under a sound form of agriculture are available to crops and consequently to animals and people, we nevertheless keep a mixture of twenty of these elements constantly available to all livestock.

We have never been troubled by Bang's disease save for mildly positive reactions in two or three cows tested just before or after the birth of a calf. And it is possible that this is so because these elements are available in the soils and accessible to the animals in the forage with the extremely high mineral content described elsewhere. Pushing this theory still further, an interrogation of local veterinarians with records of long years of practice showed me that cases of Bang's disease were extremely rare or virtually non-existent in our glacial area among cattle *bred* and *raised* in the area and not *brought in*. On the other hand, in the same county, beyond the line where the glacial moraines melt away into flat country and the sandy soils of the old lake bottom exist, Bang's disease showed a much higher incidence. Curiously the pattern of corn-borer infestation follows very closely the pattern of the incidence of Bang's disease. In other words, the heavy infestation of the corn borer and the evidence of Bang's disease both follow the line of the original comparatively mineral-deficient areas of the lake bottom and the Black Swamp areas but both largely disappear as the topography rises into the hilly country of the glacial moraine area.

Because our cattle have been consistently and almost entirely fed on forage and grains raised on our own glacial soils, the relation of mineral balance and trace elements to Bang's disease infection was difficult to trace; the case of range paralysis in the poultry houses was exactly the opposite.

For the first four years our poultry was fed entirely upon poultry mashes coming from soils other than our own and during the whole of that period we experienced continual infection and losses of poultry through range paralysis, although we changed hatcheries every year in order if possible to avoid infection from the original chicks. It was not until we took to cafeteria feeding, i.e. placing before the hens meat scraps, mash, whole oats, corn and alfalfa grown on the place and began feeding mixtures of trace elements that range paralysis *disappeared completely* from the poultry houses. Each hen was, of course, permitted to balance her own diet. We also cut feed costs at least 30 per cent and increased production by an even greater figure. It is also worth noting that under the *balanced* cafeteria feeding all cannibalism disappeared from the poultry houses.

The only deduction to be drawn was that all chicks, regardless of the hatchery, carried in themselves the germs or virus of range paralysis and that when there was a deficiency or unbalance of minerals and trace elements, the metabolism of the hens and their capacity for producing disease-resistant antibodies through hormones, enzymes etc. was so deranged or weakened that the disease took over. We also found that a 100 per cent resistance to range paralysis and indeed to apparently virtually all poultry diseases existed among the fighting chickens and the wild poultry. These groups represented a considerable number of fowls over a period of years, fighting cocks as well as stray chickens mostly of the Leghorn and Plymouth Rock variety. These roamed barnyards and near-by fields during all seasons and had access to spilled grain and the vegetation growing upon glacial soils but among them no case of range paralysis has ever appeared.

These observations both with regard to at least two notable livestock and poultry plagues, Bang's disease and range paralysis, have led me to suppose that nutrition and especially mineral nutrition has a great deal to do with disease control.

Some of the most valuable scientific contributions to the specific relation of trace elements to control of Bang's disease have been made by J. F. Wischusen of the Cleveland Research and Development Foundation. These consist of his own scientific research as well as the assimilated and co-ordinated reports of other research specialists in the field. He points out that as yet the field is insufficiently explored and that many things—such as the relation of certain trace elements to (for example) the formation of protein, enzymes, hormones, etc., which may and do lead to the creation of antibodies or in other ways to disease resistance—are not yet fully understood although the whole field in animal and human physiology and pathology is advancing rapidly. He intimates, rightly I think, that much of our research and science is bogged down firmly within the limitations of the school of vaccination and inoculation, a valuable step in relation to health but probably not the final one.

Mr. Wischusen lists twenty-two elements, together with their functions, that are believed necessary to human, animal and plant nutrition, healthy resistant life. That few soils contain *all* of the essentials is a well-established fact. That many soils, especially those originally deficient or those depleted by poor and greedy farming, lack a large percentage of the necessary elements is a well-established fact. It is clear, I think, that when the deficiencies occur the plants, animals and people existing on the given deficient soils and feeding from them will suffer from physical defects and from weakened resistance to disease in all its forms. Of course the effect of deficiencies of iodine, cobalt and fluorine, to name only three, are well- and long-established scientific facts. Mr. Wischusen also points out that these elements even in soils where they exist may not be in available form to plants and hence unavailable to animals and people; care must be taken that, when these elements are fed in mixtures to livestock, that each one exists in a chemical combination which makes it available. Most reliable feed companies providing these elements for feeding have taken care that they exist in form available to animal use. The same is true of the elements sold for incorporation into the soil by reliable fertilizer companies.

Mr. Wischusen also summons the highly interesting and effective results of the use of trace elements in dealing with undulant fever, the human form of Bang's disease—results which point in exactly the same direction as the research regarding certain trace elements in relation not only to resistance but also to alleviation of the disease.

351

Some of the experiments recounted in relation to cattle are dramatically striking in their results, notably the case of two cows, one infected with Bang's disease and one clean, both stabled in the same stall for a long period. The healthy cow was fed a balanced diet of minerals and never acquired the disease, popularly held to be highly contagious. Two other cases are recounted in which the cows of infected herds were put on to a balanced ration of minerals; practically all recovered in a comparatively short space of time and from then on produced living, healthy calves.

I recommend to the reading of all intelligent, practical farmers the pamphlet, *The Role of Manganese, Copper and Cobalt in the Bang's Disease of Cattle*, obtained by addressing J. F. Wischusen, Manganese Research and Development Foundation, Cleveland 10, Ohio.

Every livestock breeder knows that iodized salt must be fed to livestock in iodine-deficient areas. He also knows that all animals, given an opportunity to balance their own diets, will balance them exactly according to their individual needs, far more intelligently than humans will do. A brood sow, faced with a deficiency of calcium will tear up and chew the cement of her pen floor in order to get lime and a sow fed upon a minerally and protein deficient diet will eat her own young. A pregnant cow, like a pregnant woman suffering from a deficiency of calcium in her diet will take the calcium out of her bones or her teeth in order to provide the necessary mineral to herself or the baby she is carrying. The rooting of hogs in a field arises almost entirely from their search for protein nutrients and minerals which they are not receiving in proper quantities. A protein deficient diet will cause a hog to tear up the sod in search of worms and grubs and even when given unlimited quantities of protein it may still root in search of major or minor elements which are lacking or almost wholly lacking from its diet. Often enough, a half-wild sow left in a swamp to her own resources will farrow and bring up a much healthier and more vigorous litter of pigs than a sow kept penned under the most sanitary and luxurious conditions by a farmer who does not understand animal feeding. A sow knows better than any farmer, perhaps than any professor or mixed-feed manufacturer, what she needs in her diet. So does, in varying degrees of acuteness, every other animal.

In the case of a human being the *instinct* for recognizing the deficiency has been partly lost, and with it the instinctive hunger for the corrective minerals, vitamins, etc. He merely develops goitre or bad teeth or anemia or poor eyesight or a "tired feeling." He does not know instinctively what is the matter with him, as do most animals, nor how to cure it. Instead he begins taking quantities of patent medicines or vitamin pills. If he lived upon foods produced from minerally well-balanced soils, it is highly probable that most of the ills would never develop at all and that health and vigor would stay with him so long as he received no physical injury.

In children instincts and cravings regarding nutrition, deficiencies, etc., still possess an acuteness akin to those of animals. With this under consideration, one school of medical and nutritional thought is inclined to pamper children by permitting them to eat what they crave violently regardless of whether parent or doctor thinks it good for them. But even a child, affected by the long chain of habit and "civilizing" influences is less likely to possess the strong and *correct* nutritional instincts of almost any animal. Who has not seen peasant children eating whatever they chose within reach who were infinitely more tough, solid, healthy and resistant than some of the big, soft, pink and white children brought up on diets carefully supervised by "specialists" in nutrition? The frequent cases of small children "eating" dirt are evidence of the animal instinct to correct some deficiency in their carefully planned diets. Among the animals there is no evidence of any such foolish diet as a lunch made on a pickle and ice-cream soda. Animals have too much sense. Nor do animals by preference eat such nutritionally useless food as refined sugar and overprocessed white breads.

The causes of cancer, the most dreaded scourge of the human race still are almost entirely unknown yet it is perfectly reasonable to assume that they may, like goitre or decaying teeth, arise from or at least be induced by mineral deficiencies which cause in time certain glandular derangements. The connection between leukemia (a cancer relative) and deficiencies of zinc has already been established.

On the northern borders of India there exists a half-wild tribe known as the Hunzas in which no case of cancer nor any tribal record of the disease has ever been known. Sir Albert Howard, who has studied these people, has pointed out that they have practiced for hundreds of years in their narrow valley a particularly fine form of terraced agriculture in which a finely balanced mineral replenishment in the form of sand and gravel saved from the beds of rivers flowing from the Himalayas is brought up each year to the hillside terraces as fertilizer. Nor should it be overlooked that among these people all waste, both animal and human, is returned to the earth instead of being dumped into their streams to pollute them on their way to the sea from which they cannot be recovered. Not only are the Hunzas[1] known for their freedom from cancer but they are also known for extraordinary vitality, vigor, resistance, health, and longevity.

In a speech before the National Association of Hothouse Vegetable Growers the author made recently a speculation which he considered revolutionary. He suggested that one day not too far away there would be a law regarding green vegetables, similar in purpose to the existing Pure Food Act with regard to tinned foods, which would require fresh vegetables to be labeled A, B, C, or D, etc., according to the mineral content and balance of the soils upon which they were grown so that consumers, when they were buying vegetables, might know whether they were really getting the proper minerals and vitamins, or merely nitrogen, carbon, and water, in the form of luxuriant-appearing vegetation like that upon which feed the perpetually skinny and listless cattle of certain minerally deficient areas. The hothouse vegetable growers, however, showed no astonishment. Not only did they believe that such a law would eventually be enacted, they were enthusiastic about passing its enactment.

The truth was that nearly all of them clearly understood the value of a balanced mineral content in the soil and were practicing it. They knew it in a thoroughly practical dollar and cents fashion in relation to the health of the plants they

[1] *The Wheel of Life* is a book devoted to a scientific study of the Hunza people over a period of many years. Sir Albert Howard also devotes considerable space to them in two books, *An Agricultural Testament* and *The Soil and Health*.

grew. They *knew* that a deficiency of manganese, even in minute quantities, could cause splitting in the outside stems of celery and result in a loss of hundreds and perhaps thousands of dollars. They knew that deficiencies of other trace elements could cause cracking in tomatoes, or uneven ripening or poor anemic color. They knew too that plants suffering from mineral deficiencies were, like animals and people under the same circumstances, sickly and lacking in resistance and therefore subject to blights, diseases, and even attacks by insects from which wholly healthy plants receiving a balanced diet of minerals would be wholly or partly immune. In some cases the hothouse vegetable growers produced three and four crops in one year in the same soil and the tone and mineral balances of that soil *had* to be preserved if they were to continue to prosper as businessmen. Not only their health but their pocketbooks—like the health and pocketbooks of people over large areas of the United States—were dependent upon maintained balance and a living fertility.

It is only recently that a few agronomists have begun exploring the whole relationship of mineral balance to the health and productivity of soils. Most of them have been content to turn out treatises upon amounts and formulas of chemical fertilizers containing only the major elements—nitrogen, phosphorus and potassium—and to advocate the use of lime upon a calcium-deficient or calcium-depleted soil. Very little research has occurred in most state colleges concerning the relationship of minerally balanced soils to health and fertility in plants, animals, and people.

The whole theory of the ability of healthy plants grown in organically balanced and complete, mineralized soils to resist disease and even to some extent attacks by insects is not altogether new, either in the field of research among highly skilled market gardeners or among intelligent amateurs, but it is largely unknown in general agriculture. The theory of putting into the soil the means of resistance rather than applying it externally by dusts and sprays is much more revolutionary and comparatively little research has been done along these lines.

Certainly one of the most interesting evidences of the effects of a trace element upon the resistance to insects is set forth by Glen Fuller of the Battelle Memorial Institute of Columbus, Ohio in a pamphlet called Selenium in Plants.

It relates not only to the results of research by Mr. Fuller himself but is based upon the published results of research by other well-known horticulturists, entomologists, and bio chemists. It was found that the application of so small an amount as ¼ gram of sodium selenate per square foot of soil or one pound per 1800 square feet was quickly absorbed by the plants and immediately made the plants im mune to the attack of aphids, red spiders, leaf nematods and other equally stubborn and difficult pests. In some cases the effect upon the insects was actually toxic, killing them off in great numbers.

Selenium salts dissolved in water and applied to soil are widely used today by expert greenhouse growers, particularly of carnations and chrysanthemums. Not only is the process more effective than spraying and dusting but in some instances it is completely effective where the superficial process of spraying or dusting is not effective. Needless to say the old-fashioned methods of spraying and dusting are infinitely more expensive as to amounts of material, labor, and the need for constant and repeated applications.

The experiments and results with regard to selenium have opened the door on the relationship of trace elements to resistance in plants. Selenium was an obvious choice since it was already known to be an element toxic to animals and people and even to some plants in any considerable quantity. The presence of excessive amounts of selenium in vegetation was discovered some years ago to be the cause of "alkali disease" among cattle in certain parts of the west. It may even have made a small contribution to Custer's Massacre for it is known that the horses of his cavalry regiment were all suffering at the time of the Little Big Horn disaster from "alkali disease," after having fed for days on the vegetation of an area now long established as one where an excess of selenium exists in the soil.

The selenium research does not fix definitely and as a fact the efficiency of selenium *alone* as a source of resistance. It is possible that other trace elements or combinations of trace elements have a similar effect and that when one or some of these are wholly absent from the soil, the deficiency

356

causes a weakening of resistance both to disease and insect attack. Our whole experience with trace elements in plants in relation to resistance to disease and insects tends to indicate this possibility. As I have pointed out elsewhere, our glacial soil contains a great number of these trace elements, perhaps more than any other soils save those of marine origin. This fact, I repeat, makes our soil an ungrateful field for making effective tests since there is little margin in which to work. A more deficient soil would provide a better testing ground. Nevertheless, the application, in a somewhat helter-skelter fashion, of some twenty trace minerals has undoubtedly increased the resistance to disease and insects of the whole range of vegetables and fruits grown at Malabar. Which elements or combination of elements are effective we do not pretend to know save in the case of the major element potassium and the minor elements boron and manganese. When in any area there is a deficiency of any of these three, the plants display symptoms as marked as any case of measles or smallpox. We have at Malabar neither the time nor the equipment for pure and effective scientific research. We are in the main, simply keen observers, who believe in what works. The field of soils and minerals in relation to the health in plants, animals, and people, both in its purely chemical and mineral aspects as well as in the biochemical aspects of moulds, fungi, bacteria, antibodies, etc., is still almost wholly unexplored.

Contrary to fact it is the assumption of the average citizen that all virgin soils are good and well-balanced soils. It is common belief that by removing forest growth one finds in the earth beneath ancient soil of almost unbelievable fertility or that by draining a bog one makes available a completely balanced, productive, and healthy soil. Very few virgin soils are anywhere near perfect soils for they are no more than the result in most cases of the vegetation which has grown upon them, died and decayed to mix their organic material with the decaying rock, clay, or gravel in which they have grown. Minerally speaking, the dead and decaying vegetation is nothing more than the mineral material of the subsoil itself transmuted into organic form and therefore much more quickly available to the growth of the plants or trees which succeed the earlier vegetation in the eternal cycle of death, growth, decay, and rebirth. Therefore, vegetation growing upon primeval subsoil or decayed rock which is deficient in calcium or phosphorus or potassium will, so far as we know now, be equally deficient in these elements as will the organic topsoil which gradually is built up out of the death and decay of that vegetation.

The popular idea that the drained Everglades area of Florida was and is a region of unbounded virgin fertility is a complete fallacy, generally accepted by laymen and a great many farmers. When first drained, and put into cultivation and pasture, the vegetation and the condition of the cattle quickly revealed that this virgin soil, like most muck soils everywhere, consisted largely of nitrogen and carbon with almost every sort of mineral deficiency. On a recent visit to the area, the county agent who conducted me on the tour warned me in advance of the conditions, saying, "Of course, what you are going to see is not really normal agriculture but only a glorified form of hydroponics." In other words, the virgin muck soil was simply the base for operations as gravel or cinders are the base for growing plants in water, saturated with minerals. The original deficiencies of minerals necessary to the healthy growth of plants, animals and people were enormous and both vegetables and animals grown in the area were sickly, diseased and subject to the attack of almost every pest. As one grower said in 1924, "We always plant everything and never harvest anything."

It was in 1927 when experiments with trace elements were applied to over sixty species of feed and vegetable crops that the vast possibilities for vegetable growing in the Everglades region began to be revealed. Among these elements were copper, manganese, zinc and cobalt. The applications of these elements produced an almost immediate effect—in soil where until then virtually all vegetables were sickly and failed to reach maturity, the plants attained virtually normal growth and a high degree of productivity. Since then the trace elements together with major elements, phosphorus, potassium and calcium, have been applied in increasing quantities with the result that the areas today produce fat, healthy cattle and a really fabulous production of fruit and marketable vegetables. This is what my county agent friend meant when he said that agriculture in this area was largely "glorified hydroponics" in which almost everything was added to the soil.

The same area is, of course, one of the best arguments against the extreme exponents of the composting-organic school of agriculture. In other words because the vital elements, both major and trace, were not present in the subsoil no amount of composting of the indigenous vegetable would have put those vitally necessary elements back into the soils. Actually nature had been composting the vegetation of the Everglades area for millions of years and succeeded in producing a highly nitrogenous, carboniferous soil still deficient in the elements necessary for the healthy growth of animals and of all vegetation except those comparatively simple and nonnutritious forms of plant life adapted to fresh-water, marsh areas.

As Dr. Gratz, of the Florida Agricultural Experiment Station, puts it, "Without the use of minor elements the rapid progress in agricultural production in Florida would not have taken place."

In neighboring citrus-growing areas where citrus trees showed signs of deformation and diseases of all sorts, intensive applications of the major elements—nitrogen, phosphorus and potassium seemed only to increase the decline in the trees. It was not until compounds of copper, zinc, manganese and cobalt were applied that the trees began to recover their health and resistance and to produce fruit once more. Since then the other trace elements have been added to soils with the result of marked increase in health, productivity and resistance to disease. Of course the rare areas of Florida with soils having an original limestone do not fit into the same category as the deficient soils of the Everglades and the sandy areas.

As has been pointed out elsewhere, limestone is the product of minute marine animal life formed in sea water and in addition to high amounts of calcium also contains a whole category of important trace elements.

A brief report of the problem and its solution is contained in *Chemical Treatment of Florida Soil Increases Yield Threefold*, by L. O. Gratz, Assistant Director of Research, Florida Agricultural Experiment Station. In a series of pamphlets, Dr. Gratz has set forth the history of trace minerals in relation to fruit, vegetables and cattle growing in Florida. Other valuable information can be obtained from the Everglades Experiment Station, Florida.

Many forested areas of the United States have in the past been cleared of their timber in the assumption that the freed soil would be good agricultural land. On a similar assumption some millions of acres of bog land have been drained at great expense only to reach the ultimate discovery that the cleared or drained land was so deficient and unbalanced minerally that it was useless as agricultural land and could not be made productive by any process which, under the existing economy of the nation and the world, was either profitable or possible. In Michigan and Wisconsin, millions of acres of cleared timberland is being reforested because the populations which attempted to use it as agricultural land virtually starved to death since the land was wholly unproductive, or because the vegetation it produced was so deficient minerally as to provide little real nourishment for man or beast.

A little of the Michigan land by intensive use of chemical fertilizer and green manures has been made highly productive for potatoes and strawberries, two crops which bring in high cash returns per acre and justify the expense of feeding the land with the minerals it originally lacked. An expert of the Department of Agriculture conducting the writer on a tour of the drained Everglade swamps of Florida now employed for heavy agricultural production said, "There is no use trying to kid you. The agricultural processes practiced here are no more than a glorified hydroponics in which virtually *all* minerals down to the trace elements have to be put into the soil annually."

Elsewhere, notably in the great swamp area of Minnesota, hundreds of thousands of acres of supposedly rich bog land were drained for agricultural use at great expense by WPA labor during the early Thirties only to reach the same discovery—that as agricultural land it was unproductive and virtually useless for anything but scrub timber, marsh vegetation and wildlife.

One legal absurdity arose in the case of the restoration of the great Minnesota swamps. When the work of blocking the drainage ditches built by WPA was about to begin it was discovered that a State law forbade the blocking of any drainage ditch. The problem was solved by the beavers which already existed in certain areas and by other beavers imported and let loose to increase their population and the fur industry of Minnesota. They flourished in the natural wild conditions and quickly bred colony after colony which spread out damming up the expensive, useless ditches and have done their best to restore the drained areas to proper land use which in this case was wildlife, fur production, and some timber.

This lack of *un*balance of minerals over large areas of the world's surface limits greatly the future food production of the world. One hears often enough observations from travelers to the effect that there seems to be vast areas of land visible from car, train or airplane windows which are still open to cultivation and that there seems still to be unlimited supplies of food-producing land not being utilized. The answer, known only to those whose business is agricultural land, is that those areas which have not been utilized or on which unsuccessful attempts at agriculture have been made, are unbalanced or comparatively unproductive soil because of mineral lack or difficult soil structure or aridity. In their present state they cannot be cultivated with any profit and the expenditure of money in making them cultivatable by the addition of minerals and organic material is so great that their conversion into productive soils is economically impossible under existing conditions. It may be that under the pressure of a rapidly increasing world population and the decline of production upon the land already under cultivation in the world, it will become *necessary* to convert these lands into productive agricultural soils regardless of cost in order to prevent wholesale malnutrition, depressed living standards and even actual starvation of large segments of the world's population. But the expense will be enormous and will be far beyond the capacity of individuals or private enterprise; it will become the project of government or of international commissions with the expense borne by taxpayers, principally those taxpayers who live in the great congested cities who, even now, are paying heavily in order to get enough to eat at prices commensurate with the wages and economy of our times.

All of this is why it becomes vitally necessary for reasons not only of national or international economy but of health and social conditions that the destruction of existing good agricultural land through erosion and poor and wasteful agriculture be checked and that available possible agricultural land be made to produce its maximum without destruction of its fertility or mineral balance.

The mineral deficiencies of poor or worn-out soil affect not only the living standards of people attempting to make a living upon it but also standards of health, vitality, intelligence and initiative which are so fundamental a part of the *real* wealth of nations. There exist in America pockets and areas of population of the best biological stock which, having some generations ago chosen to pioneer nonagricultural forest regions as farmers, have sunk not only to the economic level of the present European peasant but have become rapidly enfeebled mentally and physically by the limited diets and the mineral deficiencies of the agriculturally poor soils upon which they have attempted to live. This is largely the history of the fine pioneering biological stock which filtered into the forest and poor land areas of the mountains and hills of the Middle South. It is also the case of a great part of the population of the Deep South which settled upon once minerally rich land long since leached-out, farmed-out, and eroded. Through failure to maintain a good mineral balance, together with a high level of organic material, the soil over large areas has become thoroughly depleted and has in time produced a population so lacking in vitality, intelligence, and initiative that it can no longer really help itself or gain any real advantage through schools, school teachers, agricultural bulletins, or other methods of a purely intellectual sort. The problem has indeed become so great and so hopeless that not only government supervision but government direct action is a primary necessity in order to make the population physically and mentally capable of absorbing education and of practicing a good and intelligent agriculture.

It is true that some progress toward a better agriculture is being made by individuals in the Deep South but the cases are largely isolated and involve only a tiny minority, still possessed of intelligence and enterprise. By far the greater percentage of the population is, through limited diet and

362

mineral deficiencies, inert and helpless. It is an interesting scientific fact that despite generations of living upon poor diets and mineral deficiencies, the biological germ stock remains undeteriorated. There is abundant evidence that sickly, apparently deficient, children of good biological stock when transferred from poor or depleted areas to minerally rich ones will lose their apparent deficiencies and develop into first-rate physical specimens.

It is impossible not to point out that it is the Deep South and in the bordering states that our greatest agricultural slums exist. Here too exist unbelievably low family incomes (as low as five dollars spending money a year), and the areas where ignorance and prejudice are by far the most prevalent and powerful.

There is indeed an interesting experiment which any reader may make who possesses a map of the United States. It is a simple one and requires merely two sheets of thin tissue paper. Place one of these over the map of the nation and trace out those agricultural areas where income, agricultural fertility, and living standards are low, where the population is deficient physically and mentally, and ignorance and prejudice run rampant. Then take the second sheet and trace out the agricultural areas where the soils were originally deficient minerally or became so through erosion, depletion, and greedy farming. You will find that the two areas coincide almost exactly even to those "pockets" of such land as exist even in the newer, less depleted middle and northern states. You will find such "pockets" in rich states like Illinois and Indiana, Ohio, and Missouri, states commonly believed to possess an inexhaustible fertility. Some of those areas have become depleted in only two or three generations of farming. Some areas like those in Oklahoma have become eroded and depleted within a single generation.

Probably the soils best balanced minerally on the surface of the earth are those with a base of limestone or those composed of glacial gravel loam. This is so because both soils contain a high degree of nearly all minerals thoroughly mixed. Limestone is the product of silt and the bodies and calcareous shells of uncountable trillions of sea organisms and as the sea became eventually the depository of all minerals poured into it from the eroding land surfaces of the earth those minerals exist in good balance in any soils or rocks of marine origin. Because of this fact the creatures of the sea are in a sense the best nourished of all living creatures and in the deposits of their dead bodies at the bottom of the sea lie the richest and best balanced soil on the earth. Limestone is little more than this soil raised above the level of the sea and hardened into rock during prehistoric time. Dolomitic limestone is not only of value to soil for the calcium it contains but for the considerable quantities of other major elements and of many of the trace elements.

Vegetation feeding and growing upon this limestone for countless centuries has transmitted these minerals into organic material which in turn through the process of growth, death, and decay has deposited them *on top* of the original limestone rock in the form of topsoil in which they are no longer rock but highly available organic and mineral material for the vegetation which succeeds them and for the healthy, vigorous animals and people who are fortunate enough to inhabit those areas where such soil exists.

It is not without reason that the best race horses in the world are bred and raised in Ireland and in the bluegrass, limestone areas of Kentucky. It is so because both soils were limestone soils containing also high percentages of phosphorus. These two elements in conjunction with the trace elements existing in limestone not only produce, but are essential to, the production of bone, stamina, vigor, and intelligence. They produce healthy, long-lived, vigorous, and intelligent people as well as animals.

Although both areas began, as one might say, from scratch, with the same advantages, the bluegrass area of Kentucky has been subject to depletion at an infinitely more rapid rate. Indeed there are, in the very heart of the bluegrass region, farms as badly depleted and eroded as are to be found in the whole of the nation, despite the fact that on some of them the topsoil lies only a foot or two above the limestone which gave it its original fertility.

There are many reasons why the Irish soil has retained its qualities longer than the soil of the Kentucky area. It is a much deeper soil and is not subject to the violent rainfalls and climatic temperature variations of Kenturky. The annual total rainfall of Ireland and that of Kentucky are about the same with the advantage in most years on the side of Kentucky but Irish rainfall is more evenly distributed throughout the year and falls most of the time in the form of a gentle drizzle. The violent thunderstorms and cloudbursts of Kentucky in which an inch or more of rain will fall in an hour or less are virtually unknown in Ireland. Perhaps most important of all is the fact that in Ireland the only open-row crop grown outside cottage gardens is potatoes and with potatoes and the rapid growth of potato vines the soil is left bare to rainfall, leaching and erosion for only a very brief period of three to four weeks.

The bluegrass areas of Kentucky, save for the great horse-breeding farms kept almost wholly in grass like the Irish countryside, are largely devoted to a general farming program which favors tobacco and corn, two of the most destructive of crops from the point of view of leaching, erosion, and mineral depletion. In the case of both crops the soil, clean-cultivated under old traditional agricultural methods, is left bare to wind, sun, and torrential rain throughout nearly all the year. At the same time the clean cultivation and constant tillage of the earth under the higher summer temperature of Kentucky burns out at a prodigious rate the organic material so vital to the absorption of rainfall, the retention of moisture, the existence of living bacteria, and the processes which help to break down minerals and make them available to plant and eventually to human and animal life.

As a result of all these forces and customs the Kentucky area has worn out quickly in comparison with the Irish country. In the very heart of the bluegrass country I have seen worn-out and eroded farms which in four or five generations have virtually been destroyed. The old-fashioned farmer in the area will tell you that his soil does not need lime because the limestone lies just beneath his topsoil and in places actually crops out of the ground. On one occasion a farmer of the "what was good enough for grandpappy was good enough for me" school was giving me the usual story when I chanced to look down on the "pasture" where we were standing. It was worn-out, sickly, weedy pasture with no white clover in sight and the only visible bluegrass was yellowish and tough although we were only in the month of May at Derby time when it should have been luxuriant. There at our very feet was an actual outcrop of limestone with sorrel, an acid-loving plant which abhors lime, displaying a luxuriant growth less than a foot from the limestone itself.

Of course the truth was that the pasture field in which we stood had long since become depleted through erosion, leaching, and overgrazing, of the original calcium and phosphorus in available form so that it would no longer grow decent crops of successive corn and tobacco. It had been turned into permanent pasture and what traces of minerals remained had been continually carried off for years in the form of bones, meat, and milk until in the end it was utterly impoverished. The merciful grass cover which prevented erosion and leaching and held the organic material, had come too late, only when the fertility of the field and its lime and phosphorus content was almost entirely consumed.

That is the tragic story of almost all pasture land in the Deep and Middle South and of much of it in the middle and northern states. It is converted to grass or rather is allowed to revert only when it has become useless and worn out as open cultivated, row-crop land. It is the reason why cattle upon such land are rough-coated and produce little milk or appear in the end at the stockyards as rough-coated, tough animals that brings prices far below those paid for quality beef. You simply cannot produce good meat, good milk, good animals or people upon worn-out land. The cattle in the field with the limestone cropping out at our feet were just such animals.

In his argument that he did not need lime because the limestone cropped out of the very surface of his pasture, the old farmer lacked knowledge, thinking power, and indeed was unable to understand the evidence of his own eyes in the case of the flourishing sorrel. It never occurred to him that the lime and phosphorus which long ago had made his soil one of the richest in the world had come there through millions of years of weathering of the stone and of transmutation into availability through millions of years of vegetation passing through the cycle of birth, growth, death, decay, and rebirth. How could that mineral content be replenished or even maintained under a violent agriculture, especially when all vegetation such as the tobacco plants and corn stover was constantly and persistently being removed from the soil, burned, allowed to rot in piles or fed to cattle which returned less than a fifth of the minerals to the soil in the form of manure. The limestone which lay beneath his soil and at our feet was flint hard. It would require more millions of years to weather and become available, unless human intelligence quarried, crushed it and applied it in semi-available form to the depleted fields.

I happened to be standing in that particular pasture because the farmer who believed "what was good enough for grandpappy was good enough for me" had farmed himself out. He had reached that level where the yield per acre of his fields was so low that he could no longer keep up to the mere level of taxes and interest. His farm had been purchased by a famous neighboring horse-breeder who realized that the land was worse than useless for grazing his horses. The forage raised on that farm, either as green pasture or as hay, would soon have put his horses out of the running and made their offspring valueless at the annual horse sales. He had flown me by plane to have a look at it and to find for him a young man practicing the New Agriculture who could put the farm back into circulation and make its soil once more productive of vigorous, healthy vegetation and healthy animals and people.

The old-fashioned farmer standing there beside us looked like his own cattle. He was tired, prematurely aged and had only three or four teeth, although he had lived all his life on a farm in the very midst of a region once famous for the calcium and phosphorus content of its soils. Although the farm had already been sold over his head he was permitted to remain until he found work as a common laborer in the near-by town of Lexington. He had indeed farmed his land, his cattle, and himself very nearly out of existence.

I have told in *Pleasant Valley* the story of another famous race-horse establishment in the bluegrass area not far from the old man's worn-out farm. It is one of the most famous in the world with breeding stock which contained the finest of racing blood lines, yet there arrived a time about fifteen years ago when it became virtually impossible to sell the colts produced in its stables at the great annual sales because they had achieved an increasingly bad reputation for split hooves, poor bones and lack of stamina. The owner, one of America's richest men, became desperate and spent great sums upon veterinarians, feed experts and even soil experts who at that period knew far less about soil and minerals than they do today, but no improvement came about until a polo-playing English friend expressed the belief that the sad condition of the farm's colts came about through soil deficiencies and said that he believed he could cure the condition. The owner, in desperation, gave his consent and the polo-playing friend, who had never been to an agricultural college, but knew horses as he knew the back of his hand, went to work on the soil of the farm with lime, phosphorus, and other minerals, and with a system of composting the manure. The end of the story is the obvious one. The colts produced by the farm are now back at the top of the market and selling for top prices at the annual sales. One of them ran one of the most famous races in Derby history at the 1947 race meeting.

Probably one of the richest and best balanced of all soils is that existing in the famous "black belts" of Texas, Mississippi, Alabama, and the Ukraine. These are, or were, deep soils containing quantities of the major minerals and most of the trace elements. They represent rich deposits of decayed organic material lying over limestone or various kinds of marl which is, broadly speaking, limestone that is not yet hardened. Its productivity as virgin soil was enormous, but virtually no major area of such soil remains undiscovered or unexploited in the world.

The tragedy is that these black soils have been so rapidly destroyed by erosion in most of the Alabama and Mississippi areas. Over great areas the soil is no longer black but gray. The same process has been under way for a shorter time in Texas. In both areas the organic content of the soil has been rapidly burned out through the cultivation of row crops, notably cotton or corn, in a climate of high temperatures and heavy seasonal rains, where the process is seldom arrested or wholly checked by low temperatures and freezing. In the Texas area the mineral content is still so high and so well balanced that the use of chemical fertilizers gives no perceptible increase of yields but the organic material has been so far dissipated, that a crop of hubam, or annual sweet clover, plowed into the soil will bring immediate increases in yields as high as thirty to forty per cent. Fortunately because of the marl base of much of the soil the destruction of its fertility is not hopeless. By proper farming methods most of its tremendous fertility can be restored.

In the Black Belt of the Ukraine the process of destruction has been much less rapid for the region lies in a northern temperate zone, the rainfall is more evenly distributed and the process of destruction has not been hastened by the sometimes reckless and unintelligent use of modern agricultural machinery.

It is a great error to suppose that modern agricultural machinery is in itself the means of better farming, better crop yields or of maintaining or increasing the fertility of the soil. It may cut production costs, do away with drudgery, and increase speed of operation but *per se* it may do as much damage as good in relation to soil fertility and productivity. The good or bad is determined by the intelligence of its use. Modern machinery badly or unintelligently used may simply intensify soil destruction by making it possible to farm more acres carelessly, rapidly, and badly.

It is quite possible that with the knowledge of soil now existing or in the process of discovery, man will soon be able, if he is not already able, to construct a better, more balanced, more productive soil than most virgin soils existing in nature. In a shrinking world with its increasing network of transportation he is able to bring together in one spot most of the elements vital to highly productive soil as only the sea has been able to do in the past. It is possible that in this new understanding he can create soils which in time will produce food that will alter wholly the health, vigor, intelligence, longevity, and character of whole peoples. In a sense the people of our great cities already benefit by the shrinking of this world and the growth of its transportation facilities since the food which they eat does not come from a single region but from *all* parts of the nation and they are therefore not subject to the same ills and deficiencies as a rural or village area which is dependent for its food upon a single area which may contain only depleted or minerally deficient soils. The city dweller undoubtedly consumes much food, aside from the processed white sugar and white bread, which is highly deficient in minerals and virtually useless save for its bulk, but it is also true that he consumes much good food grown upon minerally rich ground and containing high amounts of minerals and vitamins. As yet he has no means of determining which vegetables and fruits are grown upon poor soils and which ones are grown upon good, minerally balanced soils.

Regional afflictions such as goitre, bad teeth, and many other illnesses as yet untraced or unfixed are *regional* because they result from deficiencies of minerals within a given area.

The formula for a minerally well-balanced soil capable of producing healthy plants, animals, and people, as we know it today, should contain abundant organic material in the process of decay, bacteria, moulds, fungi, earthworms, calcium, phosphorus, potassium, nitrogen and a wide variety of trace elements such as manganese, magnesium, boron, copper, cobalt, iron, and at least twenty or thirty others. It should be soil in which the whole eternal cycle of life, growth, death, and rebirth should be constantly in progress.

Streptomycin, which has surpassed penicillin in effectiveness both in scope and curative properties, is known to come from rich, well-balanced soils, preferably those which have been heavily fertilized with good barnyard manure. Penicillin is the product of a beneficent mould which plays its part in the cosmic cycle of death, decay, and rebirth. Recently a new and highly potent antibody christened chloromycetin, the product of moulds produced in mulched soils, has been discovered and is being tested. Initial tests have shown it to be highly effective against both tuberculosis and undulant fever. At Malabar we have had some remarkable experiences with the effect of increasingly fertile soil upon infections and general health of animals. When the depleted farms were first taken over we were troubled by a mysterious foot infection which appeared in cattle in the open fields with no access to barnyards. As the fertility increased the infections disappeared completely. The experience leads to the supposition that fertile, well-balanced soils may possess organisms or substances perhaps in the form of benevolent moulds and fungi like streptomycin which themselves fight to annihilate disease. Of course the crudest example of the efficacy of benevolent bacteria fighting and annihilating malignant bacteria lies in the functioning of a well-managed septic tank. The disappearance from the poultry houses of range paralysis with the increasing fertility and mineral balance of the soil and the direct feeding of trace minerals in addition to the calcium oyster shell has already been noted and a possible control of Bang's disease through proper mineral balance has already been suggested. Certainly the increasing fertility and mineral balance of the soil has increased beyond all dispute the fertility and *breedability* of the farm animals as well as the yields of grain and seed and the efficacy of pollenization and germination. All of this despite the apparent law of nature that shortages of food often occurring in wartime cause increases in the birthrates of both animals and humans. Shortages of food, however, are not the same as mineral deficiencies in food. It is well known to stock breeders that animals which are too fat from too much food will not breed as eagerly or be as fecund as animals on a controlled diet. Thus animals suffering from a shortage of accustomed, well-balanced foods will undoubtedly breed more rapidly than animals fed in abundance on minerally deficient foods. The same probably holds true in the case of humans.

In short, a cubic foot of fertile earth capable of producing health in plants, animals, and people should contain in itself the pattern of the universe. Today it is possible for man to construct such a pattern of fertile earth, but his ability to do so indefinitely in the future is limited by many things.

One of the more serious limitations is the amount of land suitable to conversion into man-made, highly productive, well-balanced soil. Millions of acres of the soil already destroyed in this country could not be brought back by any known economically possible means because the subsurface material laid bare in many cases by erosion is poor, unprofitable stuff difficult or impossible to restore save at an economic cost which is beyond consideration. Some of it is rock, some shale of various kinds, some is tough hardpan clay.

And there is the question of mineral supplies, transportation costs and the costs of processing various minerals to make them suitable for shipment and for agricultural use. Limestone, the very base of all good agriculture, exists in vast quantities on the surface of the earth. Its quality varies as widely as does its total mineral content. Nitrogen follows directly in the path of lime for on limed or limestone soils the whole family of legumes can be grown and the legumes are of immense importance to any soil restoration process. They produce subsoil nitrogen in huge quantities and can also be the

371

source of vast quantities of organic material in the form of green manures, both in the roots and the top vegetation of the legumes. The limestone, as has already been pointed out, contains in varying amounts many of the valuable trace elements. Modern methods have also made possible the reduction of nitrogen from the air itself and the cost of that reduction will decrease. There also remain the by-product nitrogens coming from industry in the form of sulphate of ammonia and nitrate of soda, although both are expensive. The agricultural supplies both of limestone and nitrogen seem to be unlimited so long as the universe exists upon its present pattern.

Potassium, also invaluable to growth, strength and health, is in smaller supply and the processing and shipping costs make it expensive. Like all minerals the world supply has definite limitations and these are by no means as abundant as limestone.

Phosphorus, absolutely essential to the existence of man upon this earth, is shortest in supply with definite limitations in sight unless considerable new deposits are discovered. It does exist in great quantities in the sea but no economically practical method of extracting it has yet been discovered. The present cost of such processing makes its utilization in the form of fertilizer impossible except upon a basis of enormously increased food costs or heavy government subsidies in turn paid by the taxpayer, plus the expense of a complicated bureaucracy to handle this subsidy.

Virtually all the trace elements exist in sufficient quantities to provide adequate supplies at reasonable costs for centuries to come.

To be sure all of these elements are available in sea water for they have been eroding into the sea for millions of years and it may be that in the end man in order to survive will be forced to recover them from the sea. None of these elements are destroyed; they become transmuted into different forms and chemical combinations and are constantly being redistributed over the surface of the earth. The loss of precious minerals by which man exists and their concentration in the sea has been greatly hastened by the practices of man himself in an agriculture which encourages erosion and depletion and by the concentration of great populations into constricted urban areas which dump all their sewage wastes into streams or lakes whence they are eventually carried to the sea.

One factor in the burden placed upon the still rich countries by the feeding of poorer countries has been almost entirely overlooked by those concerned with the distribution of food through the world. It is that the still rich are not only exporting a certain *money* value in the foodstuffs shipped abroad but are exporting at the same time huge quantities of food producing minerals. Actually each huge shipment of food out of this or any other country contains many tons of calcium, potassium, and phosphorus which will not be returned. Much of it is exported to nations which in the past have dissipated their own native supplies of these things as we have done and still are doing in this country. The steady drain of fertility is probably in the end more costly than the money value represented by these shipments. The same holds true in another sense of the iron, copper, zinc, and other minerals exported as processed articles such as automobiles and refrigerators, etc. In every case we are exporting our real material wealth and the real sources of our strength and power as a nation. We are, in fact, steadily exporting the foundations of our living standards and our existence as a great nation. Money represents in no sense a return value for these things unless that money is spent upon the purchasing and stock-piling of new amounts of raw materials or real wealth equal to those exported. All this is in line with the statement of Bernard Baruch made to Congress that before we continue distributing our real wealth wholesale around the earth we had best take an invoice of what real wealth remains to us.

In the sense of real wealth the lend-lease arrangement was the most costly material contribution ever made by any nation to any war or series of wars in the history of the world. We exported vast quantities of real *wealth* to half the nations of the world in return for which we received only a tiny proportion of real wealth in the form of raw materials or processed raw materials although the American citizenry was led to believe by President Roosevelt that we should be repaid in kind. The small payments in exchange for these things was of utter insignificance. Billions of dollars worth of our real wealth in the form of iron, copper, aluminum, timber, etc., today lies scattered over the four quarters of the globe. We have received nothing or next to nothing in return for it. This loss, far more than money, represents the material cost of the war. It will affect adversely the lives and living standards of generations born five hundred years hence in this country.

Short of war there is no greater spectacle of human inbecility than this funneling off of our mineral fertility into the sea. It was as if man were bent upon destroying his vitality, his health, his power of procreation and in the end, himself. These sewage wastes are by far the greater source of pollution in our streams and lakes, far greater than the pollution created by industrial wastes. In countless instances cities and towns befoul their water supplies and then, before their citizens drink it, add chlorine and other chemicals in order to render harmless the noxious germs contained in the wholesale outpouring of excrement into the waters.

This whole process of decontamination is a part of the "patent medicine" philosophy of the immediate past, the same process of locking the stable after the horse has been stolen. And no one knows yet what ill effects to humans may be created by the absorption of great quantities of chemicals used in "purifying" the polluted water. Even to a child it must seem obvious that manipulators could better spend the taxpayers' money upon plants which reduced both garbage and sewage to fertilizer, a process which would in the end pay most or all of the expense of such a process, provide many cities with an unpolluted source of water, preserve the beauty and utility of our streams and most of all preserve the *concentration* of precious, life and health-giving minerals to be returned to the soil rather than being dumped wholesale into the sea.

There are times when the human race seems scarcely civilized at all and possessed of a mentality little above that of the Java ape-man. While a government sponsors an atomic project to destroy mankind, while a concentration of scientists shamefully work out the engine of destruction, and taxpayers painfully contribute nearly three billions of dollars to create it, the ills of mankind and the approaching specter of the destruction of his health and indeed of his slow starvation through a rapidly increasing world population and a decreasing food production goes, by comparison, almost unnoticed.

Out of the earth we came and to the earth we return, and it is the earth itself which determines largely our health, our longevity, our vigor, even our character. In the broadest sense any nation is as vigorous and as powerful as its natural resources, and among them the most important are agriculture and forests, for these are eternally renewable and productive if managed properly. Upon them, and largely upon agriculture depends another vast source of any nation's power—the health, vigor, intelligence and ingenuity of its citizens. One has only to look at an ignorant disease-ridden mongrel Bedouin seated among the marble ruins of the once great Roman cities of North Africa to see and to understand what happens to countries and nations when their agriculture fades, their soil becomes worn out and their peoples lose their economic independence, their health, their vigor and their intelligence.

# XV:  THE BAD YEAR
## OR
## PRIDE GOETH BEFORE A FALL

... For the Father of Agriculture
Gave us a hard calling; he first decreed it an art
To work the fields, sent worries to sharpen our mortal
    wits
And would not allow his realm to grow listless with
    lethargy
                    *—The Georgics of Virgil*

THE rains began, cold and dreary at the beginning of the
month of April and day after day they continued through
April, through May and into June. Meanwhile, the fields
grew wetter and wetter, until at last the hillsides themselves
began to weep, the water oozing out of their sides down the
slopes onto the lower ground. In the flat country to the west
of us the fields became lakes of water, sometimes almost un-
broken for miles across the level rich fields.

In our county oats, if one is to have a good crop, should
be planted as early as possible, for winter oats, seeded in the
autumn, rarely weather the rigors of the northern winter and a
farmer cannot afford to gamble on them. Oats planted in
March have the best chance of success. Planted after the
middle of April the chances of vigor and yield are lessened.
Planted after the middle of May the yield is cut in half or if
hot, dry weather comes on the results may be utter failure. In
1947 planting in March was out of the question for the fields
were still frozen and covered with snow. The usual "false
spring" which allowed us to put in early oats did not come at
all, and then the rains began, falling day after day, in showers

some days, in drenching downpours on others. And always it was cold, so cold that even the wild flowers and the morels (those first delicious woodsy fungi that grow in the deep forests under ash trees or in old and dying orchards) grew confused. A sudden burst of sunlight brought some of them into flower and fruition only to meet disaster on cold frosty moonlit nights. The delicate, tiny Dutchman's breeches all met a frosty death while in full flower and the trilliums turned up stunted, brown-fringed petals toward the gray skies instead of the usual luxuriant blossoms that sometimes covered whole acres of our deep woodlands in drifts of white. The bluegrass, water-soaked and cold, languished instead of growing and kept the restless cattle (who knew better than we do when spring should be at hand) prisoners in the barns and soggy barnyards. They mooed and cried out in their restlessness, the sound of their mournful voices drifting far across the woods and hills.

And slowly, throughout all our county, the complaints of the farmers, impatient to get into their fields and worried over the cold, soggy fields, began to raise into a wail.

Charlie Schrack, standing in the doorway of the barn, watching the fields drenched by gray rains said, "I can't remember anything like it in fifty years." Lots of farmers talk that way when drought or floods by persistent rain begin to spell disaster, but this time it seemed to me that Charlie was right, for it rained when it seemed impossible. Rain seemed to fall in cold, frosty weather out of skies that were comparatively free of clouds. It was as if the heavens were a gigantic showerbath with a small irresponsible child playing with the chain which released the water.

And Nanny said, "I'm beginning to wonder if the Atomic bomb didn't have something to do with all this rain. Maybe the scientists had better stop discovering things before they destroy us altogether. It begins to make you believe in the story of the Tower of Babel. Man can become too pretentious."

And the next morning I read in the papers that government agencies had warned planes to keep below the level of twelve thousand feet since the Atomic cloud from the Bikini tests was passing for the third time around the earth and had just reached us again. That night and for two days, it rained without ceasing.

Walter Pretzer, a prosperous hothouse grower came down from Cleveland for a dreary, water-soaked week end. Curiously enough he is both an immensely practical man and a mystic. He said, "The rains are only balancing out. We're getting what we missed during the past four or five years." To which I replied cynically, "Yes, but it isn't raining into your greenhouses."

But he answered me, "Nor is the sun shining." Sun, or lack of sun can make all the difference to the grower of hothouse vegetables. The lack of it can delay the crop until fresh vegetables, field grown from some other part of the country, come onto the market and run the prices of hothouse vegetables below the level at which it is even worth harvesting them. Sometimes it can ruin a crop altogether.

In modern agriculture, the weather is about the only thing which a farmer cannot somehow control. Against the next most disastrous potential—a sharp disastrous fall in prices—the good farmer can protect himself and manage to survive, but when the rain comes in floods at planting time or refuses to come at all for one dreary week after another, there is not much that he can do. And flooding rains are worse than drought; a farmer can irrigate dry burning soil if he possesses the facilities; he cannot mop up heavy persistent floods.

At Malabar and among the hills of our neighbors we were better off than the flat country people, for the water did not stand in lakes on our hills of glacial gravel loam. The worst we had to face were the seepage spots and "wet weather springs" which appeared here and there, sometimes at the very top of a hill. These we could plow around, leaving them water-logged and fallow, for another and better year. Our soil was loose and open and you could work it wet without too much damage if there was enough organic material mixed with it. And we had the advantage of mechanization—that when there was a break in the weather we could get into the fields and with tractor lights burning, work on shifts all through the night.

And that was what we did during the awful spring of 1947 and so somehow we got ninety acres of oats into the ground, some of it in land which had been rough plowed through Bob's foresight the autumn before and was all ready for disking, fitting, and drilling. We got in our oats in one of those two-day breaks when, if the sun did not shine, the rain at least did not fall. Then the rains broke again and the cold persisted and in three or four days the oats were through the ground in a pale, misty shimmer of lettuce green across the wet, brown fields. And our hearts and stomachs felt better and our pride rose, because we had in the ground probably more oats than any farmer from the Appalachians to the Great Divide. On our loose, well-drained soil, oats did not mind the cold nor the rain. It was the kind of weather from which it benefited in the early stages. We were having March weather at least a month after March had passed.

There is in every good farmer a curious, overwhelming, almost malicious pride common to the human race but especially well-developed in the cultivator. It is born of satisfaction in being "smarter" than his neighbor, in having his acres look greener, in getting in his crops earlier, in having fields where the hay or the pasture is heavier. And conversely there is in every good farmer a kind of perverse satisfaction in the discovery that his neighbor's fields look poorly. The sight of a poor crop in someone else's field somehow warms the heart of the farmer whose own fields are lush and green.

Often when I have been driving across Ohio with Bob, he will grin, as we pass a miserable pasture or field of yellowish weedy hay and say, "I suppose that makes you feel awfully good." And I'm afraid that sometimes it does. The pride of a good farmer is often his worst sin, but it is also what makes a good farmer and what helped to feed this nation and the rest of the world in the difficult years when lack of machinery and labor made farming a back-breaking, long-houred job. It is that same pride which makes the good farmer resist subsidies and government payments and all the paraphernalia of a "kept" agriculture. In his heart a good farmer wants to show that he cannot be "licked," and that without help from any one he can grow abundant crops despite every handicap.

That is why a good farmer grows short-tempered and desperate when the weather turns against him. With each day of drought or flooding rain, he becomes more frustrated and savage, because the weather alone he cannot lick altogether either by machines or muscle or long hours in the field.

And so farmers everywhere that spring of 1947 grew ill-

tempered and angry. They did not wail. It is only the poor farmer who wails and looks for scapegoats or excuses for his own failures of energy or intelligence. But that, of course, may be true of the whole human race. It just stands out clearly in the case of the farmer who long ago discovered what many others rarely discover—that in life there are no "breaks" except as one makes them for himself.

Still it did not stop raining. Time for planting oats receded into the distant unchangeable past and time for corn plowing came along, and still it rained and stayed cold. It was the year when Al Jolson's old song, "April Showers"[1] had a great revival and every juke-box and every radio program was blaring forth:

> "Though April showers may come your way
> They bring the flowers that bloom in May
> And when it's raining, have no regrets
> Because it isn't raining rain you know
> It's raining violets."

[1] Copyright 1921 by Harms, Inc. Used by permission.

It was a song that sounded very sour to the farmer that spring. The violets, which grew on banks like weeds in our country, were small, shriveled and frost-bitten. There were no warm showers. There were only flooding downpours, day after day as May slipped past toward June and Ellen said, "They ought to change that song to April Showers that bring the flowers that bloom in July."

Slowly countless farmers abandoned all hope of planting oats. They talked of other crops and of putting all their land into corn. Corn planting time came along and still it rained. Here and there in our hill country one could see farmers dripping wet on their tractors, turning over sod ground for corn planting. Sod ground, especially in soil like that of our county, can be plowed fairly safely when it is still too wet because the roots and vegetation help to keep the ground open, aerated and keep it from packing. We too plowed sod in the rain and turned under the acres of rank sweet clover on the loose, alluvial soil of the farm we rent from the Muskingum Conservancy. We dared not even put a tractor wheel on the small acreage of water-logged clay.

But even after the ground was plowed it was too wet to fit for planting. Day after day went by, each rain bringing us nearer to the last date at which corn could be planted and have any chance of maturing before the average frost date of October fourth. Then the rain stopped for a couple of days and again we worked night and day until all but ten acres of corn were in the ground. By our own standards at Malabar, we were three weeks late but with luck that corn, changed at the last moment to a quick ripening, short season hybrid, would mature if the frost held off.

We were thankful that we had all our corn in save for the ten acres of clay which we could not touch because it was as wet and sticky as glue. So we planned to put that into buckwheat, let it serve the bees and then plow it into the soil for the benefits it would give us the following year. "At any rate," said Bob, "it will look pretty, and it's better than leaving the ground bare or to grow up in weeds."

And again, smugly and pridefully, we settled back aware that we had probably more corn in the ground than any of the farmers to the west of us all the way into the corn country where the fields were still more like the carp ponds of Austria and Czechoslovakia than the fertile fields of the mid-western bread-basket country. But still it rained and remained cold, and we began to worry over whether the seed would rot in the ground. Then for three days the rain suddenly stopped and capriciously the weather changed from cold to oppressively hot with a hot baking sun and a new peril developed—that even with all the organic material we had pumped into the soil for years and the fresh crop of sweet clover turned under, the soil was so wet that the hot sun might bake the surface and prevent the tender, germinating corn from piercing the surface. So on the third day I climbed aboard the tractor, attached the rotary hoe and drove it full speed back and forth across the surface of the cornfield because the faster you drive it, the more efficiently it works, breaking up the surface and throwing the tiny weed seedlings and bits of crumbling earth high into the air.

Driving at full tractor speed, I felt good. The sun was shining. The alluvial gravel loam was dry enough for the rotary hoe to work efficiently. The Conservancy farm lay alongside the big artificial lake formed by one of the dams of the Muskingum Flood Prevention Project. The lake beneath the clear skies and hot sun was a brilliant blue. The distant wooded hills were tropically green and lush from all the rain. The birds, mute during the weeks of downpour, chorused from every tree, bush and hedgerow and from the marshy land along the lake came the sound of splashing caused by the thrashing about of the big carp engaged in an orgy of reproduction. And in my heart was that gnawing old farmer's pride that we had outwitted even the weather. It was one of those fine days which is recompense for weeks of bad weather.

At sundown I drove happily home and ran the rotary hoe briskly over the plantations of beans, peas and sweet corn. And then at supper time as the shadows began to fall across the valley and the lush forest, there came a sinister note of warning. Out of the symphony of birds singing and the music of the frogs in the ponds below the house, there emerged a note which fell on the ears and assaulted my senses as violently as a shrill fife playing loudly and discordantly in the midst of a great orchestra. It was the cry of the tree frogs calling for rain. It came from all sides, the same monotonous, trilled note which in time of drought can be the most lovely instrument in the whole symphony of nature.

I said, "Listen to those damned tree frogs! Haven't they had enough? I'd like to go out and strangle every one of them!" And from across the big table I heard a loud chuckle from Anne.

When I asked, "What's so funny?" She said, "Just the picture of you going around the farm strangling every tree frog with your bare hands."

Tree frogs do not, as legend has it, "call for rain." On the contrary they call when the atmospheric conditions foretell rain. They are not suppliants; they are prophets. I looked out of the window and against the brilliant sunset, big, dark, unmistakably wet clouds were piling up at the end of the valley. I couldn't believe it could rain again. There couldn't be any more water in the skies.

That evening everybody on the farm was feeling good and on such evenings the men and the kids on the place are all likely to gravitate to the lower farm. It is a kind of public forum in the center of the thousand acres and when the rain is falling people gather in the machine shop where Kenneth is kept busy during the bad weather repairing machinery or ingeniously making machines which we can't buy because they are in short supply or don't exist. On fine evenings we seem to gather there spontaneously just to talk or enjoy the evening or sometimes to go fishing in the pond that lies below the shop.

We were feeling pretty good because our oats stood high and strong and green in the fields, and because our corn was in the ground, the grains swelling and popping, in the damp ground, warmed for the first time by a hot sun. While we talked, pridefully, the dark clouds at the head of the valley piled up higher and higher and the tree frogs sang more and more shrilly. When I pointed out the clouds, Bob said, "Well, we haven't got anything to worry about. Think of those poor guys in the flat country with their fields still under water. Even if it stopped raining it would take two weeks for the ground to dry out enough to get a plow into them."

Yes, we all felt pretty good.

We all went home at last, still feeling good. Two things were certain—that we were ahead of most farmers and that no matter how hard it rained we had lost and were losing none of our precious soil. It stayed where it was meant to stay, held in place by that thick pasture and hay sod or the protecting sodded strip which prevented it ever getting away from us.

Tired from the all-day jolting ride on the rotary hoe, I fell into that deep sleep that comes only after physical labor in the open air, the kind of sleep which you can *feel* yourself enjoying with an almost voluptuous pleasure. Even the dogs were tired from the long day in the field and forgot their snack in their eagerness to go to bed. They fell asleep in their chairs even before I found myself lying with eyes closed and the book I was reading fallen aside. I awakened long enough to turn out the lights and fell into that warm, pleasant oblivious sleep which must be like the reward of death to very old people who have led long, full and happy lives.

I slept "like a log" until about two in the morning when a prodigious clap of thunder which rocked the whole house awakened me. The thunder was bad enough but there was another sound even worse. It was the sound of rain on the roof, a sound which in the dry hot days of August comes like a celestial benediction. Now it sounded like a curse from Hell for not only was it the sound of unwanted rain but of ropes and buckets and torrents of it, the sound of Niagaras of unwanted water streaming from gutters and spouts which could not carry it off fast enough. And above and through the sound of the rain on the roof came another sound of water even more menacing—that of the spring brook which ran through the garden below the house.

It was a sound I had not heard in seven years, since first we controlled run-off water on the hills and pastures above. Now, after all these years, the clear little creek was roaring again. It meant not only that it was raining hard and that the water-soaked land could drink up not one more rain drop, but that this was flood and perhaps disaster. I rose and went to the door and Prince who sleeps on the foot of the bed, jumped up and went with me. There I heard another sound, even more ominous—the roar of Switzer's Creek a quarter of a mile away which had been clear and well-behaved, never going out of its banks since farmers upstream had begun taking proper care of their fields. Now it was roaring again. It could only mean flood.

With a feeling of helplessness I went back to bed, to lie there sleepless and worrying over the fact that all the work I had done with the rotary hoe was useless since these torrents of water would pack the earth harder than ever, worrying over the cattle, the calves, the horses in the bottom fields. I knew from the roar of Switzer's Creek that this time it was not merely rain but a cloudburst of the proportions that sweep away bridges and houses and drown livestock in the fields. I slept a little more, fitfully, and each time I wakened I heard the unwanted hateful rains streaming down and the increasing roar of the streams.

At daylight I went to the door and looked out over the valley. Part of the lower pasture was flooded but the livestock was safe on high ground, drenched and grazing peacefully in the downpour. Through the middle of the flooded field ran the swift, muddy current carrying with it whole fences, trees, rubbish, bits of hog pens and even a brand new milk can bobbing along on its way from some spring house upstream to the reservoir lake below.

It rained thus until nine o'clock in the morning when suddenly the awful downpour ceased and everyone on the farm—men, women and children streamed out of the houses toward the bridge over Switzer's Creek. There was the kind of excitement among us which comes perhaps as a recompense to people in the face of destruction and disaster, a kind of exhilaration which brings all people, whatever their temperaments or differences of character, together on a common level.

The first concern of the men was the new floodgate that Bob and Kenneth and Jesse had constructed only a day or two before to separate the two bottom pastures. It hung from a heavy piece of steel pipe between the two concrete buttresses of the township bridge, made thus so that when the water rose it would swing out and float. To build it had taken a great deal of time and hard work.

The gate was still there, swinging out almost flat on the surface of the rushing water. Now and then a log or a whole tree swept swiftly beneath it without lodging or tearing it loose. It was a good piece of engineering. Everybody was proud of it.

Then with all the dogs, the men crowded into the jeep to inspect the rest of the farm. The wheat fields, so green and lush even the day before, were beaten down in spots as if a

386

giant had flung great pails of water against the wheat. In the wild swamp and woodland we call the Jungle, the water poured through the trees high above the banks. Here and there a log or a tree had become lodged, collected a bundle of flotsam and jetsam and the diverted waters had cut out a whole new channel. We stood there on a high bank, silent, watching the flood, awed yet somehow exhilarated by the terrible, unpredictable, incalculable power of rushing water.

And last of all we set out for the Conservancy farm on the edge of Pleasant Hill lake built years ago to check just such floods as this. We went with forebodings for we knew that the dam would be kept closed to hold back the water and protect the helpless people in the towns downstream along the Muskingum River all the way to the Ohio and perhaps even down the Mississippi to the Gulf of Mexico. As we neared the Conservancy farm the forebodings grew for the rising waters of the lake had already covered the lower road. There had never been such a flood before in all our experience so we could not know what that high water meant to the fields of which we had been so proud because our oats were all above ground and flourishing and our corn planted even in the midst of the weeks-old rain.

Cautiously I felt my way with the jeep through the high water. We just made it and as we came out the other side on the high ground we found out what the water on the road meant. It meant that our pride, the oats field on the Conservancy farm lay under four to six feet of muddy water. In the shallow water near the banks we could see the rippling wakes left by the big carp as they moved in to take advantage of the plowed muddy oats field which they found ideal for spawning. For a long time we stood there watching the water-traced movements of the big invisible carp.

Then Kenneth said, "I guess we might as well make something out of this mess. I think if you all make a drive we might corner some of these big carp." So the men and the boys down to George Cook who is nine took off their pants and waded out in their shorts into the cold water making a chain to trap the carp in shallow water. Even the five Boxers joined in. As if they understood the game they moved forward in a line with the men and boys trying to drive the carp into the shallows. Only Bobby, who was four and might have found the water over his head, stood on the bank and shouted advice as one big carp after another turned swiftly and darted between us, sometimes even between one's legs.

It wasn't any good. Every carp escaped but somehow the game raised our spirits. We all decided that probably the water would be released quickly from the dam and the oats field would be left free of it again before the crop and the beautiful stand of sweet clover sowed in it would suffer any damage.

At last we made our way home to disperse to the monotony of regular tasks which could and did bring a kind of numb solace and resignation in such occasions.

That afternoon the air cooled and the bright sun came out and two days later the gravelly cornfield was dry enough to repeat the whole process with the rotary hoe, all the long hours of rough tractor riding at top speed, to break up the crust all over again and let the young seedlings through. While I worked back and forth across a big sixty acre field, the air turned muggy and hot once more and the wind shifted a little to the south which is always a bad sign. I kept listening above the rumble of the tractor for the sound of train whistles. In our country when one hears the whistles of the Pennsylvania locomotives it means dry weather; when one hears the B & O, it means rain. In midsummer one prays for the B & O. For once I wanted to hear a Pennsylvania whistle. Presently as I was finishing the job with the rotary hoe, I heard a whistle. It came from a B & O freight train pulling up the long grade to Butler and never have I heard it more clearly!

At about the same time great black clouds began to appear again at the head of the valley and the accursed tree frogs began to sing. I knew that once again I had gone over that cornfield only to have all my work undone.

At twilight I rode the tractor the two miles back to the house. The setting sun disappeared beneath clouds and as I rode the drive up to the Big House, great solitary drops of rain began to fall. Before I got into the house the drops began to come down by the trillions, in torrents. I thought, trying to deceive myself, "Very likely it's only a big thunderstorm and will quickly be over." The water in the reservoir had already gone down about two feet in two days leaving part of our oats field bare in time to save it. If we had another heavy rain it would mean, with the lake level about flood stage, that instead of the young oats plants being released before they were drowned, the whole field would be flooded again and perhaps the cornfield that lay above it.

I was wrong. The rain was no thunderstorm. It was the same kind of flooding rain that had come down two nights earlier. Indeed it was worse, if possible. Eight o'clock came and nine and ten and still it poured. The little brook in the garden began to roar and then from the valley came the louder roar of Switzer's Creek.

I took a couple of good drinks and went to bed to read, thinking I could take my mind off what could only be disaster. But it wasn't any good. I tried reading novels, agricultural editorials, magazines, but through all the print and ideas, good and bad, came the devilish sound of torrents of water pouring off the roofs and the rising roar of the little brook. And at last when my eyes grew tired and I began to feel drowsy, I heard the ring of the telephone. I knew it was someone on the farm ringing because the sound is different when the ring is made by cranking the phone handle instead of pushing a button in the central office. I thought, "This is it. Something bad has happened on the farm!"

Bob's voice answered me. He was calling from his house below not far from the creek. He said, "I think we've got a job. The horses in the bottom are scared. They're running up and down crying out. One of them tried to get across the creek and is marooned on the island. We've got to look after them and the cattle."

I asked, "Is it worse down by the bridge?" And his voice came back, "Brother, you ain't seen nothing."

I dressed, gloomily, worrying about the animals and especially the horses. Cows and steers are generally phlegmatic. They either take things calmly or go completely wild, but horses and especially saddle horses, get frightened, like people, and for me the horses, like dogs, are people. I took only one of the dogs with me. I chose Prince because Prince owns me—I don't own Prince—and he is the steadiest of them all save old Gina who has always been wise and calm. But Gina was too old and plump for wild adventure. Too many dogs might only make confusion. And besides they were likely to follow me into the water if I had to go there and be carried away in the flood. Prince was a good swimmer and he would obey me and not get panicky. So Prince, delighted and excited, jumped to the seat of the jeep.

Bob met me at the bridge, water streaming from his hat and jacket. He had an electric torch and with that and the lights of the jeep I saw quickly enough that I hadn't seen anything until now. The water was so high that it was seeping through the wooden floor of the bridge and sliding past beneath with a terrifying speed. A whole log struck the edge of the bridge and made it shudder and then slipped under the water out of sight in a second. In the earlier flood there had been backwaters and whirlpools beneath the bridge where rubbish gathered but now there was nothing but rushing water going past so fast that I felt a sudden dizziness and instinctively stepped back from the edge.

He told me about the panic of the horses. "I heard them all the way up at the house."

I said, "Get in. We'll take the jeep out in the field and use the lights." He didn't think we could make it with the jeep but I knew better than he did what it could do.

He said, "I'll get my car, leave it on the road and put all the lights on the field and join you."

While he got his car I opened the pasture gate and drove through. Even the high ground was running with water and wherever there was a depression the water stood in deep pools. I put the jeep into four-wheel drive in low gear and she did what she was supposed to do. She plowed through mud and water until the lights penetrated a little distance into the mist and driving rain, enough for me to see that only a rim of bluegrass remained above the flood. The lights picked up two things, both white, the white spots on the Holstein cows who had gone to the high ground and were either grazing or lying down and the white blaze on the forehead of Tex, my own mare, as she came toward me splashing through two feet of water.

Tex is a beautiful Kentucky mare, chestnut with a white blaze, and the proudest and the most spirited of horses. She rules the others and it is impossible to catch any of the others in the field until you have first captured Tex. The other horses follow her with docility. But she is not too easy to catch and likes to play a game of enticing you near to her and then suddenly kicking her heels and rushing off. But in the flooded fields she wasn't behaving that way and now ran straight toward the lights of the jeep followed by another horse. As I got down she came up close and whickered. There were no antics now. She was afraid and wanted to be taken care of. Then the lights of Bob's car were turned into the field and I saw that the other horse was Tony, Hope's horse, young and strong, who is by nature, a clown. But tonight he wasn't clowning. He too whickered when I spoke to him.

I recognized Tony with a sinking heart because I knew then that the missing horse marooned on the island in the flood was Old Red. Either of the others were strong and spirited and could have taken care of themselves even in the terrible current that was running, but Old Red was old and tired. He was a little deaf and nearly blind. He was the one you felt sorry for.

Old Red had brought up the little children until they had learned to ride well enough to handle the younger, more spirited horses. If they fell off he would stand still until they picked themselves up and climbed back on. He never got flustered or showed off and reared like Tex and never clowned as Tony did. He was twenty-one years old when we bought him, because he was calm and docile. He was just a horse, never a high-spirited queen like the thoroughbred Tex nor a wild, impish polo pony like Tony. Sometime in his youth when perhaps he had been a carriage horse on some farm, he had been abused for on his shoulder he bore the scars of old galls from a collar. He wasn't a clever horse or a spirited horse or a beautiful one. He was always just a kind, patient, old slob. And now, at thirty years of age with his joints stiffened and his teeth mostly gone, he was marooned on an island in the midst of a roaring flood such as the county had not seen in half a century. I wished it had been one of the others.

As I took hold of Tex's halter, for the first time without her giving an indignant toss of the head, Bob came up out of the darkness and rain and mist with the light. He was carrying a long rope.

"I thought," he said, "we might need this to get over to the island to get the horse off."

I told him the missing horse was Old Red and that I'd better take the other two to the barn before they turned completely panicky and uncatchable.

Tex led easily enough. She wanted the dry safety of the barn and Tony followed as always at her heels. Prince, despite the fact that, like all Boxers, he hates getting wet, trudged along beside us, his ears down and his stub of a tail pressed low in an effort to get it between his legs. Bob went off through the water to check on the cattle on the high ground. On the way back the roar of the flood seemed to grow steadily louder. After the two horses were safely in the barn, I discovered on my return to the field that the water was still rising.

Far off through the rain I could see the faint glare of Bob's torch as he checked the cattle and in the light from the two cars I could see the stream of logs, trees and driftwood moving swiftly down on the surface of the current, but I couldn't see the island or Old Red.

I waded into the water and was joined presently by Bob but as the water rose deeper and deeper above our ankles and knees, it was clear that we were never going to make the island.

Then out of the mist, the willows of the island emerged but there was no island. There was only swift flowing water covered with leaves, bits of sod and branches. And then out of the mist, catching the light from the cars, appeared a ghostly Old Red. He was walking up and down, whickering loud enough to be heard above the sound of the water.

I called out to him and he stopped, looked toward me and then started in my direction but as soon as he reached deeper water he turned back to the island and the shallow water.

There wasn't any way to get to him. The water had risen so high that on the whole of the farm there wasn't a rope long enough to permit us to reach the island, and even with a rope tied about your waist, there wouldn't be much hope of getting through the torrent. Knowing horses, I knew that even if you made it, there was small chance of getting a horse in a panic to follow you.

I shouted to him again and again and each time the old horse started toward me and each time when he got into deep water he turned back to the island.

Meanwhile both Bob and I were drenched. The water ran inside our jackets and down our bodies. Prince, miserable in the dampness, crouched beside me. At last I gave up.

"There's nothing to do," I said, "but hope that he'll stay there and that the water won't get much higher."

And so we turned away with a sickening feeling through the rain and water, leaving the old horse where he was. The other horses were in the barn and the cattle all safe on high ground. There wasn't anything to do but go home. We had hot coffee at Bob's house and as I said good night to Bob, he said, "Maybe I opened my big mouth too soon—saying we hadn't anything to worry about." I laughed but I knew what he meant—that probably sunrise would find most of our corn and oats deep under the waters of the big lake.

By the time I got back to the bridge the planks were under water and before I drove across it I got down to make sure that the planks were still there and the bridge safe. You could not make sure but I got back into the jeep and took a chance. I speeded up the jeep and made a dash for it. The water flew high on both sides so that together with the pouring rain and the rushing water it seemed for a moment that all of us, Prince, myself and the jeep were caught in a raging torrent of water. The planks were still there and we made it.

At home Prince and I dried ourselves off and joined Mary

for hot soup and a snack with all the dogs, who treated the wet and miserable Prince with such resentment for having been the chosen one on the expedition that a fight developed between him and his brother, Baby. Then I went to bed after taking two sleeping pills so that I would not waken in the still early hours of the morning and hear the terrible rain and think of Old Red marooned alone on the island in the rising flood.

It was nearly eight when I wakened and the rain had stopped. The old orchard on the hill above my room was streaked with early morning sunlight and the red sandstone rock looked brighter and the trees lusher and more green than I had ever seen them. But in the back of my mind there was a sore spot which could not be healed until I went to the windows at the other side of the house which overlooked the bottom pasture. I had to know what had happened to Old Red.

It must have stopped raining some time during the night for the water had gone down and the surface of the island, littered with branches and trees and old boards, was now above the flood. But among the willows there was no sign of Old Red. I felt suddenly sick and in a last hope I thought, "Perhaps he is all right after all. Perhaps he's just around the corner below the slope." And I went back to the far end of the house and looked out, and there behind the slope, peacefully munching bluegrass with the few teeth he had left, was Old Red, behaving as if nothing had happened.

After breakfast Kenneth and I climbed into the jeep with the dogs and set out for the Conservancy farm. The jeep was the only car which had a chance of making it. We already knew the worst for from the Bailey Hill we could see the lake—an enormously enlarged lake covering twice its usual area with clumps of trees here and there barely visible above the water. This time we couldn't get through the lower road at all. Not only was the road under ten feet of water but Charley Tom's pasture was under ten feet of water also. The bridge structure was out of sight.

So, turning round, we took the only other course of reaching the Conservancy farm; we took to a rutted abandoned old lane and the open, soggy fields and somehow we made it. As we came over the crest of a slope we saw the full extent of the disaster. All the oat fields and half the corn land was covered by water and here and there in low spots in the field there were great ponds of water as big as small lakes.

This was, in reality, a disaster. We sat for a time in silence looking at the wreckage. It wasn't only the money loss but the loss of the long hours of work and care we had all put into these fields.

Then Kenneth said, "There's a new milk can bobbing on the edge of the current. We might as well salvage something."

So together we set to work to get that solitary milk can out of the swirling torrent. It was not easy but by the use of long tree branches and poles we maneuvered the floating milk can to a point where, wading in up to his hips, Kenneth salvaged it. He fastened it to the back of the jeep and we climbed in and set out for home. There wouldn't be any recompense in cash for the damage done by the waters of the lake; we rented the whole farm from the state with the gamble that some day there might be just such a flood. And anyway money is poor recompense to a good farmer; he wants his crops and the satisfaction that goes with raising them.

For three weeks most of the Conservancy farm remained under from five to twenty feet of impounded water, kept there to prevent its menace from being added to the already disastrous floods on the Mississippi. When the water went down at last not one living thing remained but only the desolation of logs and fence posts and driftwood scattered across the barren fields. Even the trees were killed along with the blackberries and elderberries that filled the hedgerows. We had not only lost our crops, but we had to clear the fields of their desolation. What little corn or oats remained on dry ground was growing but looked pale and yellowish in the water-soaked ground.

And elsewhere on the upper farm more rich wheat was beaten to the earth to mildew and smother the precious seedings. The bluegrass behaved in the water-soaked earth exactly as it did in time of drought. It grew tough and went to seed early and it was possible to clip it only on the high ground. Everywhere else in the fields, the power mower bogged down and had to be pulled out.

Good farmers are by nature optimistic; otherwise the uncontrollable vagaries of Nature—the floods, the droughts, the plagues of locusts—would long ago have discouraged them and the world would have been left starving. We were no different from other farmers—we hoped that the great flood had marked the end of the persistent intolerable rains.

We were wrong. June passed into July and still the rain continued, not simply showers or simple rains but cloudbursts coming sometimes twice a day. Even the fish ponds fed from tight sod-covered land and springs overflowed their barriers and big trout and bass escaped into the Clear Fork and the lake below. Came time to fill the silos with grass silage and we began cutting and hauling but quickly found that every tractor had to carry a log chain so that we could pull each other out of the mud, a minor disaster which happened ten or fifteen times a day. Twice the big John Deere dug itself into the mud up to its belly and a string of four lighter tractors, chained together, could not drag it out. In the end with four-by-fours chained to its giant wheels it succeeded in lifting itself out of the mud.

Somehow the silos got filled with the lush, heavy alfalfa, brome grass and ladino, but even the grass was so filled with moisture that it had to be wilted a long time before it could be safely put away. Weeds grew in the corn and more wheat was beaten down in the fields of which we had been so proud. The oats which remained grew more and more lushly and all but the tough, stiff-stemmed new Clinton variety were beaten to the ground while weeds began to grow up through them.

Then the weather turned warm but the rains continued and at night when the air cooled the whole valley was blanketed in heavy white mists which appeared at sundown, rising in smokelike writhing veils above the trees. For days the valley seemed more like Sumatra or Java than midsummer Ohio country. Rust appeared for the first time in our experience on the ripening wheat and mildew on the leaves and fruit of the fruit trees. Some of the grapevines began to die back from the tops, a sign that their water-logged roots could no longer stand the lack of oxygen and the wetness of the earth. Three times the vegetable garden was replanted and three times drowned out, sometimes standing for days under three or four inches of water.

Then came a brief respite which in itself was very nearly a

disaster. There was no rain but in its place there was a brilliant, burning sun accompanied by hot winds which burned the moisture out of the topsoil but not out of the subsoil where the water still soaked the roots of all vegetation. It baked a crust over open ground and burned the over-lush leaves of the crops. At night the moisture still rose from the soaked ground in heavy blankets of fog. It was as if now it was the earth rather than the sky which was raining.

Somehow we managed to combine the wheat, although we lost from five to fifteen bushels per acre of wheat literally beaten into the earth by the torrents of water. Except for thirty acres of good oats on the highest ground, the crop was ruined. In the heads there were no grains at all but only chaff. And from over the rest of the Middle West there arose a cry that drought was ruining the corn crop just at the crucial moment of tasselling and pollenization. Because there had been so much rain the corn had set shallow roots on the surface of the soil and now suddenly that surface had been burned, baked and hardened.

But in our valley even the short, vicious heat was only a delusion. As it came time to make hay and clip and bale straw, the rains began again, not simply rains but the old cloudbursts. Ragweed grew higher and higher in the standing straw and the hay, partly dry and then soaked, rotted in the fields. Weeds everywhere grew like the fierce tropical growth that overwhelms settlements and plantations in a few weeks in the Tropics when the battle against them is relaxed for a season. The whole farm, usually so neatly and proudly kept, acquired a disheveled, unkempt, half-tropical appearance.

And so it went, on and on, through the end of July and then August and well into September. There was no hay-making season at all, even for the second cutting, and when there was a day or two of sunshine the hay, dried during the day, became drenched again each night from the moisture rising out of the water-soaked ground and from the heavy, damp fogs which settled each night in the valley. At last we took in hay which was still damp. Some of it moulded, some of it heated and turned brown and a little came through as the good green hay which we always made in a summer that was even vaguely reasonable.

397

Only the pastures and the new seedings gave us any pleasure or satisfaction, for they were lush and green but even this was small compensation for all the lost labor and seed and fertilizer and the depression which arose from the sight of wet hay and weed-choked cornfields. The buckwheat planted later on wet ground produced a bumper crop but few farmers take pride in lowly buckwheat and the season was so wet that the bees could not even work the blossoms.

And then presently in the beginning of September the rains stopped and miraculously two weeks of hot weather day and night set in, and suddenly the corn, after dawdling along all of the summer, began to show signs of ripening and making a crop. The soil began to dry out for wheat plowing and that miraculous resiliency which preserves farmers against utter and paralyzing despair began to assert itself.

Gradually the season began to recede into the past. It was becoming the "old season." It was time now to plow and fit for wheat, to clip the bluegrass pastures and the weeds for the last time in the evil year of nineteen forty seven. With the turning of the first furrow the pride which was humbled began to rise again. The fields were full of moisture and the plowing was easy. The earth turned over behind the plow, dark and crumbling, and you smelled already the wheat harvest of the coming season which you knew would be the greatest harvest we had ever known. The lime trucks began moving across the remaining wornout high pastures raising visions of deep, thick clover. In the desolated oat fields of the Conservancy farm and on the poor strips of the Bailey Place the sweet clover stood deep and rank. The new season had begun.

One more disaster in the "Bad Year" still lay ahead—a hard frost with a clear, full moon which burned the alfalfa and the grapes before they were ripe and covered all the landscape of Pleasant Valley with glittering white rime. For a moment our pride rose again, even in a bad year, for our corn was ripe and hard, while to the west of us in *real* corn country thousands of acres of corn had been frosted while still green and soft. And then came the warm, clear weather of October, brilliant with the deep green of the new springing rye and wheat and the burning colors of the forest. From brilliant blue skies the sun shone all day long while the work for the new season went on its way and all hearts sang.

What was past was past but 1947 would go down among the legends of our valley as the "Bad Year," the worst year that any of us, even old Mr. Tucker who was over ninety-one and had lived all his life in the valley, could remember. We would be proud again of our fields and we would feel a certain wicked satisfaction when other fields looked worse than our own but after the bad year it would always be a pride that was not quite so confident.

# XVI: SPORTMEN'S PARADISE

> For the pursuit of farming is in some sense a luxury.
> . . . The earth yields first of all to those who farm of
> necessity, but she yields also the luxuries of life. And
> though she supplies good things in abundance, she suf-
> fers them not to be won without toil, but accustoms
> men to endure winter's cold and summer's heat. . . .
> And the land helps in a measure to arouse a liking for
> the strenuous activity of hunting . . . it affords facilities
> for keeping hounds and at the same time supplies food
> for the wild game that preys on the land.
>
> —Xenophon

THERE is no greater beneficiary of good agriculture and proper
land use than the sportsman. As a member of the Ohio Conservation Commission which devotes itself to the propagation
of fish and wild life and as a farmer who recognizes that the
benefits of wild birds and animals on a farm far outweigh the
liabilities, I have pushed a good wild life program at Malabar
and as far as possible in Ohio and other states.

I am not much of a hunter. I can say honestly that I have
never shot anything, beyond a couple of poisonous snakes,
except lions, tigers, leopards and panthers, and then without
much enthusiasm and only out of politeness when the animals
were beaten out for my own benefit when I was the honored
guest at an Indian shooting party. Even then, at the last moment, as a tiger or a panther appeared out of the thick jungle
I fired with reluctance to kill an animal so beautiful, despite
the fact that in most cases the beast had been driven and cor-
nered because it had become a menace to the local communities, by killing goats, cattle, dogs, and sometimes people.
I am, however, a great fisherman and enjoy fishing in any

fashion from a bent pin and string method on upward. Catching any fish from a minnow or a sluggish carp to a barracuda gives me a much greater excitement than shooting a big Mysore tiger.

I do have, however, no objection to the great pleasure derived by scores of sportsmen in shooting and hunting and recognize that in some instances, where natural controls have been upset by the advance of civilization, the shooting of certain predatory animals at least becomes a necessity. In Cooch-Behar in North Bengal in the wild jungle country where the plains reach the foothills of the Himalayas, the population of leopards and panthers is so great that if it were not controlled, life on the farms and in the villages would become impossible. In that wild and beautiful country the state elephants go out each day to kill panthers and leopards much as we go upon a campaign to exterminate rats. Fortunately or otherwise, leopards and panthers do not exist in Ohio and Ohio is what I am writing about. Indian and African life is another story.

Our Ohio State Conservation Commission has long recognized the fact that Ohio has a special problem among the States. Except for a few counties, it is largely a rich, agricultural area, but it is not agricultural alone, for distributed over the entire state are great industrial cities like Cleveland, Cincinnati, Youngstown, Akron, Columbus, Dayton, Toledo and a whole second chain of smaller, industrial cities like Lima, Canton, Springfield, Mansfield, Massillon and so on. This means that at least half or more of the eight million population dwells in or near cities. This same population, almost evenly dispersed, has need of recreation and sport which must come largely from agricultural areas, often enough intensively cultivated.

The problem of the Commission concerned with fish and wild life is largely one of providing sport and recreation for millions of city and suburban dwellers. Partly with the aid of experts and research men and partly the hard way, the commission has set up gradually a permanent policy based primarily, not upon artificial hatcheries, but upon natural habitat and food. This policy in turn is largely dependent for its success upon proper land use by the farmers themselves, upon proper disposals of industrial and city sewage wastes and upon the establishment of headwater lakes as fish breeding areas and of suitable parks, sanctuaries and game propagation areas.

The fight against pollution of landscapes and streams is one that has been going on continuously since the beginning of the industrial revolution and the parallel growth of our great cities and is continuing with increasing intensity. Eventually it will be won on the grounds of health if for no other reason, but also because the time is not far distant when, with an increasing population and a decreasing fertility, the world and this nation in particular will no longer be able to afford (if its living standards and high level of diet are to continue) the vast waste achieved by the funnelling of our mineral and elemental fertility into our great metropolitan areas and thence, as sewage and garbage, into our streams and rivers. Pollution of streams and lakes by industrial wastes is at all times inexcusable and gradually the average citizen is becoming aware of the simple principle that streams and lakes belong to the people and that industry has no more right to dump its unprocessed wastes into the streams than the citizen has to dump garbage and chamber pots out of the windows onto the sidewalk. The two cases are exactly parallel but it will require a long battle, even at this late date, to win this struggle for human decency, health, and civilization against lobbies, vested interests, and even short-sighted and greedy Chambers of Commerce.

The Ohio policy of establishing headwater lakes, farm ponds, fish and game sanctuaries, and propagation areas has made considerable progress in Ohio. Sites for headwater lakes and ponds are chosen in suitable areas with regard both to water supply and distribution. These provide spawning areas and refuges for young fish which later grow into big fish within the area or find their way into other lakes and adjoining streams to grow into big fish and good sport for the dwellers of our big, congested cities. They also provide other benefits, for the policy includes the purchase of land surrounding the lakes to provide recreation areas for all those devoted to outdoor life. Hot-dog stands and honky-tonks are rigidly excluded. The ponds and lakes and the marshy areas surrounding many of them, also serve in some degree, to help raise the lowering water table of the state—a condition which has caused great concern to industries, to cities, and even to farmers who, in certain areas of this well-watered state, are forced to haul water to their livestock for periods as long as six months of the year.[1]

Perhaps the most fortunate thing ever to have happened to the State of Ohio was the establishment, following the terrible and disastrous flood of 1913, of the Muskingum Valley Flood Control Project. Its establishment more or less paralleled that of the Tennessee Valley Authority and its immense benefits, alike to sportsmen and taxpayers of the area, follows out the parallel between the two projects.

As the name implies, the district was set up to prevent the recurrence of a flood which in the area in 1913 caused some forty millions of property loss and damage as well as the loss of scores of lives. In one sense the project was revolutionary for it sought to control floods at their source rather than by expensive and futile dams, levees and other means at the bottoms of rivers—a costly and hopelessly ineffective pattern which until very recently was followed consistently by the War Department and Army Engineers. As in the case of the TVA which sought also to control floods at their source, the plan met with much opposition, nearly all of it hidebound and senseless. As in the case of the TVA wisdom and intelligence won the battle after a long, hard fight.

The flood control plan resulted in the construction of fourteen dams along the stream beds of the principal tributaries of the Muskingum River. All but two of these were, after another long battle, established to create permanent pool levels or lakes, with allowance made above the permanent level for impounding flood waters. Finally, the areas surrounding the lakes were set aside as recreation areas and for development into state forests. Thus, after a long struggle against a combination of ignorance, reaction, lobbying, and influence, there emerged the Muskingum Flood Control District. It could have been developed further to create even greater benefits along the lines of the TVA but as it stands, the man-made district provides what, with Lake Erie and the Ohio River, is one of Ohio's greatest assets.

[1] The serious economic and health aspects of the underground water problem in Ohio and in other states is discussed at length in the author's earlier book, *Pleasant Valley*.

The dams and lakes served to impound flood waters absolutely and in a year or two virtually paid for themselves in prevented losses to property holders, farmers, insurance companies, and municipalities located within the area. In the spring of 1947 when in most of the area more rain fell in a given period than in the great disaster of 1913, the dams impounded easily *all* the flood waters and there was not a life lost nor one cent of property damage. The efficacy of a joint federal, state and local watershed development, managed autonomously by a local control board of able citizens proved its great benefits in a score of ways. The District has had too little publicity and its effectiveness is still little known outside the state. This is a pity for it is a pattern which could well be followed with great benefit on most of the secondary watersheds of every state in the nation. It is a pattern, I believe, which eventually will be accepted and put into use on most of the watersheds of the nation, but much must still be accomplished in the realm of education and the abolition of ignorance and reactionary sentiment.

Not only has the District proved a great economic asset, it has also proved a paradise for sportsmen and a huge recreation area for the dwellers in our great Ohio industrial cities. The whole area is hilly and largely wooded and is that beautiful combination, so rare in the world, of rich farm land, interspersed with woods, hills, marshes, and wild country. It is a natural habitat for game and fish. The Conservation Commission leases from the district the hunting and fishing rights for the benefit of Ohio sportsmen and develops these in cooperation with the District authorities.

Within the area, both in the wooded country and the farms leased out to neighboring farmers, the principles of good land use are followed and enforced. Reforestation of worn-out eroded farms is proceeding rapidly and much of the area is being put back into grass land. No skinflint or ignorant farmer may lease any land from the District for the conditions of land use are set up in every lease, and, if these are violated, the lease is automatically cancelled.

The imposition of these rules of good land use have already had a great effect upon the fish and wild life populations of the area. Siltation from eroding farms is the greatest source of stream and lake pollution—greater even than that of sewage

406

and industrial pollution—and as the district-owned land has become properly managed, the rate of siltation has declined, not only removing a peril to the dams and artificial lakes, but bringing about a decline in the carp and mud-fish population and an increase in the game fish population. The bare eroded hillsides are covered by trees, the more possible slopes with grass land and the rolling farm land is terraced, contoured, limed at the expense of the district and treated according to intelligent agricultural principles.

One of the facts overlooked frequently enough both by sportsmen and farmers, is that game animals and birds will not stay on eroded and depleted lands. No living creature, including man, recognizes so well as wild birds and animals the barrenness of worn-out farms. As regions begin to be farmed out, even though they return to a tax-delinquent state of wilderness, game will move out, into more fertile areas, leaving the wrecked countryside to complete and desolate loneliness. Perhaps a few squirrels or deer will remain in the deserted areas which are wooded and a rabbit or two but that is about all. Even the bird population of worn-out agricultural areas declines, and as every sportsman knows these desolate areas provide poor picking.

In certain areas where a poor agriculture has worn out or is wearing out the land, the wholesale slaughter of wild life on the roads has become a serious problem for game management. It is only lately that research authorities have established the fact that the slaughter comes about because the wild life migrates to the roadside at night to feed off vegetation which, often enough, is growing on virgin land or on soil heavily impregnated by the lime and other minerals coming from the stone used to surface the roads. Both taste and instinct tell them that the roadside vegetation is far richer and healthier than that growing in the depleted farm fields on the other side of the fence.

One of the perpetual problems facing the Ohio Commission is the misplacement of the wild rabbit populations. It is probable today that the town and suburban population of rabbits far exceeds the rural population. As Ohio farm land in many regions has become depleted, the rabbits have moved in upon town and suburban gardens where forage is not only easier to obtain but is of a much tastier quality owing to the use of minerals, fertilizers, and composts in more intensively cropped garden areas. Maintaining any sort of rabbit population for sportsmen in the fifteen or more deforested and agriculturally wornout counties of southeastern Ohio has become a permanent problem which appears almost insoluble although these counties are the wildest in Ohio and many of the depleted farms have reverted to the state of complete wilderness. Virtually the *only* rabbits in the area are confined to the town, village, and suburban districts. If rabbits are trapped and sent into the wilder parts of the area, they quickly disappear having undoubtedly moved out of the area altogether or into the gardens of the districts where there is a concentration of human populations and good agriculture is practiced in the form of gardening.

Both research and the amateur observation of sportsmen has proven beyond all doubt that abundant fish and game are linked directly to good agriculture and to proper land use. Fortunately, the sportsmen's organizations of Ohio have come to take official recognition of this principle and have given both approval and support to the policies of the Commission to co-operate with the farmer and to establish food, habitat and proper conditions for living and propagation rather than to follow the old expensive and unsporting practice of artificially hatching, breeding and raising game and fish to be put in the field or stream the day before the season opens. Not only does such a system cost the sportsmen sums amounting to three or four dollars per bird or fish in license money, but it provides tame pheasant which offer less sport than many of the wilder leghorn chickens at Malabar. In the case of hand-fed hatchery fish, it frequently produces a bass or a trout which will virtually follow you along the stream bank waiting for a hand-out in the form of a fly or a plug. Unfortunately there are among the hunters and fishermen of the United States a good many who are not sportsmen at all but what might be described as "chicken killers" and "bent-pin" fishermen.

In the field of abundant fish and game in heavily populated but good agricultural areas, I have had much experience while living in Europe. At our small farm, less than twenty-five miles from Paris, and in the surrounding region of the Oise, there was always an abundance of quail, pheasant, partridge, grouse, deer, and even wild boar were a common sight within view of the Eiffel Tower and the Sacré Coeur. The streams in the same area provided some of the best trout fishing I have ever had. (We were indeed able to take trout and salmon trout from our sitting-room window out of the stream which flowed against the foundations of the house.) The same could be said to be true of the country surrounding almost any city in France, Germany or Austria. The abundance of fish and game, existing at virtually a level representing maximum of potentiality, existed in those European areas because there was sufficient cover, natural or artificially created, a good agriculture and no flood or siltation from eroding farms.

The same conditions could be established almost anywhere in the United States, even in the most thickly populated areas, if our agriculture were better and if steps were taken to provide the conditions under which wild life may live and propagate. In all of Europe there are no clean, wire fence rows, idiotically burned over or mowed two or three times a summer. In their place are hedgerows or stone walls overgrown with vegetation which provides food, cover and nesting places for birds and other wild life. In the great wheat and sugar-beet areas of the Valois where the pheasant and partridge shooting is famous, small strips and patches are left deliberately here and there in the fields to grow up in briars and shrubbery as refuges. Often enough they are planted artificially to shrubs and trees and ground cover which provides food for wild life. The farmer does this for three reasons: (1) Because he recognizes the great value of an abundant bird population as a control of insect pests. (2) Because the birds he protects and feeds provide him with sport and a rich and delicious addition to the family larder. (3) Because, when the shooting season opens, he frequently reaps a considerable harvest of fees charged for shooting rights on his place. The old square-field farmer with his burned-over fence rows has not only caused much damage to agriculture and soil in the United States but he has also been the worst enemy of sportsmen and wild life generally.

With all of the above facts and elements in mind, the Ohio Commission has set out upon a long range policy similar in its fundamentals to that pattern which has, in European areas similar to that of Ohio, with large populations in regions shared by both big industrial cities and agriculture, succeeded in producing a wild-life population at maximum of potentiality; or in other words a Paradise for real sportsmen.

Occasionally some mechanical or technological development arrives in a highly populated or agricultural area which proves a menace to wild life. The development of the automobile and the consequent slaughter of wild life along the high roads is one of these.

Another and perhaps more serious menace has developed recently in Ohio with specific relation to the pheasant population. Most of Ohio's pheasants exist in the agriculturally rich flat western and northwestern portions of the state. It is typical "pheasant" country, save that in some areas there is insufficient cover and that many farmers follow the old habit of burning over fence rows. At one period, some eight or ten years ago, the size of the pheasant population and the excellence of the shooting threatened to rival that of South Dakota. From that period onward, however, the pheasant population has been declining and sportsmen have made more and greater complaints.

Many things—rainy springs, bad winters, and one or two other factors entered into the decline in the number of pheasants but investigation seemed to confirm the fact that the greatest damage had been done not by seasonal conditions but rather by technological changes introduced into agriculture and changes in agricultural programs.

About five years ago many of the farms in the area began to turn from a wholesale program of corn farming to putting out larger areas in grass, mostly alfalfa. This was partly so because alfalfa, when dried artificially and sold as supplementary high protein feed for hogs and poultry brought at retail sale as much as 75 to 80 dollars a ton. In the case of the more intelligent and informed farmers, the change was made from one crop or short rotation farming in order to increase the organic content of their soil, which through persistent row-crop farming had become so depleted that the flat ground was becoming more and more like cement and ceased to drain properly even through the most complicated tillage systems. Under the new alfalfa industry, the existing fields were enlarged and what little shrubbery and wild cover remained in them was destroyed.

All of these changes were detrimental to pheasant maintenance and propagation, but the real reason for the decline was a purely technological one—arising from the way the alfalfa was harvested. In order to obtain the highest protein content and therefore the highest price per ton the farmers began mowing the first cutting of alfalfa from two to three weeks earlier than in the past, thus catching the hen pheasants when they were nesting, before the young birds were hatched and able to escape; and they began mowing alfalfa at night when in the darkness even the bewildered hen was rarely able to escape the destruction which fell upon her nest and eggs. Investigations showed loads of green alfalfa filled with slaughtered pheasant hens caught while nesting. One load was discovered which contained 27 dead birds. This, of course, meant not only the death of 27 pheasants but of a minimum of 216 young birds which would never be hatched. It is not difficult to see how great was the holocaust created by the new farming practices.

The situation created a dilemma for the Ohio Commission. Obviously it was impossible for the Commission, or the sportsmen's organizations or indeed the government itself, to forbid farmers to continue an enterprise which increased their incomes by as much as 50 per cent. It was equally unlikely that gentle persuasion would have any effect worth consideration. The Commission could do only two things, both of which it did. (1) To increase the number of its own purchases or leases upon land which could be used as refuges or pheasant propagation areas. (2) To pay farmers in the area to set aside a small acreage each year to be put into sweet clover or other crops which went unharvested or which were not harvested until after the hatching season when hen and young birds were able to take care of themselves.

The program has only been inaugurated and its success is as yet undetermined. That it would help the situation on a reasonable and economic basis is certain but that it would restore the old abundant pheasant population remains to be seen. Certainly, many a farmer, by providing small shelter and nesting areas on his land, could do much toward increasing sport and outdoor recreation for himself, his friends, and many an office or industrial worker from the cities. Whether they will do so or not also remains to be seen.

411

Not the least important step taken by the Ohio Commission has been the contracts made with individual farmers and landowners to maintain their farms as game refuges and propagation areas. The contract provides for the maintenance or establishment of proper cover and food plantings for wild life and frequently for the establishment of farm ponds with surrounding areas of cover. Lately emphasis has been placed as well upon good agricultural practices since these automatically produce abundant fish and game populations just as bad practices reduce populations.

To be sure, all good farmers engaged in a good program of land use automatically produce conditions favorable to the potential maximum population of fish and game. Some farmers and landowners with the tastes and instincts of sportsmen or naturalists voluntarily lay emphasis on the side of wild life and take measures which have greatly increased game and fish population within a comparatively short space of time. Among the Ohio farms aiming at proper land use with emphasis upon wild-life protection and propagation, Malabar is one.

The natural topography with its combination of thick woods, marsh, springs and streams with productive agricultural land interspersed among them had inherent advantages and these have been steadily exploited and improved.

In the beginning the 140 acres of woodland scarcely provided shelter for more than a few birds and a few squirrels since the whole woodland area had been heavily pastured for years and consisted entirely of large mature trees with the ground beneath bare of cover or tree seedlings. As such the woodland provided little or no cover or shelter for wild life. The first and most effective step taken was simply to fence the cattle and sheep out of the area and allow the bare, sometimes gullied earth to grow again the natural, thick cover which was normally characteristic of our beautiful, virgin, hardwood forests in Ohio. Once the step was taken, nature provided the cover with a rush. Ferns and wild flowers came back in abundance and with them hundreds of thousands of seedlings of the native trees, among them hundreds of those important nut and food trees—the beeches, the walnuts, the hickories and the lovely dogwood, with its white blossoms in spring and its scarlet berries in the autumn. New wild grape seedlings appeared and flourished and the Solomon seal berries and the creeping partridge berries began again to spread. (We did not agree with the advocated forestry practice of cutting out dogwood and wild grape, both of which contribute beauty as well as food for wild birds and game.)

The results of allowing nature instead of undernourished sheep and cattle to take over the woodland have been satisfactory and in some senses miraculous for in a period of eight years, the woods have regained that almost tropical appearance which the first settlers found on entering Ohio. In spring the woodland floor is carpeted with great patches of white, purple and yellow violets, trilliums, Dutchman's breeches, Canadian lilies, Wild Bouncing Bet, bloodroot, and wood anemones. The cover has grown so thick that, in portions of the woods, it is impossible to see a deer a few feet away in the undergrowth and during the summer months it is possible to lose oneself completely. There are many seedling trees of valuable timber—white ash, red, white and brown oak, walnut as well as the less valuable beech and maple which have grown to a height of twenty feet or more since we protected the woods.

And with the regrowth of the cover, the wild life has returned in abundance. In the daytime one is aware that the thick undergrowth is filled with small birds and animals and at night an electric torch turned in almost any direction catches the gleam of some pair of wild eyes. Bjonne Bremer, a Bostonian friend, recently spent two or three nights in a sleeping bag high on the Ferguson Place on the edge of the woodland and got little sleep because of his curiosity concerning the wild life in the dark woods surrounding him. The beam of his electric torch revealed raccoon, and skunk, rabbit and opossum, fox and deer.

Below the Ferguson woods lies a marshy area through which Switzer's Creek follows a meandering course. It is known on the farm as the Jungle because some of the deeper parts are completely impenetrable. There are springs everywhere and numbers of wild apple trees and of the beautiful and wild black raspberries scattered among a considerable amount of valuable second growth timber. It is a perfect game refuge and propagation area, especially since it adjoins the restored fertility of the rolling bottom fields of the Fleming and Bailey Places. And we have added to its protections by bulldozing down into its depth old trees and brush and great bundles of rusty wire fence. These are quickly overgrown with blackberry bushes and elderberry bushes so that they become citadels unassailable by dogs or even by foxes. The Jungle is alive with wild life, for added to all the other creatures which frequent the higher woodland, there are mink and muskrat as well as red-winged blackbirds and wading birds, the kingfishers, the common heron and a pair of great blue herons which stay with us the year round. And in spring, all the wet ground is a mass of great tropical green skunk cabbage leaves rising above the bright gold carpet of the marsh marigold.

Occasionally during the raccoon season the hounds get out of hand and run raccoon into the sacred propagation area. Almost invariably the pursued raccoon follows the same tactics, heading for the Jungle to take refuge inside the great and impenetrable tangles of brush and old wire fence where in perfect safety they can thumb their noses at the baffled hounds.

The efficacy of the tangled piles of wire fence as a refuge last summer provided the scene of a comedy in which a flock of sparrows and a sparrow hawk were the principal actors. The sparrows had been feeding on the ripening wheat in an adjoining field when the sparrow hawk appeared overhead. At the signal of alarm, the sparrows headed for the tangle of wire and once safe inside, chattered and swore at the hawk. As soon as he was gone to some neighboring high tree, they returned to the feast in the wheat field. Within a little time the hawk again dived toward them and again they took refuge in the pile of old fence, chattering and swearing. While I watched, for a period of perhaps twenty minutes, the comedy was repeated three or four times until at last the discouraged hawk flew away for good.

In the course of changing the landscape at Malabar not only the shape but the size of the fields was altered greatly. This meant taking out many old fence rows that bordered the old-fashioned square fields. Many of these had long since become hedgerows, grown up in berries of all kinds and some sassafras and wild cherry trees up to nine or ten inches in diameter. The destruction of these ancient fence rows with their thick cover was recognized as a serious loss to wild life protection since it not only destroyed cover, nesting places and shelter but also the means of moving from one part of the farm to another without coming into the open field.

To compensate for this destruction regular plans were laid out to leave here or there in the new and larger fields, patches of shelter. In many fields of the originally neglected and run-down farms these patches already existed in wet land or on the edges of gullies where stones culled from the fields had been heaped in piles about some ancient 40-ton glacial boulder. Many of these copses were left as they were and encouraged to thicken. They represented only a minute percentage of withdrawal from production of productive land and we felt that by maintaining and increasing the shelter for bird life we were actually making a gain through the power of wild birds to control insect pests.

We not only left some of the existing patches of shelter and cover but actually constructed, after the fashion I learned in France, new patches of shelter located more strategically than some of the original patches. One patch was constructed about the heap of great glacial boulders we bulldozed out of the fields and piled together in a great heap. The areas surrounding the farm ponds planted in game cover and food plants have been described elsewhere. Even the small area surrounding the pond at the Big House is frequented by all sorts of wild life including wild duck, although the pond is only fifty feet from the house, the big, dairy barn and all the hub-bub which surrounds the two establishments. Much of the garden at the Big House is planted to ornamental and flowering shrubs among them viburnums, honey locusts, mountain ash, dogwood, flowering crab, and standing honeysuckle all of which provide quantities of food for both animals and birds. The shrubs are interplanted with cedars, arbor vitae and Pfitzers whose thick evergreen foliage provides a windless and snowless shelter for birds throughout the worst winter weather. This, together with a good supply of grains, is undoubtedly one of the reasons why some naturally migratory or semi-migratory birds stay with us throughout the winter.

The drainage tank in the wide expanse of the lower Bailey field became a natural gathering place for wild life almost the moment it was established even before the willows or any vegetation had been planted on its edges. Rosa Multiflora plantations together with the willows are making of the drainage tank a thick protection for wild life. I visited it only today and the mud around the edge (for the water level is low in the late autumn) was covered with the footprints of deer, raccoon, and pheasant.

A plentiful supply of water is a necessity in any good pheasant territory. In northern Ohio I have seen dozens of pheasants in dry weather drinking from the water troughs between the railroad tracks where engines, passing at full speed, scoop up water on the run. As a train approached they would scatter to adjoining fields only to return later to what in a dry, hot summer was probably the only and certainly the cleanest water supply within miles.

As a partial replacement of the old, demolished fence rows the banks of dynamited drainage ditches are being utilized as shelter and as passage from one field to another. Planted with willows and Rosa Multiflora, the areas immediately bordering the ditches become thickly overgrown very quickly. Elderberry, wild black raspberry and blackberries follow with the result that in short order wild life has both plentiful food and shelter. The willow roots serve also to tie together the loose soil on the edges of the ditches to prevent caving in through frost action. The willows themselves serve to evaporate thousands of gallons of water a year.

Certainly the virtues of Rosa Multiflora in any wild life or good land use program, deserve a paragraph. It is an extremely hardy and thorny rose resembling the common eglantine save that instead of trailing it has a thick, upright sturdy growth. It has long been used in the Deep South for quail shelter and food. After a few years its growth becomes so thick and thorny as to be impenetrable save for small animals and birds. Within the past few years it has been greatly promoted by the U.S. Soil Conservation Service for two reasons. (1) As a hedge substitute for fence along the borders of curving strips and contours where it is difficult to build substantial permanent fencing on a curve. (2) As game cover, food, and protection as a passageway from one part of a farm to another.

An experimental planting made at Malabar produced at the end of three years a hedge effective enough to turn cattle. In another two or three years the hedge will turn even a razorback hog. Each year it sends up more and more shoots which turn woody and extremely thorny within a year. The rapidity of its growth depends largely upon soil and climate. In the longer growing season of the Deep South it will grow and thicken about twice as rapidly as in our part of the country.

Unlike the old osage and "bodark" hedges it does not grow into tree size to rob the adjoining field of moisture and fertility. Any tendency of the rose to spread out into adjoining fields can easily be corrected by running a plow furrow along both sides of the hedges. It has other virtues as well as those of hedge and shelter for it produces immense quantities of small rose pips much appreciated by quail, pheasant and other wild birds during the hard winter months. Its virtues on the score of beauty are not to be overlooked; its foliage, very thick, is a deep green in color, its growth vigorous and it is not subject to blights or insect attack, at least in our area. In June it produces great panicles and sprays of tiny white roses each centered by a large cluster of gold-dusted anthers.

Gradually we are working out a program of multiflora rose not only for use in game shelter and food patches but as a means of replacing expensive permanent wire fencing. As time and labor permits, we shall plant all newly constructed fence on both sides with Rosa Multiflora and by the time the fence deteriorates over a period of ten years or more we should have thick *growing* fences with the forgotten fence virtually encased by a woody, thorny wall on both sides—a barrier which is there forever. This rose hedge is extremely hardy. It ignores the winter and in one case where fire got accidentally in the hedge and destroyed a short stretch of it, vigorous new shoots came up immediately to replace the old. Within two years the damage was completely repaired with no mark of the fire damage remaining. Quite naturally the rose grows better on good land than poor but in the case of poor land, a mulch of barnyard manure quickly repairs the deficiencies of both minerals and moisture and a rapid, quick growth follows immediately.[1]

[1] Rosa Multiflora is being more and more widely propagated by the Soil Conservation nurseries and by other government and state agencies. Any soil conservation agent or any state fish and game commission or the U. S. Wild Life Department, Washington, D. C., can supply information regarding it.

All the measures taken at Malabar and at many other farms in Ohio have been inexpensive; indeed in many states, as in Ohio, food and shelter plants and trees are provided free by soil conservation and fish and game agencies. And in many states the survey and planning of farm ponds is done without cost by state wild life agencies; some even provide heavy machinery and labor to accomplish the actual construction.

At Malabar we look upon all these measures as economically profitable. They represent, it is true, a revolution away from the old square field, clean wire fence row, over-draining, penny-wise, pound-foolish American agriculture, but that agriculture has worn itself out, destroying itself more quickly than any agriculture in the history of the world. And not only has it destroyed soil and wild life but very largely it has brutalized the farmer, made a drudge of his wife and driven his children off the farm into the cities. There are spiritual and aesthetic values to good farming just as there are brutal economic ones, and all contribute to a good agriculture, good land use, good and healthy citizens and, above all, happy ones with minds which are intelligent, alert and adventurous.

I can think of no greater contrast to the life of any good, well-managed farm, where game and wild life play a large part in the picture, than that of the old square field, clean fence row school of farming, with the fields stretching flat to the horizon without a tree or shrub, or a wandering willow-bordered stream to obstruct the view, with fields that are lifeless save for the crops grown upon them. And there can be no greater contrast in our own hilly country to a good, well-managed farm in proper land use teeming with life than the miserable worn-out gullied acres of a poorly used farm abhorred even by the rabbits and the wild birds and the field mice because it is a miserable, depleted thing.

At Malabar the life of the children and young people is one long excitement not only because of the burgeoning fields and the livestock but because of the wild things which exist there in abundance. There is swimming, there is good fishing. There are thick woods that become in the mind of a small boy the jungles of the Congo. Who can gauge the delight of the heart of a child at the sight of a young faun or of a big red fox squirrel scuttering about under a hickory tree gathering nuts for the winter? Or the pleasure of a boy with his first big trout on a line? Or the excitement of his first shotgun as he trudges across a field behind the beagles? If you have never seen the look in the eye of a small boy as he says, "Pop, what do you think I saw? Six deer! In the bottom pasture!" you have missed something.

All of these things go with good farming and a good life and they go, too, with keeping the best of young farm boys and girls on the farm where, by the nation and the world, they are desperately needed.

But beyond all that there is an even broader purpose behind the men and women who are working for proper land use, for wild life, for a wider and better understanding of the pleasures of which nature can provide in such abundance if helped only a little. Speaking broadly, it is a goal which seeks to make of the whole American countryside, even in our thickly populated industrial areas and within a few miles of our great cities, a world in which the streams and lakes are clean and clear and filled with fish, where there is wild game in abundance and there are trees and hills and hidden ravines and valleys where city people can get away for a little while from concrete pavements and subways and the noise and stench of motor traffic.

Have you ever stood by the toy farm at Bronx Park Zoo and watched the faces of children from New York tenements who are seeing their first lamb or baby pig? Go there some time and watch. The sight will tell you far more than all the words set down here. In that moment of his first encounter with that lamb or baby pig, something has happened to the child which will remain with him all his life.

I have lived in France and Germany in thickly populated areas where sportsmen had good sport almost at the limits of the city, where farms were green and rich, where the streams were filled with trout, where there were green fields and forests in which to lose oneself as remotely as if one were in the depths of the Rockies or the Jungles of Sumatra, where there were no deserted, wretched farms empty of all life.

It can be done, here in my own Ohio, with its great cities and its big population. The change is coming about as farmers learn better how to use their land and real sportsmen lose the idea of slaughtering game wholesale, of cutting farmers' fences and leaving his gates open and shooting his cattle. The whole of this state or any state can become a sportsman's paradise and an area of clean streams and beautiful forests and rich, productive farms to be enjoyed not only by the prosperous farmer who loves his land but by the city dweller seeking escape and relaxation from the pressures and artificialities and nerve-wracking cities. The change will be profitable for everyone in terms of economics, of sport, of the spirit and in terms of real civilization.

# XVII: MALABAR JOURNAL

## Summer (2) 1945

> I was tired of the idle and turbulent life of Paris: of
> the crowd of *petits maîtres*, the bad books printed with
> official approval and royal patronage: the cabals of the
> literary world.
>
> —Voltaire at Ferney

AUGUST 10: The construction of the pond has turned out to
be a bigger job than any of us including the engineer and the
caterpillar driver anticipated. It is always like this, especially
with myself who is always inclined to be optimistic and
brush away small difficulties. Although it was not yet finished,
the water was turned in today in order to make the fill in
the old course of the stream. It will take a week or ten days
to fill up the whole of the big pond. Next spring we will
plant the borders with willows, French poplars and shrubs that
give shelter and food to game of all kinds.

This evening we found Harry and Naomi's pet gosling in-
specting the big caterpillar and making curious peeping noises
of excitement. She is half grown and very friendly, the sole
survivor of three Harry and Naomi hatched from eggs sent
by Charley's brother. The foxes got one and one drowned
(literally)—a strange fate for a gosling. I bought her on the
spot and brought her up to the big house where she will be
safe from "varmints." She is very tame and keeps peeping all
the time. By common consent she is called Inez after Inez
Robb of International News. There is a certain resemblance
in the way she talks back.

Gilbert and Bea, the turkeys, seemed puzzled by Inez and

421

apparently unable to decide exactly what she was. They circled her for a long time making curious gobbling noises.

Today I heard from Hatch in Mexico. He is a remarkable fellow. McEvoy did a piece about him in the August *Reader's Digest*. It was good but there is much more to the story of the remarkable things he accomplished on the Indian farms and villages and is now accomplishing among the miserably poor Indians and peasants of Mexico. I met him first in Baroda where he had come to discuss with the old Maharajah and Krishnamacharia, the Dewan, a program of agricultural reform in the villages and farms. He is a fundamentalist and began with one Indian village teaching sanitation to the villagers.

In a short time by the installation of latrines and treatment of tanks and marshes, he eliminated hookworm and in the dry season at least the malarial mosquito. He brought in Italian bees, and white leghorn chickens to cross with the hardy native chicken which is very close to the wild jungle fowl ancestor of all chickens. He brought in good Karachi bulls and he-goats. Within three years he had, in his first Mysore village, revolutionized the health and the economic status, and even the culture of the village. Not the least important and beneficial accomplishment was the organization of village co-operatives which packed and shipped eggs, honey and cheese to Madras and Bombay and the bigger near-by cities like Bangalore and Mysore City. The crossed chickens laid four to five times as many eggs as the original half-wild stock and the eggs were of better size and quality. Packaged, they sold from ten to twenty times the price formerly received in the local markets. From among the bright boys of the village, he selected six whom he educated in the plan so that they in turn went to other villages, reorganized them and taught other bright boys to accomplish the same results. Some such plan is as necessary in our own South and Southwest where much of the village and rural population lives below the level of a European peasant, and many of the people on the level of Indian peasants. A good many people, talking big about this country, forget this population which is a very large one.

We are in the middle of the sweetcorn season and our own plantings have furnished us and scores of friends and neighbors with some the best sweetcorn I've ever eaten. The variety is Golden Cross which in our soils seems to produce both abundance and excellent flavor. I have never seen corn so well filled out. The fat, sweet grains run to the very top of the ear. Whether it is because of soil, of variety, or because the weather has been exceptionally favorable to pollenization I don't know. Very possibly it is a little of all three—which is just another argument for sound balance in agriculture.

It isn't only our friends and neighbors who have benefited by the glut of sweetcorn but our furred and feathered friends as well. The woodchucks and the raccoon and possum have been growing fat on it. The corn grows close to the Jungle, the wooded swampy area which we keep closed as a game propagation area, and at night possums and coon raid the patch. In the daytime the woodchucks help themselves. I've caught a fat woodchuck on the job two or three times. He pulls down the whole stalk and gorges himself, running his fine, sharp teeth along the rows of grains exactly as a person eats corn, turning it over as he eats. If he can get the corn loose from the stalk he will sit up and hold it in his paws while he eats—a comical sight.

I've also caught the slow-witted, slow-moving possum working on the corn at night. He seems to finish up the partly eaten ears which the woodchuck and raccoon leave on the ground.

That bespectacled rascal, the raccoon, has his own fashion of eating and is as selective as a gourmet in choosing his ears. He doesn't pull one off and eat it unless it is exactly to his taste, neither too green nor overripe. He goes along the row husking ears until he finds just what he wants and pulls it off, husks it, and eats it on the spot. Apparently he considers sweetcorn fresh out of the husk sanitary enough for his finicky tastes and does not carry it to a brook or spring to wash it first as he does with most things he eats. His habit of partially husking ears to find one to suit his taste is annoying for he leaves part of the ear open to the attacks of insects. Also he is always operating in direct competition because he selects exactly the ears you want yourself. Moreover he gets people into trouble.

Day before yesterday Bob asked, "You've lived most of

your life in the country. Can't you tell by the feel of an ear of sweetcorn when it's ripe?"

"What do you mean?"

"Well, somebody's going through the sweetcorn pulling part of the husk off each ear to see if it's ready."

"Listen!" I said, "If you're out to lecture, go and tell it to the raccoons!"

While I've caught possum and woodchucks at work on the sweetcorn I've never caught Stinky Raccoon no matter how carefully I've approached the sweetcorn patch or operated an electric torch. He always hears me first and scuttles into the corn or the thick alfalfa nearby. I never take the dogs on my after-dark excursions to the corn patch for fear that a mother raccoon has her family out teaching them how to steal sweetcorn and select only the best ears. No animal is more attractive or comical than a young raccoon.

In the daytime pheasants and quail clean up the corn left uneaten by the furry animals. Usually at this season the young of both are pretty well grown but still stick together with the hen.

I don't know how much corn the wild things take and I don't much care, especially in a season like this when the corn grows in such abundance. Planting a couple of extra rows will provide for them all and a couple of rows is a small share of the abundance at Malabar. It's a small enough reward for the job the quail and pheasant do on the insects.

AUGUST 14: Went to Miami University yesterday to do a speech at the Summer Seminar on the need of decentralizing our nightmarish industrial cities. It was a long trip—170 miles by car, in hot weather but it was worth it—nearly all the way through rich agricultural country, most of it very well farmed. The corn in the flat country has come on remarkably considering the cold wet spring. Some of it was the finest corn I have ever seen, very different from the drought ridden corn of last summer. Some fields looked like great blocks of lush green food, an even, thick, dark green with a layer of pale yellow tassels on the top like frosting on a cake. The occasional sight of a rich field of middle-western corn was one of the things I missed during all the years of life in Europe.

The pastures were not so good, none of them indeed as good as our own, but of course most of the rich region is not really forage or dairy country but corn and hog country with some beef feeding. However I did not see a single herd of feeder cattle, which certainly does not augur well for the beef supply—only half a dozen steers here and there which I suspect were all ear-marked for private consumption through dubious channels.

The campus of Miami University, one of the oldest state colleges in Ohio, is very beautiful. By some stroke of fortune it seems to have escaped the buildings and architecture of the *awful* period from about 1885 to 1915. The old buildings have taste and scale and line and the new ones are beautiful, mostly in the style of Williamsburg. The trees, as everywhere in Ohio, are magnificent, all save the elms which are dying tragically on one of the two diseases that have attacked elms everywhere. It will be tragic if they go the way of the chestnut.

*Note:* A later study of the trees affected by the elm disease shows a definite relationship between the incidence of the disease and the falling water table of Ohio. The trees affected are all in paved city areas or in those areas where the water table has fallen seriously. Most elms are water loving trees and the deduction is that as the water supply fails the tree is weakened and falls a victim to disease. The same situation is true regarding the white ash, one of our most valuable trees which is dying off as it attains a height of thirty feet. The falling water table is a direct result of poor farming and forestry practices. At Malabar where, owing to the geological formation, the water table has been fairly static and has been greatly improved by soil conservation and forestry practices, there has been no vestige of the elm disease and the white ash flourishes in abundance.

Late that afternoon the students were shouting and singing to celebrate the capitulation of Japan—not yet definite, but fairly certain. All the way home we kept the radio of the car in operation, listening to the cloud of confused reports and rumors from Berne, Tokyo, Guam, Chung King, London, Paris—a fantastic world when a car driving along a road in Ohio is in communication with the whole of the world, And on top of this the Atomic bomb!

Tried out today the new "Scotch" plow sent me by Roger Keyes. It is the type of plow used in the British Isles and almost entirely in French Canada. Both Jim Cook and I who tried it out are enthusiastic. It is longer, slimmer and the moldboard has a more acute curve than our conventional moldboard plow. It also has a deep notch just behind the point. Its real value is that it actually *breaks up* sod or stubble rather than simply turning it upside down and burying it. With the simple adjustment of the Ferguson tractor it is possible to make it do any kind of job you want. I started plowing a poor field on the Bailey Place, part mammoth clover and part weeds which had been twice mowed during the summer with the residue left on the surface of the ground. There was a thick accumulation of decaying organic material, with mould and bacteria and weeds for perhaps the first time in years since Bailey stopped using organic material and depended entirely on chemical fertilizer. Also the ground underneath, although almost like cement in texture because it contained *no* humus, was moist and friable. With the Scotch plow properly adjusted I was able to "layer" the decaying residue *into* the starved soil—not turning it over and burying it to be smashed down by the weight of the earth and the implements passing over it during the fitting of the ground but sandwiched in upright sections, running vertically so that with a disking all the decaying rubbish will be thoroughly mixed into the poor, cement-like soil. This will check almost completely the erosion which is inevitable even on flat ground with soil totally devoid of organic material and *life*.

All this is the first step in bringing soil like that on the Bailey Place back to life and productivity. The layering with the Scotch plow followed by fairly deep disking, plus chemical fertilizer and some barnyard manure and the invaluable conservation of moisture which allows life to return to the soil, will increase the yield of that particular field by at least 500 per cent in one year—which is a great increase but less impressive when one considers that the production base of this field was less than five bushels of wheat per acre. With other fields on the Bailey Place where we have jumped wheat production from under five bushels to thirty-five bushels, the process was more clumsily and less efficiently accomplished than with the Scotch plow. In French Canada there is virtually no market for our conventional moldboard plow and after using the Scotch plow I can understand why. I suspect that Kenneth, Bob, and Jim may become converts and want to shift over once they have used the new plow. It also stays in the ground on gravel mounds and in bare hard subsoil far better than the conventional plow. I am plowing as deeply as possible, between ten inches and a foot, in order to bring up as much as I can of our minerally valuable subsoil which is sometimes potentially more fertile than some of our worn-out topsoil. Quantities of humus added to it make it strong, alive, and highly productive.

AUGUST 15: The new plow continues up to expectations. It is especially valuable on land which has been freshly limed as, instead of turning the lime over and burying it seven to ten inches deep (where it remains until the land is plowed again), it *layers* the lime vertically *mixing* it with the soil to the same depth.

We have had a curious and interesting experience with the effect of lime on production and fertility. The 160 acres of the Conservancy Farm is bisected by a state road which is usually dry-surfaced with limestone and occasionally with the local glacial gravel. In midsummer great clouds of dust rise from it with the passing of each car and drift across the fields. The land is potentially good land but farmed out and in four years we have raised production enormously by the use of lime, sweet clover and the great amounts of humus from the clover, and the plowed-in cornstalks and oats straw which the mechanical picker and combine leave on the field. In other words nothing is taken off the field but the grain of the oats and the ear of the corn. None of the content of straw, cornstalks, sweet clover and weeds are removed from the fields —only the grain which draws heavily on minerals. In addition the straw and cornstalks draw approximately 90 per cent of their bulk out of sun and air and this is added to the soil plus the 100 per cent return of both minerals and bulk from the growth of all the sweet clover and the weeds. Naturally this has increased the organic *humus* content of the soil enormously. Liming, of course, did much to improve the growth of everything on the fields, particularly the legumes.

A couple of years ago Bob proposed protesting to the state highway authorities regarding the vast clouds of dust which in dry weather rose from the road and blew across our fields, covering the crops with a fine dust until the first rain washed them clean. Half jestingly, I said, "Why do that? We're getting a lot of free limestone quickly available to the crops."

Observation has shown that this is true. The prevailing winds are from the northwest and all the fields south and east of the road show the effects of the cover of limestone dust. It is most evident from a distance of about seventy-five feet from the road itself and diminishes gradually to the far side of the field. Occasionally before a rain the wind turns to the southeast and carries the dust across the fields on the other side of the road. Here the evidence in the growth and yield of crops is even more striking but only on a narrowly limed strip next to the road. There is no doubt about the benefits the fields receive from the dust. It is also probable that the dust contains also valuable trace minerals from the pulverized glacial gravel which is sometimes used for surfacing the road. In any case, both crops and weeds on the fields bordering the road are among the healthiest on the whole farm, even in comparison with the fields where we have worked intensively in restoring humus and minerals.

Just came in from looking at the sows which are all having pigs about the same time, and found a new litter of ten just born. There may be more which would be a fine record for a gilt with her first litter. As each pig was born, it stood up, shook itself and went immediately to feeding. Hogs are very remarkable animals in their intelligence, adaptability, and natural vigor. It is easy to see why they can go wild and survive easily. A sow could travel right across country with her litter, taking care of herself and family, feeding them, watering them, defending them from dogs. Sometimes here they do take to traveling. It is the worst thing about them. I find them among the most sympathetic animals on the farm. There is certainly nothing more amusing than a smart, clean little pig with his curious face and bright intelligent almost human eyes.

Usually we buy pigs to follow the steers but this year Bob thought they would be scarce and high-priced and bought ten gilts from Vane Close and a boar from the Areharts. He was right. Pigs are almost unfindable and black marketeers are going about in trucks offering $25 a piece for weanling pigs —a terrific price.

It will be good to see subsidies, price ceilings and all that nonsense done away with and the return of abundance and the process of produce finding its own sound price level. That is the only way to cure black markets. There is no other. It is also the only way to achieve quantity food production. I doubt seriously that in a free production market the prices would have been as high as some of the ceilings that have been imposed and would have been 200 per cent less than some black-market prices. Certainly all green vegetables would have been cheaper. Day before yesterday I stopped in Springfield in a market to buy sweetcorn and a watermelon. The sweetcorn was 60c a dozen and the smallest watermelon $1.25. These are prices unheard of, even in the first World War when there was no price ceiling. Tomatoes are selling wholesale at $1.50 a basket and peaches at $8.00 a bushel. Yet OPA officials have the face to tell the public that living costs have not increased more than 15 per cent. Each of the these items represents a jump in price over 1939 prices of 100 per cent to 300 percent. Ask any housewife whether the cost of feeding her family has not doubled in the items where production has not been limited to too low ceilings and are at the moment virtually unavailable save in the black market where in the case of poultry the city price, if poultry can be found, is up 300 per cent. And poultry has been 85 per cent in the black market since the very beginning because no farmer, let alone a big poultry feeder who buys feed could possibly produce poultry at 28 cents a pound. The regulations only resulted in driving all those who observed ceiling regulations out of business.

Two farmers in Southern Ohio have just been fined and sent to prison for butchering and selling poultry and meat at black market prices. This is the drop in the bucket of the sensational war promised by the OPA against black markets and highly publicized by the newspapermen and writers employed by the OWI. What a farce all this government control of information, prices, etc., has been—not because it *could* not work but because it has largely been in the hands of theorists, incompetents and the sweepings of professional classes—lawyers, writers, and professors. I find few individuals more contemptible than the small-fry New Dealers who have gone from government job to government job in the last twelve years—always taken care of, through the NYA, OWI,

OPA, WXYZ and all other conflicting and overlapping agencies. Few of, them had put in a full day's work since 1933 and on the score of efficiency or ability the score is even worse. It is a whole class, such as European bureaucracy has known for a couple of generations, but it is new here. No wonder that one of the strongest expressions of contempt in the French language is the word *fonctionaire* which translated means no more than bureaucrat. Its meaning in common French usage is a small-minded, incompetent fellow, pompous and self-authoritative, a goldbricker without initiative or such ability, who is always taken care of by government political machinery. Too many of them wangle their way into posts from which under Civil Service regulations it is almost impossible eventually to dislodge them. The French look upon such bureaucratic service as a kind of WPA which it is.

The stigma acquired by the New Deal bureaucrat is hard on the original meaning of the word in this country, for in the permanent services such as agriculture and forestry there are many excellent, intelligent, and devoted servants of the people. After the last twelve years many words will need re-definition, among them the words "bureaucrat" and "liberal." Both have been debased from an honorable status and meaning.

While Fred Herring's machinery has been working on the new road above Pleasant Hill lake, we have done some horse-trading for the use of the big bulldozers. Fred has a farm near Lucas and we have traded the use of our combine and hay-baler for the heavy road machinery. The balance runs against us but the extra payment we consider an excellent investment and a considerable economy.

Today (Sunday) there were two big fourteen-ton bulldozers at work, one on the old-line fence-row between the Bailey and the Fleming Places and the other busy with a scoop building a drainage pond on the Bailey Place.

The fence-row had been in existence for perhaps a hundred and thirty years and after years of neglect and tenant farming had become virtually a jungle pile, including a half-ruined fence, piles of glacial "niggerheads," old rubbish as well as a thick growth of poison ivy, elderberries, blackberries and wild cherry and sassafras trees as much as twelve inches in diameter. We wanted it out of the way because it prevented us from running long strips and contours across both farms from one township road to another, a distance of a mile or more. The prospect of clearing it out of the way by hand appeared very nearly insuperable and extremely expensive. Very likely it would have taken two or three men all winter, hacking, digging, wrestling and when they had finished the job would still be unsatisfactory. We figure that it would cost us at least a thousand dollars. With the fourteen-ton bulldozer the story was quite different.

The big affair moved in about ten in the morning and went to work moving along the fence-row. With no effort at all it pushed over and uprooted the twelve-inch trees. Its big blade scooped up the old ruined fence, the underbrush, the rocks and rubbish and pushed them down into the swampy part of the Jungle where the great piles of rubbish make wonderful shelter for wild game. (No dog could dig his way into those tangles of old wire, roots, branches and rubbish and it is doubtful if even a fox could make much headway through them.)

Everybody was on hand all through the middle of the day watching the operation and all the kids had to take turns riding on the seat high up beside the tough and capable driver who manipulated the big engine as if he were playing a pipe-organ. By three o'clock the job was done and the driver was running the big blade up and down the road smoothing the site of the old fence-row to the level of the fields on each side, leaving behind not a rock or a root. In four hours the place was as clean as if there had never been any line fence on the site. The job cost exactly sixty dollars. Three hours and sixty dollars for a job that would have taken three men (if you could have found them) all winter at a cost of a thousand dollars or more!

When he had finished, the driver moved up to the bottom bluegrass pasture on the Fleming Place and went to work leveling off the last vestiges of the steep high millrace which had once fed the mill owned by Ceely Rose's father. It had bothered us for a long time because its sides were too steep for pasture mowing and each year grew up in coarse weeds. The job took him about forty minutes and he went off across the fields to the paddock across from the Big House to clear out the rocks and trees and underbrush of an area which

432

was neither forest nor pasture but only a mess. We wanted it for a calf paddock because there was shade there and spring water and it was near the barn. After two hours more the big bulldozer had cleared the paddock and left it ready for seeding with all the rubbish pushed deep into the adjoining woods for game shelter—and again a job that would have taken three or four men all winter was done in a couple of hours at a small fraction of hand-labor costs.

Meanwhile the other bulldozer with a great scoop attached was doing another job in the middle of the bottom fields on the Bailey Place. There the swirling waters of the melting glacier had formed a hollow some twenty or thirty acres in extent with no drainage outlet. All around the area the land rose to a height of twenty or thirty feet. In the center of this bowl lay a smaller flattish area in which each winter the water collected, drowning out all crops and preventing us from working the land until late in the summer. Not only was it unworkable but it made a weedy, unsightly spot in the middle of the neat strips and contours laid out across those bottom fields. Any conventional means of draining the area seemed out of the question. To have put in tile drainage we should have been forced to dig to a depth of twenty or thirty feet through the surrounding rim in order to get proper fall and we avoid tile drainage whenever possible because it drains off our much desired moisture as well as much expensive lime and fertilizer in solution. In addition we should have had to run the tiling for at least a quarter of a mile, and after it was installed, suffer all the troubles and expense of breakage and stoppage which go with tiling.

After striving over the problem for two years, inspiration or rather memory came to the rescue. I remembered suddenly the drainage tanks used sometimes in Europe and in India to drain off flat land. Why not follow that pattern and simply dig a deep pit lower than the surrounding land, spread out the earth excavated over the surrounding area and let the water settle into the tank. I did not know whether it would work in this kind of area but with the big bulldozer and scoop it would not cost much and it was worth trying.

So the bulldozer and scoop went to work and in three hours excavated a hole eighty by twenty feet and about ten feet deep in the very center of the bottom of the bowl. In three hours at the cost of something less than fifty dollars the drainage tank was completed with all the earth taken out and spread level and smooth over the surrounding area. I hope it will work!

(Note: November 1947. It did work. Water which formerly drained into the bottom of the bowl and remained there until well into the summer drained into the new pit making a permanent pond or tank. Even during the heavy, persistent flood rains of the spring of 1947, it reduced enormously the amount of water standing on the field, even though the tank filled to the top and overflowed. At wheat plowing time we were able to plow to within two or three feet of the edge of the tank and the ground was moist, as it should be, but not wet. Fortunately, most of the water which formerly stood in the basin has found a natural drainage outlet through subterranean gravel, apparently blocked until the pit was dug. We planted Babylonica willows at intervals of six to eight feet along the edges of the tank. These serve two purposes: (1) The rapid growth of the intricate roots hold the steep sides together preventing cave-ins from winter frost action and prevent any siltation. (2) As the willows grow they will in themselves serve to evaporate scores of gallons of water a day through their leaves, thus absorbing much of the unwanted excess water. Actually, the tank has become a fourth farm pond in which sunfish and big bullfrogs are flourishing. All during the summer the mud about the edges is covered with the tracks of raccoon, pheasant, quail and other game which come there to drink. As the tank lies in the very midst of a wide open stretch of field, we plan next spring to plant Rosa Multiflora, standing honeysuckle and other food and shelter plants to give the game better cover and security.)

The day was an exciting one and proved beyond much doubt the great contribution which modern heavy machinery can make toward land restoration and farm maintenance. For something less than two hundred dollars we had literally changed the landscape at Malabar in a single day as well as putting into production some thirty or forty acres of what had not only been a series of eyesores but useless and unproductive land. Without the machinery the same job would have been impossible or prohibitively expensive. The possibilities in the business of reclaiming potentially good land which has been misused and exists in millions of acres in the United States, seem almost limitless.

While making the excavation we watched closely the soil structure and discovered many interesting things. Perhaps the most interesting was the evidence of natural erosion at the period between the two great glaciers. At a depth of ten feet we found a ten inch layer of what must have been topsoil antedating the glaciers or at least topsoil built up during the thousands of years that passed between the two glaciers. This was buried beneath a mixture of clay and gravel deposited by the second glacier. And of course at the very top level we found about three feet of topsoil which had been eroded from the surrounding slopes through the effects of a poor agriculture in our own times. Nearly all the soil excavated had the *deadness* of soil long water-soaked in which anaerobic action had destroyed very nearly all life or at least all life contributing anything of value to productive agriculture.

(Note: Afterward we ran a field cultivator to a depth of ten inches through the layer of dead soil excavated from the pit in order to admit air and sunlight which in turn would change the action of anaerobic to the healthy aerobic action which is so important to productive agriculture. The excavated soil was also given a coating of barnyard manure to impregnate it with the beneficent moulds, fungi, and bacteria which would eventually turn it from *dead* into *living* soil and therefore productive of life in all its forms. In the following summer the soil still showed signs of being dead and unproductive but in the second summer it began to come to life and really produce. One of the signs was the appearance of earthworms.)

August 18: Came across a quotation from Thoreau in this week's *New Yorker*. It was written concerning museums but it might well be applied to this half-mad, materialist, decadent, industrial world in which we live: "One green bud of spring, one willow catkin, one faint trill from a migrating sparrow would set the world on its legs again. The life that is in a single green weed is of more worth than all this death."

One might add that all this is true and that it might save the world if the trill from a migrating sparrow could be heard above the clamor for higher wages, higher profits, election promises, water closets and automobiles, above all the outcry for materialistic things and standards by which man does *not* live, by which eventually he dies the death of the soul, of the spirit, of all understanding and growth, in the end, of decency itself. An age in which God is represented by the Holy Trinity of plumbing, overtime and assembly lines is not a great age, unless man learns to use these things for his freedom and the growth of his spirit rather than his brutalization.

In all the oceans of printer's ink used by columnists regarding the Atomic bomb I have seen no mention of its true and profound horror—that it is the symbol of the fact of utter destruction and negation to which so many brilliant minds have devoted their energies. It is appalling to reflect on how much of human thought, of spirit, of creative force either in the polished beauty of a turbine or the quiet still beauty of a garden, can be annihilated by a single Atomic bomb. The deepest horror of war is not the death of individual men but the destruction of so much that man has striven painfully and eagerly to build up in his slow, aspiring climb upward out of the steaming swamps of the primeval world. As in an ant-hill kicked over by the careless foot of a passerby, there will always be a few ants and a few men to cherish the impulse and the aspiration to carry on and build another ant-hill or another civilization elsewhere. The impulse and aspiration is the most profound justification for the existence both of the ant and of man himself. I have heard that a few scientists refused to lend their brilliant talents to the creation of the Atomic bomb. It is possible that in a century or two these men will be honored above those whose names and faces appear everywhere in the press today.

Perhaps it is that the world needs not a dictator or Communism or technology or any of the other materialistic doctrinaires of doctrines but another Jean Jacques Rousseau who with all the snobberies, and affectations and romanticism which followed in his trail like the tail of a comet had as much to do with revitalizing the European world of the tired, cynical, brilliant eighteenth century as the steelyminded Voltaire. Together they and their followers planted the seed of a revolution which revitalized the civilization of the world and brought man another step upward in the long, slow ascent of his development.

Reason, machines and guaranteed wages are not enough because man does not live by these things alone and if the spirit and nature itself are ignored, they lead him only into the blind alley of defeat and eventually of annihilation. Mankind can do without plumbing but not without Saint Francis of Assisi. It can survive without automobiles but scarcely without the leavening experience, wisdom and faith of Saint Augustine, Russia found that man could *exist* on the bare, materialistic skeleton of the Marxian system with its machines and lavishly decorated Moscow subway but he could not *live* without the writers and the actors and the dancers of the ballet, and in the end that he could not *live* without even the dubious splendors of the Orthodox Church. It is simply that in all life on this earth as in all good agriculture there are no short-cuts that by-pass Nature and the nature of man himself and animals, trees, rocks, and streams. Every attempt at a formula, a short-cut, a panacea, always ends in negation and destruction. And the worst violation of all is the negation of the nature of man and his relation to the universe and eternity. In that lies the whole answer to the eternal and inevitable failure of a pure Marxian doctrine. It is like trying to farm by chemical fertilizer alone, ignoring the immense powers of rain and water, the beetles, the bumble bees, the fungi and moulds, the earthworms, and the minute invisible bacteria deep in the soil without which the whole scheme of the universe and man's relation to it and his whole life would in the end be annihilated. Marxian Communism is philosophically and socially a shallow, short-cut, cure-all formula and in the natural order of life and human nature there is no such thing. Man's progress toward the Light can never be achieved by any mass formula which ignores the individual and certain rights bestowed upon him by God and Nature. Eliminate them and man becomes no more than a brute or another cog in an assembly line. Those who believe in industry and technology as the *sole* means of man's advance and liberation are as far wrong as the Marxian doctrinaire.

437

Jimmy has talked to Bob and me and decided to stay on here instead of returning to school in Cleveland in the autumn. He is a remarkable boy, mature, serious as a man of thirty yet there is nothing stuffy about him. I feel that when I am with him I have the companionship of a mature and intelligent man yet when he is out with the kids no one of them has such a capacity for enjoying himself. He came here when he was fifteen to work during the summer to keep in training for football and became so interested in agriculture that he came back for the Christmas and Easter holidays. The interest has grown steadily until this year he has decided to take up farming as a career and eventually to have a place of his own. Being a bright fellow, he has finished high school in three years and has only a history credit to make if he should want to go to college. He plans to do it at the Lucas High School.

This summer he acted as foreman of the other boys and began by helping in the dairy with Harry who in the shortage of manpower has been in charge of both dairy and poultry. About a month ago Jimmy took over a good-sized dairy and the hogs single-handed and has done a good job.

He is one of those who cannot be deprived of an education and really has little need of college. He learns not only from books but from the fields, the animals and the earth itself. College on the other hand could not harm him by fixing in his mind theories and ideas which in time will become inert, outdated and embalmed, for he has a *live* and growing mind like that of both my grandfathers which continued to grow after seventy up to the day of their deaths in their nineties. And he will escape the specialization which so many of our schools seek to impose and which has done much injury to the growth and advance of education in this country. It has produced too many single-track limited minds which act always upon the assumption that the narrow field in which they are utterly absorbed has found the key to the universe; and the universe is quite a tall order. The worst offender is perhaps the mechanical mind which assumes that because it has evolved a new carburetor it is final authority upon economics, history, philosophy and God knows what. Any reader can pick out without much trouble a dozen such minds among men famous in the mechanical-industrial world of America.

Many of our engineers are great offenders. They believe quite seriously, that steel, cement and logarithms are the whole solution to problems of floods and drouths, overlooking completely such elements as erosion, bare earth, siltation, rainfall, the actual *value* of marshes. There are in America millions of dollars wasted in the dams, flood control and water supply measures which have become useless after a few years through flooding or siltation, because the mind of the man who built the dam was limited by cement, steel, and logarithms. As often as not that sort of mind knows nothing whatever of their ramifications or implications. The most colossal example of the limitations of an engineering mind is the billions of dollars spent in constructing levees on the lower Mississippi to control waters which can only be controlled by forests and marshes and proper land use and dams along the tributaries and *headwaters* of the great and turbulent rivers. We have only begun to understand that fundamental truth. In the meanwhile we have not only lost the vast sums spent annually for a century by the nation in building levees but have suffered year after year the flooding and destruction of valuable land, property and lives. The vast achievements of the Tennessee Valley Authority are the product not of a specialist engineer's mind but of the minds of a handful of really *educated* engineers such as those of Lilienthal and the two Morgans, encouraged and supported by a really educated political mind like that of the late George Norris.

One finds the same kind of specialized mind in agriculture. The soil man trained primarily as a chemist all too often sees soil only in terms of chemistry, ignoring the very principle of life itself and the life which is perpetually born of death itself. The specialist in botany sees hybrid corn as the panacea of corn-hog production. While it increases corn yields by a fourth and is resistant to disease, yet even the added yield has not kept the annual *average* yield in our great corn areas from declining steadily each year, because the hybrid corn rooter and the average farmer have forgotten that the fundamental of corn production is still the *soil* and that the hybrid corn which yields 25 per cent more also takes more out of the soil. The man who believed after Leibig that chemical fertilizer was the sole element in soil fertility ended up with barren fields of the consistency of cement with traces of acid. The whole South and some of the Middle West is an awful testament of this specialized belief.

Jimmy is certain to escape these errors of specialization whether he goes to college or not because he has a live, inquiring mind, interested in *everything* and coupled with it is the immense force of a mind which forgets nothing.

Last night just at twilight I came upon one of those sights which occur now and then in the life of a farm—a moment of arrested beauty which brings the satisfaction and delight of merely being alive. I had been up on the high Ferguson Place looking for a heifer who had hidden herself away somewhere in the underbrush to have a calf and as I came down off the high plateau I noticed in the evening light what appeared at first to be the cattle gathered around the salt block. Almost at once, however, I discovered the mistake. They were deer—six of them—a big-antlered stag, three does and two partly grown fawns. I stood quite still watching them until the breeze carried my scent downwind. The big buck raised his head and looked toward me, stamping his hooves. Then in a second, all six turned and cleared the high fence bordered by barbed-wire as if it were no obstacle at all. The flash of their white tails was the last I saw of them as they vanished into the darkening thick woods.

Always there are deer tracks in abundance around the salt block and in the sand along the spring brook at the bottom of the deep Ferguson ravine and although I have tried again and again to find them this is the first time I had ever seen more than a faint, distant shadow of brown moving quietly and quickly through the underbrush.

AUGUST 20: Back from two days in Detroit where we went for agricultural reasons to talk with Roger Keyes and others at Harry Ferguson, Inc., concerning new agricultural implements for the New Agriculture and with officials of the Stran-Steel, a subsidiary of Great Lakes Steel Corporation, regarding their plans for farm buildings. Growing production has swamped us and we need new dairy buildings to house a bigger herd, new feeding barns for more beef cattle and poultry buildings for several thousand more chickens or turkeys. Harry is enthusiastic over turkeys but I remain cynical and dubious. They represent a big investment, a low will to live—less even than sheep—and a brainlessness that is virtually unexcelled. Incidentally, it would appear in the case of many animals that the will to live is somehow related to intelligence and to a greater *internal* resistance to illness and death. A ewe or a turkey, both stupid creatures, if it feels badly, will simply lie down and die with serenity, almost with pleasure. The hog, perhaps the most intelligent of farm animals, will fight with all its wits and spirit against illness and death.

The steel dairy units, standardized but flexible enough for adaptation, have immense possibilities on the grounds of fire resistance, durability, moving and general convenience. In a short time we have evolved plans for a really modern and practical dairy unit, in which the cows would run free in covered feeding sheds, partly open all the year round for health's sake, with a milking-parlor where they would be fed silage and grains. Hay would be fed actually in the mow or storage room itself where they would be walled in by the bales of hay and straw. It would of course be a one-story, ground floor mow and as they consumed the hay the cows would gradually eat their way out until spring pasture was ready. We had the idea of using movable hayracks so that as the bales were consumed the racks could be moved back and out. Thus they would always be exactly next to the hay so that no carrying and little labor would be involved. All the mow and feeding shed would be kept bedded all winter and the manure removed as the occasion permitted. All of his plan has its origins in the mind of H. E. Babcock of Cornell University, perhaps the best, most co-ordinated and comprehensive mind in American agriculture.

If our plan works out we shall put the new dairy unit on the plot next to Bob's house at the crossroads by the red school house. It will make an interesting contrast with the older farm buildings of the Beck Place just across the road— the one steel, fireproof, practical and completely modern, the other modern, somewhat old-fashioned, subject to fire and wasteful of labor. It seems to me that the need for two- or

three-story farm buildings has largely disappeared. So far as we are concerned, baling is the only practical way of handling hay and straw, and forage in bales can be stored much more easily on the ground level than overhead in the huge, high, old-fashioned mows. This is especially true when the bales are kept, as we plan, exactly next to the cattle and actually form a part of their shelter. Few things can increase the profits and efficiency of a farm so much as modern buildings conceived and planned for saving labor and with consideration for modern machinery and feeding methods.

Dr. Borst of the Zanesville, Ohio, U.S. Soil Conservation Station, who discovered and developed the use of alfalfa as a poor-land crop, spent all of Sunday with us. We went over the whole farm, field by field, and showed him with a good deal of pride the fine thirty-acre field of alfalfa high up on the top of the hill on the Ferguson Place on what was only four years earlier a barren eroded hilltop. Also the fine two-head-per-acre bluegrass–white clover permanent pasture next to it established on the same sort of land.

We found a lot more evidence of the ecological fact of the effect of minerally balanced soil and abundant organic material in relation to disease and insects. The only alfalfa attacked by leaf-hoppers is on spots, usually on the flat spots where the terribly depleted topsoil remains. Here even our concentrated efforts have not yet been able to restore the soil to full life and strength. The leaf hoppers simply do not attack the healthy plants on good, well-balanced soil.

The same evidence showed up brilliantly in the vegetable garden where a large plot given over to tomatoes, canteloupe, sweet pepper, cucumbers, and late sweetcorn exist in abundant health absolutely free from insects, blight or disease although *no* dusting or spraying has been done. The melons are absolutely free from the blight which usually attacks them. For the first time in our experience we have not lost a single canteloupe plant after germination, and this in a patch representing about a third of an acre.

Most of the time with Dr. Borst was interrupted by farmer visitors, some of whom stayed with us to complete the tour. It was the first Sunday without gas rationing and visitors descended like locusts upon Egypt. Some came simply out of curiosity but a good many were farmers or soil men whom I always find interesting and am glad to see. Very often I learn much from them. One party which I found the most interesting was made up of three boys from Clark County, more than a hundred miles away, with their girls. They were all under eighteen and very much alive, intelligent and full of ideas. They stayed with us all the afternoon and at the end asked shyly if I would come down to Clark County during the winter to talk to the 4-H Clubs and the farmers. It is clearly evident that the future of our agriculture, and therefore the future of a large segment of our complex and interlocking economy, lies in the hands of our young people. With them the land-grant colleges, the extension service and the soil conservation service are doing a wonderful job. Very likely the government money spent on their education is the best investment made of government money and its good results affect us all, even in the congested areas of our unhealthy cities—a fact which too few people understand.

One of the striking things we have discovered slowly is the relation between animal secretions and droppings and the germination and vigor of meadow seedlings. Without exception in the fields where cattle and sheep were allowed to wander, the germination and vigor of seedlings is much higher than in the fields, even with much better soil, from which they have been excluded. This fact is also true on the poor areas where barnyard manure has been used. The most striking example which caused Dr. Borst to whistle and say, "Jehosaphat!" was the cemetery field, once perhaps the poorest field on the Fleming farm, mostly steep and rough, which had been destroyed by row crops and erosion. Lime, a mixed legume seeding, and turning over the field to cattle for two years achieved a miraculous result. The seeding, even on the poor, bare, mound-tops and steep slopes is fantastically thick and vigorous. It is a mixture of ladino, alfalfa and brome grass. As we stood in the deep growth talking about that particular field, Dr. Borst said, "We still know practically nothing about these things." I do know that if virgin leaf mould topsoil out of our virgin woodlots is used alone in the greenhouse or in window-boxes, the plants grown in it are feeble and spindly. A little lime and a little barnyard manure completely alter its character and the resulting germination and vigor of growth is astonishing.

During the middle of the day we, with the help of the kids and visitors, drove the shorthorn herd with Blondy, the Angus bull, from the Bailey hill pasture to the Ferguson Place to join the blue-roan herd running with Elmer, the white Shorthorn bull, a distance of about a mile and a half, mostly along highways. Everything went wrong—calves got lost, one ran back up to the 120-acre Bailey pasture. One of the cows was in season which added to the confusion. In order to rescue one little two-day-old calf, we had to drive the whole herd back so that his mother could find him. Each time we sought to round him up, he high-tailed it up over the hilltop where he found a clump of bushes or a patch of blackberries to hide in, staring out and watching us with comical, very bright black eyes. When we tried to surround him, he would break through and with his tail straight up in the air take up over the hill. I am sure the little stinker enjoyed every minute of it. It was a hot day and all of us felt like killing him but we couldn't help laughing.

As we passed the bottom pasture all the yearling beef cattle crowded up to the fence bawling with curiosity and sociability, perhaps recognizing their mothers of last season or wanting to meet their brothers and sisters born this year. In the uproar and confusion a white calf got through the fence to join them and Jimmy, the high-school athlete and Harry ran him down on foot and finally returned him to the herd. Harry put him in the back seat of Jimmy's car and sat on him to keep him quiet.

Once we reached the Ferguson Place, Blondy and Elmer engaged in a first class bullfight surrounded by admiring and very vocal cows of both herds. Blondy, the big Angus is heavier and older but Elmer had the advantage of having horns. They pushed each other around, bellowing and pawing for a long time until Blondy decided he had had enough. He wanted to quit but Elmer pressed the issue and finally Blondy simply broke down the heavy gate and set off down the Ferguson lane through the thick woods with Elmer behind him. The chase continued all the way back to the Bailey Place along the highway and over and through fences to the elation of the Sunday tourists on the road.

Finally we gave up and simply put up the gates leaving the two gentlemen in the big Bailey Hill pasture. The pursuit continued at a slowing pace until dark. We could see them from across the valley—big, black Blondy walking ahead, willing to call the whole thing off and followed at exactly the same speed by Elmer about ten feet behind. In the morning when we passed the Bailey pasture on the way to Cleveland, they were eating peacefully side by side without their harems, who, with all the calves, were eating rich alfalfa and clover on the high, distant Ferguson Place.

The two bulls have always run together before with the combined herds after breeding season, but up till this year Blondy was the pusher and kept the younger Elmer in his proper place. Apparently Elmer considers himself grown up now and will take no more pushing around. Of the two I am afraid that for reasons of personality and charm my sympathies are with Blondy, the Angus. He is a very gentle fellow with great dignity who allows you to come up and scratch his ears in the open field. Elmer, the Shorthorn, has always been a little dumb and shy.

Spent Monday in Cleveland for a meeting of the Mayor's Committee on the new farm Cleveland plans to set up on the lake front in the very heart of the city about two minutes from the public square. It will be a real farm of about 160 acres—a unique development among farms and cities in that it will be in the heart of the city itself. It will provide a spectacle of great interest to city folk, especially the children, and do a good deal toward bringing about some degree of understanding between city and country people. It is planned also to have exhibitions of farm machinery and products of all kinds—in other words, to make an agricultural center in the heart of a large area which is one of the richest agricultural and industrial areas in the world.

I have also been made Vice-President of the new association which is establishing a new international horse and livestock show in Cleveland. It will fall in the week between the Toronto and Chicago International and permit exhibitors to show during the intermediate week instead of having to lay off. Cleveland has great advantages with its auditorium and exhibition hall in the very middle of the city adjoining the proposed site of the farm, with railway sidings only five minutes away. The site of the Chicago show is more than an hour's drive from the center of the town. I am honored by the two appointments as I am not a Clevelander but live 75 miles away, down in Richland County.

We shall be a full household over the week end with Ramona Herdman of Harpers, Freddy Spencer convalescing after illness in the Navy hospital in Washington, Mimi Rand and Muriel King motoring east from the Pacific Coast and Mac coming down from Detroit for Saturday and Sunday.

AUGUST 21: Folly home from Dr. Wadsworth's with six good strong pups. They are beauties with black faces that look as if they had been smudged with soot. Knowing her frivolous, charming character I was afraid that she wouldn't be a good mother but the type that leaves the babies at home to go out to the nearest beer-parlor. Just the contrary is true. She is a demon mother and won't leave the pups and turns into a fury when any of the other dogs come near. We have set up the family in a basket full of straw in the cellar assembly room. This suits her fine as every now and then she will leave them long enough to run up the stairs to my room to say "hello." She is a fantastically intelligent and sympathetic dog—pretty, vain, affectionate, and sociable with eyes that really talk.

The demand for Boxers is extraordinary. It appears that there are at least ten customers for every pup that's born. I must say I understand it. Every customer is a satisfied customer, and they are the best dogs in the world with children. The farm is full of kids and they put up with all sorts of prodding, pushing and pulling. When they can't take any more, they simply walk off, but there is never a growl out of them.

Mimi Rand and Muriel King arrived last night to spend a couple of days on their way through by car from San Francisco to New York. George Rand is at present on Okinawa.

Certainly no nation in history has ever been defeated as the Japanese have been. It appears that MacArthur was made for the role of military governor. Some of his communiques read as if they were sent down out of a cloud by God himself. It may be that the Japanese will become utterly confused and mistake him in the end for their Emperor. Why not? It would be a good solution and MacArthur would have no objections whatever to being descended from the Sun-God.

Yesterday in the new pond I came across an almost inexplicable circumstance which perhaps an ecologist or a botanist could explain although I have never heard one of them do so. The new pond was constructed to fill a hollow in the fields below the Bailey house and in the deeper parts as much as 12 to 15 feet of earth was removed. Most of this was filled-in, eroded topsoil from the fields above—the result of years of abominable farming. The record was all there like the excavated records of past civilizations. About three feet down we came across an old string of blocked tile put there for drainage purposes and then six feet below the level of the first string we uncovered another that had been put in earlier. I doubt that the second string was put in more than thirty years ago because tiling for drainage was scarcely in general use anywhere before that. And the tiles were of a comparatively modern type of manufacture. In other words approximately nine feet of good topsoil had moved down from the fields above in less than thirty years. (For the past three years under our management *none* has moved.)

But the remarkable discovery came on the surface of the bare, scraped, subsoil five or six feet further down. There, during the last few days, weed seeds have begun to germinate. The only deduction is that they have been buried at a depth of about twelve feet for at least thirty years and all that time have remained dormant. One explanation might be that the seeds were carried in and dropped on the bare, scraped excavation by the scraper during its operations, but this is nullified by the fact that, on investigation, the tiny seedlings proved to be growing from seeds germinating an inch or two below the surface of the scraped subsoil. More than that, some of the seedlings were those of a great cockle-burr which we have a mile and a half away in the Conservancy bottom alluvial soil but have never been seen by us on the Bailey Place. The only conclusion is that the seeds have remained in damp, almost wet ground for at least thirty years without germinating.

One circumstance is even more remarkable and that is that the seeds existed not in the layer of silted-in topsoil but well below that level, or that the level of the original virgin forest topsoil actually is the silt clay loam piled up by the second great glacier. This leads to the fantastic speculation that the seeds have been buried there and remained dormant for over

200 thousand years, waiting only for the elements of light and heat to start them into life. I cannot figure it out otherwise, yet it is unbelievable. Sauvagot, of the French Ministry of Agriculture, told me when he was here that he was convinced that in France there existed wheat grain from grains which had lain stored in Egyptian tombs without light, moisture or heat for over five thousand years. He showed me pictures of the grain—a heavily bearded tall growing wheat which gave good yields. The story is a classic one in agricultural circles but has been denied again and again by agriculture experts. The experience with the excavation here leads me to believe that there might be some truth in it.

Paul Sears has recovered the pollen of various varieties of evergreen trees from borings penetrating the layers of silt deposit by the second glacier lying deep underground. I have seen a bottle of the pollen on his desk and it resembles the pollen of certain evergreens existing today. Possibly some of it comes from varieties of trees long since extinct. I am going to transfer some of the cockle-burr seedlings into pots and let them develop to see whether they exactly resemble the varieties now growing in the Conservancy land or whether they are variations as in a plant from seeds that have been dormant for centuries. Most of the other seedlings are of the common pigweed which is everywhere in the cornfields and gardens and which germinates only under the proper conditions—that is in plowed and cultivated ground that is well-fertilized. One never finds it in a wheat field or a meadow, yet once such fields are plowed and cultivated it appears at once.

All these and many other things lead me to believe that there are vast unexplored fields or knowledge concerning germination *stimuli* and the behavior of plants in relation to soil of which we know little or nothing. Again and again we have had evidence in our fields that legume seed falling on knolls and mounds eroded down to the dry silt subsoil will not germinate at all, *unless* cattle have had access to the fields for long periods. On those same bare knolls the legume seed which in some cases has been completely dormant for three or four years will spring into life and germinate with the first application of animal manure. We have just had evidence of this on the bare, eroded Bailey Hill where seeds of mammoth clover seeded three years ago suddenly came to life in considerable quantities during the heat of mid-August upon the application of barnyard manure.

*Note*: Further examples of delayed germination on the same Bailey Place Hills have been astonishing. On fields where broom sedge, sorrel, tansy, poverty grass, etc., were the only vegetation, these disappear sometimes in a single season following the application of lime, chemical fertilizer and barnyard manure. In their place appear millions of volunteer seedlings or redtop, mammoth, red and alsike clovers in some areas so thick that no hand seeding would have been necessary. The seedlings appear in our planned seedings of alfalfa brome grass and ladino. In one four-acre area of wet ground, a thick sod of redtop formed within a year of the application of lime and fertilizer. Until then the area had grown *only* weeds and marsh grasses. Only two assumptions are possible: (1) That the seeds of the *volunteer* legumes and grasses did not germinate until lime and fertilizer had been applied. (2) That any seedlings from seeds which did germinate could not make any growth or were crowded out by the acid-soil-loving plants. The area had not been seeded to any of the volunteer plants for at least a generation and redtop, a native grass like the white clover, had never been seeded on the Bailey Hills. In our experience with renovating old, weedy, worn-out bluegrass pasture, applications of lime and fertilizer together with pasture clipping produce within two or three years beautiful heavy sods of almost pure bluegrass and white clover without any seeding whatever.

Two mysteries have impressed government scientists and practical farmers this season. One is the widespread spontaneous appearance of leguminous plants everywhere through the Middle West followed by a tremendous growth. This is particularly true of our native wild white clover. The other mystery is the veritable plague of wild carrot which literally infests the whole middle-western region. It is a weed which always *exists*, particularly in run-down, semi-barren fields, but this year it is everywhere in vast numbers—in fence rows, pastures, meadows and even cultivated land. The year has been an abnormal one—cool and wet, with many inches more than normal rainfall. Did this produce the germination of wild carrot and legume seeds which had lain dormant for perhaps many years? The wild carrot is evident everywhere I have gone in the Middle West as if it had been sown broadcast over the whole region.

Conversely the tent caterpillar which infested all Ohio during the drouth season of last year for the first time in my memory is virtually nowhere in evidence at all this year. At this time last year whole landscapes were desecrated by masses of dreary cobwebs hanging on denuded wild cherry and black walnut trees. This year in all my travels over Ohio I have seen only two or three nests of the tent caterpillar.

Freddy Spencer arrived from the Navy hospital in Washington to spend a week or two convalescing from the results of the Pacific campaign. Commander Frazer flew him out, stayed for lunch and went back to Washington in the afternoon. The trip takes under two hours by plane. When we established ourselves here we figured we were beyond the Bucks County, Connecticut, Long Island area and could thus avoid some of the "drop in" visitors, but planes have cut all that out and people drop in frequently from Washington and New York for a meal. I've never liked suburbs or suburban life and now planes have made nearly every place a suburb of some place else.

Had a long and interesting letter today from Frederico Rangel, head of the Brazilian Farm Bureau, who visited us here in the spring. He is back in Rio and wrote a lot about politics and agricultural conditions in Brazil. He urged me to pay Brazil a visit in the near future, saying that I'd have not only a good reception from the agricultural but the literary people as well. It's a good idea if ever there is time.

AUGUST 27: This entry is largely a paean of praise to a plow, a small, light, two-bottom plow which is a honey. It is the Scotch plow I wrote of some days ago.

For two days we had been plowing a tough run-out field of alfalfa, ladino and brome grass. Some of it was fairly heavy clay that is wet in spring and from time to time cattle had run over it. Now at the end of August it was tough and hard and the heavy, conventional moldboard plow kept riding out of the ground in the hard clay and the gravelly knolls. Late in the afternoon I took over from Jim Cook and exhausted myself swearing at the difficulty of keeping the plow in the ground.

At last I called to Bob who was fitting the same field and told him that if this modern moldboard plow was the best agricultural engineers could produce, then I was through with agriculture and he could have the tractors, plow and all. He turned the cultipacker and spring tooth over to me and went back to the machine shop to put on new points. In a little while he returned and I got back on the tractor without looking at the plow. It did no better than before and when I stopped cursing, Bob came over and said, "It was a dirty trick I played, but that's your own pet Scotch plow."

Sourly I started out again and began working with the adjustment which regulates the pitch of the blades. Suddenly I hit exactly the right angle and the little beauty bit into the earth down to six, eight, nine inches through hard clay and gravel. The joke wasn't any longer on me. It was on Bob and Kenneth who had treated my light, small plow with cynicism and even contempt. (The truth is that at times all of us fall into that cursed attitude of "What was good enough for granpappy is good enough for me.") The little beauty, by the perfection of line and design, did what their big moldboard plow couldn't do.

They watched while I made two more rounds with the Scotch plow sticking right down to eight or nine inches, "layering" the soil and alfalfa and throwing a little fillip of soil over the ridges of sod. By the time I came up to them they were talking about changing the heavy moldboards for the Scotch plow. For myself I cannot see why more farmers haven't discovered it before now, except that the implement companies have not promoted it.

AUGUST 26: Drove to Mansfield today for the first time in months except to take a train. The trip was to help the Workman sisters and the dog refuge which they set up some years ago. They are unmarried, very intelligent and share my feeling about animals. Some Mansfielders regard them as eccentric, which they are not. The opinion is born of limited experience and understanding. They are very good citizens and far above the average in character, intelligence, and education, using virtually the whole of their small income for the dog shelter.

The need for it arose out of the mismanagement of the whole dog fund by County Commissioners in the past who used even the office of the dog warden to bolster their political positions.

On the way in I felt again that evil satisfaction which all good farmers feel at some time—that his crops look better than any of his neighbors. On the way into town the only corn I saw which was not "fired" was on Ralph Mengert's place. Even Heldenbrand's showed signs and always he has the finest corn in the valley, because he loves his land, but for the last two years he has been in poor health and with the shortage of labor he has had to leave most of his farming to two boys under eighteen. They do a good job but it is not the same as if Heldenbrand was in the field himself. Our own corn, especially on the upper farms, is green, tall, fresh and unwithered despite the heat and a three-day hot wind which has dried everything—perhaps the tail-end of the Galveston hurricane.

The good condition of the corn results from four things: (1) Because it is planted on contour in strips and no rainfall has been lost by runoff. (2) Because of an abundance of organic material in the soil which holds the moisture and makes the fertilizer available. (3) The presence of hay beans and weeds in the rows which blocks the drying winds, shades the soil and keeps it cool and moist and serves to break up the heavy drops from cloudbursts and thunderstorms into a fine mist which is absorbed 100 per cent by the soil instead of the drops sealing up a dusty soil and running off. (4) Bob's use of fertilizer and his refusal to be "penny-wise, pound foolish."

All these conditions except the hay beans and weeds are present in Roy Mengert's fields and even on his steep hillside the corn looks lush and green.

On the way to Cleveland the other day through parts of Wayne and Medina Counties, once two of our richest Ohio counties, I saw only two or three fields which you could call first-class corn.

The odd thing is that it takes no more labor and no more money to farm well than to farm badly—usually it means much less labor—yet a lot of farmers won't change their ways and spend a good part of their time finding excuses why their crops don't look well.

On the whole, this has been rather a tart entry.

AUGUST 31: Another year gone—a crowded year which has passed quickly, ending as it began with watching the barometer. Both wars are finished and the difficult peace begun.

We have had for five days a hot sun and a hot wind, evil, dehydrating and devitalizing for man and beast alike. It is extraordinary how rapidly and how deeply a hot wind can dry out the soil to a great depth, even when it is covered by sod or mulch. Life in a country of dry, hot winds would be intolerable to me. It is easy to understand why people in such countries develop eccentricities that sometimes come close to madness. Much of the corn in the neighborhood is fired although our own, save in the spots where there is a deficiency of organic material, still looks green and lush. The hot dry weather comes at a bad time for much corn in the Middle West, as it is in the grain forming stage when moisture is vital.

The barometer this morning has gone down for the first time. There are clouds but the atmosphere is dry and dusty with that feeling of still suffocation which makes it difficult to perform any task well whether it be writing or thinking or working in the fields. August—particularly the end of August— is not my favorite month. It has neither the lush promise of spring nor the promise of ripening harvest which comes with September. In our country it is usually hot and dry with the bluegrass dormant and the clover withering in the heat. All the livestock looks fat and well for most of them have ladino and alfalfa to fall back upon. I think all of us will be really happy only when the whole of our 960 acres is knee-deep in ladino, alfalfa and brome grass, with the steepest hillsides and wet bottoms in bluegrass and white clover. That is still two or three years away but we are making rapid progress. It is good to see the deep green marching across the hill pastures which only a little while ago were so thin and barren and weedy.

Of course conditions are exceptional at Malabar but loneliness what with telephones and radios and automobiles and new aeroplanes, is a thing of the past save on farms in remote areas.

Yesterday we christened the new pond by all knocking off work in the middle of the afternoon for a swim—all the kids, Bob, Harry, Jimmy, and Naomi and the little Hellers who waded around the edges. The dogs went in too, swimming around among us. Heidi, the St. Bernard puppy, takes to the water like a fish. In the hot weather she walks in casually and

454

swims around until she has had enough. She is a comic puppy, very good-natured and already bigger than the Boxers, although she is only about one-third grown. Her paws are so big that they *flap* when she walks and sometimes become unmanageable when she is trying to hold a bone.

The water in the new pond is all spring water from the big spring on the Bailey Place which gushes out of the rocks at a temperature of 50 degrees. There is no bare watershed so that there is no siltation or discoloration. All the surface water comes off sod. It is so clear that when seen from a distance it is the color of turquoise and when you stand above it the color is that of clear jade. Swimming in it had a special sensual pleasure. The water is already about six feet deep and it will be up to a fourteen-foot depth in another week. It cost very little money and was made in two days. The delights of a pond are so endless that I wonder more people do not construct them.

Last evening after supper Bob, Kenneth, Tom, Charley, Freddy Spencer and I fished for bluegills and sunfish in the pond by the Big House. It is overpopulated and we had not the time during the war to fish it enough to keep the population within proper limits, even with the kids helping. After a hot day the fish were sluggish and all we got was about twenty which we put in a big milk-can to transfer to the new pond where they will breed and serve to feed the brown and rainbow trout with which we are stocking it in the spring. The new pond should make an ideal fish pond for the water is perfect and we left a good deal of topsoil in the shallow areas to grow vegetation, food, and shelter.

Already the pond lies like a jewel in a setting of deep-green alfalfa and corn below the road where passers-by as well as ourselves can enjoy its beauty. Willows, poplars and flowering shrubs will add immeasurably to its beauty.

One of the fish we transplanted to the new pond died today and the giant water beetles were working on it. Where they came from I do not know, but there were three of them, diving like divers working on a sunken submarine and rising again to the surface after a minute or two. The life of a pond is a fabulous, intricate thing, a whole universe in itself, near at times to the very steaming slime out of which all of us rose and are still rising, painfully in the long ladder of evolution. Perhaps when I am older and less rushed, I can sometime take a whole year simply to *watch* one of the ponds and what goes on in the depths, on the surface and along the shoreline.

The first pair of mallards appeared on the pond and went away again. I doubt that any wild ducks will stay there, even over night, for it is too new. Hope, Mac, and I worked all afternoon with the tiller and the bush and bog harrow making the borders on the pond ready for planting.

It has been a good year despite the hard work, the rain, and the cold, and the shortage of help. The livestock has all been healthy and the crops abundant and we have managed to do much more work than we counted on doing, particularly in the spreading of lime and the improvement of pasture. The results of past years have begun to pile up in abundance.

If we did not know from our own records and from the record of the fields themselves that we have been doing a successful job, we should know from the increasing number of farmers who come to us to ask how we have achieved this or that improvement or increase in yield. More and more they come, not only from considerable distance but from among our neighbors, some of whom were among the greatest skeptics in the beginning. We have never preached or given advice but have kept our noses to the grindstone working for results, knowing that most farmers believe only what they see. Fortunately they can see almost everything we do and the results we obtain. Except for the high, lost Ferguson Place almost the whole area of every farm is visible from the township and county roads.

Passers-by have seen the bottom pastures carrying more and more livestock through each season. They have seen green expanses of alfalfa and sweet clover in country where tradition had it neither crop could be grown. They have seen, if they cared to climb the long hill "up Ferguson way" thirty acres of beautiful alfalfa growing on the top of what was once a barren, eroded hill. They have seen wheat yields jump on the Bailey Place in two years from less than five bushels to thirty-three bushels against a nation-wide average of twenty bushels per acre. Yesterday the neighbor who sells us our hybrid seed-corn came to look over the various cornfields. On the Bailey Place where only three years ago there was scarcely a cornstalk more than three or four feet high, with ears that were nubbins, he saw corn ten and eleven feet high, lush and green despite the hot, dry weather, which will yield well above seventy-five baskets to the acre. He said, "I still don't believe what I am seeing. The Bailey Place as far back as I can remember has always been known as the thinnest farm between Newville and Little Washington."

All these things have been the *real* satisfaction, more even than the economic gains which have come with them. One neighbor slipping in "casually" to come round presently after much "made" talk to the question he came to ask is the greatest reward we can have. A farmer likes to see: he does not like to be told. He is the king of pragmatists and rightly so, for in no other skilled profession is it more necessary to know that one thing *works* and another does *not*.

Best of all, we have not made a single improvement or employed a single practice which is not within the economic means of any farmer who is able to get a loan from a bank or from the Farm Security Administration. The scale has been larger than that of most farmers but acre by acre both costs and practices are within the limits of any average farmer on the scores of labor, of time, and of cash expenditure. And during the past three years we have been gravely handicapped by shortage of labor and above all of skilled capable help and materials with which to work.

It must be admitted that the larger scale has brought us some benefits, chiefly in the field of mechanical equipment, for the larger acreage permits us to support such expensive pieces of machinery as a cornpicker, a combine, and an automatic baler. Such machinery can, however, be owned co-operatively by a group of farmers, or in most fairly good agricultural areas of hours of work for neighboring farms during the last few years.

All of our experience boils down in the end to the soil and consequently to a better agriculture. We believe that an agriculture which raises 100 per cent of the potential production per acre without loss of fertility, cannot help being a prosperous agriculture. Too many farmers are farming two and three and sometimes as high as five acres to produce what one acre should, if properly farmed, produce. Too many farmers when they seek to increase production and income, go out and buy another farm instead of gaining the increase by properly farming the land they already possess. The farmer who farms five acres to produce what one should produce is destined for eternal defeat, for his costs in labor, taxes, interest, time, gasoline and wear and tear are five times what they should be and will constantly defeat him. Expansion horizontally in terms of land rather than vertically in terms of production was responsible for the ruin of most of those farmers who went down in defeat after the first world war. It will be the ruin of more farmers in the years following the second world war, although the number is less because the methods of American agriculture have undeniably been improved and because a good many farmers remember what happened the last time. But there are many farms too which have been overworked to produce crops at high war prices, farms which have lost in fundamental fertility far more than their owners gained through flash high prices during the war years. In many cases they can be restored but the process of restoring fertility is a slower one than destroying it and many farmers who will not make the effort or the expenditure of time, intelligence and money to restore it are already on the down grade, with the wheel rolling faster and faster down hill toward final destruction.

In the deepest sense, no farmer can *overwork* his soil, so long as he puts back into it as much or preferably a little more than he takes out of it, both in organic material and in minerals. Too many farmers follow a "pennywise, pound foolish" policy. Some of them will save a dollar or two per acre on fertilizer and risk the failure of a crop when the extra dollar or two would have brought a return of fifty times the expenditure, or even made the difference between success and total failure in a crop.

One of the things we have learned, partly from those good men whose lives are devoted to problems of soil and partly from our soil itself, is the relation between the health of plants and the health of animals, birds and humans and the health and balance of our soil itself. As we have increased the mineral and organic content along parallel paths, the health of crops in field and garden and their resistance to disease and insects has steadily increased. So in exact ratio has increased the health and resistance of poultry and cattle and ultimately of the people living off the crops and animals grown on soil to which mineral and organic material has been

458

restored. There are few places in the world where a better record of health and vigor can be shown by a small community comparable in size to that at Malabar. This is particularly true of the children. Scientifically, logically, it is perfectly evident to any thinking mind that you cannot produce off soil that is deficient in calcium and phosphorus and many other elements, either plants, animals, or human stock which possess resistance, vitality and in the case of humans, energy or intelligence.

It is safe to say that the greater part of the agricultural land of America is a depleted soil, deficient both in organic material and in minerals, and in the older regions of the East and Deep South, the deficiency has reached proportions which made it virtually impossible in some areas to produce people who are capable of learning or of helping themselves, even with the aid of schools and expenditures of money in terms of subsidy and relief. The economic and social problems of large depleted areas of the United States are, as they are in the case of an individual farm, largely those of soil and secondarily of diet.

# FINIS

*Another Letter to a Sergeant*

Malabar Farm, 1947

MY DEAR SERGEANT:

On reading over *Malabar Farm* I am aware that I am guilty of many sins of omission and commission as well as of repetition.

As for the sins of omission, they are inevitable for agriculture and horticulture are at once arts, professions, and sciences, and their range is so vast, so complex and so intricate, that it is impossible to encompass their ramifications in a whole book or indeed a whole lifetime of steady writing. Their horizons are entirely without limit since they encompass the whole pattern of the universe, of man and his existence. Each time that one reaches the top of one hill another lies just beyond. In this it is very like our own country in Pleasant Valley. It is probable that the *science* of agriculture has made more progress in the preceding generation or two than in all the history of the world up to then; yet we have really only scratched the surface of the mysteries. As Wheeler McMillen has said in the quotation I used a little earlier in the book, "I do not believe that anyone knows very much about farming."

As to sins of commission, I no doubt have been guilty of many—in drawing false deductions, in making assertions which may turn out any day, month or year, from our own experience, to be wrong. I do not, however, believe that these particular sins of commission are very serious. They may even be of considerable value in creating controversy and exploration and research. An agriculture or research or a pedagogy which is not controversial, inquisitive and even at times a little angry, is a dead agriculture, a dead research and a dead pedagogy. In this aspect of controversy lies the value of

463

men like Ed Faulkner and his controversial *Plowman's Folly* and *A Second Look*, by Sir Albert Howard, who is much more a pure scientist than Ed or myself, in his books *An Agriculture Testament* and *The Soil and Health*. They have the power to stir up things, to ignite a spark in the hundreds of thousands of farmers, researchers, gardeners, amateurs and the young men and women who, in the end, must make our agriculture and that of the world sounder and more productive. The good farmer has always been and always will be a man with great powers of observation and great intellectual curiosity.

It has always seemed to me that our great agricultural educational structure—the greatest and most expensive in the world—has been guilty of two great weaknesses: (1) That it has too often been a closed affair in which professors and research men wrote papers at each other and that much of the material sent out to farmers is so technical and so dull as to be unreadable and at times unbearable. Agriculture is an exciting profession, one of the most exciting on earth but, save in the case of a few men like Liberty Hyde Bailey, Hugh H. Bennett, Aldo Leopold and H. E. Babcock, little of that excitement has ever reached the average practicing farmer or the young men and women about to enter the profession. Of course these men, and others like them, are essentially both great crusaders and great teachers, and are born, not made. (2) That all too often the farmer is told to adopt certain practices because he will get better yields and make more money or even improve his soil, but all too rarely is he told why this is so, or are the processes by which improvements and better yields come about explained to him.

If more were explained to him of what goes on in soils, in plants, in livestock and explained in an interesting and stimulating and even controversial fashion, progress toward a better agriculture would be infinitely more sound and rapid. It would inevitably bring about more and greater contributions from the farmer himself to the science of agriculture. It could ignite a thousand sparks in a thousand young men and women who might one day make immensely important contributions to the science. The good farmer is no fool and he need not be treated as a child. He can understand the "mysteries" if given half a chance.

Again and again I have heard a middle-aged farmer say, "Why didn't somebody tell me that? I would have understood how the thing worked and it would have made all the difference." And you could read in his sun-burned face the disappointment at the interest and satisfaction he had missed by not knowing how a "thing worked."

I know of no element of our population more intelligent or more eager for information and scientific knowledge than our average good farmer. It is difficult or impossible for him to obtain good books and treatises existing only in distant libraries or in the archives in the Department of Agriculture. I would suggest that the Department, and our State Agricultural Colleges, could undertake no better or more profitable project than to issue a series of pamphlets, written simply and with some degree of enthusiasm, upon the almost endless subjects which arise from the science of agriculture. One on "Bacteria" perhaps, one on "Plowing and Fitting in All Their Phases," one on "Organic Material and what goes on in the Soil," and so on.[1]

As to sins of repetition in this book, they are many but most of them, I believe, are inevitable since agriculture is so intricate, complex and interwoven a science. That is why keeping books on a farm as one might keep them for a retail store has baffled and still baffles the agricultural economist. The question is always, "What to charge off to what?" because no single aspect of agriculture exists alone or can be isolated. How is one to charge against the costs of a bushel of wheat the benefits of the lime put on the soil six or seven years earlier, of the nitrogen and organic material produced by the legumes and grass plowed in before the wheat was seeded, or the value of the straw once it has been worked through the barns and returns to the soil of another and different field as life-giving manure, or the benefits of the sunlight, air, and water which have contributed more than 90 per cent to the growth of the crop or any of at least a dozen other elements which go into agriculture?

Or how can one estimate merely in terms of cash the

[1] The nearest approach to such a project is the excellent agricultural year book edited by Gove Hambidge and put out annually by the Department of Agriculture. Any farmer can obtain it by writing to his congressman.

benefits of the monthly milk check which is the backbone of many a dairy farm family's economy? It is impossible to analyze it in dollars and cents and charge off debits and credits. The evidence of its value is none the less there. It is evident in the greener fields, the better buildings and maintenance and greater productivity and the better fencing, which are characteristic of almost every good dairy farm.

All of these things remove farming from the realm of pure business and make of it an art as well as a science. Even the philosophy or religious sense or the temperament of a farmer may well pay off in dollars and cents in a fashion which can never be entered in the ledger. In our own case at Malabar enthusiasm and curiosity and pride of accomplishment have paid even bigger dividends in dollars and cents than the lime and the fertilizer or the modern machinery.

That is why there are repetitions in this book. I found almost at once that, whether I was dealing with health in plants, animals, and people, or the virtues of grass and legumes, or wild life, or farm economy or almost any other element of a sound agriculture, the individual aspects could not be separated because their fundamentals were hopelessly and intricately interwoven into a pattern which resembled that of the universe itself. That is why agriculture to the good farmer is a calling of intricate variety and fascination which he would not exchange for any other regardless of rewards in money. So if repetitions have annoyed you here and there in this book, forgive them. They could not be avoided.

On reading over this book, I have noted that it appears a little like a many-layered sandwich in which heavy foods were alternated with light ones. This was a pattern which was partly conscious and partly unconscious but it is, I think, somewhat symbolic of the life of a good farmer. There are periods of hard work and worry, alternating with periods of relaxation, delight, and satisfaction, but again they are interwoven and overlapping, and contribute to the fascination which a good farmer finds in his profession.

I have noticed that a great many pages are given over to weather and to other manifestations of nature but these too play great parts in the richness of life in the country. I have observed, as I reread the record, that I am no different from any other farmer in the fact that I find the weather very rarely perfect.

A farm, especially a diversified farm, is itself a whole world, a cosmos in miniature in which the farmer like the sailor and the fisherman lives intimately with the fundamental realities of our existence in the universe. Like the sailor or the fisherman, a farmer always has an eye turned toward the sky, watching the quarter from which the weather comes. Like the sailor and the fisherman he lives by the barometer and learns to observe small things which indicate the weather—the turning of leaves on the trees, the frantic efforts of the flies to enter the house or the dairy, the behavior of cattle and the anguished singing or the silence of the tree frogs. When the turkeys start oiling their feathers you can look for rain or at least a thunderstorm. When they quit their bare exposed perches in the trees in the winter and take to the barn you can make ready to stoke up the big fires and get out the snow plow.

All of these signs are more infallible than the reports of the scientific weatherman sitting high atop a skyscraper in some distant city, and they are a great deal more interesting.

Weather for the farm is rarely the right weather. If you need rain for the corn, the pastures, and the new seedings, it may be a disaster for the hay cut and drying in the field or for the grain that is just dry enough for combining. If you have good haymaking and harvesting weather—bright and hot and dry—it may be bad for the corn and the pasture. Weather is the principal reason why the farmer has gained the reputation of being a "grumbler." Rarely is the weather right for everything. On those days, not more than half a dozen times a year, when the weather is right, the good farmer is the happiest man in the world and would not change places with any man.

City folks rarely understand what disasters and what delights weather can bring to the farmer. In their physically limited and protected lives, rain means merely that the buses and street cars will be overcrowded, or a hot spell means only that they will be uncomfortable and will grumble, louder perhaps than the most discontented farmer. Weather does not mean to them floods or droughts which may ruin their income and destroy the rewards of a whole year's work, with whole fields ruined perhaps for years to come. It does not mean the loss perhaps of hundreds of cattle snowed in on the range.

Because of the weather and the fact that good farmers live close to the earth, to the trees, to the animals and are aware, whether they choose or not, of the eternal, inexorable, ruthless and beautiful laws of creation and nature, all of them are religious men in one way or another. I do not mean by this that every farmer is a fanatic church-goer or a "shouter." That kind of farmer lives usually on marginal land, too poor even to provide a decent living. Often enough his motivation springs largely from fear and the hope for a future life less bitter and poverty-stricken than this one. Your good farmer on good land is constantly aware, perhaps more than any other element of the population, save the sailors and the fishermen, of an immense plan in which compensation, order and precision are all involved. It is a plan and a force with which he must live and he learns by necessity to understand and respect it. A church may be an instrument of great good in a rural community or it may be a dead thing, or it may be merely a force to promote ignorance, bigotry, and evil. Usually it depends upon the pastor or the priest who heads it. Too many of our rural churches serve more as social meeting places than as houses in which to worship God. Too many of them have little or no relation to the daily lives of the people in the neighborhood. A rural pastor has in his grasp potentialities for immense good if he chooses to use them.

The religion of the good farmer goes far beyond all this. He has faith in the Great Plan with which he must live daily, as an infinitesimal part of the whole divine scheme. He knows that he must adjust himself to the immutable laws of that Plan. If he is clever or wise he will learn even to turn these laws to his own advantage. He will understand them and plan so that the rain becomes a blessing rather than a curse. He will learn new ways of combatting a drought and even perhaps of turning it into a profit. He is a foolish man who sets himself in ignorance or defiance in opposition to the laws of nature for in the end he will be defeated and crushed.

A good many of the best farmers I have known were not

regular church-goers, usually because the church in their community was a dead or sometimes even an evil thing. When the weather is against them, they will work on the Sabbath, for the sin of waste, as our Lord made clear, is a far worse sin than that of missing a service and never was this truer than in the starving world of today. The faith of a good farmer is far beyond church-going or the conventional fears or superstitions of the ordinary man. It is a direct faith in God himself, in the very universe with which he lives in so close an association. The church can minister to and support that faith or show the way to use it to the advantage of one's fellow man, but even the church is an insignificant thing in relation to the greater faith, no more than a feeble attempt of man to understand and formalize the greater law, to reach up and bring down to earth for the limited understanding of man what is essentially beyond understanding.

Well, Sergeant, here is the book. I hope you found at least some partial answers to the questions you ask but I hope most of all that it may act as a spark plug. Knowing you a little better after your visit, I would say that you'll find agriculture a pretty satisfactory profession. It's very different from what it was in your grandfather's day, particularly in its economic, technological, and scientific aspects, although the fundamental satisfaction of rural living recorded long ago by Hesiod and Virgil and Voltaire and countless others remains the same. The old-fashioned frontier farm, with its rigors and its sometimes bitter satisfactions, is gone and in its place is the farm in which business, science, and even philosophy and art play their roles.

Some people are born for country life and others for city life, but the old bromide, "You can take the boy out of the farm but you can't take the farm out of the boy," is still true and it would, I think, be true in your case, no matter what success or wealth you might amass in any other calling you might undertake. I have seen that old saying in operation a hundred times with men who have made great successes in other fields and amassed great fortunes and fame but about middle-age or later, they get themselves a farm and from then on that farm becomes something of an obsession in which virtually all other interests become lost and absorbed.

In a world and in a nation where the opportunities of the

Horatio Alger hero become steadily more restricted and the acquisition of vast money fortunes like those of the nineteenth century Robber Barons has become an impossibility, the farm is a good place to be and agriculture is a good field in which not only to find security but satisfaction in living. In good or average times the income of the average good farmer is far larger than that of 85 per cent of the rest of the population. In bad times the difference between the status of the good farmer and of most of the rest of the population is the difference between that of a roof, good food, security and that of destitution and public relief. In other words, I think you are making a sound choice. What we need is young men who *want* to be farmers rather than young men who, as so often in the past, became farmers merely through indifference and lack of gumption.

We hope to see you now and then and to hear how things are going with you. In the meanwhile good luck to you in a profession which is the oldest in the world and certainly one of the most important, worthy, satisfactory and dignified.

L. B.